LETTERS TO TIMOTHY AND TITUS

Letters
to
Timothy and Titus

SOUND WORDS
FOR ECCLESIAS UNDER PRESSURE

Alfred Nicholls

THE CHRISTADELPHIAN
404 SHAFTMOOR LANE
BIRMINGHAM B28 8SZ

1991

First published 1991

ISBN 0 85189 132 2

Reproduced from copy supplied.
Printed and bound in Great Britain by
Billing & Sons Ltd., Worcester

PREFACE

THE chapters in this book began as a series of articles with the same title in the Special Study Section of *The Christadelphian* from April 1977 to December 1980. As the study developed, so the importance of these Letters for the twentieth century ecclesias as well as for those of the first became more and more evident. It was therefore decided to deal fully with the Letters to Timothy in the Magazine and redeem the implied promise of the title by publishing the articles together with chapters on Titus in book form.

The wealth of material contained in the Letters has been set out in introductory chapters and a commentary of the verse-by-verse type. With the text has been incorporated a series of 52 Essays of an expository or informative nature, so that the richness of the Apostle's thought and his grasp of the essentials of ecclesial life and behaviour in a pagan world, strangely like our own in many ways, can be thoroughly appreciated.

The book is earnestly commended to the reader in the hope that the author's own fascination with the Pastoral Epistles and the undoubted profit to be derived from seeking to understand them a little better can be more widely shared.

"For God hath not given us the spirit of fear; but of power, and of love, and of a sound mind."

Halesowen.   ALFRED NICHOLLS

FOREWORD

THE sub-title of this book, "Sound Words for Ecclesias under Pressure", conveys precisely the character of Paul's Letters to Timothy and Titus. In Ephesus and Crete, respectively, Paul's sons in the faith were being exhorted by his emphasis on "sound doctrine" and his "faithful sayings" (and warnings against the "other-teachers") to be strong, to fulfil the charges committed to them, and in their turn to pass on to others "the things that thou hast heard of me".

The author draws out from the words, allusions and metaphors used by Paul a wealth of absorbing detail and practical exhortation which is as relevant today as it was then. Highly instructive are the parallels between the rigour of the godly life and the training and discipline of the athlete, the soldier or the labourer. There are countless examples of "oncers"—those words and idioms in the original text which are unique to these Epistles. Throughout, we are given fascinating glimpses of the era in which the writer and his readers lived—the religious practices, the vanities and vices from which followers of the Lord Jesus had been called.

It follows that, perhaps more so than for other New Testament epistles, the exposition of the Letters to Timothy and Titus calls for an acquaintance with the First Century world and with the language of the times. Before he undertook the Editorship of *The Christadelphian*, Brother Alfred Nicholls had been a teacher of Classics and had special opportunities for study in these matters. Yet, as he would himself be quick to add, an understanding of Classical themes is not a sufficient accomplishment on its own: the principal qualification is a love of the Scriptures. The author's lifelong devotion to God's Word shines through this work: it is, in a very real sense, the outcome and fulfilment of his studies both secular and spiritual—but especially the latter. It is lovingly commended to all who would "live godly in Christ Jesus".

JOHN MORRIS

CONTENTS

The First Letter to Timothy

The Second Letter to Timothy

The Letter to Titus

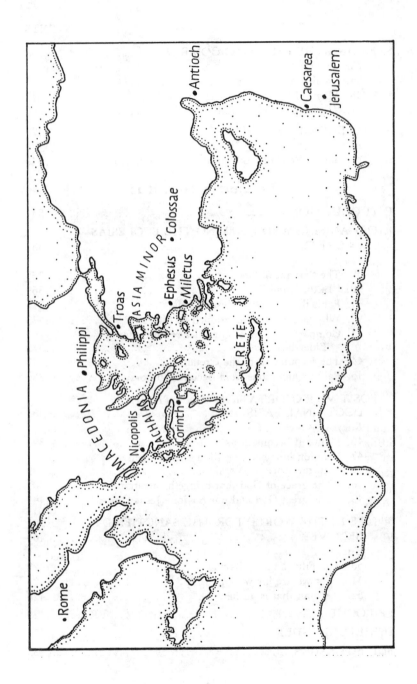

INTRODUCTION

THE Letters to Timothy and Titus are very much for our time. Written at a time of crisis and change and giving practical advice soundly based on doctrinal principles, they will help us, if we will only pay heed to their message, to clarify our vision and strike right balances in ecclesial life.

Throughout this book it is assumed, without discussion of all the arguments which lead to this conclusion, that the Apostle Paul was released from prison in Rome at the end of the two years described in Acts 28, only to be imprisoned again and put to death after a period of which these Letters alone give any Scriptural information. The length of time after his release could have been as much as five years, from AD 63 to early 68, although it is impossible to give precise dates, nor is our understanding dependent upon them.

Reference will be made to some of these points in the detailed commentary and in a separate table of the last years of Paul's life. Suffice it to say that this period, long or short, must have been an active as well as an anxious one for Paul: active because, according to the testimony of the Letters, he travelled once more in Asia Minor, Macedonia and some parts of Achaia, and possibly in Crete; anxious, because of the circumstances which called forth these epistles, aptly named for the last two hundred and fifty years or so *The Pastoral Epistles*.

The distinctive nature and style of these letters addressed to individual men with a pastoral responsibility, and their lessons for us, will be the theme of our study.

THE BACKGROUND OF THE LETTERS

AT the time of his first Roman imprisonment there had been no legal reason why Paul should be detained beyond the statutory

1

two years if his enemies did not themselves make the journey to Rome to accuse him before the emperor's court of appeal. The relative freedom he enjoyed throughout the period and the optimism concerning his release expressed in his letters from Rome, confirm the theory that he was in fact set free (Philippians 2:23,24; Philemon 22). Christianity, still officially regarded as a sect of the Jews, was not a proscribed religion. Indeed, Luke is at pains to demonstrate in the Acts that the Roman authorities found nothing in it contrary to the law.

The situation was, however, to change dramatically. The Great Fire of Rome in July 64 was attributed to the Christians and immediate and dreadful persecution began in the city itself. It was a period of great danger for the brethren in Rome, and particularly for those regarded as leaders, and the effects of the changed official attitude spread to other parts of the Empire; it may also be assumed that Jewish leaders lost no opportunity of aggravating the hostility of local magistrates against the disciples. When the Jewish insurrection against Rome that was to lead to the destruction of Jerusalem began two years later, there were thus two probable reasons why a prominent figure like Paul should be arrested and brought to a trial that ended in death. That he himself expected no other release is very plain from the whole tenor of 2 Timothy.

It is tempting to follow early traditions which speak of his going to "the boundary of the West", and preaching in Spain; we at least know that he had had that intention (Romans 15:24). But much had happened to cause him to modify his original plans. The prosperous journey to Rome he had hoped for (Romans 1:10) was made under armed guard, and took two years in its prospering; on the other hand, although he had not expected to see the elders of Ephesus again, he was in fact to pay them another visit. What he saw there gave him cause for great concern.

Words to the Elders of Ephesus

With distinct echoes of Moses' charge to the elders of Israel (Deuteronomy 31:29), Paul had said to them on the shore at Miletus: "For I know this, that after my departing shall grievous wolves enter in among you, not sparing the flock. Also of your own selves shall men arise, speaking perverse things, to draw away disciples after them. Therefore watch, and remember . . ." (Acts

2

20:28-31). Two years afterwards the process he had foreseen was only too well advanced and immediate remedies were called for. Being himself about to go on into Macedonia he "besought (Timothy) to abide still at Ephesus" (1 Timothy 1:3), and gave him a charge to keep for himself and to pass on to the ecclesia, so that in a man he could trust to "take heed to himself and to the doctrine", a worthy example of pastoral care would counteract the effects of the heretical teaching and the irresponsibility of the elders.

The *First Letter to Timothy* is a private letter, parts of which were no doubt intended for the ecclesia's ears since its purpose was not only to give Timothy instructions for his delicate and responsible task, but also to make it perfectly clear that he was acting with full authority from Paul, "an apostle of Jesus Christ by the commandment of God our Saviour".

"These things write I unto thee, hoping to come unto thee shortly: but if I tarry long, that thou mayest know how thou oughtest to behave thyself in the house of God, which is the church of the living God, the pillar and ground of the truth."

(1 Timothy 3:14,15)

The instructions were designed to exhort Timothy personally, to provide a set of basic doctrinal principles which would raise the moral tone, and to give practical advice on ecclesial organisation and the responsibilities of ecclesial life. The Apostle's methods and priorities are worthy of our diligent study.

The *Second Letter to Timothy*, the last Paul ever wrote, is more intensely personal. Written from prison, full of fatherly feeling for a "dearly beloved son" in the faith, it displays earnest longing to see a familiar face once more, an anxious concern for the physical and spiritual welfare of a man whose strong faith and timidity of nature had been rightly assessed, and again a charge to the young shepherd of the flock to counteract evil tendencies in the ecclesia by strong personal example, mingled with a gentleness, a patience and meekness in his instruction of "those that oppose themselves" (2 Timothy 2:24-26). Truly a document for our times!

There is no certain record of when Paul visited Crete, but the indication that he did so is plain enough from the *Letter to Titus*.

3

Here we have to deal not with one ecclesia as in Ephesus, but with several, for Titus was given the task of appointing "elders in every city". Probably he and Paul had visited the island together, but the Apostle had not had time to carry out his usual practice of "ordaining them elders in every church" (Acts 14:23), and so Titus had been left behind in Crete "to set in order the things that were wanting". The question of the qualifications of those to undertake responsibility arises immediately in Titus, therefore, but not until chapter 3 in 1 Timothy.

In this epistle, moreover, Paul addresses himself to the special characteristics of the people of Crete which influenced some of the ecclesial attitudes of mind and called for rebuke. The nature of the problems is somewhat different at first sight from those in Ephesus, although the Apostle's method of describing and dealing with them is the same: their teaching was vain talking and subversive of faith; the remedy was sound doctrine expressed in personal integrity and exhortation upon the real practical implications of the principles of the faith.

Elders to take the Oversight

The choice of the men addressed in these letters must have been a matter of careful thought. Although Paul had ordained elders to take the oversight of ecclesias to whom he had brought the Gospel, he retained strong personal links with them to whom he was "willing to have imparted . . . not the gospel of God only, but also our own souls, because ye were dear unto us" (1 Thessalonians 2:8). The care of, or anxiety for, all the churches came upon him daily, whether he was present with them or not.

But the apostolic age was to come to an end, and the time of his own departure would come—indeed, had come by the time 2 Timothy was written. To whom should the task of continuing his work be committed? To whom, other than to those who would "hold fast the form of sound words" which they had heard of him, and would commit the same "to faithful men, who shall be able to teach others also"? And who better able than a man like Timothy who had from his youth known the holy Scriptures; who had known from his first contact with the preaching of the Gospel that it meant persecution and, observing in his long companionship with the Apostle what faith and endurance meant, was not likely to be ashamed of the Gospel of Christ; who had borne the

4

Apostle's Letter to the Corinthians, and was under no illusions about the problems connected with ecclesial oversight? Or a man like Titus, of whom we know just enough to realise that, in spite of his early daunting experiences amongst false brethren (Galatians 2:3-4), he grew in spiritual stature, to become capable of showing uncorruptness in doctrine, sound speech that cannot be condemned, a man who could refresh Paul's spirit by his presence (2 Corinthians 2:13)?

The Ecclesial Guide

Such were the young men to whom the Apostle entrusted the delicate task of organising, edifying and reproving ecclesias. No one was to despise them because they were young, but they were to be examples first and reprovers afterwards. Nor did their apostolic authority give them the right to overstep bounds of prudence or propriety: differences of age, rank and sex, as well as the nature of the need to be filled, were all to be taken into consideration to discipline their approach to their task, for only so would they both save themselves and them that heard them.

The Pastoral Epistles were their ecclesial guide, and the fascinating study of the distinctive style, the special vocabulary, the "faithful sayings", the nature and treatment of heresy, the true function of the ecclesia, will inform our hearts as well as our heads. In this, the second half of the twentieth century, we are in a similar position to those in the second half of the first. They like us had lost some of the single-minded enthusiasm kindled by the need to contend for the faith against that which was without: the dangers and the questionings came from within. The remedy for our disease is surely to be found in theirs, and amongst the thirty or more people mentioned by name in the thirteen short chapters of the Pastorals—"a panorama of judgement day", since they either helped or hindered, did much evil or refreshed the saints, spoke wholesome or cankerous words, loved this present world or were not ashamed of an apostle's chain—there were those who resembled ourselves. Which shall we take for our personal examples?

THE VOCABULARY OF THE LETTERS

THE language of the Letters to Timothy and Titus differs in many respects from all other in the New Testament, not least in the unusual vocabulary used by the Apostle. The fact that between 146 and 188 words in these letters occur nowhere else in the New Testament (the exact number depends on the method of computation employed and whether proper names are included), has been used as an argument against their authenticity. These *hapaxes* ('oncers') as they are usually called, together with other words used here for the first time by Paul although other New Testament writers use them, provide a fascinating study in themselves and, incidentally, evidence *against* the hostile critic.

Reference to some of these words characteristic of the Pastoral Epistles will be made as they occur; here we briefly consider the reasons for their use. Other letters of Paul contain words used only once, although not in such large proportion. The fact that they are unusual to the author is not of itself evidence of some other hand. Indeed it has been shown in the case of Shakespeare's works that relatively three times as many *hapaxes* occur in *Hamlet* as in some earlier plays, and that plays on a specialised theme contain words which appear nowhere else in all his works.

The same reasoning applied to the Pastoral Epistles suggests that they are either among the Apostle's later writings or are concerned with a different problem from, say, the Letter to the Romans. In fact, both conclusions are valid. For if they are to be placed somewhere between AD 65 and 68, as is now commonly accepted, they belong to a period in the Apostle's life when, released from his first Roman imprisonment, he has added to his experience in further travel and his command of language has increased.

Moreover, a new type of theme calls into use a fresh vocabulary, and greater preoccupation with an old subject means a more extensive use of words previously employed. When Paul wrote these letters, the conflict with Judaism was over and men had begun to arise "of their own selves, speaking perverse things to draw away disciples after them". His concern, therefore, was not to lay again the foundation of doctrine, but to exhort to faithfulness and sound ecclesial life. To do this he draws on a range of vocabulary taken from the *koinē* or common speech of the Hellenistic world, and also from the Septuagint (Greek) version of the Old Testament, in which some 78 of the *hapaxes* are to be found. Even a casual survey of the language gives a consistent picture of a man progressively enriching his mind by travel and observation, by contact with his friends, especially Luke, and above all by diligent study of the Greek Old Testament.

But it is of prime importance to realise that Paul's *use* of his vocabulary, as distinct from his *choice* of it, is always with a characteristically Biblical "flavour". We meet, for example, in 1 Timothy 3, a wide range of moral attributes described in words familiar to any prospective candidate for a magistracy in a provincial town who studies the list of qualifications. Their connotation for Paul, however, is not the ideal qualification for an elected secular official, but the sense of spiritual responsibility essential in anyone accepting the oversight of "the church of the living God, the pillar and ground of the truth".

A Healthy Community
In writing to the Ephesians, Paul had visualised the church as a body that was growing and developing into a mature man, and so needed edifying (Ephesians 4:12-16). In the situation confronting Timothy and Titus, however, it was a body needing to be kept healthy. It is possible that his close companionship with Luke, the beloved physician, influenced Paul's choice of medical metaphors for this soundness of the church as a body.

The words used imply soundness and wholesomeness, and the same idea is to be found in Luke 5:31—"They that be *whole* need not a physician, but they that are sick." So the emphasis is not so much upon restating first principles, which are assumed, as upon sound moral and spiritual judgement in the expression of belief in them. The kind of teaching contrary to sound doctrine and destructive of faith is compared with gangrene and sickness. 2 Tim 2 v 17

Significant too, is Paul's reference to "conscience", a common enough word in the New Testament, but in the sense of a Scripturally-informed conscience Paul attaches great importance to it, as well as to the effects of rendering it insensitive to spiritual things. The word he uses so frequently for "good" (*kalos*) is appropriate to the theme of these Letters, implying as it does beauty as well as the intrinsic quality of goodness, and so refers to the well-balanced character as well as to the individual acts of goodness which are its expression.

These and other words characteristic of these Epistles— military, athletic, and other metaphors concerning self-control

7

and discipline, words for strife and debate and the nature of true godliness—we shall see in their place in the text. They will appear especially appropriate to the theme and occasion of the writing; while the new emphasis laid on ideas dealt with before, gives evidence of the Apostle's concern for the healthy faith and conduct of the community he had laboured to build up. There was nothing he could say that he had not already said. It remained for faithful men, grounded and settled in the faith, with a due sense of their public and private responsibilities in the sight of God, "the Saviour of all men, and especially of them that believe", to preach by word of mouth and personal example the sound doctrine they had received of him.

This responsibility devolves upon the community of the twentieth century as much as upon the men of Ephesus and Crete.

NEW TESTAMENT LETTERS

THE Ancient World had its own conventions and variations in letter-writing, some of them consequent upon the actual physical form of the letter and the method of its delivery. Once the letter was written on papyrus, it was rolled and sealed. Shorter messages would be inscribed by means of a stylus on wax tablets in a wooden frame, which was then closed and the seal affixed. Therefore the name and address of the recipient was written on the outside, especially when the special messenger—there was no "post" or "mail" in our sense except for Roman government correspondence—had several letters to deliver. Inside, although the individual writer's choice of phrase might vary, the letter contained the following conventional divisions besides the main body of the letter:

Superscription: mentioning the name of the sender.

Ascription: or inside address, giving the name of the person to whom the letter was sent.

Salutation: some form of greeting.

Subscription: some final expression of goodwill or farewell.

In Roman official correspondence some of these forms might be reduced to abbreviations or even initial letters only, as in "Caius Senatui S.V.V.B.E.E.Q.V.", or "Caius to the Senate: If you are in health it is well: I and the army are in health".

The Apostle's Adaptation

The apostolic letters display some of the features of ordinary correspondence of the day. Usually all the traditional beginnings and endings are employed in a structural sense; what distinguishes these letters, at least those of Paul, is the solemnity of the words which replace the purely conventional phrases, to make of the formulae sometimes an expression of affection based upon fellowship in Christ, often acting as a pointer to the doctrinal content of the epistle which follows, and even giving a kind of résumé of the whole Gospel in the opening ascription and greeting (see Titus 1).

In Acts 23:26, in the letter of Claudius Lysias to Felix, the New Testament contains an example of official correspondence with conventional greeting and farewell. The first "official" letter of the Christian Church is to be found in Acts 15:23-29, and uses the normal greeting adapted to the occasion:

"The apostles and elders and brethren send greeting unto the brethren which are of the Gentiles in Antioch and Syria and Cilicia ... Fare ye well."

Other letters of Peter, James and Jude show interesting variations, some lacking a formal opening, others without the final greeting; but in general there is special mention of the value and privilege of the relationship of both writer and readers with God and the Lord Jesus Christ.

A New Content

It was Paul, however, who above all impressed upon the formal style of letter-writing the mark of his own style and devotion to Christ, and, while retaining the usual forms of polite communication, gave them a specifically religious content and transformed the whole epistolary art into a unique form of communication of Divine things. It is this fact, of course, which renders futile any attempts to decide the authorship of the letters on any principle which could be applied to Classical authors, by computer or any other means employed by modern critics.

The plain fact is that Classical authors paid conscious attention to their literary style, even their private correspondence having a wider public in view, and much polishing and re-writing went into it. Paul wrote as he was moved to do so, with his message and

9

his readers in the forefront of his mind, adapting his style to the matter in hand and enlarging his vocabulary to suit his theme in a way which defies mechanical analysis. Above all, it is his use of the greeting and farewell which sets the seal of authenticity on all his work.

The development of Paul's thought can be seen in the *superscriptions* to his letters. 1 and 2 Thessalonians contain merely his own name and those of his colleagues, Silas and Timothy. The Letter to the Ephesians contains (in Greek) seven words, 1 Corinthians eight, 1 Timothy fifteen, Titus forty-seven and Romans seventy-two. It is not merely the length but the content of the title which is instructive. Among his earlier letters, 1 and 2 Thessalonians are the nearest in style to private correspondence. Galatians, with twenty-six words, contains in its opening Paul's own title of "an apostle . . . by Jesus Christ, and God the Father". Thenceforward every letter, with the exception of Philemon and Philippians (for which ecclesia Paul seems to have had a special affection), bears the mark of Paul's apostolic authority in its title. Sometimes there are additions or modifications in the formula, as in 1 Timothy and Titus where the precise instructions for the good of the churches in question come from "Paul, an apostle . . . by the *commandment* of God", a word of almost military significance which makes him an officer passing on the orders of no less an authority than God Himself.

Again, Paul abandons the strictly impersonal form of traditional usage—"Gaius to Titus gives greeting"—and uses "I", "me" and "us" in a more intimate and personal way. In short, although he writes as an apostle, a delegate of the Lord Jesus Christ, and his words are authoritative, he is still addressing communities of men and women for whom he has a concern, so that there is no "officialese" even in his more "official" letters.

A Guide to Tone

In the *ascription* Paul allows the reader to gauge the tone of the letter to follow. Compare, for example, Romans 1:7—"To all that be in Rome, beloved of God, called to be saints"; or 1 Corinthians 1:2, another affectionate greeting, with the rather curt "Unto the churches of Galatia" (Galatians 1:2). On the other hand, 2 Timothy, which has only three Greek words in the ascription, is to "Timothy, my dearly beloved son", while the shortest letter of them all, Philemon, has twenty-one words of introduction. Yet both letters associate Paul with his correspondents in a personal and characteristically Christian way.

Indeed, the Christian character of the recipients is always expressed. The Thessalonians are addressed as "the church ... which is in God the Father and in the Lord Jesus Christ"; the Corinthians, Romans and Philippians are all "saints" or "sanctified"; the Ephesians and Colossians are "faithful" or "faithful brethren" in Christ; and the relationship with Timothy and Titus is one "in the faith" or "in the common faith". Here again there are no empty phrases demanded by a code of etiquette and, as Spicq says (*Les Épîtres Pastorales*), in the Pastoral Letters especially "it is God Himself who, by the voice of His herald, addresses Himself to His children newly-begotten, to educate them as men of God according to the Scripture".

Mercy, Grace and Peace

The *salutation* is thus made all the more a Christian greeting at the hands of Paul. Ordinary letter-writers contented themselves with a single word of greeting, often identical with that exchanged between passers-by in the street, a brief equivalent of our "Good day!" (Perhaps one could usefully meditate on the differences in national character and hope implied in the Roman greeting, which meant literally "Good health", the Greek "Be happy" and the Hebrew "Peace".) For the single word of greeting Paul substitutes a Christian wish for grace and peace. In a skilful way he replaces the conventional *chairein* (Be happy!) with the word *charis* (Grace), keeping an almost familiar sound but enriching the meaning. Often he adds the source of the blessings: they are from "God the Father and our Lord Jesus Christ". For it is of the great mercy of God that His grace has been revealed in our Lord Jesus, through whom we have the peace of God that passeth all understanding.

It is significant, too, that in the last letters he wrote—these to Timothy and Titus—increasingly conscious of the need for the Divine mercy both for himself and for the community, he adds the wish for "mercy" to "grace and peace". No doubt he was responding to, or more probably initiating, a development in the style of greeting between Christian brethren everywhere in the ancient world. At any rate we can surely take a lesson from Paul who was no longer concerned with the worldly happiness and good fortune of his correspondents, but with their spiritual well-being and their response to the greatest of all gifts—those of grace, mercy and peace.

Expressive Subscriptions

There followed the main body of the letter, and the final close or greeting. The *subscription* of Greek letters contained compliments, polite expressions, a final wish, and then the date. If the last ever appeared on the letters of Paul it has nowhere survived. To give lists of people to whom he pays his respects (as in Romans) or people the apostle associates with himself in greeting, seems to have been an innovation of Paul himself, unknown in ordinary correspondence. It is a mark of his concern for, and knowledge of the circumstances of his readers, consistent with his concept of Christian ministry. Indeed, only Galatians and 1 Timothy end without some such mention. "Greet all the brethren", "Salute the brethren"—these are common phrases as the end of Paul's epistles.

Additional exhortations and wishes show slight variations but amount in principle to the same thing. The Apostle never uses the conventional secular wishes for good health or earthly fortune, but always seeks for the brethren the gifts of grace and peace, often bringing the name of the Lord Jesus into his farewell blessing. Perhaps the most expressive of them all is the conclusion of 2 Corinthians:

"The grace of the Lord Jesus Christ, and the love of God, and the communion of the Holy Spirit, be with you all. Amen."

There was no need of signature. The name of the sender was in the superscription anyway. Nor was there any need for Paul to seal up the letters, for they were taken by trusty messengers, such as Timothy, Phoebe (Romans 16:1) and the former runaway slave, Onesimus, who (a nice touch of Paul's here) was associated with Tychicus in the letter to the Colossians, as well as bearing that to Philemon. But whoever was his secretary or his courier, Paul seems invariably to have finished the letter, the final greeting, with his own hand. So the personal sentiments and the large handwriting (Colossians 4:18; 1 Corinthians 16:21; 2 Thessalonians 3:17; Galatians 6:11, etc.) were the hall-mark of the work of the great apostle who, through the medium of ordinary correspondence and in the framework of the conventions of his day, fulfilled the charge laid upon him, and manifested his care for all the churches.

SUGGESTED TABLE OF THE LAST YEARS OF PAUL'S LIFE

AD

61	Spring	Reaches Rome.
62		*At Rome:* Writes Philemon, Colossians, Ephesians; in autumn, Philippians.
63	Spring	Released; goes to Macedonia (Philippians 2:24), Asia Minor (Philemon 22).
64-65		Visits Spain (see Romans 15:24,28). Great Fire at Rome: persecution of Christians begins.
66	Summer	To Asia Minor (1 Timothy 1:3). Finds that process foreseen in Acts 20 has begun. Goes to Macedonia. Jewish War begins. Letter to Hebrews probably written about this time.
67	Summer	Writes 1 Timothy from Macedonia. Returns to Ephesus (1 Timothy 3:14,15) via Troas? (2 Timothy 4:13). Short expedition to Crete. Letter to Titus. Via Miletus to Corinth (2 Timothy 4:20).
	Winter	Nicopolis (Titus 3:12); re-arrested, after Titus had gone north (2 Timothy 4:10).
68		*In prison at Rome again.*
	Spring	Writes 2 Timothy.
	Summer	Executed (Nero died mid-June same year).

(Collated and adapted from various authorities)

The First Letter to Timothy

CHAPTER 1

The Importance of Sound Doctrine

IT is impossible to fix a precise date for the First Letter. There are many difficulties in the way of harmonising the indications of time and place in it with any of the details given in the Acts. Even if we accept the suggestion in the Introduction that the epistle relates to a period between two imprisonments, we can do no more than put forward the possibility that the date of writing was towards the end of that period, say AD 66 or 67, as in the Table set out on the previous page.

Paul says that he had given Timothy a charge "when I went into Macedonia" (1 Timothy 1:3), which is no certain indication that Paul was now writing from there; or if he were, that he had not been further afield beforehand. That he was on his way back to Ephesus seems probable from 1 Timothy 3:14. But wherever he had been, perhaps even to Spain as some suggest (see Romans 15:28), what more natural than a sojourn amongst his beloved Philippians on the return journey?

The contents of this Epistle afford confirmation of the later date suggested by the more advanced state of ecclesial organisation they envisage and the stage of development of the false teaching frequently alluded to. The object of the Epistle is plain enough: it was to warn and exhort Timothy personally and reinforce him with the Apostle's own written authority to counteract the undesirable trends in the ecclesia at Ephesus, by sound organisation, positive teaching and, above all, his personal integrity in doctrine and life.

1:1-2—Address and Salutation

The superscription is *"Paul, an apostle ... "* An apostle was a messenger, 'one sent', and the Greek *apostolos* is so translated in

14

2 Corinthians 8:23 and Philippians 2:25. There a representative of the local ecclesia seems to be in view. But Paul's apostleship was of a higher status: he was commissioned personally by Christ as his ambassador (2 Corinthians 5:20; Ephesians 6:20), and belonged to him as his minister and servant. Thus the letter, though addressed to Timothy personally, is an "open letter" in the best sense: not one offering criticism to an individual, to which the writer wished to give the widest publicity, but one the recipient can use publicly for the effective discharge of his duty. Timothy now has written apostolic authority for his delicate and responsible task.

"Christ Jesus": Most versions give this order of words here. "Jesus Christ" expresses briefly the idea that Jesus is the Christ; "Christ Jesus" emphasises the title rather than the person of the Lord.

"According to the commandment": The commandment is clearly expressed in Acts 13:2—"Separate me Barnabas and Saul for the work whereunto I have called them." The same phrase occurs in Titus 1:3. The word is *epitagē*, and its use in Titus 2:15 helps to define its sense: "rebuke with all *authority*." Paul's usual words defining his commission are according to "the *will* of God" (1 Corinthians 1:1; 2 Corinthians 1:1; Ephesians 1:1; Colossians 1:1; 2 Timothy 1:1), but perhaps "commandment" is a more appropriate word when God and Christ are joined in the same phrase: God commanded and Christ gave the actual order. See also 1 Corinthians 7:6, where *epitagē*, 'commandment', is contrasted with *sugnomē*, 'concession'.

"God our Saviour": The application of the title Saviour to God instead of to Christ is characteristic of the Pastoral Epistles and of no other letters of Paul (1 Timothy 2:3; 4:10; Titus 1:3; 2:10,13; 3:4). Its use there and in Jude 25, another late New Testament writing, has given rise to the idea that it was a counter to the growing tendency to attribute the title of Saviour to the pagan emperors. Elsewhere in Paul the title is given to Christ as being the one through whom the great deliverance from sin and death was wrought.

In fact, God is frequently described as Saviour in the Old Testament, notably in the Psalms (24:5; 25:5; 27:1,9; 62:2,6; 65:5; 70:4; 95:1) and Isaiah (12:2; 17:10; 25:9; 45:15) and it is a thoroughly Old Testament idea to which Mary gives expression in Luke 1:47—"My spirit hath rejoiced in God *my Saviour.*" For she was to bring forth God's only begotten Son and call his name Jesus ('the Lord is salvation'), because he would "save his people from their sins". He would also be Immanuel, "the Holy One in the midst of thee".

"The Lord Jesus Christ, which is our hope": A profound truth lies in these words. God has become our salvation because He "hath begotten us again unto a lively hope by the resurrection of Jesus Christ from the dead" (1 Peter 1:3). He is the ground of our "hope of glory" (Colossians 1:27). In these two expressions ("Saviour" and "hope") the present and future aspects of salvation are clearly seen. God *saved* us, potentially (2 Timothy 1:9; Titus 2:11; 3:4,5—tenses are all aorist, expressing completed "once for all" action), but we still look "for that blessed hope, and the glorious appearing of the great God and our Saviour Jesus Christ" for the full realisation. See also 1 Peter 1:20,21, where the sense could probably be better expressed as "so that your faith might be your hope in God".

"Unto Timothy, my own son in the faith": This form of address, with its tender gentleness, speaks volumes about the mind of the Apostle and his feelings towards Timothy. "Ye have ten thousand instructors in Christ", he wrote to the Corinthians, "yet have ye not many fathers: for in Christ Jesus I have begotten you through the gospel" (1 Corinthians 4:15). Just as those who are led by the Spirit of God are His beloved sons by adoption, so Timothy and Titus (1:4) were Paul's spiritual sons, begotten, cherished and now made his worthy representatives. *Gnēsios*, 'true-born', 'legitimate', is found in the New Testament only in Paul. In 2 Corinthians 8:8 it refers to the *sincerity* of love and in Philippians 4:3 to a *true* yokefellow, expressions which illuminate the quality of Paul's relationship with Timothy just as the word *teknon*, 'child', expresses affection as well as a spiritual relationship (see also Acts 16:1-3). The Greek text omits the definite article before "faith", another characteristic of the Pastoral Letters when dealing with familiar Christian terms.

"Grace, mercy, peace from God our Father and Christ Jesus our Lord": "Grace" and "peace" form the salutation to all the other Pauline epistles, and to Peter's epistles and Revelation: "mercy" is added

in the Pastorals and 2 John (see "Introduction", page 11). Grace is the mark of God's condescension towards sinful men, the strong coming to the help of the weak—"by grace ye are saved, and that not of yourselves". To wish that the beauty of God's holiness and of His loving kindness should be upon those with whom we too correspond is to wish them all that can be desired, especially when coupled with "the peace of God that passeth all understanding".

It is the hall-mark of the Scripturally ordered life of the man "whose mind is stayed on thee: because he trusteth in thee" (Isaiah 26:3). But man needs pardon for the past as well as strength for the future, and the sense of the wideness of God's mercy had evidently grown in the Apostle's mind over the years since first he, "a blasphemer, and a persecutor", had become a very pattern to them that believe of the long-suffering of God in action (1 Timothy 1:12-16). What more natural then than that a spiritual father, now ageing and approaching the hour of his appearing before the righteous Judge, should adapt once more an old Jewish blessing of mercy and peace (Galatians 6:16) with which to bless his own son in the faith?

1:3-7—Paul's Charge to Timothy

Verses 3-4: That Paul is now sending a written memorandum of previous oral instructions, given as he was on the point of departure (RV), appears from verse 3. The original text reveals one of the peculiarities of the Apostle's style, when he begins a sentence of which the strict grammatical conclusion seems to be temporarily lost sight of in the full flow of his thought. Examples are to be found in Romans 5:12; Galatians 2:4; Ephesians 3:1, where the conclusion of the sentence is delayed unto 4:1. *"As I exhorted thee"* has a conclusion supplied in italics by both AV and RV in verse 4: *"So do"*. The thought is in fact sustained until 2:1, "I exhort therefore", where the practical measures to be taken by Timothy are spelt out. For all his apostolic authority, clearly emphasised in most of the epistles, Paul prefers to exhort or beseech his readers. The verb *parakaleō* is used about 50 times in this sense (it also means 'to comfort') throughout his works.

As already pointed out, the historical details of Paul's stay with Timothy at Ephesus and his visit to Macedonia (verse 3) cannot be accurately defined. No such doubt surrounds the Apostle's exhortation: Timothy was to *"abide still": prosmenō* is used by Paul only in this letter: in 5:5 it refers to the "widow indeed, and desolate" who *"continueth* in prayers and supplications night and day". In Acts 11:23 Barnabas urged the brethren at Antioch "that with purpose of heart they would *cleave* unto the Lord"; and Paul, in spite of all the difficulties that beset him *"tarried* yet" in Corinth (Acts 18:18): so Timothy was to 'remain at his post'.

The military metaphor in fact suits the task entrusted to him: he was to *"charge some that they teach no other doctrine"*. The charge was committed to him (1:18) that he might pass it on, as from the higher command. This idea is present throughout the Pastoral Letters, since Paul derived his authority as an apostle from the Lord Jesus, and what he committed to Timothy, the younger man was to commit to "faithful men . . . able to teach others also" (2 Timothy 2:2).

The strength of the words for "charge" (*parangello* and *parangellia*), both verb and noun, can be gauged from their use elsewhere in the New Testament. In the Gospels (Matthew 10:5; Mark 6:8; 8:6; Luke 5:14; 8:29,56; 9:21) it is always the Lord's commandment; in Acts it is either the categorical instructions of the Sanhedrin that the apostles should not preach the resurrection, the charge to the gaoler at Philippi, or some other military occasion, or else a command of the Lord Jesus to his apostles, or one made in his name to cast out an evil spirit (Acts 16:18). It appears elsewhere only in 1 Corinthians, Thessalonians and, significantly, seven times in 1 Timothy. We shall note these occurrences in their place.

Timothy was to charge "some". It is probable that Paul is being intentionally vague rather than contemptuous here, although he does name two in particular later. The number of Timothy's potential opponents might well have been small at this stage. It is characteristic of Paul, however, to name names in a critical way only when he has to, preferring generally to keep the personal element out of his censure, since his purpose is to reform and not to provoke. For examples, see 1 Corinthians 4:18; 2 Corinthians 3:1; Galatians 1:7. We can gather from the same epistles that his opponents were not equally generous, but we shall do well to follow Paul's example rather than theirs.

18

To describe the work of the brethren who were putting the faith of others at risk Paul apparently coined a new word, "to other-teach", which is found in 1 Timothy 1:3 and 6:3 and nowhere else in Greek literature up to that time. Emphasis on "teaching", both in content and method, is a characteristic of these letters, as will become apparent later, and two other compound words are used, for "law-teachers" (*nomodidaskaloi*, 1:7) and "good-teachers" (*kalodidaskaloi*, Titus 2:3), the latter being a "oncer", like "false-teachers" (*pseudodidaskaloi*) in 2 Peter 2:1.

The force of the word "other-teach", or rather "to be an other-teacher", as it applies directly to the theme of 1 Timothy will become more apparent from the verses which follow (and see Essay 1, page 41). Such teaching overthrew the faith of some because it ignored vital elements of the Gospel and it needed a workman who could rightly divide the word of truth to combat it (2 Timothy 2:15). The content of the teaching in Ephesus is suggested by the phrase *"fables and endless genealogies"* (see Essay 2, page 42). In Titus the fables or myths are defined as Jewish (1:14), and all five occurrences of the word *muthoi* can be so connected with Jewish traditions. Four of them are in the Pastorals (1 Timothy 1:4; 4:7; 2 Timothy 4:4; Titus 1:14) and the other in 2 Peter 1:16, where Peter is contrasting the true word of God with what the false prophets among the people were proclaiming (2:1). It is significant that this word, "other-teach", enters late into the vocabulary of the New Testament, suggesting that the earlier circumcision controversy (the word "circumcision" appears but once, in Titus 1:10) had given way to debates about the content and use of Scripture.

Building up the Ecclesia

The many further references in the three Epistles to the effects of false teachings leave no doubt as to the urgent necessity for the charge: there would arise "strifes of words" (*logomachini*, lit. 'word-battles') and many other things destructive of ecclesial life. The AV of 1 Timothy 1:4 adopts the reading *oikodomia*, "edifying", and certainly the other-teachers did nothing to minister to that, for there was no content to their doctrine which could be productive of faith. In the Letter to the Ephesians the Apostle had been concerned with the edifying, or building up of the church in love and unity. The other-teaching would have divided between

Jew and Gentile as effectively as would the earlier Judaising controversy, had not Paul opposed its protagonists. In the one case insistence on conformity to the Law and in the other on the possession of a secret, exclusive knowledge as essential for salvation, would make void the work of him through whom both Jew and Gentile have access by one Spirit unto the Father.

Perhaps the more usually adopted reading *oikonomia*, 'dispensation' or 'stewardship', yields even better sense as part of the charge to one who was to tend the flock. The word can mean either the office of the steward, or the method by which he carries out his duties. Both meanings are appropriate, in view of the fact that Paul had written to Timothy (3:15) that he might know how he ought to behave himself in the house of God, and by taking heed unto himself and his teaching save himself and them that heard him (4:16).

Paul now feels the need to break off the grammatical sequence of his sentence (see above) to explain further about the trust committed to him and Timothy, the "dispensation of God" (RV).

The End of the Charge

Verses 5-7: The RV *"But"* introducing verse 5 is surely correct: the whole purpose Paul has in view, the whole concept of good stewardship in the house of God, is the fostering of love, the greatest of the three abiding qualities, of the very nature of God Himself (1 John 4:16). The immediate reference here is to the promotion of love in the place of the strife caused by the false teachers, but the links are plainly with such passages as "love is the fulfilling of the law" (Romans 13:10); "Christ is the *end* of the law for righteousness to every one that believeth" (Romans 10:4).

So Timothy receives no profound arguments to combat the other-teachers. He is to concern himself with the positive instruction of which the ensuing letter is full, and the test of its validity would be the restoration of that loving spirit which seems to have characterised the Ephesian ecclesia in its earlier days (Acts 20:36-38). It would be interesting to know how well the balance was maintained in the ecclesia after Timothy's day. In Revelation 2:1-5 the ecclesia is highly commended for their zeal and the way in which they had dealt with the false apostles. But they had "left their first love", which, in view of the foregoing, can hardly mean their early love of the Truth; rather, "they did not love as they

20

used to do'', and this in the Lord's eyes was "somewhat against thee" (see Essay 3, "The Three-fold Origin of Love", page 44).

"Missing the mark"

"*Some*" in Ephesus "*swerved*" from these three things or rather "missed their aim". The word appears only here and in 6:21 and 2 Timothy 2:18, where it is translated as "erred" concerning the faith or the truth, in each case referring to the other-teachers. They may well have had good intentions, but failed because of a lack of sound method in handling Scripture. It seems clear that they were still members of the ecclesia, for otherwise Timothy could have no jurisdiction over them.

The picture is consistent with what is described in Acts 20, where a united body of elders came to see Paul at Miletus, but there were among them those who would later fall into error: "Of your own selves shall men arise, speaking perverse things" (verse 30). They would thus "*turn aside*", or swerve from the path, in which the true "workmen needing not to be ashamed" would "hold a straight course in the word of truth" (2 Timothy 2:15). "Turn aside" is a typical word from these Letters: some widows were "already *turned aside* after Satan" (5:15); Timothy was to see to it that he "*avoided*" completely "profane and vain babblings" (6:20); while the followers of the other-teachers would themselves be "*turned* unto fables" (2 Timothy 4:4).

The only other New Testament use (Hebrews 12:13) is equally revealing: "Make straight paths for your feet, lest that which is lame be *turned out of the way*". Or, as the Old Testament passage on which the verse is based has it: "Make level the path of thy feet ... *Turn not* to the right hand nor to the left" (Proverbs 4:26,27, RV).

There is a practical as well as a theoretical need to hold a straight course in the word of truth: having defined the way, one then has to walk in it. Otherwise, all is "*vain jangling*", or empty talk (see Titus 1:10), a special characteristic of the other-teachers. This "oncer" in the Pastorals is related to the "vain conversation" or traditional way of life (1 Peter 1:18), "vain thoughts" of the wise (1 Corinthians 3:20), "vain religion", of the man without control of his tongue (James 1:26), and "vain imaginations" of those who "changed the truth of God into a lie" (Romans 1:21).

21

Yet what the *other*-teachers had sought was the honourable title of "*law-teachers*", or "doctors of the law" (Luke 5:17; Acts 5:34; and verse 7 only), with all the respect and influence of a Gamaliel at whose feet Paul himself had been brought up. Verse 7 confirms that the content of the teaching was concerned more with Jewish than with Gnostic learning, although the false teachers had departed a long way from the conservative Judaisers who wanted to impose the Law as a way of life. Rather had they sought to emulate the intellectual skill of contemporary Rabbinical commentators, and in doing so missed the point of both the Old Testament and the Gospel. For a teacher must first of all understand what he teaches and be perfectly clear in his own mind that it is true. The false teachers are charged with the exact opposite: they understood "*neither what they say, nor whereof they confidently affirm*" (RV).

The scene is a familiar one: the dogmatism with which a theory is propounded is no guide to its validity. Again a word familiar enough in the cultured Hellenistic world (*diabebaiousthai*, 'confidently affirm') finds its only place in the Greek Bible here and Titus 3:8. The positive affirmation and entire confidence of the "other-teachers" must be matched by the man of God's equally confident and constant exhortations to the ecclesia to maintain good works, profitable to men, and "avoid foolish questions, and genealogies, and contentions, and strivings about the law; for they are unprofitable and vain" (Titus 3:9).

1:8-11—The Right Use of the Law

Verse 8: Paul immediately guards against possible misunderstanding of his attitude to the law, as distinct from the professed teachers of it, by a comment upon its quality and purpose: "*But we know that the law is good.*" The context demands that we understand not "law" in general, but the Law of Moses in particular. He is not decrying the validity of that Law but opposing the futility of the speculations of the other-teachers about it. The word *kalos*, 'good' or 'beautiful', is used 24 times in the Pastoral Letters, compared with 16 in other letters of Paul, and it has a shade of meaning which *agathos*, 'intrinsic goodness', has not. For the Greek philosophers, their studies led them to the pursuit of the *kalos kai agathos*—"the beautiful and the good", or the quality of beauty and nobility that springs from excellence. It has been

22

suggested that in a Biblical context "the beauty of holiness" is expressed by *kalos* in a way no single English word can reproduce. It is applied to God's law in Romans 7:16—"If then I do that which I would not, I consent unto the law that it is good (*kalos*)."

The Law is good "*if a man use it lawfully*", that is, suitably for the purpose for which it is intended. Paul's word-play on "*law . . . lawfully*" is equally apparent in the Greek *nomos . . . nomimōs*, the latter word being found elsewhere only in 2 Timothy 2:5 and once in the Apocrypha.

Verse 9: "*Knowing this*" is grammatically attached to the preceding "a man", and refers to the essential view to be taken of the Law by the true teacher, a view to be expounded in the verses that follow. "Knowing this" is characteristic of Paul, as in the original of Romans 5:3; 6:6; 2 Corinthians 4:14; Galatians 2:16; Colossians 3:24, and something of its force can be learned from consulting these passages. Being "well aware" of certain things, the disciple believes or acts accordingly. In this case it is the fact that law is not "*made* (or ordained) *for the righteous*" but for the wicked of various classes which must be borne in mind. Its practical end was to make men righteous, which it could not actually do, as Paul is at pains elsewhere to point out (e.g. Galatians 3:21); therefore its spiritual end was to bring men unto Christ (Galatians 3:24), "that we might be justified by faith".

It will be noticed that in the list that follows, the acts of impiety, profanity and defilement are the grossest forms of what the Ten Commandments prohibit for the people of God. They are all expounded in practical terms in the Book of Deuteronomy, in which the Law of God in its principles is expressed in terms of the laws of the land, the centre of the worship of God and the throne of His Kingdom.

"*Lawless and disobedient*" is a general description of those who are unwilling to submit to restraints upon their behaviour. *Anomos*, the word that describes the "wicked" that crucified Christ, the deeds of Sodom, and the thieves executed with the Lord, appears here only in the Pastorals. It is coupled with *anupotaktos* (peculiar to the Pastorals and Hebrews 2:8), usually translated "unruly" (see RV) as in Titus 1:6,10, which has a positive verbal form, "be in subjection (to higher powers)" in Romans 13:1,5.

The rest of Paul's list contains several words peculiar to these Letters, or found only in the Septuagint or later New Testament writings like 2 Peter or Jude. *"The ungodly and sinners"* (*asebēs* and *hamartōlos*) are joined together also in 1 Peter 4:18 (from Proverbs 11:31) and Jude 15. For those without reverence for God or who actually deny Him, the Lord is not merciful, gracious, long-suffering and abundant in goodness and truth: they hate Him and are therefore outside His covenant.

This idea is well taken up in the words *"unholy and profane"* (*anosios* and *bebēlos*). As one commentator (J. H. Bernard, *The Pastoral Epistles*, Cambridge Greek Testament for Schools and Colleges) has put it: "Such is the temper which lies at the root of the sin of perjury, explicitly forbidden in the Third Commandment." *Anosios* occurs in the LXX, but only again in 2 Timothy 3:2; *bebēlos* is an instructive word, especially in its application to Esau. Its basic idea is that of ground which can be walked on— that is, outside the sanctuary, and so 'secular' (cf. Exodus 3:5 —"Put off thy shoes from off thy feet, for the place whereon thou standest is holy ground"). Esau, having despised his birthright, placed himself outside the covenant and so could not inherit the blessing. "A root of bitterness" sprang up and defiled him (Hebrews 12:15), and the context in Deuteronomy 29:18 of that quotation shows that it refers to turning away the heart from the Lord our God. This background will help us understand more accurately Paul's use of *bebēlos* when we consider the later references.

"Smiters (RV margin) *of fathers and mothers"* were extreme and outrageous violators of the Fifth Commandment, as "man-slayers" (a "oncer" in the New Testament) were of the Sixth.

Verse 10: *"Fornicators and sodomites"* broke the Seventh Commandment. *"Menstealers"*, despising the Eighth Commandment, practised the most despicable of all theft—that of a man's own self, and the practice is specifically condemned in Exodus 21:16 and Deuteronomy 24:7. The word itself appears nowhere else in the Greek Bible, but the idea it represented carried severe condemnation (see also Amos 1:6,9).

Of the words for *"liars and perjurers"*, the latter is also a *hapax* ("oncer") in the New Testament, although it comes from the same root as the verb used by the Lord in Matthew 5:33, meaning 'to foreswear'. "To suppress the truth is a form of 'false witness', but the worst form is a false charge made on oath" (Bernard); the Apostle's reference is clearly to the Ninth Commandment.

It is to be noticed, however, that in his use of words and ideas in these verses, Paul is following the thought of the Master. It is not to be assumed that in giving examples of the grossest forms of wickedness with which the *anomoi*, 'the lawless', violate the Ten Commandments, the Apostle thinks that only such men are sinners. Rather is he reminding us that by the law sin is revealed to be "exceeding sinful" (Romans 7:13), and that all departures from the Divine standards are gross. The Lord made the same point (Matthew 5:21-37) when he declared that murder was unreasonable anger, adultery the lustful glance, and the disciple's lightly given "yea, yea or nay, nay" could take God's name in vain: "When lust hath conceived, it bringeth forth sin" (James 1:15).

Only those sins have been actually specified in Paul's list which can be regulated by law, in the sense that their effects are observable by others. But there are sins, such as covetousness, to which only the heart of the sinner and, of course, God Himself are privy. Perhaps covetousness is in the Apostle's mind when he concludes his list of things which God's law is designed to combat with *"and if there be any other thing which is contrary to sound doctrine"* (see Essay 4, page 46), arising out of "the lust of the flesh, the lust of the eyes, and the pride of life" (1 John 2:16).

The Apostle applies the word "sound" to *healthy* doctrine, and contrasts this with error when he adds that "if any man teach otherwise ('other-teach') . . . he is *ailing* (AV, *doting*)" (1 Timothy 6:3,4). Although this term was applied especially to the situation prevailing in Ephesus at the time, the warning against discussion of questions ultimately destructive of faith is timely for us. After all, everyone is just not capable of striking the right balance between possible opinions, and those who are have the responsibility of not "helping the unbelief" of the others in the wrong direction. There are "words which will eat as doth a canker" (2 Timothy 2:17) now, as then, often of the same type as those of Hymenaeus and Philetus who were guilty of wrong emphasis to the point of missing the mark as far as the truth was concerned. It is true that every baptized believer has passed through a sort

25

of resurrection when raised to newness of life. To say, however, that this was the true meaning of resurrection, which was therefore past already, overthrew the faith of some not capable of evaluating the statement for what it was worth.

It is imperative that the Brotherhood become more sensitive to the distinction between the profitable and the unprofitable, the helpful and the unhelpful, that it avoid both the shut mind unreceptive to the full implications of Christian teaching, and also the mind so open that it is willing to accept anything at all. Moreover, the raising of doubtful issues and the pressing of personal opinions in a way which tends to form partisan groups is what is meant by the word "heretic" in Titus 3:10, and it is condemned by the Apostle in no uncertain terms.

Verse 11: *"The glorious gospel of the blessed God"*: the nature of the sound doctrine is thus further defined, in this Hebraism for "the gospel of the glory". The false teachers asserted that the Law was designed for a righteous man and urged their interpretations as a necessary appendix to the Gospel. Their doctrine, like the wickedness of men itself, was not answerable to the true message of the Gospel.

It is highly appropriate that Paul should refer to the glory of God immediately after his catalogue of vices for which the restraint of law is necessary. "For all have sinned, and come short of the glory of God" (Romans 3:23). The "glory of the Lord" first appeared in the cloud to Israel at a time when they were manifesting their sinfulness, to leave them in no doubt as to the nature of their "shortcoming" (Exodus 16:4-10). The Gospel likewise revealed the glory of the Lord (with rich harmonies of Exodus 34:6,7), in its message of the grace and truth, the righteousness of God, and the wrath of God against every evil work (John 1:17; Romans 1:17-19). Only in this verse and in 6:15 is the term *makarios*, 'blessed', applied to God in the whole of Scripture. It is not only that men bless the Lord *(eulogeō,* 'to speak well'): He is the source of all blessedness in Himself, and the hope in Him and His salvation is therefore a *blessed* hope (Titus 2:13).

"Committed to my trust": Paul was always acutely conscious of his responsibility as an apostle of the Lord Jesus, and a preacher of the Gospel. We shall consider this point in further detail when

we discuss 1 Timothy 6:20 and Titus 1:9, under the title of "the good deposit", a banker's term expressing all that "committing to" and "trust" implies in that profession (see page 201). For the present we refer the reader to 1 Corinthians 9:17; Galatians 2:7; Colossians 1:25; 1 Thessalonians 2:4 (especially); 2 Timothy 1:11 and Titus 1:3. Paul's contemplation of both his responsibility and privilege (1 Thessalonians 2:4), and the bountiful mercy and longsuffering of God thus displayed to him personally, leads naturally to the next section. This is in the form of a parenthesis in which thankfulness, praise, wonder and adoration are expressed as his personal experience of the truth that "Christ Jesus came into the world to save sinners" (verse 15). No clearer indication of the practical aspect of "doctrine" and the necessity for such a statement of the faith could be given us.

1:12-17—Paul's own experience of the Gospel

Some commentators think that it was sometimes a convention in ancient letters to include expressions of praise and thanks to a god. Even if this were so, however, there is no following of a convention in the thankfulness of the Apostle, ending as it does in an outburst of "wonder, love and praise" characteristic of the man so responsive to the grace of God towards him—cf. the ending of Romans 11 and 1 Timothy 6:16. The very mention of "the gospel of the glory of the blessed God" (verse 11, RV) leads him to describe in gratitude his personal experience of its power unto salvation, which made him "a pattern to them which should hereafter believe".

Verse 12: "I thank Christ Jesus our Lord": The Apostle's usual word for "I thank" is *eucharistō*, but here and in 2 Timothy 1:3 he uses the rarer *charin echō*, found elsewhere in the New Testament only in Luke 17:9 and Hebrews 12:28—"let us *have grace*" being a literal translation of the expression. (It is worth noting in passing the links between the vocabulary of the Pastoral Epistles and that of Luke, and some of the later epistles, specially Hebrews.) *Charin echō* was common enough in New Testament times, but it has been suggested that Paul adopted it after his stay in Rome, where he became acquainted with the Latin idiom, *gratiam habeo*, which is the exact equivalent.

"Who hath enabled me": The idea of power and strength *(dunamis)* with reference to the grace of the Lord Jesus Christ is a favourite

one of Paul's. The word here is a verb, *endunamō*, and three of Paul's six uses of it appear in 1 and 2 Timothy; again it is used in Acts and Hebrews, where the exact sense in which it is to be understood in Paul's reference to his own experience is plain to read. After his conversion and baptism "Saul *increased* the more in *strength*" (Acts 9:22) as he preached Christ in the synagogues. The Lord who had called him equipped him for the task, just as God's faithful servants through the ages "out of weakness were *made strong*" (Hebrews 11:34), so that they could say with Paul, "I can do all things through Christ which *strengtheneth* me" (Philippians 4:13; see 2 Timothy 2:1; 4:17). Thus did he prove that Jesus was "the very Christ" (Acts 9:22).

"For that he counted me faithful": Paul had already written to the Corinthians (1 Corinthians 4:2) that "it is required in stewards, that a man be found *faithful*", and the sense is clearly *trustworthy*. We shall consider some aspects of the word for "faithful" later, since it is used repeatedly in these letters. In fact, trustworthiness both in handling the Word of God and in the conduct of ecclesial affairs is the basis of Paul's solution for the problems affecting the ecclesias in Ephesus and Crete—and the same is true today.

"The ministry"

For "the ministry" referred to in verse 12 is to be understood in the general sense, not the technical as in 1 Timothy 3:8-13. The *diakonia* is the service rendered to the Lord in love and devotion, and the very use of this word in this sense is an argument against a date in the second or third century for the writing of these letters, which the critics suggest. By that date the word was used of a lower rank of Church servant and would never have referred to an apostle.

Such characteristic words and usages of Paul stamp the letters with the seal of authenticity, as does the word "count" in "*counted* me faithful", in the sense of "esteem". The thankfulness he felt at being held in some esteem by the Lord whom he had persecuted lent force to his exhortations to the brethren at Philippi to have lowliness of mind and "each *esteem* other better than themselves" (2:3; see also 1 Thessalonians 5:13).

"Putting me into the ministry": "putting" is a weak expression to describe the purpose of the Lord himself in making Paul a

"chosen vessel" and ordering the affairs of the ecclesias. For all the main uses of the Greek word in the New Testament, the subject is God Himself, working through Christ or the Holy Spirit. So He *made* the overseers in Ephesus (Acts 20:28), *made* Abraham father of many nations (Romans 4:17), *set* the members in the body and "some" in the church in various capacities, and *appointed* some to wrath and others to escape it (1 Thessalonians 5:9). Likewise Paul was *ordained* a preacher and an apostle—an unworthy man (in his own estimation), entrusted to proclaim God's grace with the conviction that he was a living example of what that grace really was.

Verse 13: "A blasphemer, and a persecutor, and injurious": Paul describes his former conduct in the strongest possible terms. In them he takes to himself the lesson of what the purpose of the Law was, and on his own principle of being a debtor to the whole Law if a man offend in one particular, confessed that he was chief of sinners. A *blasphemer* offended against the first and great commandment, which summed up the first Table of the Law: he spoke against God, by denying the resurrection and Divine Sonship of the Lord, whom God had declared to be "the Son of God with power . . . by the resurrection of the dead" (Romans 1:4, RV). It was in the very context of his persuading Agrippa that there was nothing incredible in the thought of God raising the dead, that he declared: "I verily thought with myself, that I ought to do many things *contrary to the name of Jesus of Nazareth*" (Acts 26:9). In his being "exceedingly mad against them", he even compelled Christ's brethren to blaspheme (verse 11).

He had been pulled up short, however, in the realisation that as *a persecutor* of the disciples he was persecuting Jesus himself as well as breaking the Second Commandment, which was "like unto" the First; in that very act (Acts 9:1,4,5 etc.) he had been made a witness of the fact that Christ was risen indeed.

He had indeed been injurious, a wanton aggressor, almost a "bully", using one of the words with which he had earlier described those who had not retained a true sense of the living God in their minds, "despiteful" (Romans 1:30). Indeed, only in these two passages does the adjective *hubristēs* occur in the whole of the New Testament, although the verb "to treat shamefully or spitefully" is used in connection with persecution and stoning, such as Paul had suffered himself at the hands of his countrymen

(Acts 14:5; 1 Thessalonians 2:2; see also Matthew 22:6; Luke 18:32). It is interesting to see from the use of this word in Luke 11:45 how the lawyers smarted under the Lord's words: "Thou *reproachest* us also."

"But I obtained mercy": the contrast between what he had been and what he was allowed to become—a minister of the Gospel— was clearly always in the Apostle's thoughts. It was a living testimony as to the nature of God's mercy. *He* is faithful, though man be not; His covenant love extends to those who fail to keep His standards, His glory is not obscured by those who come short of it. So the Lord is plenteous in mercy, and Paul had obtained it, undeserving though he felt himself to be.

Obtaining or receiving mercy is a characteristic phrase of Paul's, especially in the Letter to the Romans, and the verb used appears frequently in the Gospels, usually in the form of an appeal to "the Son of David" to have compassion on the sick. In 1 Corinthians 7:25, Paul gives his opinion on a marital problem "as *one that hath obtained mercy* of the Lord to be faithful" (see 1 Timothy 1:12 again)—a powerful lesson in the spirit with which we should approach such difficulties in our own time: as faithful stewards, who have themselves obtained mercy of the Lord and therefore count the showing of compassion as an important element in a faithful ministry.

But if Paul had been a blasphemer, he was no blasphemer against the Holy Spirit. He obtained mercy because he acted *"ignorantly in unbelief"*. Unbelief or *apistia*, 'lack of faith', goes hand in hand with ignorance, as the Jews themselves were witnesses. Their rulers who had admitted that Christ had done many miracles yet deliberately plotted his death (John 12:47; cf. Acts 4:16), were in a dangerous spiritual condition.

The people, too, were counted as having taken him by wicked hands to slay him (Acts 2:23). But in the spirit of the Lord Jesus, who had prayed, "Father, forgive them, for they know not what they do", Peter could say to the Jews, "And now, brethren, I wot that through *ignorance* ye did it, as did also your rulers" (3:17). They believed also that they were doing God service, by killing the disciples, as the Lord had foretold (John 16:2), a motive to which Paul also confessed (Acts 26:9). When the true nature of God's service *(diakonia)* was brought home to him, "he was not disobedient to the heavenly vision". The quality of our own service, personal and ecclesial, will be commensurate with our estimate of the grace we have received.

Verse 14: *"The grace of our Lord was exceeding abundant":* Paul's own estimate was a very high one indeed, and again his vocabulary accurately reveals his thought, and again the authenticity of these letters as his work is also revealed. Expressions like *abounding* grace, faith that *grows exceedingly*, the glory that *excels*, all contain the Greek prefix *hyper*, and are one of the marks of the Apostle's writings (see Romans 8:37; 1 Corinthians 10:13; 2 Corinthians 7:4; Philippians 2:9; 4:7; 1 Thessalonians 3:10; 4:6; 5:13; 2 Thessalonians 1:3, in any Greek Testament or Concordance). Although the actual word in this verse 14 *(hyperpleonazō)* is a very rare word, appearing nowhere else in the Greek Scriptures, the thought is no doubt consciously reproduced from Romans 5:20, which Paul is here applying to himself: "But where sin *abounded (pleonazō,* without the *hyper),* grace did *much more abound (hyperperissuō)."*

Grace and mercy must be linked together, and are no abstract concepts for Paul: as his sin manifested itself in real acts, so every act of service Paul was privileged to perform testified that *through* His grace God had granted him mercy.

The simple title "our Lord", is used once more by Paul (2 Timothy 1:8), and occurs in Hebrews 7:14 also—one more link in the chain of evidence which suggests that Hebrews was, after all, written by the Apostle to the Gentiles.

"Grace, faith and love" are also frequently joined together in Paul's writings. True faith believes in the grace and love which is in Christ Jesus, and as the disciple responds in love so the grace abounds. So disciples "abide in his love" if they keep his commandments (John 15:10) and, with "the breastplate of faith and love" (1 Thessalonians 5:8), grow in the "faith which worketh by love" (Galatians 5:6), manifesting such qualities as "work of faith, labour of love, patience of hope", which rejoice an Apostle's heart (1 Thessalonians 1:3; 3:6). Such qualities he commends to Timothy as the true end of the charge given to him (1 Timothy 1:5) and to Titus (2:2) as the basis of the example the older men are to set the young. And what better benediction can be said than,

31

"Peace to the brethren, and *love with faith*, from God the Father and the Lord Jesus Christ" (Ephesians 6:23)?

Verse 15: *"Christ Jesus came into the world to save sinners"*: this, the first of the "faithful words" (see Essay 5, page 49), like that in 4:9, is qualified as being *"worthy of all acceptation"*. The last word, like its related adjective "acceptable" (1 Timothy 2:3; 5:4) occurs only in the Pastoral Letters, although the verb, which is variously translated "receive" or "welcome hospitality", is more common, and is in fact applied to the cordial reception of apostolic preaching in Acts 2:41—"They that *gladly received* his word were baptized." Why the particular saying now under consideration should be declared "worthy of all acceptation", that is, worthy to be received gladly by all men as well as accepted unreservedly, will become plain when we examine it further.

Paul's reference to "the glorious gospel of the blessed God which was committed to my trust" has led him to express his deep gratitude to Christ for the manifestation of his grace which allowed the man who had been a blasphemer and a "bully" to become a messenger of that grace. If, therefore, the expression "Christ Jesus came into the world to save sinners" is indeed a terse "statement of the faith" such as might find its way into a catechism of the early community, Paul has made it characteristically a personal statement of faith, related directly to his own experience. For him the salvation in Christ was, as we have seen, no mere theological point; he was the living example of the power and scope of the Divine mercy. He enables us to gain a deep insight into what happened to him on the Damascus road where the conviction of personal sinfulness was borne in upon him more deeply than by any requirements of the law of which he had been so zealous an upholder.

It was no mock modesty which caused him to describe himself as the *"chief"* of sinners or, elsewhere, as "the least of the Apostles" and "less than the least of all saints" (1 Corinthians 15:9; Ephesians 3:8). Indeed, his use of the present tense, "I *am*" instead of "I *was* the chief" emphasises this point, and gives added force to his claim to be "a pattern to them which should hereafter believe" in Christ, a living example of what that grace and mercy can accomplish and a source of genuine hope and comfort to all weighed down by a sense of personal failure to reach the standard set in Christ. The Greek word translated "first" in the AV of verse 16 is the same as "chief", and refers not to time but to degree: his active opposition to the members of the Church had been a persecution of Christ himself, the very type of rebellion against God.

"Came into the world" reminds us both of Christ's own words, "The Son of man *came* to seek and to save what was lost", and also of the words of John's Gospel in several passages (Luke 19:10; John 1:9; 12:46; 16:28). The expression does not imply the pre-existence of Jesus as commentators suggest, although the grace and mercy of which he was the manifestation existed from the beginning. Commenting on the verse, "For the law was given by Moses, but grace and truth came by Jesus Christ", John Carter wrote: "Mark the precision of John's words: the law was *given;* grace *came.* Moses was the mediator of a covenant in which the favour of God made Israel His own nation, but he was only the channel of this grace which bestowed this privilege on Israel ... Jesus is also the mediator of a covenant, but of better things, and the grace of this covenant *was*—it *came to be*—it resided in Jesus and remained in him. One was but the channel; the other the embodiment of all embraced in the covenant established in him" (*The Gospel of John*, page 27).

Thus, "the coming into the world to save sinners" means that the eternal purpose of God includes, even necessitates, the salvation of sinners and that this Word, this purpose, was made flesh and dwelt among us. "And we know that *the Son of God is come*, and hath given us an understanding, that we may know him that is true ... This is the true God, and eternal life" (1 John 5:20). We "believe on him to life everlasting" (1 Timothy 1:16).

We have already noted (page 15) two other characteristic features of the Pastoral Epistles, which illustrate the Apostle's awareness of the need for salvation in God's purpose and of the central rôle of Christ in its accomplishment. One is the constant emphasis on the special qualification of Jesus for his work. He was anointed of God to be the saviour of men, and the title regularly afforded him in the Letters to Timothy is *Christ Jesus* rather than *Jesus Christ*. The name occurs in this form 13 times in the two Letters, surely more than a mere change for the sake of variety

33

(1 Timothy 1:12,14,15; 2;5; 3:13; 6:13; 2 Timothy 1:1,9,13; 2:1,10; 3:12,15).

The other feature is the application of the title of "saviour" to God Himself. In the three Letters Christ is referred to as "saviour" four times, and God Himself six times (1 Timothy 1:1; 2:3; 4:10; Titus 1:3; 2:10; 3:4); in some cases the title is ascribed to each of them in consecutive verses. God is so described outside the Pastorals only in Jude 25 and Luke 1:47 in the New Testament, although it is a familiar concept in the Old. The point is interesting and important enough to warrant a study on its own, but is mentioned here to show that it is in the thought that God is the ultimate source of salvation—that He is "the saviour of all men, specially of those that believe" (1 Timothy 4:10)—that Paul finds his personal inspiration and on which he builds his exhortations to keep the glorious gospel of the blessed God unchanged. It is the responsibility of the community thus redeemed to hold fast to the sound teaching about its salvation.

It is easy to see, then, why such a faithful saying should be *"worthy of all acceptation"*. It is in the nature of God to save and the coming of Christ into the world was the manifestation of that salvation. But "after that the kindness and love of God our Saviour toward man appeared" (Titus 3:4), its effectiveness towards the individual depends upon a man's personal acceptance of it. Should not all men be eager to accept it and to accept it all? And should not a community built upon faith in Christ live quiet and peaceable lives "in all godliness and honesty"? "For this is good and acceptable in the sight of God our Saviour; who will have all men to be saved, and to come unto the knowledge of the truth" (2:3,4).

Finally, in an age when we too need the exhortation to hold fast the form of sound teaching and distinguish between the vital and the unprofitable question, we would do well to remember that the important theological points are those which affect us personally and have the power to change our lives as completely as does the faithful saying that Jesus Christ came into the world to save sinners.

Verse 16: *"For this cause I obtained mercy"*: with great emphasis Paul reinforces his words about the purpose of God in salvation through Christ, as it had been illustrated in himself. That he was a "chosen vessel" the Lord had made clear, both to Ananias at the first and to Paul himself in the commission he had been given (Acts 9:15; 22:21; 26:16-18). The choice was evidently made, not solely on the basis of his suitability as a preacher to the Gentiles: he was a living example of "the power of God unto salvation" in the Gospel he preached. The Lord had, in him *"as chief"*, revealed the very nature of Divine mercy, and illustrated the point to which Paul returns in 2:4 and Peter spells out in 2 Peter 3:9—that God desired the salvation of all men and that *"longsuffering"* was an important attribute of His holy Name (Exodus 34). And in the same man the principles upon which mercy would be granted were illustrated also—confession, repentance and obedience. The force of *"all* longsuffering" should not be missed.

So Paul was *"a pattern to them which should hereafter believe"* on Jesus. The word for pattern is *hupotupōsis*, which occurs elsewhere only in 2 Timothy 1:13—"the *form* of sound words". The idea is that of a detailed sketch from which a skilled craftsman may work to reproduce an exact copy of an original. The skilled preacher or teacher, for example, handles his material in the spirit and style of the Master whose Gospel it is. Likewise every potential disciple experiences the long suffering and Divine forgiveness, the example and pattern of Paul's experience being plainly set before him. As Paul could say: "Be ye *imitators (mimētēs)* of me, even as I also am of Christ" (1 Corinthians 11:1, RV); "Be ye therefore *imitators* of God as dear children" (Ephesians 5:1; also 1 Corinthians 4:16; 1 Thessalonians 1:6, all RV, etc.). Saved by this grace we are quickened, even *"to life everlasting"*. At this point it is worth reading through carefully Ephesians 2:1-7, for all the rich associations with the theme of this section of the Pastorals. The passage ends: "That in the ages to come he might show the exceeding riches of his grace in his kindness toward us through Christ Jesus."

Verse 17: *"Now unto the King eternal, immortal, invisible":* praise and thanksgiving are never far from the lips of Paul, as we have remarked above. Characteristic of the expressions of them in these letters, here and in 1 Timothy 6:16; 2 Timothy 4:18, is the tendency to dwell upon the absolute eternity, power and unity of God, *"the only wise God"* (AV) or *"the only God"* (RV). The exact expression, "King eternal", occurs nowhere else in the New

Testament, unless we adopt the RV for Revelation 15:3, and read *basileus tōn ainōn* instead of *basileus tōn hagiōn*, "King of saints". It is soundly based in the Old Testament, however, as in Exodus 15:18—"The Lord shall reign for ever and ever", and in Psalm 145:13—"Thy kingdom is an everlasting kingdom".

Through the grace of the God "who only hath immortality", the source of light and life, is "brought life and immortality to light through the gospel" (2 Timothy 1:10). The fact that God dwells in light unapproachable, exalts Him above the ways and thoughts of men, rendering all the greater the privileges of drawing nigh to His throne of grace and of rejoicing in the revelation of the glory of His Name—things which being unseen are eternal, making it possible for us to be related to eternity. For the glory granted to those privileged to be with Christ where he is and behold the glory which he had with the Father from the beginning (John 17), will be likewise *"for ever and ever. Amen"*, indeed.

1:18-20—The Charge Committed to Timothy's Trust

Verse 18: *"This charge I commit unto thee":* here Paul takes up the thought suspended at the end of verse 4, which the English versions there complete for us by the addition of the words "so do", or their equivalent, in italics. He is saying, "As I besought thee to abide still at Ephesus, that thou mightest command some not to other-teach . . . this charge I commit unto thee". In the long intervening passage, "the end of the charge" and the deep responsibility it brings has been brought out, in a way which could leave Timothy in no doubt that his commission was related to the eternal things of the Gospel and salvation, both his and that of the ecclesia under his care. Such are the responsibilities, personal and corporate, of the life in Christ. The ideas behind the word "charge" and the Apostle's understanding of "the gospel . . . committed to my trust", have already been considered (pages 17, 18). The word "commit" is used again in 2 Timothy 2:2, where Timothy is in his turn to commit to faithful men that which he has received—the true "apostolic succession". See page 16 also for *"son Timothy"*.

"According to the prophecies which went before on thee": it is tempting to see in this phrase a parallel with "the commandment going before" of Hebrews 7:18. But the RV margin translation of the succeeding phrase, "led the way to thee", indicates that we are

here concerned with utterances which pointed out Timothy as a person suitable for the ministry, rather than prophecies about how he was to act in the future. This interpretation agrees with the whole concept of the apostolic mission. For since Paul had been charged with the work of preaching and edifying, it is evident that the Spirit would guide him in carrying out that work. There had in fact been "prophecies" connected with his own special mission delivered in some way in the Antioch ecclesia, for "the Holy Spirit said", no doubt through the "certain prophets and teachers" that were there, "Separate me Barnabas and Saul, for the work whereunto I have called them" (Acts 13:1-2).

The ecclesial "laying on of hands" which followed was not an act of "ordaining", which the Spirit had already done, but of fellowship and association with the work. See 2 Timothy 1:6; the question of the laying on of hands will be discussed further when this verse is dealt with later. It is, of course, quite consistent with the New Testament usage of the word "prophecy" that it should imply some "predictions" of Timothy's future progress, as is suggested in 4:14. The fact that Paul now commits this responsible charge to Timothy in accordance with the prophecies suggests that the other view is more probable.

"That thou mightest war a good warfare": consistent with the military metaphor underlying the word *parangellia*, 'charge', Paul exhorts Timothy to war a good warfare. "By them", or "in them", means the prophecies referred to which are the source of his confidence, perhaps even with the idea of their being the armour in which he goes forth to his spiritual warfare. The concept gives strength to the interpretation of the prophecies referred to above, since it means that Timothy is buoyed up not by a prediction of success but by the knowledge that his task was for God and therefore could be carried out in the strength of God.

The meaning of the word *kalos*, 'good', characteristic of the Pastoral Letters, has been discussed before (page 22). It is to be noted that Timothy's work is not a *battle* but a *campaign*, the service of the good soldier of Jesus Christ (2 Timothy 2:3,4) in all its details, calling for endurance and separation from the things of this life. We shall further discuss the military metaphor in its later context, but simply note here that the links of this passage are with 2 Timothy 2:3,4 and not 1 Timothy 6:12 ("Fight the good fight'') or 2 Timothy 4:7, which are concerned with athletics. All the passages, however, reveal Paul's fondness for the cognate accusative, as it is called—*fight* a *fight*, *war* a *warfare*, *sin* a *sin*, or even *run* a *race*, which is not so plainly the same class of expression in English as it is in other languages.

Verse 19: *"Holding faith, and a good conscience":* "holding" is literally 'having' or 'holding fast to', which is surely the meaning. Timothy is not "holding faith" as a shield, although in Ephesians 6:16 faith is the shield of the man of God. But *echōn* is used in connection with faith (1 Timothy 3:9), sound words (2 Timothy 1:13) and a form of godliness (3:5), in the sense of "possessing", and the linking of "faith and a good conscience" is a reference back to verse 5 and "the end of the charge". If Timothy is rightly to carry out his duty, in the spirit of charity, then he must himself have "faith and a good conscience" (page 44).

"Some", on the other hand, had *"thrust away"* (RV) the good conscience, going further than "neglecting" faith or "missing the mark" (verse 6 margin): they had rejected it and so had "tossed conscience away", like the jettisoning of the ballast or cargo of a vessel. The positive, wilful nature of the act can be gauged from the use of the verb in such passages as Acts 13:46, RV—"Ye *thrust* (eternal life) from you"; Acts 7:27—"He that did his neighbour wrong *thrust him away*"; 7:39—"Our fathers would not obey but *thrust* him *from* them".

The natural result of such conduct is to make *"shipwreck concerning the faith"*. With no conscience of Divine things there can be no faith, since faith is more than intellectual assent or a drawing nigh with the lips: "The devils also *believe*" (James 2:19). Faith is manifested in the deeds of a man sensitive to God's commands because he believes in them.

We are justified, however, in taking faith here as meaning also "the faith", as the RV does. This is consistent with the entire range of thought in these letters, concerned as they are with sound words, sound doctrine, and five faithful sayings, or "statements of the faith". Out of 33 occurrences of the word *pistis*, at least eight including this one bear this objective sense. The others are 4:1,6; 5:8; 6:10,21; 2 Timothy 3:8; 4:7; Titus 1:13. In these passages men are said to depart from, deny, err from, or be reprobate concerning, keep, or be sound in "the faith". Loyalty to a body of revealed doctrine and to the community founded upon it are clearly implied, which makes the quality of the subjective faith of the individual of even greater importance.

"To make or suffer shipwreck" is a "Pauline" word, appearing in the New Testament only here and in 2 Corinthians 11:25. To go through the actual experience three times would leave Paul with a vivid impression of the nature of such a disaster, with its loss of wealth and potential loss of life, and his realisation of the meaning of a shipwrecked faith was equally vivid. Men do survive, however, and Paul's dealings with such were designed to save and not to cast away.

Verse 20: "Of whom is Hymenaeus and Alexander": Both these names occur in the Second Letter, but there is no certain proof that the same persons are referred to in each case. This Hymenaeus is probably the one associated with Philetus (2 Timothy 2:17) as author of a "cankerous word". The fact that by their teaching, which was a clever denial of the literal resurrection in favour of a purely "spiritual" one (based on a misapplication of Romans 6 and a shutting of the eyes to 1 Corinthians 15), they "overthrew the faith of some" is a good indication that Philetus' colleague was the one also who "made shipwreck concerning the faith".

The other two Alexanders mentioned are the Jews' spokesman at Ephesus (Acts 19:33) and the coppersmith who did Paul "much evil" (2 Timothy 4:14). There are some grounds—the fact that one was a *Jew* who might have joined the ecclesia at Ephesus and leaned towards the Jewish fables, and the other occasioned Paul much distress—for thinking that one of them is referred to in this verse 20, but we cannot be sure. Alexander the coppersmith may be so named to distinguish him from the other one, and he was apparently at Rome or possibly had been in the place where Paul was arrested the second time.

"That they may learn not to blaspheme": This is surely decisive when determining what *"delivered unto Satan"* actually means (see Essay 6, page 52). It was not solely punitive but disciplinary, as the word for "learn" shows. *Paideuō* is often translated *"chasten"*, especially in Hebrews 12:6-10, referring to the Lord's education of His sons. Timothy was in meekness to *"instruct"* his opponents (2 Timothy 2:25), while the revelation of the salvation of God in Christ should *"teach"* us to deny ungodliness and worldly lusts

39

while we wait for the glorious manifestation of the Saviour who is still to come (Titus 2:11-14). The "blasphemy" in view in the verse we are considering is in fact a speaking against God, by declaring that His grace and salvation is other than He has declared it to be. "Faith" is a Scripturally definable thing, as is also "the faith"; and "a good conscience" is one "void of offence toward God", not because we *feel* "not guilty" but because we are not in fact so in His sight. This as we have seen is the true end of *the charge* (1:5), the true charity, which is not the declaring of the guilty to be innocent, but the compassionate re-education in spiritual things of those whose conscience has been pricked.

No doubt there are lessons here for us today. There might well be fewer "automatic" withdrawals, or less abandoning of those who have been withdrawn from, if there were in fact more true ecclesial *discipline* exercised in the spirit of helping one another towards a spiritual maturity, and a fuller realisation that forgiveness and restoration are complete in God's sight for those who at least attempt to mortify the flesh.

ESSAY 1

The "Other-Teachers"

IF the word "other-teachers" (1 Timothy 1:3 etc.) was new to Paul, the idea was not, and a brief study of it will help to define the nature and the danger of the unsound teaching in Ephesus.

The key passages are in 2 Corinthians 11:3,4,13-15 and Galatians 1:6-9. The first is concerned with subtlety and beguiling which, after the manner of the serpent with Eve, can nullify the force of Divine truth by a false emphasis. God had indeed made the tree of knowledge as Eve saw it, "good for food, pleasant to the eyes, and much to be desired to make one wise". It was reasoning in the place of simple faith that made the word of God of none effect. Rarely does the direct negation of the Truth go unrecognised for what it is.

But if what is preached is *Jesus, other* than as he is presented in the Scripture, or the Gospel be proclaimed for what it is not, then that is the work of *apostles*, but *false* ones, of *workers* who are in fact *deceitful*. Their skill and zeal may be exemplary, but the effect of their work devastating to the life of the ecclesia. Similarly in Galatia: there could be no doubt about the excellence of the Law nor of the necessity for a Jew born under it to be circumcised.

Where observance of the Law excluded the grace of Christ, however, then the Gospel was made "other" than it was intended to be. In fact, says Paul, it is no Gospel at all (Galatians 1:7), and even he himself or an angel from heaven, would lie under a curse for so denying the validity of the work of God in Christ. (Compare also the word "to other-yoke" in 2 Corinthians 6:14, to express incompatibility in essentials which hinders any spiritual enterprise.)

41

ESSAY 2

Myths and Genealogies

THE myths were Rabbinical tales, incorporating some wise teachings and many legendary histories, which formed the subject of comment and discussion. The parable of the Rich Man and Lazarus is based on such a tale, skilfully used by the Lord to drive home a point. The danger was that such fables, together with the traditional oral commentary on the Law which often accompanied them, assumed all the authority of the Word of God, and in many cases made it void, as Jesus was at pains to point out (e.g. in Matthew 15:1-9). The parallels with the serpent's other-teaching are obvious.

"Endless genealogies"

The "endless genealogies" may well have been genealogies in the proper sense of the word—authentic lists of names such as occur in the Pentateuch and 1 Chronicles particularly, but with wild allegorical interpretations added to make them "endless". The word "genealogy" occurs in 1 Timothy 1:4 and in Titus 3:9 only, although there is a related verb in Hebrews 7:6; elsewhere the term "generations" is used. The *Book of Jubilees* written about 135-105 BC contains many examples of genealogies of Biblical characters. It has been assumed by some commentators that the Letters to Timothy and Titus presuppose a form of the Gnostic heresy which troubled the ecclesias later in the first century and particularly in the second; in which case the "genealogies" would be the succession of personal emanations from God, of which Jesus Christ was one, by which God was separated from the material world.

Though there probably was an incipient form of this heresy in

42

Ephesus, the evidence of the Pastoral Letters themselves favours the Jewish theory, especially since there had been a growing tendency amongst some of the Jews of the Dispersion to follow the teachings of Philo of Alexandria, a Jewish thinker of the early first century (see also page 365). His greatest contribution to thought is said to have been his linking of Hellenistic philosophy with the forms of the Mosaic Law. His main works were expositions of the Pentateuch, and included a commentary on Genesis: *The Allegory of the Laws*. There is little doubt that the influence of his ideas of allegory and typology were felt in Ephesus and Crete. As he himself commented on a community called the Therapeutae, among whom he may have spent his youth: "They read the holy Scriptures, and explain the philosophy of their fathers in an allegorical manner, regarding the written word as symbols of hidden truth which is communicated in obscure figures" *(Concerning the Contemplative Life)*.

No wonder such discussions were described as "endless". They could lead to no firm conclusion and since they were not concerned with realities, the choice of interpretation was largely a matter of taste. To what could they lead, then, other than to "questionings", to which no answer could be given, and which were not worth answering in any case. The charge was therefore not only to refrain from teaching such things but "to give no heed" to them either.

ESSAY 3

The Threefold Origin of Love

THE love of which Paul is writing in 1 Timothy 1:5 has a threefold origin. It is:

(i) *"out of a pure heart"*, and could not, therefore, be displayed by "men of corrupt minds" (1 Timothy 6:5). The "pure heart" is an Old Testament concept, referring to the moral and intellectual as well as emotional dispositions of a man. "He that hath ... a pure heart" would ascend into the hill of the Lord and stand in His holy place (Psalm 24:3,4); he will "see God" (Matthew 5:8); and for such a "clean heart" David most earnestly prayed, that he might be restored to the Divine fellowship (Psalm 51). It is obviously inseparable then, from

(ii) *"and of a good conscience"*: "conscience" was a familiar word in the Hellenistic world of the day, a favourite theme of the Stoic philosophers. Its literal meaning concerns that which a man "knows with himself", but Paul's usage has nothing to do with the Greek concept of "the god within", although the world "conscience" is emphasised in the Pastoral Epistles, as for example in 1 Timothy 1:19; 3:9; 2 Timothy 1:3, where the conscience is "good" or "pure"; and in 1 Timothy 4:2; Titus 1:15, where, in reference to the false teachers, it is "seared" or "defiled". For the true Scriptural idea of conscience, we can go to Hebrews 5:12-14: the mark of spiritual maturity is "by reason of use to have (their) senses exercised to discern both good and evil". Those who have their "conscience purged from dead works" are able to "serve the living and true God" (Hebrews 9:14). So Paul exercised himself "to have a conscience void of offence toward God, and toward men" (Acts 24:16; see also Acts 20 for how he conducted himself in Ephesus). Such a *Scripturally informed conscience* is consistent

44

with "rightly dividing the word of truth", in practice as well as theory. The other essential element is:

(iii) *"and of faith unfeigned"*: an unhypocritical faith, such as dwelt in Timothy himself and his forebears (2 Timothy 1:5). It is a faith that "worketh by love" (Galatians 5:6) and "purifies the heart" (Acts 15:9). With wrong or inadequate ideas about God true faith is impossible, and without faith in Him and His purpose in Christ there could be no purging of the conscience or creating of a clean heart. What a responsibility devolved upon Timothy and the faithful men who were able to teach others also!

ESSAY 4

"Sound doctrine"

THE words "sound" and "doctrine" are so characteristic of the Pastoral Epistles as to call for a special note. In fact, "sound doctrine"—both in the teaching and practice of it—is the only remedy which Paul sees for the problems of the ecclesias in Ephesus and Crete.

It is evident from its use in the context of his description of those for whom law is necessary that Paul views *doctrine* as the basis of a way of life and not as a theological code. *Didaskalia* is the word he uses 14 times in these letters (1 Timothy 1:10; 4:1,13,16; 5:17; 6:1,3; 2 Timothy 3:10,16; 4:3; Titus 1:9; 2:1,7,10), and it occurs elsewhere in the New Testament only in Matthew 15:9; Mark 7:7; Ephesians 4:14; Colossians 2:22; Romans 12:7; 15:4. The more usual word is *didachē*. We have already met a related verb form in the word for "other-teaching" (page 19).

It means not only the *content* but the *art* and *method* of teaching, such as is displayed by a *didaskalos*, 'teacher' or 'master', the very title by which the Lord Jesus was usually addressed by his disciples in the days of his flesh. (After the resurrection he was invariably "the Lord".) His is the pattern, therefore, for "sound doctrine".

"Sound" and "Wholesome"

The two related Greek words represented by "sound" *(hugiēs, hugiainō)* appear nowhere else in Paul's letters, and nowhere else in the New Testament in the sense in which they are used here. Their basic meaning concerns the health of the body, and they form the root of the English word "hygiene". They are frequently used in the Gospels with reference to miracles of healing, when "they were made *whole* that had been sick". The prodigal son's father rejoiced because he had received him "safe and *sound*", and John wished the beloved Gaius to prosper and "be in health" (Mark 3:5; Luke 7:10; 15:27; 3 John 2).

It is possible, since the Apostle wrote the Pastoral Letters late in his career, that these words were added to his vocabulary as a result of his long association with Luke, the beloved physician. Secular writers used them in the sense of 'sane' and 'wholesome' as applied to thoughts and speech, and it is a metaphor which Paul found peculiarly suited to the purpose in hand. In his earlier ministry he had been concerned with the building up of the body of Christ, and his metaphors had been taken from building construction and the nourishment of the body (Ephesians 4:12-16). Now the process foreseen in Acts 20 was sufficiently advanced for him to realise that the speaking of perverse things was seriously endangering the spiritual health of the Christian community in Ephesus and Crete. Hence his insistence that both Timothy and Titus should devote their talents and energies to healthful teaching, encouraging responsible members of the church to do likewise and shunning those who would not consent to *wholesome* words (1 Timothy 6:3; Titus 2:1,2).

Two passages particularly throw light on the nature of this teaching, and offer us a useful guide in days when our problems as a community seem to arise as much within as from without. In 1 Timothy 6:3 the wholesome words are qualified as being "the words of our Lord Jesus Christ". While it is tempting to see in this phrase confirmation of the existence of a collection of sayings of the Master recorded at quite an early date (see also Paul's words to the elders of Ephesus in this connection, Acts 20:35), the translation is not without its difficulties, and commentators are divided on the exact interpretation. But even if they do not bear the sense of "the actual words of the Lord Jesus", they certainly mean that the Lord himself is the ultimate source and theme of the sound doctrine the Apostle had in mind, especially since it is further qualified as "according to godliness"—teaching wherewith a man can approach the standard which God has revealed in Christ.

The other passage is 2 Timothy 1:13, where Timothy is exhorted to "hold fast the form of sound words" which he had heard from Paul. The word "form", the same as that translated "pattern" in 1 Timothy 1:16, means 'an outline sketch or ground-plan used by an artist or, in literature, the rough draft forming the basis of a fuller exposition'. Timothy, therefore, should be unswervingly loyal to Paul's message, regarding it as his pattern. Furthermore, this must be done "in faith and love in Christ Jesus".

The spiritual health of the community, therefore, is affected to a great extent by the sense of responsibility of its members towards the splendid trust committed unto them (2 Timothy 1:14). This is a responsibility of which all speakers, writers, editors and publishers should be especially aware. It does not mean that they are confined to the repetition of what has been already said, or that there should be no free and open discussion of difficult problems.

A living witness is a personal witness, and it is still true that a body is fitly joined together and compacted by that which every joint supplieth, and so is edified; but it must grow up into him in all things which is the head, even Christ (Ephesians 4:15,16). There is all the difference in the world between the free and frank discussion of problems which are recognised as such and the publication of one's personal doubts or the discussion of questions in a way which undermines the faith of those who would otherwise not have been troubled by such doubts. Especially is this true when theories are put forward with all the assurance of authoritative teaching.

ESSAY 5

The Faithful Sayings

AMONG the interesting and unique features of the Pastoral Epistles are the five "faithful sayings". The phrase consistently rendered by the Revised Version as "Faithful is the saying" occurs in 1 Timothy 1:15; 3:1; 4:9; 2 Timothy 2:11 and Titus 3:8. There has been some discussion as to whether the words preceding or immediately following this expression form the saying thus referred to; but, as we shall see when we come to consider each saying separately, a careful reading of the text usually removes all ambiguity. This note is concerned with the "Faithful Sayings" as a group.

Most commentators agree that they are in fact sayings which had become proverbial in the church at the stage of development implied in the Pastoral Letters, and are either statements of doctrine tersely expressed, or maxims of Christian conduct. This is most probably the case, but the interest attached to the question of their origin is increased by the use made of them by Paul and the insight they give into his mind and thought. The position of the adjective is emphatic, "*Faithful* the word" *(pistos ho logos)* being the literal translation of the Greek in each case.

There is an Old Testament parallel in the words of the Queen of Sheba to Solomon: "*True the word* which I heard in my land concerning thy words and concerning thy wisdom" (1 Kings 10:6; 2 Chronicles 9:5). Even more significant is the precedent of a phrase in use in the worship of the synagogue, apparently from the earliest times, which can be found in the Hebrew Prayer Book even today. Although Paul felt keenly the separation from his own people and tradition caused by his preaching the Gospel to the Gentiles, he took great pride in his upbringing and refers,

49

evidently with gratitude, to the religion of his forefathers which found its "proper development and flowering" in Christ (see 2 Timothy 1:3).

It could well be that Paul's "Faithful the saying" is an echo of a prayer which followed the recital of the words, "Hear, O Israel: The Lord our God, the Lord is One": "*True* and firm, established and enduring, right and *faithful*, beloved and precious, desirable and pleasant, revered and mighty, well-ordered and acceptable, good and beautiful *is thy word* unto us for ever" (see *Authorized Daily Prayer Book,* Hebrew-English version, 1924 edn., page 42, and page 98 for a similar expression). For in these Letters, whether he is quoting a popular saying, a fragment of a Christian hymn or a doctrinal statement, the Apostle relates it to the purpose he has in hand, the restraint of false teaching and the edification of the ecclesia through the wise guidance of responsible members. However he speaks, then, he speaks as the oracles of God.

Some New Testament parallels to the phrase "Faithful the saying" provide further illustration of this. "*Faithful is he that calleth you,* who also will do it", Paul wrote to the Thessalonians, when encouraging them to hold fast under persecution by the reminder that "the God of peace would sanctify them wholly, and preserve them blameless at the coming of the Lord Jesus Christ" (1 Thessalonians 5:24). Such exhortation was valueless if its basis was insecure. But it was God who had called them to sanctification, and His faithfulness made the Apostle's exhortation effective and powerful.

Again, on the same theme in 1 Corinthians, Paul speaks of believers being confirmed unto the end because "*Faithful is the God,* by whom ye were called unto the fellowship of his Son Jesus Christ our Lord" (1 Corinthians 1:9). And again, in the same letter, "There hath no temptation taken you but such as is common to man: but *faithful is God*, who will not suffer you to be tempted above that ye are able" (1 Corinthians 10:13). So keenly aware was Paul that he was put in trust with the Gospel of God, that he set himself the highest possible standards of truth and faithfulness in his handling of it and the people with whom it brought him into contact. When he discusses with the Corinthians his intention to visit them he declares that even in this matter he did not purpose according to the flesh, "But *faithful is God*, and *so our word* to you was not yea and nay" (2 Corinthians 1:15-24).

Just as God was a God of truth (Hebrew: *amēn*), and as the Lord prefaced some of his emphatic utterances with the words, "Verily, verily *(amēn, amēn)* I say unto you" (e.g. John 3:3,5,11; 5:24,25; 10:7), and as "all the promises of God in him are yea, and in him Amen" (2 Corinthians 1:20), so the sayings of the Apostle bore the same stamp of faithfulness and authenticity. As we consider each of the faithful sayings of the Pastoral Epistles separately we shall see their force and beauty and the characteristic way in which Paul uses them to express the teaching of him who said to another Apostle, also traditionally of Ephesus: "Write: *for these words* (sayings) *are true and faithful*" (Revelation 21:5; 19:9; 22:6).

ESSAY 6

Delivering unto Satan

MUCH discussion has been centred around the meaning of this phrase in 1 Timothy 1:20, which is parallelled in 1 Corinthians 5:5—*"to deliver such an one unto Satan"*. There it refers apparently to a formal act, when the ecclesia was to be assembled "in the name of our Lord Jesus . . . and my spirit, with the power of our Lord Jesus Christ" (verse 4). It is even possible that the phrase is an almost technical formula, based upon the idea of Job 2:6, where Job was put into Satan's hand by the Lord God Himself. The detailed discussion of the issues raised would demand a separate treatise on the Devil and Satan, of which there is already a good example in the book *The Devil—The Great Deceiver,* by Peter Watkins. Perhaps some immediate help with this passage can be gained from Acts 26:18, where the purpose of the apostolic mission is described as "To open their eyes, and to turn them from *darkness to light,* and from the *power of Satan unto God,* that they may receive forgiveness of sins, and inheritance among them which are sanctified by faith that is in me."

"Deliverance unto Satan", therefore, could be anything from the formal pronouncement of the apostle, or the ecclesia under his guidance, that the words or works of an offender were sinful and would, apart from his repentance, leave him in darkness, or in the power of Satan, and exclude from the life of God, to an actual act of disfellowship. The latter would be the logical sequel to the former, until the repentance was manifested, since it was a practical consequence of a spiritual state. It has been well said that "more often than we know, religious error has its roots in moral rather than intellectual causes". Such an interpretation accords well with the context of 1 Timothy 1:19; Hymenaeus and

52

Alexander had *thrust away a good conscience*, doing violence both to their own faith and to "the faith", and besides being in a dangerous spiritual condition themselves were liable, in the absence of ecclesial discipline, to "overthrow the faith of some" of their brethren (2 Timothy 2:18).

The question then arises as to whether some physical penalty were attached to this act of excommunication, in view of 1 Corinthians 5:5—"For the destruction of the flesh, that the spirit may be saved in the day of the Lord Jesus." That the apostles had power to do such a thing is plain enough, when we consider the case of Ananias and Sapphira (Acts 5:1-11) and Elymas the sorcerer (13:8-12). But the first case was an act of judgement for "lying against the Holy Spirit", the eternal issues of which we cannot begin to discuss here. The flesh was quite literally destroyed, but there was no possibility of the reclamation or re-education of the sufferers.

In the case of Elymas, the temporary physical blindness which matched his spiritual blindness, was more of a sign than a discipline, since he was not a disciple anyway. In any case, it is almost certain that Paul would have used the word "body" for "flesh" if he was talking in physical terms, since the contrast between "flesh" and "spirit" is essentially a *moral* one. "Flesh" stands for that which opposes God, which is not the body but wrong thoughts or deeds done in the body. If we are humble enough to repent and seek forgiveness, then indeed to that extent the flesh has been destroyed and the spirit revived. That certain acts involve physical consequences of course goes without saying, but that is not what is meant here.

The First Letter to Timothy

CHAPTER 2

Practical Aspects of Sound Doctrine

PAUL now takes up the theme of "the charge" in its practical aspect, as he gives directions as to how it is to be carried out. It is this aspect of his teaching which gives these letters their pastoral quality.

2:1-2—Prayer to be made for all men

"Sound doctrine" has its basis in a set of revealed facts about God, His purpose, His relationship with men and their redemption and salvation, without a knowledge of which there can be no Christian living. The quality of that life, both personal and in the ecclesia, Paul does not leave to be deduced by Timothy, and therein lies the supreme value of the Pastorals as a document for our times.

Sound ecclesial organisation, in which all the details are treated as spiritual matters rather than practical or business arrangements, will promote a healthy corporate body, where the cankerous word or the morbid preoccupation with questions that minister strifes can gain no hold. We must therefore pay careful heed to Paul's exhortation and the doctrines upon which they are based.

Verse 1: *"I exhort, therefore, first of all"*: The word *parakaleō*, with its idea of calling someone to your side, has the force of urging on a matter of extreme importance: it is not a matter of mild exhortation. "Therefore" makes the transition from the general charge to the particular instuctions which make it up.

"First of all", a "oncer" in the New Testament, means more than first in the list of injunctions: it means that Paul's exhortation is of outstanding importance, since it is based upon an understanding of the very nature of salvation and of the duties of the ecclesia in its inner life and outward relations with the world.

The ecclesia should be a "house of prayer", as the record of the early apostolic church reveals. "They continued steadfastly in the apostle's doctrine ... and in the prayers" (Acts 2:42); and individually and collectively, at times of crisis or great enterprise, they were found at prayer. It is fitting that the subject of prayer should take first place, since the health of ecclesial life is to be gauged from ecclesial *attitudes*.

"Supplications, prayers, intercessions and giving of thanks": It is probably mood or attitude of mind which distinguishes the first three words from one another, rather than any outward form of presentation, but unless they are to be regarded as rather meaningless repetitions there must be some purpose in the threefold classification.

"Supplications", in the Greek original, expresses a sense of need, as for example in the prayer of Zacharias who resorted to the Lord because he was childless, and his *supplication* was heard (Luke 1:13, RV); or the desolate widow who "continueth in *supplications* and prayers night and day" (1 Timothy 5:5; cf. also Luke 2:37—Anna served God with fastings and *prayer* or *supplication*); or perhaps the most powerful example of all, that of the Lord Jesus who "offered up *prayers* and supplications (entreaties) with strong crying and tears unto him that was able to save him from death" (Hebrews 5:7). So, says Paul, "in every thing by prayer and *supplication* with thanksgiving let your requests be made known unto God" (Philippians 4:6).

This word, like that for "intercessions", is also used for requests and petitions made to men, but "prayers" *(prosuechē)* is always used of address to God (cf. the expression "house of prayer") with the idea of fervent wish or desire underlying it and so it is often associated with supplication as in some of the passages referred to above.

The Greek noun for "intercessions" is used again by Paul in 4:5 ("prayer"), but that is its only other occurrence in the Greek Bible, if one excludes the non-canonical 2 Maccabees. The verb, however, appears in Acts, Romans and Hebrews, consistent with its basic meaning of petition to a superior—the governor or God Himself. Thus Festus said that "the Jews have *dealt with me*" (Acts

25:24), and Elijah made *"intercession* to God *against Israel"* (Romans 11:2). In Hebrews 7:25 it is Christ who "is able also to save them to the uttermost that come unto God by him, seeing he ever liveth to *make intercession* for them", which is the thought behind Romans 8:27,34.

The words combine, then, to express the earnest desire and sense of dependence upon God which should characterise a reverent approach to Him in prayer as part of our Divine service, with an urgency arising from the particular object of the prayers which Paul has here in view: an urgency which his "first of all" reveals. But "thanksgivings" *(eucharistia)* form an integral part of such worship. To receive God's material gifts with thanksgiving is fundamental to the process of sanctification "by the word of God and intercession", which is of the very purpose of God in creating the gifts (4:3-5). As the very word implies, one has the *grace* to respond to the *grace* of God, and it figures largely in the Apostle's exhortations and personal example, as a glance at a concordance will readily show. In corporate life also we should be "giving thanks always for all things in the name of our Lord Jesus Christ" (Ephesians 5:20, RV); "In every thing give thanks: for this is the will of God in Christ Jesus concerning you" (1 Thessalonians 5:18).

We have never followed the practice of calling the weekly remembrance of the death and resurrection of Christ the *eucharist*, preferring the descriptive term "breaking of bread" or, more rarely, "communion" or act of fellowship. Nothing is implied here to suggest we should change our vocabulary—there are, indeed, powerful reasons why we should *not*—but the great importance of a thankful attitude towards our heavenly Father comes home to us as we remember that His "love in creation" and "grace of salvation" are fittingly brought to a focus when we break the bread of life and drink the wine of the covenant in what we call so often "the central object of our coming together"; remembering also that the central act is invariably coupled with *eucharistia*—the giving of thanks, after the Lord's own pattern. The essence of paganism is that men "glorified him not as God, neither were thankful" (Romans 1:21).

"Be made for all men": The doctrinal basis of this injunction will be seen when we come to verse 4. Here it is important to realise

that "all" is "all without distinction" rather than "all without exception", and the following words— *"for kings, and for all that are in authority"*—are by way of example and not of limitation. The phrase "all men" with this interpretation is the only possible one in many Scriptural contexts, as for example in Titus 2:11, which does not really teach that every member of the human race has been made aware of the grace of God unto salvation; nor was the belief that John the Baptist was a prophet a universal one (Mark 11:32). And it is certain that not every human being is justified (Romans 5:18).

Verse 2: The exhortation is no doubt against the exclusivism of some of the heretics at Ephesus, but it is also against the temptation to limit our prayers to our own narrow interests (see Essay 7, "Prayer for Those in Authority", page 81). For the purpose of God is with "all men" in the terms of verse 4, and it is with His purpose in mind that the prayers are to be offered. There is a *discipline of prayer*, such as with the command to "pray for them which despitefully use you, and persecute you" (Matthew 5:44).

The Apostle's petition corresponds exactly with Paul's charge: it is *"that we may lead a quiet and peaceable life in all godliness and honesty"*. The meaning is not at all that we would merely seek a quiet life for ourselves, but that we should seek the honour and glory of God and the opportunities for His service. *Tranquil* and *quiet* and rare adjectives, the first *(ēremos)* a oncer here, and the other *(hēsukios)* also in 1 Peter 3:4. The latter passage, and the uses of the corresponding noun *hēsukia* (2 Thessalonians 3:12; 1 Timothy 2:11,12) and verb *hēsuchazo* (Luke 14:4; 23:56; Acts 11:18; 21:14; 1 Thessalonians 4:11), help us to determine the meaning.

Eremos could mean free from outward disturbance, but *hēsukios* refers to an inner peace of mind resulting from restful contemplation (for example, on the Sabbath), yielding to the will of God, studying to be quiet, or following the example of the sisters in Christ who are *in silence* and of a meek and *quiet* spirit. It represents exactly the proper attitude of the chaste bride of Christ or the people of God, who accept the responsibility of obedience and trust in the power of him who loved them and gave himself for them. So no disciple is a demonstrator or political activist, a passive resister, a "brawler" (Titus 3:2), or a striker for temporal advantage. And if our citizenship (*politeuma*, translated "conversation") is really as becometh the Gospel of Christ (Philippians 1:27), then we shall strive to rid our minds of our inbuilt socialism, conservatism or liberalism which hopes for better things for our material lives with every change of government. The whole aim and satisfaction of our lives is to live them in all godliness and honesty.

"All godliness ..."

The word for "godliness" *(eusebeia)* is a word common enough in the Greek and Hellenistic world but rare in the New Testament. Ten of its fifteen uses are found in the Pastorals, the others being in later Epistles such as Peter's, and in the Acts (1 Timothy 2:2; 3:16; 4:7,8; 6:3,5,6,11; 2 Timothy 3:5; Titus 1:1; Acts 3:12; 2 Peter 1:3,6,7; 3:11). Its related words are translated "devout", "godly", "worship". It is an interesting example of a colourless word, expressing vague religious feeling or perfunctory religious observance in everyday life, being transformed by Apostolic usage. Although the word could be used for reverence or respect for superiors, especially ancestors, in the New Testament it is restricted to reverence for God. It then exactly fits our context here. The disciples could pray *for* the emperor, but not *to* him, and they did so for the reason that Israel were to keep the commandments, especially the showing of honour to parents and respect for the aged: "I am the LORD" (Exodus 20:2; Leviticus 19:32; see also Acts 23:1-5).

The verb-form is used by Paul in his speech on Mars' Hill to describe the conventionally correct worship of the God who was, nevertheless, "unknown" to the Athenians. But when he has "declared" Him unto them it is plain that worship must be based on a response to a revealed purpose on which men can set their faith and hope, and that revelation is in the person of the "man whom he hath ordained, whereof he hath given assurance unto all men, in that he hath raised him from the dead" (Acts 17:31).

In the Pastorals, "godliness" takes on precisely this meaning. They are full of the idea that the purpose of God is the salvation of men, which is characteristic of His mercy and loving-kindness towards them; that this purpose is expressed in the historical event of the appearing of Christ Jesus at the critical time chosen by God; that true worship is based on faith in this fact, with a pure conscience; that sound teaching, as distinct from the "knowledge falsely so-called" which produces "profane and vain babblings which will increase unto more *ungodliness*" (6:20; 2 Timothy 2:16), is the means of understanding this purpose; and that right living *(kalos)* which is the only true index to right belief is the individual believer's response to this saving grace, and collective worship must be organised on the basis of the sense of responsibility of overseers and members of every age, rank and station in the Ecclesia.

Godliness, therefore, is for the Apostle God-likeness, the personal, social and ecclesial behaviour of those who adorn the doctrine of God in all things and are taught by the appearing of the grace of God that bringeth salvation to deny *ungodliness* and worldly lusts, and to live soberly, righteously and *godly* in this present world while they wait for the consummation of the purpose in the second appearing of the Saviour Jesus Christ (1 Timothy 6:20; 2 Timothy 2:16; Titus 2:11-14). Ungodliness, on the other hand, is *asebia*, the ungodly are *asebēs* and to live ungodly is *asebein*—words which figure in Romans as characteristic of the world where the power of the Gospel is not felt (Romans 1:18), of the very people for whom Christ died (4:5; 5:6), of the latter days when there will be fewer prepared to deny themselves (2 Timothy 2:16), and of the world upon whom the judgement is to fall (1 Peter 4:18; 2 Peter 2:5; 3:7; Jude 4,15,18, etc.).

The question of "the mystery of godliness" we shall consider further when we come to 1 Timothy 3:16.

"... and honesty"

"Honesty" or *semnotēs* is again peculiar to these Letters (also in 3:4 and Titus 2:7) as is its adjective *semnos*, except for Philippians 4:8, where it is one of those qualities which the brethren and sisters at Philippi are to "think on", as they banish anxiety from their minds—"but in everything by prayer and supplication with thanksgiving" let their requests be made known unto God. It is an important quality to be cultivated by arranging brethren and other ecclesial servants, indeed by all the ecclesia, and its value will appear when the requirements for the bishops, deacons and their wives are discussed.

Gravity, dignity, an intense conviction of the seriousness of the life in Christ and a concept of its high ideals—all this goes into the word, which accords well with the quiet demeanour and dignified behaviour of the saint even under great stress: the picture arises in the mind of the Lord Jesus silent before his accusers: "He was oppressed, and he was afflicted, yet he opened not his mouth." It contrasts sharply with the behaviour of those who insist upon their rights or who say in effect, "Let us do evil that good may come".

It has been suggested, with great effect, that "in godliness and honesty" is the Hellenistic counterpart of the Hebrew expression "in holiness and righteousness". This passage in Luke 1:74 connects beautifully with that presently under consideration: "That he would grant unto us, that *we being delivered out of the hand of our enemies might serve him without fear* ...."

2:3-6—The Doctrinal Basis of the Exhortation

Verse 3: *"For this is good and acceptable in the sight of God our Saviour"*: this refers back to the exhortation of verse 1 of which verse 2 is but one illustration. For a note on "good" *(kalos)* see page 22. "Acceptable" *(apodektos)* is connected with *apodochē*, "acceptation" (on which see the note on page 32), but itself recurs only in 5:4, in a phrase identical with the above. The thought is parallel also, since practical help for widows and reverence for one's elders is *eusebein*, 'the showing of piety' or 'godliness'. So prayers honouring God by expressing the qualities we have considered have an intrinsic beauty and excellence *(kalos)* and God receives both them and the offerer. The Lord's Prayer can in fact be considered as the basis of such prayers, combining as it does all the elements of reverence, worship, petition, desire and confidence.

The emphasis on the title *God our Saviour* has already been remarked upon (page 15). It is especially appropriate here since it provides the doctrinal basis which makes prayer for all men so acceptable to Him.

Verse 4: *"Who will have all men to be saved"*: the reason for the "all men" of verse 1 is now clear: all without distinction of rank, or nation, social status or sex (the word *anthropos* is comprehensive of either gender of the human race) come within the orbit of

God's purpose in salvation. He is "the Saviour of all men, especially of them that believe"—another faithful saying, worthy of all acceptation (4:10), for it sums up the Divine principle. Salvation is in a sense universal, not limited to any one group, as the covenant with Abraham concerning the blessing of all nations in his seed confirms. But the process of salvation involves men's belief: it is not something which is done to them while they remain passive.

The preaching of the Gospel must be equally non-selective since although all men will not in fact be saved, their judgement lies in the hands of Him who willeth not that any should perish, but that all should come to repentance. Paul's own example in prayer and request is instructive. In spite of what he suffered at the hand of his countrymen and his knowledge that they had judged themselves unworthy of eternal life (Acts 13:46), to those same Gentiles to whom he then turned in his preaching he said, "Brethren, my heart's desire and prayer to God for Israel is, that they might be saved" (Romans 10:1). Arraigned before one of the kings, whose genuine interest in the Gospel message as a means of salvation might well have been in doubt, Paul can still cry sincerely, "King Agrippa . . . I would to God, that not only thou, but also all that hear me this day, were both almost, and altogether such as I am, except these bonds" (Acts 26:29).

"And to come to a knowledge of the truth": knowledge of the truth is inseparably connected with salvation, a fact which solves the problem of reconciling the truth that God wills that all should be saved with the truth that He will not save every man. He who is the Way to Life is also the Truth, which men have to acknowledge. *Epignōsis alētheias,* 'knowledge or acknowledging of the Truth', occurs three times more in these Letters, in 2 Timothy 2:25; 3:7; Titus 1:1. So it is the realisation of the truth which comes with repentance, it is something which cannot be achieved simply by "ever learning", and it is closely linked with godliness and God's purpose of election.

We are dealing therefore with something deeper than head knowledge or accumulated Scriptural facts. It is a matter of joyful recognition and deep, spiritual discernment which, once being attained to, a man cannot lapse from by sinning wilfully without being in danger of the judgement (Hebrews 10:26). "May (God)

give unto you the *spirit of wisdom and revelation* in the *knowledge* of
him'' (Ephesians 1:17). ''And this I pray, that your love may
abound yet more and more in *knowledge* and all discernment''
(Philippians 1:9, RV). ''We do not cease to pray ... that ye
might be filled with the *knowledge* of his will, in all wisdom and
spiritual understanding'' (Colossians 1:9). ''All riches of the full
assurance of understanding, to the *acknowledgement* of the mystery
of God'' (2:2). No wonder, then, that Christ prays earnestly for
the sanctification of his people through the knowledge of the word
which is truth: for *''this is life eternal,* that they might know thee,
the only true God, and Jesus Christ, whom thou hast sent'' (John
17:3,17).

Verse 5: *''For there is one God'':* the doctrinal foundation for the
foregoing is now seen to be firmly based upon the unity of God
and the work of the Lord Jesus Christ. It is emphasised frequently
in the Scripture that the practical issues of life depend upon the
knowledge of God. The connecting word ''For'' is almost
equivalent to ''as we all acknowledge'', which is how F. F. Bruce
interprets it in his *Expanded Paraphrase.*

Similar passages enable us to link the verse with the great commandment to Israel, so often repeated in the synagogue
throughout Israel's history unto this day. ''But *to us* there is one
God, the Father'', Paul wrote (1 Corinthians 8:6, RV); and
James, ''Thou *believest* that there is one God'' (2:19). They both
draw the same practical conclusion from the fact that God is one
as Israel were to draw from the commandment in Deuteronomy
6:4—''Hear, O Israel: the LORD our God is *one LORD:* and thou
shalt love the LORD thy God with *all* thine heart, and with *all* thy
soul, and with *all* thy might.'' It followed from the unity of God,
or rather from the uniqueness of Yahweh who was Israel's God,
that a *singleminded* response was required from His people, the
service of the *whole man.*

For the One God had one purpose—to ''gather together in one
all things in Christ'' (Ephesians 1:10). Therefore He is God our
Saviour, a title characteristic of the Pastoral Epistles (see page
15); He is also the Saviour of ''all men''; He cannot be ''God of
the Jews'' only, without being ''of the Gentiles also: seeing it is
one God, which shall justify'' (Romans 3:28-30); ''the same Lord
over all (who) is rich unto all that call upon him'' (10:12).

The unity of God's purpose is clearly demonstrated in His ordaining of only *"one mediator between God and men"*, who, since the purpose is with "all men", is *"himself man, Christ Jesus"* (RV). The underlying significance of this fact is brought out in many another passage, especially those relating to Jew and Gentile, bond and free, male and female, and to the carefulness which ought to be exercised in dealing with "the brother for whom Christ died", and particularly in the passage we are considering where it is the ecclesia's duty to have "all men" in mind.

In the New Testament the word for "mediator" *(mesitēs)* occurs only in Galatians (3:19,20) and Hebrews (8:6; 9:15; 12:24) apart from this passage. The argument in Galatians centres around the Law and the Old Covenant. The mediator is a man, Moses, who stood between God and Israel at the people's own request. In the passage from Timothy the link is with Hebrews and the mediator of the New Covenant of forgiveness, sanctification and redemption. The work is not for angels, but for one of whom it could be said, "For both he that sanctifieth and they who are sanctified are *all of one*". A mediator, especially in matters of salvation, must be a representative, and the idea of the mediation of angels both to represent God to man and intercede with God for man is unscriptural. The superiority of Christ over Moses, as the unique mediator in the fullest sense, is seen in the fact of his Divine begettal and his partaking of flesh and blood.

The Septuagint uses the word *mesitēs* to translate "daysman" in Job 9:33. This chapter is worthy of study in this connection, since Job recognises the impossibility of a man contending with God—"How shall man be just with God?"—and the need for one to stand between God and himself to "lay his hand upon us both". It could only be a "redeemer", a *goel*, or "kinsman" of them both (Job 19:25), but how could there be such a one? Moses perceived that forgiveness depended upon the giving of a life (Exodus 32:32), and was taught that it was not to be his own, but one provided by God—even Jesus, the 'Salvation of Yah'.

Verse 6: *"Who gave himself a ransom for all":* another "oncer", *antilutron*, implies the paying of a price for something to be released. It is true that the *anti-* gives an added meaning to *lutron*, the word for "ransom" in Matthew 20:28 and Mark 10:45, where the Lord Jesus describes himself as the Son of man who came "to give his life a ransom for many". But the prefix does not imply a *substitutionary* payment but an *adequate* one, an equivalent in *value*: all that Christ resigned in a life of obedience and a death as though he were a sinner since be bore the sins of many, is that which was given back to him, even honour, glory and life everlasting, and it is given also to all those who "die in him". It was *his life* he gave as a ransom for many: he made "*his soul* an offering for sin" (Isaiah 53:10). There is no contradiction between the Lord's "for many" and Paul's "for all"; the ransom has infinite value, but the benefits require appropriation (Guthrie, *Tyndale Commentary*), and not all are prepared to receive what God has offered.

"To be testified in due time": the phrase "to be testified" is in the Greek a noun, *to marturion*, a 'testimony' or 'witness'. It is in apposition to the whole thought of verses 4-6, and signifies that the sacrifice of Christ on behalf of all men is itself the great sign or attestation of God's will to save all men. The faithfulness of Moses in God's house was for "a *marturion* of those things which were to be spoken" (Hebrews 3:5). The faithfulness of Christ as a Son over that house was the *marturion* that the things had been fulfilled *in due time*.

The phrase is literally "in its own time", the appointed time of the maturity of God's purposes. The times are in fact God's own times, to which the prophets looked forward and for which the faithful waited. So Peter says that Christ, as the spotless lamb free from blemish, "was foreknown indeed before the foundation of the world, but was manifested at the end of the times for your sake" (1 Peter 1:19,20, RV). Then "when the fulness of time was come, God sent forth his Son" (Galatians 4:4).

The actual Greek words for our passage occur twice more in the Pastorals. In 1 Timothy 6:15 it has a connotation yet future, for God, "who is the blessed and only Potentate, the King of kings, and Lord of lords" will "in his own times" manifest the Lord Jesus at his appearing and his kingdom. The other passage, however, links us with the words which follow in 1 Timothy 2:7; in Titus 1:3 Paul tells us that God our Saviour, "that cannot lie", promised eternal life before the world began. But He "hath in due times manifested his word *through preaching* which is committed unto me".

64

Verse 7: *"Whereunto I am appointed a preacher":* for while Christ is "the *faithful witness,* and the first begotten from the dead, and prince of the kings of the earth", "the Amen, *the faithful and true witness,* the beginning of the creation of God" (Revelation 1:5; 3:15), there is an ongoing testimony to the historical fact of his death, resurrection and second appearing to be borne through the preaching of the Gospel. While the verb 'to herald' is the usual one for preaching, the use of the noun *kērux,* 'a herald', is confined to this passage, 2 Timothy 1:11 and 2 Peter 2:5 (here applied to Noah): another example of a word which comes late into the vocabulary of the ecclesias, although the idea is familiar. It implies more than *evangelism,* the proclaiming of the good news: it is a more solemn, formal proclamation of all that the Gospel contains—the revelation both of the righteousness and of the wrath of God to come.

This apostolic ministry was not self-chosen: "I am ordained a preacher, *and an apostle ...* a teacher." The entire clause is repeated in 2 Timothy 1:11, where once more *kērux* describes the work and *apostolos* the mission on which he had been sent (cf. Romans 10:15—"How shall they preach *(kērussō)* except they be sent *(apostellō)*?" The "I" is emphatic, and illustrates Paul's concept of his work. His whole vocation, his very reason for living, is now to cooperate in the saving work of God in Christ and to proclaim it to "all men". The wonder of it and of his personal privilege in participating in it are never far from his thoughts, and the very mention of the reconciliation itself often leads him to mention his own mission to proclaim it: see 2 Corinthians 5:18—6:1 and Ephesians 3:6-12.

The assertion of his apostolic mission and authority is very much in place here. Beyond the fact that the authority gives support to the "charge" which Timothy has to exercise, the immediate theme of the universal nature of salvation is emphasised. Why proclaim the Gospel abroad if it is not for men to receive? And why appoint specifically a preacher to the Gentiles if the grace of God is not for them? The ministry of Paul is the final argument for the universality of salvation: *"I speak the truth in Christ, and lie not; (I am) a teacher of the Gentiles in faith and truth."* For the strong emphasis of *"I speak the truth,* I lie not", see Romans 9:1; and for the assertion of his claim to be a teacher of the Gentiles, see Romans 11:13 ("I *magnify* mine office") and Galatians 2:7-9 ("the same was *mighty in me* towards the Gentiles").

It seems better to take "in faith and truth" closely with the word "teacher" (*didaskalos*, see page 46), thus describing the *content* of the teaching. Not only is this consistent with the emphasis in these Letters on *sound* teaching, in the faith and in the truth—in contrast to the "other-teachers" (page 41), whose message brought no salvation—but the way of describing common Christian terms without the use of the definite article is also a characteristic of these Letters. See 1 Timothy 1:2 and Titus 1:4, where "in faith" and "a common faith" clearly means *the faith*.

What more appropriate, then, than to place "first of all" in his authoritative advice to an ecclesia under pressure the exhortation to pray "for all men" for the reasons Paul had given, to make of the ecclesia a veritable "house of prayer" in the sense portrayed in the early apostolic church. In Isaiah 56 we read the Lord's own exhortation: "Keep ye judgement and do justice, for *my salvation is near to come*, and my righteousness to be revealed" (verse 1).

Then the son of the stranger, the eunuch and the outcasts of Israel, "all men" who genuinely sought the Lord and joined themselves to Him, were promised that the Lord would accept them and "make them joyful in my house of prayer . . . for mine house shall be called an house of prayer for *all people*" (verse 7). The first fulfilment of this is described in Acts, where despised followers of Jesus, Samaritans, a eunuch and the Gentiles, were made glad by the salvation revealed "in due time".

Here, surely, is an exhortation that we can take to ourselves. There can be no better way to face the problems which beset the Ecclesia of God today, which threaten to impair seriously our corporate spiritual life and our effective preaching, to leave us divided into factions engaged in *logomachiai*, or 'word battles' (1 Timothy 6:4; 2 Timothy 2:14), following strained or irrelevant interpretations, making charges and countercharges, with tensions between liberal and reactionary, and a search for power or influence, than to learn the power of corporate prayer and the need for it.

Thus we can stimulate the sense of devotion and service in the ecclesias which recognises the greatness of our salvation and the responsibility of testifying to it in word and deed.

2:8-15—The Ecclesial Duties of Men and Women

Verse 8: *"I will therefore that men pray every where"*: The "therefore" takes up once more the general subject of ecclesial prayer after the exposition of its purpose and meaning in verses 3-8, and "I will" expresses the Apostle's authoritative command about the details of public worship. Nothing could be more instructive—nor apparently, then as now, more necessary—than this command for the division of ecclesial duties. The word for "men" is not the *anthrōpos* of the verses about salvation in Christ, who is himself man: it is *andres, the* men as distinct from the women. To them alone belong the public duties of the ecclesia, the leadership of the worship of the saints.

Private prayer and devotion are not under discussion here, but only those connected with the formal assembly of the believers constituted as a church. Some indication of this can be gathered from the use of the phrase "every where" or "in every place", as for example also in 1 Corinthians 1:2—"The church of God which is at Corinth, to them that are sanctified in Christ Jesus, called to be saints, with all that *in every place* call upon the name of the Lord Jesus." Again in 2 Corinthians 2:14—"God ... maketh manifest the savour of his knowledge by us *in every place*"; and in 1 Thessalonians 1:8—"*In every place* your faith to God-ward is spread abroad." So the instruction was to apply to no particular locality, but to the "brotherhood near and far", in Ephesus, Corinth, Thessalonica or wherever the saints assemble as the house of God today.

"Lifting up holy hands": There is an appropriate physical as well as mental attitude for prayer. The lifting up of the hands, in an attitude of humble supplication, was the Jewish habit of prayer, as we may gather from 1 Kings 8:22; Psalm 141:2; 143:6; Lamentations 3:41. It is also the posture adopted for blessing an assembly (Leviticus 9:22; Luke 24:50). But *standing* (Genesis 18:22; 1 Samuel 1:26; Matthew 6:5; Mark 11:25; Luke 18:11,13), *bowing the head* (Genesis 24:26,48; Exodus 12:27; 2 Chronicles 29:30; Luke 24:5), *lifting eyes to heaven* (Psalm 25:15; 121:1; 123:1,2; 141:8; 145:15; John 11:41; 17:1), *kneeling* (2 Chronicles 6:13; Psalm 95:6; Isaiah 45:23; Daniel 6:10; Matthew 17:14; Mark 1:40; Luke 22:41; Acts 7:60; 9:40; 20:36; 21:5; Ephesians 3:14) and *prostrating oneself to the ground* (Genesis

17:3; 24:26; Numbers 14:5; 16:4,22,45; 20:6; Deuteronomy 9:18,25,26; Joshua 5:14; Judges 13:20; Nehemiah 8:6; Ezekiel 1:28; 3:23; 9:8; 11:13; 43:3; 44:4; Daniel 8:17; Matthew 26:39; Mark 7:25; 14:35; Luke 5:12; 17:16; Revelation 1:17; 11:16) are all Scriptural attitudes for prayer, either public or private.

An attitude of body implies an attitude of mind, but to adopt one of reverence, humility or pleading does not necessarily condition the mind, though it may help to do so. The spiritual attitude is indicated by the injunction that the outstretched hands be holy. "The hand is the instrument privileged to act for man" (Spicq, *Les Epîtres Pastorales*), and to it in Scripture are attributed man's acts both pure and impure. "He that hath *clean hands and a pure heart*" shall stand in the Lord's holy place. So "draw nigh to God, and he will draw nigh to you. Cleanse your *hands,* ye sinners; and purify your hearts, ye double minded" (James 4:8).

"Without wrath and doubting": this injunction may well have a special relevance to the situation in Ephesus, but the principle is clearly stated in other contexts too, notably in the Lord's Prayer. God has pardoned us in Christ and we are expected to follow that example in our feelings towards others, for wrath can alienate the mind from prayer; whereas we are specifically commanded to pray even for them which persecute and despitefully use us. So also in Ephesians 4:26-32—"Be ye angry and sin not ... Let all bitterness, and wrath, and anger, and clamour, and evil speaking, be put away from you, with all malice ... forgiving one another, even as God for Christ's sake hath forgiven you." See also the Parable of the Unmerciful Servant in Matthew 18:23-25.

Dialogismos is probably better translated as "disputing" (RV) rather than "doubting", although the second has some authority, as in Luke 24:38 where the "thoughts" arising in the disciples' hearts are indeed doubts. The disciples are also exhorted to believe that they have the things they pray for, and they will then receive them (Matthew 21:22). In view of the ecclesial situation in Ephesus, however, and the general New Testament sense of the word (as in Romans 14:1, "doubtful *disputations*", and Philippians 2:14, "without murmurings and *disputings*"), the Apostle is commanding that controversy be laid aside in favour of a joint approach in prayer to the God and Saviour of all men.

The spirit of debate is not conducive to a devotional atmosphere and true godliness, which is why the warnings against it are so frequent in these Letters. Again, we have a powerful message for our time.

Verse 9: *"In like manner also, that women adorn themselves"*: equally powerful and necessary for our time is the Apostle's next injunction, for the words "I will therefore" must be supplied from verse 8. The word for "in like manner" occurs in Paul's writings in Romans 8:26 and 1 Corinthians 11:25, then *six* times in the Pastorals (1 Timothy 2:9; 3:8,11; 5:25; Titus 2:3,6). In each case it means "in like manner" (applied to "the cup after supper" for example) and a strict comparison is being made between two methods or principles of conduct. Some have stated that Paul seems to turn from his discussion of the public work of the ecclesia to the private behaviour of the women. Far from making a digression, however, his point is precisely that the public work of the men which calls for a certain attitude of mind and a rigid self-discipline, has a counterpart in feminine demeanour. It is not a comment upon *status* but upon *function* in the ecclesia, where dress, deportment and attitude on the part of the women form as vital a part of ecclesial life as any more so-called active participation.

That such emphasis should be laid upon this in the New Testament, both by Paul and Peter, is in fact remarkable, but it arises from an equally remarkable fact about the status of women in the New Testament as a whole, which will become apparent as the Apostle's words are examined phrase by phrase.

The idea of *adornment* as an expression of an attitude of mind is not confined to this passage. Peter uses the same metaphor in 1 Peter 3:1-6, where a meek and quiet spirit is regarded as a more valuable ornament than the most expensive apparel, and always formed part of the distinctive beauty of holiness of the women who trusted in God. It has a relation to the proclamation of the doctrine of God, moreover, since such demeanour could even win over unbelieving husbands "without the word". In Titus 2:9-10 faithful obedience on the part of slaves to their masters is called an "*adorning of the doctrine* of God our Saviour *in all things*". Manifestly the work of the sisters has as "public" an aspect as that of the brethren, whose behaviour in their own sphere must also match their spiritual pretensions.

"In modest apparel, with shamefacedness and sobriety": there is an interesting play upon words between "modest" *(kosmios)* and "to adorn" *(kosmeō)*, both connected with *kosmos*, an 'orderly arrangement' (also frequently, 'the world') which helps our understanding of the kind of adornment Paul has in view. The expression almost amounts to "adorned with a proper adornment", that is, with the discipline and moderation which constitutes "good taste"—in this instance a Scripturally informed good taste (see Essay 8, "Braided Hair and Costly Array", page 83). There is nothing in this to suggest that a "dowdy" appearance, or an outfit into which no thought or care has gone, is particularly acceptable, nor the kind of casual dress worn deliberately to emphasise a supposed lack of concern for conventions or ordinary standards. That can be as "immodest" in the Scriptural sense we are discussing as the other forms of extravagance with which the Apostle is concerned. There was less need for him to warn against the deliberately unkempt fashion of his day, since the only intelligent people who willingly adopted it if they could afford to be otherwise, were the Cynic philosophers (the "Dogs") who made a display of dispensing with all the standards of everyday life and comfort.

The word for "apparel" is a "oncer", although it is found in the Septuagint Version of Isaiah 61:3. It is again a word which suggests a moral quality expressed in a detail of dress, rather like the English word "habit", which can be both a vestment and the detail of a personality. Paul may well have had Isaiah's "garment of praise" in mind in his use of the word here.

Shamefacedness and Sobriety

But "shamefacedness and sobriety" were to be the keynotes. The former noun is a modified form of the Old English *shamefastness* and conveys no sense of dishonour. Its Greek original *(aidōs)* occurs here and in Hebrews 12:28, where it is the *reverence* which accompanies godly fear in service of the living God. It is in every way a noble word, rare indeed in Scripture (not at all in the Old Testament), but common enough in philosophical writers of the Hellenistic world. J. H. Bernard (*The Pastoral Epistles*, Cambridge Greek Testament for Schools and Colleges) has a note which cannot be improved upon. *Aidōs* "implies (1) a *moral* repugnance to what is base and unseemly, and (2) *self-respect*, as well as

restraint imposed on oneself from a sense of what is due to others
... Thus *aidōs* here signifies that modesty which shrinks from
overstepping the limits of womanly reserve."

Sobriety *(sōphrosunē)* is one of a group of related words for
which Paul shows a marked preference in the Pastoral Epistles.
The usual translation is some form of the word "sober", as here,
although in 2 Timothy the phrase is "sound mind" (cf. "in his
right mind", Mark 5:15) and in Titus 2 it is "temperate" in verse
2 and "discreet" in verse 5. Its primary meaning in Classical
Greek is "a command over bodily passions, a state of perfect self-
mastery in respect of appetite. It marked the attitude towards
pleasure of the man with a well balanced mind, and was equally
opposed to asceticism and to over-indulgence" (Spicq).

Although it must not be assumed that Paul uses the word with
the philosopher's virtues in mind, it is certainly another instance
of his use of current vocabulary and ideas to which he gives a
characteristically Christian meaning. In a situation such as that
reflected in the Pastoral Letters, where "swerving aside" (1
Timothy 1:6) from the true path led to false asceticism (4:1-5) or
over-indulgence (2 Timothy 3:1-6), what better virtue could be
recommended than a *true sense of responsibility* in ecclesial servants
(1 Timothy 3:2), aged men (Titus 2:2), aged women (2:3), young
women (2:4), young men (2:6), Timothy himself (2 Timothy 1:7)
and the sisters whose true influence and "public ministry" lay in
the outward indications of their godliness (1 Timothy 2:9,15)?

Verse 10: There is, however, an adorning, of which the careful
dressing with due consideration is the outward mark, even the
ornament "of a meek and quiet spirit, which is in the sight of God
of great price" (1 Peter 3:4). Peter says this is the mark of "holy
women"; Paul says it *"becometh women professing godliness"*.

Unique in all the New Testament, the word *theosebeia* ('godliness')
means reverence for God, the spirit of recognition of Him in all
one's thoughts and ways. The idea that reverence can be
displayed in a manner of dressing for the meeting is one which
needs to be emphasised today, for men as well as women. For it
is only too easy to defend the wearing of casual clothes, or clothes
which imply *carelessness*, in the ecclesia, on the ground that one
does not need "Sunday best" to worship God (which is true);
whereas one is in fact following the fashion of an age which has

no respect for anything or anyone. One can make a *display* of his lack of concern.

"Professing" is an interesting word in the context of verse 9. The usual meaning of *epangellomai* is 'to promise', used both of God and men. Only here and in 6:21 ("professing knowledge") has it this particular shade of meaning. It almost implies a covenant relationship with God, the practical response of those who have promised: "All that the Lord hath said will we do, and be obedient" (Exodus 19:8).

The *"good works"* with which the Ephesian sisters were to adorn themselves are not necessarily deeds of charity, though they may well include them. Good works were required of the church as a whole: the purification of "a peculiar people zealous of good works" was the object of Christ's redemptive work (Titus 2:14), and such a people were to be exhorted to be "prepared (equipped) for every good work" (2 Timothy 2:21; 3:17; Titus 3:1) and careful to "maintain" them (Titus 3:8,14). Especially was Titus to be "a pattern of good works" (Titus 2:7; cf. 1 Timothy 6:18). Indeed, to be an ecclesial servant was in itself a good work (3:1), and it was a characteristic of older widows that they were well reported of for good works, diligently followed (5:10).

It is probably impossible to press too closely the distinction between *kalos* and *agathos*, both meaning good (see page 22), in connection with works throughout these passages, or indeed throughout these Epistles, although the use of both these words in the last passage suggests that *kalos* is a more comprehensive term than *agathos*, including both charitable acts and other deeds which were also the right index of true belief.

In any case, the emphasis on works as a proof that what is intellectually understood about God is not being denied in practice was necessary in an ecclesia where there were those who professed to know Him but in works denied Him, and were "unto every good work reprobate" (Titus 1:16). The average Greek who dabbled in the *gnōsis*, the philosophy of his day, knew of *to kalon kai to agathon*, "the beautiful and the good", in an intellectual or abstract sense, but he would have found the idea of an actual work or deed being either *kalos* or *agathos* difficult. It is obvious from what follows that Paul is emphasising, not detracting from, the spiritual value and importance of the women's contribution to ecclesial life: it is as much "a good work" as that of the elders with different responsibilities.

Silence in the Ecclesia

Verse 11: *"Let the woman learn in silence with all subjection"*: the repetition here of teaching given in principle to the Corinthians (1 Corinthians 14:34-35) is an indication that the question of the place of women in public worship was as much of an issue in Ephesus as it was in the Greek city, and as it is today. In the first century, as we have remarked above, there were certain practical points raised by the fact that the men and the women shared an absolute equality in the spiritual sense before God according to Paul's teaching; and, in fact, the Pastoral Letters themselves do envisage a rôle for the sisters in ecclesial life, as in 1 Timothy 3:11 and 5:3-14. It is true that in 1 Corinthians 11:4-15 women apparently did pray or prophesy aloud under the direct influence of the Spirit. But we should not forget that Paul is at pains to regulate this practice, as he was the whole behaviour of the Corinthian ecclesia, to the point of bidding them refrain from some of their previous habits because they created confusion, and *in this very context* (1 Corinthians 14:34) forbade women to speak in public.

The passive rôle of learning not teaching was to be accepted "in silence", without a spirit of rebellion or fretfulness. The word for "silence" applies to quietness and calmness of spirit as well as to stillness of the tongue, and it is reinforced by the words "with all subjection", or with complete submissiveness. There were, no doubt, in Ephesus, as there are in the modern ecclesia, many able, intellectually gifted sisters for whom it could prove a sore trial to play a passive rôle when they seemed to have so much to offer. It may be, too, that not enough use is made in ecclesial life of women's talents and energy in spheres for which they are particularly suited. But now, as then, it is impossible to avoid the clear, Scriptural prohibition upon public utterance on their part.

Verse 12: *"But I suffer not a woman to teach"*: that the prohibition actually refers only to teaching in the assembly is plain enough, both from Scriptural precedent and from what follows immediately in this same verse. The teaching of children by their mother,

73

who would exercise a great influence in this sphere, is well documented. It is implied in the frequent coupling of the mother's name with that of the kings of Israel who did good or evil in the sight of the Lord (26 times from 1 Kings to 2 Chronicles); it is explicitly stated in such phrases as "the law of thy mother" (Proverbs 1:8; 6:20); it was surely a factor in the education of the young Jesus, who was subject unto both Mary and Joseph (Luke 2:51); and it was an important element in the preparatory background of Timothy himself (2 Timothy 1:5). Priscilla is coupled with her husband (and is sometimes mentioned *first*) in the work of instructing Apollos in the way of God, and in helping the Apostle, who refers to their joint work with approval (Acts 18:26; Romans 16:3; 2 Timothy 4:19).

But whatever the nature of a sister's work, it must not allow her *"to usurp authority over a man"*. The verb *authenteō* ('usurp authority') is not only a Biblical "oncer": it was apparently previously unknown in all Greek literature, although some rare related words are on record. It has a peculiar force when interpreted in the light of the explanation Paul is to give later in the chapter. The basic meaning of the verb, the ancestor of our word "authentic", is 'to act of oneself', 'to be absolute master', 'to be the instigator', 'to take the initiative', 'to assume the responsibility'.

Although it is primarily of the sphere of ecclesial life that Paul is thinking here, his words have their parallel in the domestic scene, which is a reflection of the relationship between Christ and the church—a point which it is easy for the husband to forget, since his responsibility is great when viewed in that light. The responsibility of the brethren in the ecclesia is, by the same token, equally great.

Paul recognises that for sisters a great deal of restraint needs to be exercised and rounds off his prohibition with a repetition of the words *"to be in silence"*. That a sense of restraint is involved here can be gauged from the meaning of "silence" or "rest" as used in Luke 23:56. The loving, devoted women who had waited at the foot of the cross, watched to see where and how the body of their Lord was laid. Then, eager to perform their last, sad service for him, they went home "and prepared spices and ointments; *and rested* (were quiet) *the Sabbath day according to the commandment"*.

We can imagine that it was only respect for the Law which enabled them to preserve a quiet spirit in such a circumstance. No wonder that it was "very early in the morning" that they went to the sepulchre bringing the spices which they had prepared!

The Scriptural Basis

Verse 13: *"For Adam was first formed, then Eve"*: Paul is *not*, as the modern commentators affected by the spirit of the age would have us believe, offering a personal opinion founded on prejudice. None can read his comments upon the sisters with whom he came into contact without realising his profound respect for them and gratitude for their work. See especially Romans 16. Nor can we reconcile his careful concern for the building-up and spiritual health of the ecclesia with the idea that what is now known as male chauvinism would make him deprive the ecclesias of a ministry of women if such were indeed of immense benefit both to the ecclesias and the women involved. His commands are soundly based upon principles of Scripture and the physical, emotional and psychological facts of the case. All reasoning upon contemporary conditions, social or enonomic, must give place to two abiding facts: the fact of creation and the fact of the entrance of sin.

The actual situation in Ephesus as in Corinth, both ecclesias needing to be healed of faction and strife by sound ecclesial organisation, only serves to throw these facts into relief and make the Apostle, with tender sympathy and basic understanding, forbid the sisters to enter into a sphere of activity for which they were not equipped and in which they would be exposed to much personal distress. Paul is saying more than that man is the senior partner in Divine arrangements. It was he who received and was made responsible for obedience to God's commandments; with him God began the work of the Garden and the naming of the animals.

Adam was in fact both type and fore-runner of the "man of God's right hand" whose headship in spiritual matters goes unchallenged. That man has grossly abused his position with respect to women does not alter the fact that, according to the Scripture, woman was made for the sake of man and not the other way round. She was to fill up that which he lacked, that in helping and being "meet" for him there might be seen a perfect harmonious whole. Either this is a symbol of the relationship between God and His people or Christ and the Church—in which case the nature of the relationship is as clear and unmistakable as Paul makes it in Ephesians 5 and Colossians 3—or it is not, in which case marriage has no spiritual basis at all.

Verse 14: *"And Adam was not deceived":* the mutual relationship allows woman to exercise "a gracious yet very powerful and beneficent influence" upon man which "can promote her own happiness, unto God's glory" (Hendriksen, *1 and 2 Timothy and Titus*). The fact that the influence can be otherwise, while equally powerful, results, like the nature of man himself, from the Fall, with its entail of sin and death upon Adam's sons and Eve's daughters. Paul is not excusing Adam and blaming Eve. On the contrary, Adam provides a classic example of the weight of man's responsibility in the partnership, since although Eve was *first "in the transgression"*, "by *one man* sin entered into the world, and death by sin" (Romans 5:12ff.). It was also a classic case of the dangers of a woman being "authentic" or usurping authority: she led, and the man followed.

The very emotional balance of woman's nature which enabled her to exercise that sweet and beneficent influence also allowed her to be "beguiled" (2 Corinthians 11) or "deceived", by that which was a piece of "other-teaching" on the part of the serpent. She had usurped the man's authority in saying what was and what was not to be, in connection with God's command: she had, in the very meaning of the word *authenteō* used by Paul in verse 12, 'taken the initiative', 'acted for herself', 'assumed the responsibility'. The influence upon Adam proved no less powerful because it was wrong.

There are two clear instances in Scripture where God upbraids His people because women ruled. One is in Amos 4:1, where the "kine of Bashan" are called upon to hear the judgement of the Lord upon them because they called upon their masters (surely an irony here!) saying, "Bring, and let us drink", thus causing the poor and needy to be oppressed to provide the money to satisfy their demands. The other is in Isaiah 3:12—"As for my people, children are their oppressors, and *women rule over them*. O my people, they which lead thee *cause thee to err*, and destroy the way of thy paths." There follows, remarkably, and Paul could almost have drawn his exhortation from this very passage in the prophets, a list of the extravagances in dress and attitude, of the daughters of Zion, none of which would be of any value in the day of account, when the men of war were slain by the sword and the women left desolate (verses 16-26).

A Sister's Rôle

Verse 15: *"Notwithstanding she shall be saved in childbearing":* there have been many attempts to explain the above passage, some of them satisfactory, others touching but the fringe of reason or grammatical possibility. The following are the principle explanations offered by commentators, Christadelphian and others:

1. She will be saved by means of *the* childbirth, that is, by the birth of Christ who is specifically described in Genesis 3:15 as "the seed of the woman";

2. She will come safely through childbirth;

3. She will be saved *by means of* bearing children;

4. She will be saved *by way of* her childbearing (that is, not by way of public ecclesial work, or usurping a man's place).

(1) In spite of its attractiveness as a neat explanation, Scripturally sound *as far as it goes* (it has some connection with Genesis 3), this cannot be fully acceptable in the context. It is true that some godly Hebrew women eagerly looked for the privilege of bearing the Messiah, and prepared themselves mentally and spiritually for the responsible task of bringing up and giving early training in Divine things to the Saviour—"continuing in faith and charity and holiness with sobriety". But Messiah had already been born when Paul wrote, and only one woman had known the heart-piercing joy of fulfilling that responsibility. So the "she" of verse 15 must refer to "woman" in general, and if the sense be therefore that women ("they") are saved because a woman bore Christ, then that is equally true of "all men" (verse 4) also; which is not the point Paul is making.

(2) This explanation does violence both to the context and to the sense of the word "saved". This verb must bear the meaning it has in 1:15 and 2:4, especially since the whole discussion of chapter 2 centres around the respective rôles of men and women in spiritual life in the process of salvation. Moreover, many

women of unsaintly character come safely through their ordeal; and while clean and holy living, with self-restraint, can have an effect upon physical well-being, this is surely not the Apostle's present theme.

(3) This would imply that childbearing is *of itself* a meritorious act. It is true that Paul's whole point in this chapter is that attitudes of mind and spiritual outlook make natural or necessary duties, such as the oversight of an ecclesia (3:1) and here of motherhood, into "a good work", but the spiritual merit lies in the outlook and not in the work, "for by grace are ye saved through faith . . . not of works, lest any man (or woman, see Genesis 30:1 and 1 Samuel 1:6) should boast" (Ephesians 2:8,9). And if the merit lay in the act, then the unmarried woman or the childless wife would be at a disadvantage before God— an idea quite foreign to Paul's explicit teaching and to the whole spirit of Christ (1 Corinthians 7:32; 1 Timothy 5:5, cf. Martha and Mary).

There remains for consideration explanation (4). At first sight it seems open to some of the objections mentioned above, especially if the meaning of *teknogonia* (a "oncer" in Greek, with a related "oncer", *teknogonein* in 5:14), is restricted to the physical act of giving birth. There is an extended meaning, however, which if followed illuminates this admittedly difficult passage in the light of (4), although it would not remove the objects to (1)— (3). The key lies in the relation of Genesis 3 to the argument, and especially to the conclusion of the passage in 1 Timothy 2:15— *"If they continue in faith and charity and holiness with sobriety"*.

Sōphrosunē (page 71), 'sobriety' or 'a true sense of responsibility', was precisely what Eve had failed to "continue in" when she took the lead in Eden. Her act was an act of faithlessness; she had not continued in her faith that what God had said was true. Her action placed Adam in a terrible, though till this very day a familiar, dilemma. On him lay the responsibility whichever way he went, in the way of his wife or in the way of God. Through him, when he had made the natural rather than the spiritual choice, "sin entered into the world and death by sin".

The results, which have also passed upon all men and women, were appropriate to their physical and psychological make-up: for the man it was the responsibility of labour to provide bread, with toil and sweat; for the woman the responsibility of bearing children and of submitting to the authority of the man, both rôles being attended by sorrow and frustration. The terms of God's pronouncement make it plain that what would have been natural to their life in any case would thenceforward be carried out with difficulty and excess, since they had chosen to exaggerate the importance of their natural and legitimate desires to the point of disobedience to God's commandment.

It is clear from many a New Testament passage, especially in Paul, that worship of God extends beyond the formal acts, even the formal assemblies, of what is ordinarily understood as worship. Daily labour, human relationships, due regard for one's status and condition in life, a contentment to abide in the calling wherein one is called, whether male or female, bond or free— all are service of the Lord when all is done as unto the Lord. Further, ecclesial life is a corporate existence in the family of God comparable with daily life and work in all its aspects of mutual relationships and responsibilities. (On this point see especially the qualification for eldership described in 3:4,5 following.)

Devoted Women

One can therefore almost put the words "through childbearing" in parenthesis, and read "she shall be saved ... *if they* (women) *continue in faith and love and holiness, with sobriety"*. The same qualities are required in men for their salvation, and their proper ecclesial sphere is public responsibility and that which is to be considered in the next chapter. For the reasons outlined above we cannot press the meaning of *teknogonia* to exclude the childless woman, so the wider sense of "maternal instinct" is probably nearer to the Apostle's thought as expressing the woman's rôle. The phrase sums up all those fine, gentle, self-sacrificing qualities which are important in the home, in the training and "nourishing up" of children, and in any corporate assembly, above all the house of the living God.

If these qualities have not always been utilised fully by us in ecclesial life, or their importance has been under-estimated, there is no support in Scripture for this attitude, as the story of the sisters at Bethany and frequent apostolic reference to women by name makes plain: "Phoebe .. hath been a succourer of many, and of myself also'', and she also apparently brought Paul's letter to Rome; "Priscilla and Aquila, my fellow workers in Christ Jesus ... for my life laid down their own necks, unto whom not only I give thanks, but also all the churches of the Gentiles''; "Mary, who bestowed much labour on us''; "Tryphena and Tryphosa, who labour in the Lord''; "Rufus's mother and mine'' (Romans 16); "Euodias and Syntyche ... those women which laboured with me in the gospel ... whose names are in the book of life'' (Philippians 4); "Our beloved Apphia'' (Philemon 2); "The unfeigned faith ... which dwelt first in thy grandmother Lois and thy mother Eunice'' (2 Timothy 1:5).

The list is impressive, as surely would be the list of those devoted women of the twentieth century ecclesias who labour with shamefastness, sobriety and quietness at that which they, and only they, can do so well, in home, ecclesia and other branches of the Truth's service, to train, teach and guide the young at home or in the Sunday School, to cherish and console, and with affection and skill offer rest and hospitality to the travelling speaker, or carry out many another ecclesial duty which is in effect a "washing of the feet of the saints'', or the receiving of "a prophet in the name of a prophet'', and so receiving with him "a prophet's reward''.

ESSAY 7

Prayer for Those in Authority

THE general concept of prayer for all men needs to be looked at in more detail, which Paul now proceeds to do in 1 Timothy 2:2. To specify those in high places— *"For kings and for all that are in authority"*—does not exclude lesser men, but it does enable us to see how the principles set out in these verses were actually practised by God's people. If Nero was the reigning emperor (or "king") at the time, then the thought of prayers for him would not have come easily to mind. Yet respect for and submission to the authorities *as authorities* is a prominent feature of apostolic teaching. It appears in Titus 3:1, a reminder necessary for brethren in the special circumstances of Crete; it is spelled out in some detail in Romans 13, with explanatory comment; it is part of the seemly behaviour prescribed in 1 Peter 2, where we are assured that it is answerable to Christ's own example, and is therefore "for the Lord's sake" (verse 13). One of the points which emerges clearly from the record in Acts is that the apostles and their converts were at pains to respect authority. When restrained by an official edict, sometimes itself a violation of its own principles (cf. Pilate's "I find no fault in this man—take ye him and crucify him", John 19:4,6), only then did they disobey, or *"obey God rather* than men" (Acts 5:29).

There is equally good Old Testament precedent for prayers for those in authority. Darius requested prayers "for the life of the king and his sons" of the returned exiles for whom he was providing things necessary for the rebuilding of the Temple and its worship (Ezra 6:10; 7:23). Perhaps more surprising, and in contradistinction to the falsely based "nationalism" of the rulers in Jerusalem, the captives in Babylon were commanded to "seek the peace of the city ... and pray unto the Lord for it: *for in the peace thereof shall ye have peace*" (Jeremiah 29:4-7; note the subtle play on the name Jerusalem!).

The reasons are clear. Equally clear is the fact that although two of our Pastoral words can refer to petitions offered to men as well as to God and Biblical examples may be cited for this practice also, it is prayer *to* God *for* men that Paul has in mind. For "the powers that be are ordained of God" (Romans 13:1). Therefore, although captives in Babylon or disciples in the Roman Empire might feel themselves completely at the mercy of ruthless and tyrannical rulers, or subject to the whim of a Pilate, a tetrarch, a proconsul or a town-clerk, and so recognise a sense of need or social insecurity such as those in a liberal democratic society cannot begin to understand, they were neither to rebel nor put their trust in princes: they were in a spirit of thankfulness to make supplications, prayers and intercessions unto God.

Sometimes the repressive régime brought beatings and imprisonment, and there could have been a crisis of conscience and, humanly speaking, some justification for intercession *against* the authorities. Here, too, the apostolic practice is worthy of note: "They lifted up their voice to God with one accord, and said, Lord (Greek: *despotēs;* Hebrew: *Adon*, for *true* Lord and Master), thou art God, which hast made heaven, and earth, and the sea, and all that in them is." There follows the recognition that all was happening according to the word of the Lord, "for to do whatsoever thy hand and thy counsel determined before to be done". Their petition is that the Lord would look upon their condition and grant their heart's desire—"that with all boldness they may speak thy word" (Acts 4:24-31).

ESSAY 8

Braided Hair and Costly Array

"NOT with braided hair, or gold, or pearls, or costly array" (1 Timothy 2:9): Many contemporary pictures, statues and actual objects recovered by the archaeologist, give examples of what Paul counselled his sisters in Christ to avoid. Again the emphasis is upon extravagance, which is the root meaning behind our own word luxury. At certain periods plaited or braided hair was the usual style of coiffure for women. Paul's strictures, however, are not upon a style of arranging the natural hair but upon *display*, as the other words in the phrase reveal. They imply the presence in Ephesus of some women of wealth, whose extravagant adornment would be all the more offensive in a Christian congregation which was made up of rich and poor, bond and free; although, as now, it was possible to buy certain cheap imitations which deceived no-one, except perhaps the wearer who aped a life-style beyond her means. The gold wire mesh or "hair net", the various pins, combs and false tresses needed, in extreme cases, the aid of skilful slaves with crisping pins, and hours of labour, to arrange into a complicated edifice upon the head of the lady of leisure. So it was not a question of forbidding a neat arrangement of beautiful hair, a Divine gift in itself, but of displaying or giving the impression of wealth and self-indulgence, emphasised by the wearing of pearls—sometimes of "great price", worth a merchant's whole capital—and expensive clothing.

There could be another element in the "psychology" of feminine attire and hair-style. More than one Roman author refers to the "lascivious pin" inserted into the hair, and the parting of the tresses to indicate (the word is actually to *profess*) a "loose femininity". Let it be frankly said, that if the Lord's own warning, that a man's lustful glance persisted in is tantamount to adultery, has a female counterpart it must surely be in the deliberate provocation of that glance, either in dress or deportment. If this thought be not actually expressed in the Apostle's warnings here, the principle he is enunciating clearly covers it, and his exhortation has its point today, when sisters, often all unwittingly, follow fashions which negate Scriptural principles (such as the covering of the head in ecclesial worship) or reflect the more sinister aspects of the spirit of the age.

Is Paul saying then that sisters should not dress carefully and well, or try to look attractive? Is he indulging in a conventional diatribe against female extravagance? On the contrary. What he is against is the impropriety of women *exploiting* their physical charms. In early times, even in the world outside the ecclesias, extravagance was officially frowned upon however much it was privately cultivated, and for the rural areas, still cherishing something of the traditional frugality which had, in the case of the Roman, been fostered by *leges sumptuariae*, or laws regulating expenditure, the ways of the wealthy and the manners of the city were marks of decadence. Moreover, the freedom of association between men and women which arose from the fact that "in Christ there is neither male or female" could be seriously misunderstood by those without, if it were not seen to be regulated by restraints of a spiritual nature.

The First Letter to Timothy

CHAPTER 3

The Responsibility of Ecclesial Servants

A S we have seen, Paul is outlining the practical measures by which Timothy is to carry out the "charge" given him to set things in order in Ephesus. The rebuke of the false teachers and the building up of the ecclesia on a basis of sound organisation were complementary parts of this work. Throughout Scriptural history God has worked through the medium of responsible leadership and not by any democratic process for the guidance of His people. Where the leadership has resisted or was not itself submissive to Divine authority, spiritual disaster was the result.

The work of organisation in Ephesus was to centre on Timothy himself, a personal example of all that a believer ought to be in manner of life (4:12-16). But all the ecclesia's members, individually and collectively, had their special parts to play. Neither Timothy nor anyone else, however, was to be a bishop in the ecclesiastical sense. His authority could direct and his example inspire, but the spiritual tone of the Ephesian church would depend upon the manner in which all its servants carried out their duties (see Essay 9, page 106).

3:1-7—The Office of a Bishop

Verse 1: "Faithful is the saying": for a general survey of these characteristic sayings in the Pastoral Epistles see Essay 5, page 49. The rendering of this, the second of the five "faithful words", is that of the Revised Version. Some commentators, thinking that the seeking of office is more a fleshly than a spiritual pursuit, have preferred a different reading. The Authorised Version has "a true saying" and the New English Bible, "It is a human, or popular saying". Apart from the lack of real textual evidence to support it, this rendering completely misses the point of the Apostle's argument, as does the attempt to link the phrase with the preceding verse about women and their salvation in chapter 2.

Whether the saying we are considering did in fact have its origin in a popular proverb or not is of no great importance. By his use of it Paul has made it one of the "words of the Faith", and has left us in no doubt that ecclesial organisation—or the Constitution, where it is based on sound principles—is as much a cardinal element of life and fellowship as the Statement of Faith itself. (Traditionally, the two have formed part of the same document for many decades.)

"If a man desire the office of a bishop": The word for "desire" occurs twice more in the New Testament. In 1 Timothy 6:10 it refers to the coveting of money, and so signifies the wrong kind of desire. From Hebrews 11:16, however, where it describes the eagerness with which men of faith sought "the better country, that is, an heavenly", we can see the sense with which it is being used here. In fact, in his exhortation to his fellow elders, Peter expresses the precise idea although not with the same word: "Feed the flock of God which is among you, taking the oversight thereof, *not by constraint, but willingly*; not for filthy lucre, but of *a ready mind*; neither as being lords over God's heritage, but being ensamples to the flock" (1 Peter 5:2,3).

Why should Paul feel it necessary to emphasise that it is a good work *(kalon ergon)*? The word *ergon* refers to the proper duties, not the honour of the service, and of "good works" in general we have already written (see page 72). There is some evidence of unwillingness on the part of brethren of the right calibre to undertake ecclesial office in the first century; a reluctance which seems to have had its counterpart in the political world of the Greek cities. Kelly, in *Pastoral Epistles*, page 72, makes the point that it was sometimes difficult to find enough responsible men to undertake civic duties.

As far as the early church was concerned it was becoming increasingly dangerous to be known as a prominent Christian, as Paul's own imprisonment and execution testify. The smiting of the shepherd was still a good way of scattering the sheep. Moreover, the *kalon ergon* of ecclesial administration properly discharged is onerous and should be approached with a sense of responsibility and dedication. The words which follow in 3:2

introduce the list of qualifications for service, which all who nominate or accept nomination for ecclesial service in our own day would do well to study carefully—always remembering that if we ourselves persistently refuse to accept responsibility merely to avoid its burdens, or even because of a general feeling of inadequacy, we should restrain ourselves from the carping criticism of those who prayerfully undertake it from the right motives.

The list of qualifications in 1 Timothy 3 is worth committing to memory, if only as a "check list" of our responsibilities (see Essay 10, page 107). We shall find that Paul has a characteristically Christian view of all the words he uses, wherever he has drawn them from. Indeed, it is as though he is saying to Timothy, and to us, If a town like Philippi, chief city of Macedonia, or even a small provincial town like Pompeii, demands that its officials be "worthy of the state", how much more must they be worthy, in spirit and not only in letter, who are servants "of the house of God, which is the church of the living God, the pillar and ground of the truth" (verse 15)? And not only the overseers and ministers, but all who are members of the corporate body, which is compacted together by that which every joint supplieth, must let their "conversation be as it becometh the gospel of Christ" (Philippians 1:27; "conversation" is *politeuma*, or "citizenship", as in 3:20, RV).

Verse 2: *"A bishop then must be blameless":* The order of words in the Greek text is much more emphatic: "It is *therefore essential*." *Dei oun* indicates absolute necessity, arising from what has gone before, in this case the statement that taking oversight is one of those good works of which a purchased people should be zealous in the proper sense (Titus 2:14). The verb *dei* appears three times in this chapter: again in verse 7, "he *must* have a good report", and in verse 15, "how thou *oughtest* to behave thyself" in the ecclesia. It also introduces aspects of personal behaviour, both positive and negative, in 1 Timothy 5:13, 2 Timothy 2:6 and Titus 1:7,11, the last passage being parallel to the one under consideration. It is noteworthy that we have no list of *duties*, only of *qualifications*, which makes these passages of timeless validity: the twentieth century makes its own detailed demands upon ecclesial organisation; the principles on which it is based must not change.

"Blameless": the list of seven positive qualities to be possessed by overseers is headed by a word which comprehends them all. The Greek word for "blameless", "beyond reproach", is Classical but appears in the Greek Bible only in 1 Timothy. The usage in 5:7 refers to the qualifications which made a widow eligible to come under the ecclesia's care. In 6:14 it applies to "the commandment" which Timothy was to keep unimpaired until the day of the Lord's manifestation; that is, the charge laid on him at his baptism (see 6:12) when he "professed the good profession". By living a spotless, unrebukeable life he would have kept the commandment in its entirety.

The ecclesial servant had not only to be of good report, but deserving of it also, and his reputation had to be sound outside as well as inside the church (verse 7). The standard was high, as high as that of God Himself, as we read out of the law (for example, Deuteronomy 1:16,17; see also Psalm 82): the elders and the judges acted on the Lord's behalf, and therefore they had to be like Him (Matthew 5:48) (see Essay 11, "The Husband of One Wife", page 110).

"Vigilant, sober, of good behaviour": some translators prefer "sober" for the first word (*nēphalios*, unique in the Greek Bible to the Pastoral Epistles) as it is so translated in verse 11 and Titus 2:2, and "sober" does not really carry the same sense as that of the word which follows it. It is related to the verb used for "be sober" in 1 Thessalonians 5:6,8; 1 Peter 1:13; 4:7; 5:8, although 2 Timothy 4:5 has *"watch thou* in all things"*. Although in contemporary society it could carry the sense of abstaining from wine, a wider reference is surely indicated here, since Paul deals with the question of wine-drinking in the next verse. It is, therefore, preferable to take its meaning as indicating moral restraint in general, in which the idea of "vigilance" or "watchfulness" or even "clear-headedness" is not out of place, implying as it does unceasing carefulness over every aspect of behaviour.

So regarded, the word goes well with the two words which follow it, *sōphrōn* and *kosmios*, to indicate that "mastery of oneself" which enables an ecclesial servant to carry out his duties with a dignity, reverence and restraint befitting behaviour in "the house of the living God". Such restraint extends beyond deportment to speech ("alway with grace, seasoned with salt",

Colossians 4:6), which should be free from the ribaldry and crude colloquialism which marks much of the conversation of the present-day "man in the street".

Of *sōphrosunē*, a word related to *sōphrōn* ('sober', AV) we have already written (page 70) in connection with the whole deportment of the ecclesia, amongst members of all ages, sisters and brethren alike. (See also on Titus 2:1-10, pages 385-387.) How much greater is the responsibility of the overseer or elder, or the modern "arranging brother" to display this quality: "Take heed unto thyself" (1 Timothy 4:16); "Be thou an example of the believers" (4:12); "In all things showing thyself a pattern of good works" (Titus 2:7)—these were the constant exhortations to the young men entrusted with the delicate and responsible task of guiding and, if necessary, rebuilding, ecclesias under pressure.

For *kosmios* ("of good behaviour") see the notes on 2:9 (page 69) in connection with "modest apparel". Here the meaning goes deeper than that of outward adornment, but it still carries the idea of *orderly* behaviour, reinforcing the former positive qualities which combine to give a due sense of the responsibility of ecclesial office.

"Given to hospitality": the word is literally 'a friend to strangers', a quality which has its roots deep in the Old Testament and God's relationship with His people. Frequently were they reminded of their duty to the stranger because in so acting they were manifesting God's glory:

"For the LORD your God is God of gods, and Lord of lords, a great God, a mighty, and a terrible, which regardeth not persons, nor taketh reward: he doth execute the judgment of the fatherless and widow, and *loveth the stranger*, in giving him food and raiment. Love ye therefore the stranger: for ye were strangers in the land of Egypt." (Deuteronomy 10:17-19)

This theme is taken up in Hebrews 12:29—13:1,2, where "For our God is a consuming fire" is followed immediately by "Let brotherly love continue. Be not forgetful *to entertain strangers*: for thereby some have entertained angels unawares."

There is no doubt, however, that Paul is carrying the principle over to brethren or sisters in need of a meal and bed, whether they were known to the host or not. So much is implied in 1 Timothy

5:10, "If she have lodged strangers" (*xenos*, 'stranger', is also the Greek word for 'guest') as it appears in the following verses: in Romans 12:13, "distributing to the necessity of saints; given to hospitality"; in 1 Peter 4:9, "use hospitality one to another without grudging"; and in 3 John 5, "Beloved, thou doest faithfully whatsoever thou doest to the brethren, and to strangers". Such hospitality was an act of mercy, inspired by the union in the same faith which existed between members of the same family of God, and to which was attached a special blessing.

There was, moreover, another reason for the practice of offering hospitality in the first century. The missionary age saw many brethren on the road with but slender resources, and for the new men in Christ the lodging places they could afford were unthinkable. Not only were some of them dangerous, where a man might well be exposed to robbery and violence, or worse, but the moral atmosphere would have been oppressive to a disciple who was trying earnestly to cleanse himself from all filthiness of the flesh and spirit, perfecting holiness in the fear of God (2 Corinthians 7:1). The "bishop", therefore, with a responsibility which made him a representative of the local ecclesia, had both a spiritual and practical obligation to lead his flock in this matter also.

"Apt to teach": this quality above all was required, especially in Ephesus and Crete, which needed the firm yet sympathetic guidance of one learned in the knowledge of God, especially of His ways, and skilled in teaching others by his own example. It was one of the functions of the priests of Israel, to whom Moses delivered the Law, that they should cause the people to hear it: "For the priests' lips should keep knowledge, and they should seek the law at his mouth: for he is the messenger of the LORD of hosts" (Malachi 2:7). This function seems to have distinguished the bishop from the deacons, although in Acts 6 one deacon at least in no way came behind in this gift, for no one could resist the wisdom and spirit with which Stephen spake (verse 10).

Such overseers as Timothy and Titus themselves could no doubt pick their way through the wrangling and jangling of the other-teachers with a sureness of touch which grasped the Scriptural essentials and exposed all else for what it really was. Their reorganisation of the ecclesias on sound lines called for more men of the right stamp to exercise leadership, like the elders "who labour in the word and in teaching" (1 Timothy 5:17, RV). Nor must the servant of the Lord display the self-opinionated aggressiveness which is the hall-mark of some professing exponents of the Word: he "must not strive, but be gentle unto all men, apt to teach, patient, in meekness instructing those that oppose themselves" (2 Timothy 2:24,25). The required characteristics of the bishop are given in detail in Titus 1:9—"Holding fast the faithful word as he hath been taught, that he may be able by sound doctrine both to exhort and convince the gainsayers." Or, as it might otherwise be put, he must show loyalty to the apostolic teaching, be ready to instruct the ecclesia in it, and be vigilant in confuting those who pervert it.

Verse 3: *"Not given to wine"*: the fact that this negative command is referred to three times in all (see verse 8 and Titus 1:7) shows that it was a necessary injunction. From 5:23, where Paul prescribes "a little wine for thy stomach's sake and thine often infirmities", it is clear that moderation and not total abstinence is envisaged here. But the exhortation to be no *paroinos* (used in the New Testament again only in Titus 1:7) indicates a tendency on the part of some to "add drunkenness to thirst" (Deuteronomy 29:19).

There is evidence that it was recklessness or befuddling of the wits which so clouded the judgement of Nadab and Abihu that they offered "strange fire before the LORD", and thus failed to sanctify the LORD in their approach to Him. For immediately after their burial,

> "The LORD spake unto Aaron, saying, *Do not drink wine nor strong drink*, thou nor thy sons with thee, when ye go into the tabernacle of the congregation, lest ye die: it shall be a statute for ever throughout your generations: and that ye may put difference between holy and unholy, and between unclean and clean; and that *ye may teach the children of Israel* all the statutes which the LORD hath spoken unto them by the hand of Moses."   (Leviticus 10:8-11)

Thus "apt to teach" was coupled with "not given to wine" in the "holiness code" for the priests as well as for ecclesial servants.

The warnings were necessary in an age where it was usual for the dinner-party in ordinary society to merge into the *commissatio*, or drinking-party, and "rioting and drunkenness, chambering and wantonness" and (let it be carefully noted) "strife and envying" were specifically listed as inconsistent with the behaviour of those who had "put on the Lord Jesus Christ" (Romans 13:13,14); and "such like" are listed as "the works of the flesh" (Galatians 5:19-21). When we remember that some Corinthians showed a tendency to eat and be drunken even at the Lord's supper (1 Corinthians 11:21), we are not surprised that Paul should list moderation amongst the necessary qualifications of a spiritual leader (see 1 Corinthians 10:6,7,14). The spirit of the present age and the temptations that beset young people particularly, though the old are by no means immune, make careful attention to this same point by no means unnecessary today.

"No striker, or brawler": this vice, a common outcome of being *paroinos*, is no doubt to be taken in its literal meaning. It was certainly not unknown for an unvigilant, faithless servant of a household to "begin to beat the menservants and maidens, and to eat and drink, and to be drunken" (Luke 12:45), or for masters in a position of power over their servants to use unnecessary violence in disciplining them, without being under the influence of anything but anger or frustration. Indeed, amidst the strifes about words and other disorders in the Ephesian ecclesia, the atmosphere could very well have been conducive to coming to blows.

It has not been unknown for an ecclesia in modern times to witness something very close to a brawl, when voices are raised in dispute, and brethren even claim to be defending the Truth against error when they rise in noisy interruption or accusation. This was not then, nor is it now, for the patient, gentle, meek servant of the Lord, apt to teach, who seeks to exercise a genuine spiritual influence in an ecclesia (2 Timothy 2:23 and Essay 33).

"But gentle, not contentious, no lover of money": this Revised Version rendering differs slightly from the Authorised in the order of words and it avoids the repetition of "not greedy of filthy lucre" and "not covetous". "Forbearing" is the idea behind *epieikē*, 'gentle'. It is a characteristic of "the wisdom that is from above" (James 3:17), which should be "known unto all men", a distinguishing mark of the true disciple (Philippians 4:5). Above all, it was to be seen in "the gentleness of Christ", by which Paul

exhorted his recalcitrant, critical brethren in Corinth to submit to his apostolic authority (2 Corinthians 10:1). Let this mind be in us . . .

Clearly the way to deal with contention and strife in an ecclesia is not to be oneself *contentious*. This was sound advice in Ephesus and Crete, and it is advice sorely needed today, when it is only too easy to become involved in "questions and strifes of words, whereof cometh envy, strife, railings, evil surmisings" to the point where we can even become "bereft of the truth, supposing that godliness is a way of gain" (6:4,5).

So the bishop must be "not a lover of silver": it is unlikely that financial gain is much sought after in modern ecclesial life (indeed, ecclesial servants tend to minister of their own substance far beyond what could justifiably be recouped by way of "expenses"), but the warning was obviously necessary in Paul's day. The Pharisees were "lovers of silver" (covetous) and mocked the Lord when he declared: "Ye cannot serve God and mammon" (Luke 16:13); and the treachery of Judas began with taking what was put in the bag with which he was entrusted.

A brother with a weakness in financial matters would certainly be unsuited to handle the ecclesial purse, and the temptation would be great if in fact the elders of the first century ecclesia did receive an honorarium, as some have thought. (We shall examine this point further when we come to 1 Timothy 5:17-18.) But covetousness extends to other things beside money; and gain other than financial can be sought, such as status, power, influence or anything that ministers to or satisfies the *ego*. Such is not godliness in any disciple, least of all in a spiritual leader.

3:4-5—The Ecclesia and the Family

Verse 4: "One that ruleth well his own house": perhaps insufficient attention has been paid to this necessary qualification, which must surely cause much heart-searching in the modern age, when the pressures of the outside world weigh so heavily upon our young people and their parents, and parental authority is frequently challenged by both school and society. Thereby is the parents' task rendered all the more difficult. Before taking up this point of the modern problem, we first consider the Scriptural principle.

The ecclesia is "God's house" (verse 15), and Paul's allusion to Jacob at Bethel (Genesis 28) reminds us that the building of a household was the very basis of God's covenants of promise, from the time that He blessed Abraham to the day when He made "the whole family" of Israel into His own people and covenanted to dwell with them and be their God.

The name of Father, applied to God, brings home the point Paul makes in Ephesians 3:15 that out of Him "the whole family (literally, 'every fatherhood') in heaven and earth is named". The child too young to bear a personal responsibility towards God learns to do so through his duty to his parents; and the parents, under God, the givers of life to their children, have a responsibility to care for and sustain them. "If any provide not for his own, and specially for those of his own house, he *hath denied the faith*, and is worse than an infidel" (1 Timothy 5:8).

Verse 5: Pastoral care of the flock of God calls for feeding and tending, with the compassion of a father, the gentleness of a mother in Israel, and a command of Scriptural principle: "If a man know not how to rule his own house, how shall he take care of the house of God?" But "who is sufficient for these things?" (2 Corinthians 2:16). To which the answer must be, Few, if any of us. To know and understand the idea, however, and to work towards it as far as human limitations will allow, trusting in the strength which God supplies to any who in sincerity seek to work for Him and "desire a good work", is essential. There is certainly no room for the routine "annual election of ecclesial officers" to which no prayerful thought is given; nor for the campaigning for office and influence which is more of the citizenship of this world than of that which is in heaven.

"Taking care" has a nuance which appears in Luke 10:34,35 —the only other occurrence of this verb. It was characteristic of the Good Samaritan in his gentle, thoughtful concern for the welfare of him who fell among thieves. If, therefore, in our times it seems more difficult to have *"children in subjection"*—compare the signs of the last days in 2 Timothy 3:2—one can at least show *"gravity"*, that is, a due sense of that which is honourable and right in the principles which guide the household.

In Philippians 4:8, the Revised Version "honourable" translates the adjective *semnos*, from which *semnotēs*, 'gravity', is derived. The use of both noun and adjective is otherwise confined to the Pastoral Epistles, and has already been commented upon in the note on 2:2 (page 59). If the children are in no doubt as to the parents' standards and intense conviction of the seriousness of the life in Christ, and the household is so ordered, then it will be a matter for sorrow and regret but not for self-censure on the part of the parents if their children do not ultimately share their faith, hope and ideals (see Jeremiah 31:29,30; Ezekiel 18).

Verse 6: "Not a novice": a convert newly come to the faith (literally 'newly planted', the only known example of the word used figuratively) would be quite unsuited to take charge of an ecclesia, whatever his native skills might appear to be. Of all the possible reasons—his lack of authority, his insufficient knowledge, his loyalty and constancy as yet unproved—Paul cites only one: the novice would be too easily exposed to the weakness of pride.

"Lifted up with pride", a "oncer", found again in 6:4 and 2 Timothy 3:4, is all one word, derived from the word for 'smoke'. Pride goes to the head, like smoke which blinds and confuses, and in a head so filled sureness of judgement and the standards of wise judgement cannot be guaranteed. Particularly in the Ephesian situation such a one could lose his head, teach false doctrine or show himself arrogant towards his brethren. If he is "proud" (6:4) he could be "knowing nothing, but doting about questions and strifes of words", or become "heady, *highminded*" (2 Timothy 3:4). Although special circumstances may sometimes demand otherwise—this caution is omitted in the case of elders in Crete, for example—the "two-year rule" in some ecclesial constitutions concerning the appointment of the newly baptized to office is a wise precaution.

"Lest . . . he fall into the condemnation of the devil": the orthodox view naturally sees in this the condemnation passed upon the Devil for his pride; that is, he was cast out from his high office in heaven, as Lucifer, son of the morning (Isaiah 14). The Scriptural view of the *diabolos* as sinful human nature yields good sense here, since the condemnation is that which the novice will bring upon himself for giving way to his human pride. There is a specialised use of the word in these Letters, however, occurring in verse 11 and in 2 Timothy 3:3 and Titus 2:3, where it refers to the gossip or the slanderer. It might be that the accusation laid

against the puffed-up novice would be true and not false, but in any case accusation knows few restraints and Paul would not have the overseer talked about by the slanderer within or without the ecclesia—a disaster for the person concerned and for any ecclesia under his management.

Verse 7: The bishop must, therefore, *"have a good report of them which are without"*: such was Ananias who brought Christ's message to Paul (Acts 22:12) and by such reputations Paul set great store, as he counselled the Thessalonians, "that ye may walk honestly toward them that are without" (1 Thessalonians 4:12). The unblemished reputation of the Lord Jesus ("I find no fault in this man"—John 18:38; 19:4,6) did not render him immune from the false witness who laid wait for him that they might have something to accuse him of. Nevertheless it was recognised that it was only by *false* witness that he could be condemned.

Perhaps *"lest he fall into reproach and the snare of the devil"* is best taken as meaning falling into the trap laid by the slanderer who seizes the opportunity to reproach and condemn. If the Lord himself could not escape, how much more would a novice overseer be needlessly exposed to the gossip of the *diaboloi*? Sadly it must be confessed that attacks upon reputation, justified or not, are often the tactics of those who seek occasion for their own purposes.

3:8-13—The Deacons and their Wives

Verse 8: *"Likewise must the deacons be grave"*: the very emphatic "likewise" sets the same high standard for all ecclesial servants as for those in a more prominent position. Some have seen a significance in the plural, "deacons", as distinct from the singular, "a bishop", as though we are here dealing with the kind of church hierarchy which developed in orthodox circles. From Philippians 1:1, however, we learn that this distinction need not be made and, as we have seen, there was nothing in the Scriptural "overseer" to suggest the monarchical figure who emerged in the second century. Indeed, from 1 Peter 5:12 we learn that the case was exactly the opposite. Nevertheless, the fact that deacons are referred to as a separate class does imply a function different in some measure from that of, say, Timothy himself or Titus.

The word deacon (*diakonos*) ordinarily means a servant or minister and with the noun *diakonia*, 'service', and *diakoneō*, 'to

96

serve', occurs frequently in the New Testament. These words can apply equally to the ministry of the angels to the Lord in the wilderness, the "much serving" of Martha, the ministry of the word (Acts 6:4), to the work of the Apostle Paul himself (Acts 20:24; 21:19; "mine office", Romans 11:13), the service rendered to him by his minister, John Mark (Acts 13:5), and the diverse "administrations" of the one Spirit (1 Corinthians 12:5). It would appear, therefore, that the diaconate covered the whole range of activities of those who, having decided to *serve* the Lord Jesus, follow him as his disciples. Moreover, the Lord himself was among his disciples "as he that *serveth*" (Luke 22:27).

In the passage under consideration, however, Paul obviously has in view some particular form of ecclesial service for which the same sense of responsibility is required as that for bishops, but not necessarily the same aptitudes. Acts 6:1-4 supplies the key. In the simple organisation of the church in its earliest days the Apostles gave themselves to "the ministry *(diakonia)* of the word", while others were appointed to "serve *(diakoneō))* tables". The men appointed, however, were not selected simply because of any practical, administrative skill they may have possessed: they were "men of honest report, full of the Holy Spirit and wisdom", and one of them at least was also able to speak with wisdom and with Spirit.

The deacons therefore had to be "grave", of high principle, as we have described the word in the note on 2:2 and verse 4.

"Not doubletongued, not given to much wine, not greedy of filthy lucre": "Preserve me from my calling's snare" prayed one hymn writer, conscious of a danger to which we would all do well to take heed. Differing responsibilities may call for different qualities in each one of us: they may equally expose us to different spiritual dangers, and Paul is here alive to that possibility. "Double-tongued" is a New Testament "oncer", and may mean simply "a talebearer", a damaging vice into which it would be too easy for an ecclesial visitor or other servant who needed to go from house to house to fall. The more subtle temptation would be to say one thing to one and something different to another, in the genuine attempt to be "all things to all men", in the spirit of the Apostle Paul himself. It is one thing to adapt one's manner of approach and style of address to the needs and capacity of the one

being visited. It is quite another to be doubletongued and shift ground on principles and say only what the other wishes to hear.

Perhaps the stronger emphasis upon carefulness over wine-drinking is also necessary, in view of the fact that a deacon might frequently be offered wine in his house-to-house visiting, as a gesture of hospitality. See also verse 3 above. Likewise the warning against love of money is stronger, since the deacon would probably be responsible for the administration and disbursement of ecclesial funds. He must not "greedy of base gains" (see also on Titus 1:7,11, page 364), for "the love of money is the root of all evil", and the one who undertakes this kind of "*diakonia* to the saints" (2 Corinthians 9:1) must be beyond reproach in this respect.

Titus himself was obviously trustworthy, as was the brother chosen to accompany him when they bore the proceeds of the great collection taken up in the ecclesias of Corinth and Macedonia: "(His) praise is in the gospel throughout all the churches; and not that only, but who was also chosen of the churches to travel with us with this grace, which is administered (*diakoneō*) by us ... Avoiding this, that no man should blame us in this abundance which is administered by us: providing for honest things, not only in the sight of the Lord, but also in the sight of men" (2 Corinthians 8:18-21). It is no doubt significant for the distinction between the work of the deacon and that of the overseer that he was not *necessarily* "apt to teach".

Verse 9: *"Holding the mystery of the faith in a pure conscience"*: of "the mystery of the faith" we write below when considering verse 16, but it has reference to the firm belief of the deacon in the content and practice of his faith. "In a pure conscience" may well refer here to the close relations between a sound belief and the kind of life which leaves the conscience free from stain and self-reproach. (For "pure conscience" see 1:5, page 44.) On the other hand, in this particular context the Apostle may well be warning against all reservations in belief. The unsure, the doubleminded ("unstable in all his ways", James 1:8), the unconvinced are all unqualified for ecclesial office, since the ecclesia should be led by men who believe every word they say and also believe whole-heartedly in the community they serve. Our brotherhood has suffered more from its internal critics than from any of the direct attacks from those outside.

Verse 10: *"And let these first be tested":* again we have the impression that the requirements for the deacon were more stringent than for the overseer. In fact this is not so, since the latter had also to have "a good report of them which are without" as well as of the ecclesia itself. Nor are we to understand some kind of formal examination or enquiry prior to the acceptance of men for ecclesial service. The idea is equivalent to that of "not a new convert, or novice" in verse 6: sufficient time must be allowed for the necessary qualities to be manifest in private and ecclesial behaviour. Again Acts 6:3 helps our understanding, for the multitude of the brethren were able to "look ye out among you seven men of honest report", who had already proved themselves by their conduct and demeanour and were thus able to *"use the office of a deacon, being found blameless".* The rather quaint expression, "use the office . . ." again translates the one word *diakoneō.*

Verse 11: *"Even so must their wives be grave, not slanderers, sober":* the same word "likewise" (as in verse 8) introduces the women's service and links it to that of the bishops and deacons. "Wife" and "woman" are the same word in Greek, so the question as to whether the deacons' wives or women who serve the ecclesia is intended depends upon other considerations (the word "their" does not appear in the text). It is true that the quality and demeanour of a man's wife is of great importance in his ecclesial service and her sense of responsibility provides him with a strength and stay. An onerous task becomes doubly difficult if she be a gossip, intemperate, not faithful in all things.

The sequence of thought in 1 Timothy 3 and the subject under discussion—sound ecclesial organisation and behaviour in the house of God (verse 15)—make it more likely that Paul is discussing the rôle of sisters in the service of the ecclesia. No duties are defined here, nor are they for the brethren, since it is qualifications with which Paul is concerned. The later word *diakonissa,* 'deaconess', is not found in the New Testament but there were sisters who served. Phoebe, for example, was a *"diakonos* of the church which is at Cenchrea" and had come to Rome to carry out some specific task, relying on the assistance of the brethren and sisters there "in whatsoever business she hath need of you" (Romans 16:1-2).

When we consider the wide range of ecclesial service covered by the word *diakoneō* as outlined in the note on verse 8, we can see how some of these activities could be performed equally by men or women, and at some of them the sisters would in fact excel. Indeed, as we have already indicated (pages 79-80), they bring to their work a quality of devotion and single-mindedness aptly summed up in Paul's *"faithful in all things"*. It was doubly important, therefore, to ensure that that service was not marred by gossipping. *Diaboloi* in the plural always bears the sense of 'false or loose accusation' in the New Testament, although it is not necessarily only a feminine weakness: see 2 Timothy 3:3 and Titus 2:3.

Verse 12: The importance of a solidly based family life has already been discussed in the comments on verses 4-5 (page 93).

Verse 13: *"For they that have served well as deacons gain to themselves a good standing":* the Revised Version of this verse gives the better sense, at any rate once we have determined what "a good standing" is. Since it is a New Testament "oncer" we have no good Biblical guide, for in the Septuagint it means 'threshold' (1 Samuel 5:5) or 'degree' on a sundial (2 Kings 20:9); in Classical Greek it means 'base', 'pedestal of a statue', or a 'degree', 'step' or even 'throne'. In the moral sense "standing" is as good a translation as any, and may refer to the increased reputation which men of already good repute before they were chosen could win by faithful service. It is even possible that faithful service as a deacon might be regarded as a suitable preparation for assuming the heavier responsibility of the overseer, although in view of what has been said about the corporate responsibility of all ecclesial servants in their standing before the Lord this view is not pressed.

There is another consideration, however, which all commentators seem to have overlooked. *Service* of any kind was considered to be rather degrading in the Ancient World, particularly for the Greek. There is surely intended the linking together of the "good work" (*kalon ergon*) of verse 1, the *kalōs diakonēsantes*, the good service of the deacons of verse 13 and the *bathmon kalon*, or "good standing" of the same verse. For it was the example of the Master himself, who took upon him the form of a slave, girded himself with the towel, the very badge of humility and menial service, and washed his disciples' feet (see 5:10). And when he "was set down again, he said unto them, Know ye what I have done to you? Ye call me Master and Lord: and ye say well; for so I am. If I then, your Lord and Master, have washed your feet; ye also ought to wash one another's feet. *For I have given you an example*, that ye should do as I have done to you" (John 13:12-15).

A man or woman taking Christ for an example (note the plural, "*they* that have served well") will indeed have "*great boldness in the faith which is in Christ Jesus*". It is the assurance of the Apostle who could say, "In (him) we have boldness and access in confidence (assurance) through our faith in him" (Ephesians 3:12, RV). Besides this assurance before God there is also confidence in the presence of men, born of a living faith exemplified in irreproachable conduct; and, most wonderfully, when the Lord of the watchful servants comes, "Verily I say unto you, that he shall gird himself, and make them to sit down to meat, and will come forth and serve them" (*diakoneō*, Luke 12:37)!

Verse 14: *"These things write I unto thee, hoping to come unto thee shortly":* if the sequence of events envisaged in the Introduction and the comment on 1:3-4 (pages 13,17) be correct, Paul could have been at Philippi at the time of writing, on his way to Ephesus. But whether his sojourn there was to be long or short, he wrote 1 Timothy to exhort, encourage and instruct Timothy in the responsibilities of his task.

Verse 15: *"But if I tarry long, that thou mayest know how thou oughtest to behave thyself":* as already remarked, the example of Timothy himself was of the utmost importance. The most perfect organisation with the clearest of instructions would be ineffective if the character of the leaders was defective. Especially in Ephesus the problems of the ecclesia had arisen from the irresponsibility of its elders, so Timothy was instructed to "take heed *unto thyself* and unto the doctrine ... for in doing this thou shalt both save thyself and them that hear thee" (4:16). For the sphere of his service was none other than *"the house of God"* (see Essay 12, page 113).

The right kind of preaching must be combined with the right kind of organisation, and in the Apostle's advice on this matter perhaps the key words are *"gravity"* and *"uncorruptness"* as defined above (2:2, AV "honesty"; 3:4; and especially Titus 2:7 in context)—"an intense conviction of the seriousness of life and the difficulty of realising the Christian ideal'', a sense of responsibility on the one hand, and on the other ''the singlemindedness and sincerity which a teacher of sacred things should exhibit'' (J. H. Bernard, *The Pastoral Epistles*, Cambridge Greek Testament for Schools and Colleges).

3:16—The Doctrinal Pivot of the Epistle

We come now to the doctrinal statement which is the pivot of the whole Epistle, appropriately set about midway through it. Although it is not introduced by the usual ''Faithful is the saying'', it is nevertheless a foundation statement of the faith. The entire verse provides an excellent example of how the Apostle could speak that which was exactly right for the situation with which he was dealing: it was especially applicable for the ecclesia at Ephesus, both in their problems within and the pressures from without; it is in metrical form, easily remembered, and possibly an early hymn; it links directly with the Old Testament background to the promise that the Gospel would be for Gentile as well as Jew; and it summed up the purpose of God revealed in the living Christ as the very foundation of the ecclesia which was to defend and confirm the faith.

The precise reference of *''without controversy''* seems at first sight not easy to determine. Some think that it was a liturgical formula, such as that introducing the recitation of an ode to Diana in Ephesus, and that Paul uses it to emphasise the contrast between the false mystery and the true (see Essay 13, ''Great is the Mystery of Godliness'', page 116). The rarer, but surely more apposite meaning of *homologoumenōs*, unique in the New Testament, is ''consistent with what has just been said'', or ''and this is what we all profess''. Paul has just been reminding Timothy that the concept of the Ecclesia and of his own behaviour in it springs from the fact that God was in Christ, and that He dwells in and with the community who are the custodians of this revealed truth as well as living examples of its principles at work. The verb and noun related to the Greek for ''without controversy'' confirm this interpretation. Timothy (1 Timothy 6:12,13) ''professed (*homologeō*) a good profession (*homologia*)'' before many witnesses as Christ ''witnessed a good confession (*homologia*) before Pontius Pilate''. Christ is also ''apostle and high priest of our *homologia*'' (Hebrews 3:1). There are several other uses of the words in the

New Testament, which justify our translating the opening of verse 16 as, "And as we all know, this is a fundamental of our common faith: Great is the mystery . . ."

We now resume the exposition of the hymn in 3:16, to examine its lines in detail.

"He who was manifest in the flesh": The Word was in the beginning but the Son of God was not, as becomes evident from this passage. The term "flesh" is usually employed by the Apostle to indicate the nature of man wherein sin dwells. So he writes in Romans 8:3: God sent "his own Son in the likeness of sinful flesh". Here the term indicates rather the essential humanity of Christ, "flesh" as distinct from "spirit", as in John 1:14— "The Word was made *flesh*, and dwelt among us, (and we beheld his glory, the glory as of the only begotten of the Father), full of grace and truth." When all is said and done, humans, as distinct from those of angelic nature, are subject to weakness and temptation, and so "he took not on him the nature of angels" but was manifest in the flesh. This accords well with the Apostle's theme of the Ecclesia, since he is giving us the doctrinal foundation for his definition of it in verse 15: see also Hebrews 2:12.

Being made perfect through suffering, "he is not ashamed to call them brethren, saying, I will declare thy name unto my brethren, in the midst of the *church* will I sing praise unto thee". The word "manifest" exactly counter-balances the word "mystery" throughout Paul's writings. The "purpose and grace, which was given us in Christ Jesus before the world began . . . is now *made manifest*, by the appearing of our Saviour Jesus Christ, who hath abolished death, and *hath brought life and immortality to light through the gospel*" (2 Timothy 1:9,10). "The righteousness of God without the law *is manifested* . . . even the righteousness of God which is by faith of Jesus Christ" (Romans 3:21,22).

"Justified in the Spirit": Christ never walked after the flesh, but after the Spirit, so the righteousness of God was manifest specifically in him. The reference here, however, is not so much to the blameless life of the Lord but to the resurrection by which his Father declared him to be the holy, harmless and undefiled Son of God: "For Christ also hath once suffered for sins, the just for the unjust, that he might bring us to God, being put to death

103

in the flesh, but quickened by the Spirit" (1 Peter 3:18). Or, to put it Paul's way, "Jesus Christ our Lord was . . . declared to be the Son of God with power, according to the spirit of holiness, by the resurrection from the dead" (Romans 1:3,4).

"Seen of angels, preached unto the Gentiles": here in this strong antithesis is emphasised the distinction in nature between angels and men. The angels had an immediate revelation of the Lord and his life and resurrection. They "desired to look into" the prophetic message of "the sufferings of Christ and the glory that should follow" (1 Peter 1:11), and when the time came it was they who brought to earth the tidings of great joy. They were present with Christ in his suffering, for example in the temptation in the wilderness and the agony in the Garden (Mark 1:13; Matthew 4:11; Luke 22:43). Also the angels were the first to behold him in the day of his resurrection (Matthew 28:2-6). For all the Gentiles, however, and for the majority of the Jews except those few chosen to be eye-witnesses of his resurrection, the witness to the Lord's work was through the medium of preaching, a witness which is as powerful today as it was in the first century, and to proclaim it the church has been constituted "a pillar and stay of the truth".

"Believed on in the world": the "world" has no evil connotation here. It was for the world which God so loved that He gave His only begotten Son, "that whosoever believeth in him should not perish, but have everlasting life" (John 3:16); the world was in need of salvation; the world was the scene of Christ's manifestation of the Father in flesh; and it is in the world, among men, that the saving grace of the Gospel is proclaimed, a message worthy of *all* acceptation, though, alas, all are not willing to accept it.

"Received up into glory": this is the distinctive word used for the Lord's ascension to heaven in both Mark 16:19 and Acts 1:9. He is now "where he was before", glorified with "the glory which I had with thee before the world was", because he had manifested His Father's name to them which were given to him (John 17:5,6). The prophets from the foundation of the world had spoken of the glory as well as the suffering, and Psalm 110 especially ascribed to Christ a glory "with" or "beside" the Father when "the LORD said unto my Lord, Sit thou at my right hand until I make thy foes thy footstool" (Acts 2:34,35).

So the mystery of godliness is described in a hymn which takes us from the incarnation—which as Dr. Thomas once pointed out, was not an incarnation of the Son but of the Father—to the ascension.

The sequence of thought in the hymn is logical (and poetical) rather than historical, since the Lord ascended before the Gospel was preached unto the Gentiles. The thought is matched in a similar pivotal passage in Titus 2:11-14 (see also Essay 48, page 401), which sees the ecclesia of the living God, redeemed and purified, looking forward to the consummation of their life and hope, when the Lord will come in great glory, to take his ransomed people unto himself:

"For the grace of God that bringeth salvation hath appeared to all men, teaching us that, denying ungodliness and worldly lusts, we should live soberly, righteously, and godly, in this present world; looking for that blessed hope, and the glorious appearing of the great God and our Saviour Jesus Christ; who gave himself for us, that he might redeem us from all iniquity, and purify unto himself a peculiar people, zealous of good works."

ESSAY 9

Bishops and Deacons

THE subject of "bishops and deacons" (1 Timothy 3:1-13), or overseers and ministers, in the early community has been admirably discussed *The First Century Ecclesia* (J. B. Norris) and *Letter to the Philippians* (T. J. Barling), to which the reader is commended. It is sufficient here to say that their work was the care and oversight of the flock in every department of the community's life. According to the *Manual of Discipline* of the Essene community at Qumran, the *mebaqqer*, or 'overseers', had the duty of commanding, examining, instructing, receiving alms or accusations, dealing with people's sins and generally shepherding them. No doubt that organisation had followed some of the principles of shepherding the flock established in Israel under God's law, which was the true precedent for the apostolic arrangements.

Though there are parallels with arranging brethren, sick visitors and others charged with ecclesial management and pastoral care in the twentieth century, it must be remembered that the early servants were chosen by the apostles or their representatives, such as Timothy (Acts 14:23; 2 Timothy 2:2; Titus 1:5), and some at least had a Spirit gift. The principles governing the selection of suitable candidates remain unchanged, however, and we ought to pay much more careful heed than we sometimes do to the question of "ecclesial offices" and the necessary qualities of those who hold them. To neglect this is to confess that we are not, after all, "the church of the living God, the pillar and ground of the truth" (1 Timothy 3:15). If the principle of sound organisation and a due sense of responsibility were basic to ecclesial life in Ephesus, the same prescription can promote spiritual health amongst the ecclesias of today.

ESSAY 10

The Lists of Qualifications
for Ecclesial Office

BEFORE examining the list Paul gives us in 1 Timothy 3 it will be worth considering it in general, and relating it to those in Titus 1 and other places. We have already referred to the distinctive vocabulary of these Letters and to the special circumstances which called them forth (Introduction, page 5). Many of the characteristic words used once or twice only in the New Testament occur in these lists, but are found frequently in the current Hellenistic Greek or *koinē*.

We have already noted the tendency, which will be further documented as we proceed in our study, for Paul to use tersely expressed statements of doctrine or maxims of Christian conduct (for example, in the "Faithful Sayings", pages 49-51), which may be a fragment of a hymn, or even a popular saying, but which he relates to the purpose he has in hand, thereby imparting to them a thoroughly Christian spirit.

One has the distinct impression that these lists and those of other duties outlined, are taken from catalogues of a familiar, even stereotyped character. It has been said that the lists in the Pastoral Epistles are general and vague, containing nothing specifically Christian, and are related to the paradigms or catalogues of virtues to be cultivated and vices to be avoided frequently found in philosophical writings in the contemporary Hellenistic world. It is also true that then, as now, candidates for public office had to fulfil certain requirements before their nomination could be considered, although the emphasis then seemed to be on moral quality, however colourless the terms describing it might be. For example, the electoral propaganda in first century Pompeii follows a set pattern usually reduced to abbreviations:

LUCRETIVM FRONTONEM IIVIR O.V.F.D.R.P.

which means, "Vote for Lucretius Fronto for duovir (joint mayor); he is well qualified". D.R.P. or *dignum re publica* means literally 'worthy of the state', that is, qualified for the office. O.V.F., often abbreviated into a neat monogram, is short for *oro vos faciatis*, "I urge you to elect".

There are, however, other paradigms in Paul's writings which indicate, firstly, that in his later letters he placed increased emphasis on practical morality as the visible evidence of sound understanding of the Truth; and secondly, that in making lists of obligations he followed as much a Jewish practice as a Greek one, even if his vocabulary was contemporary. He had already written in some detail about behaviour to the Ephesians (chapters 5 and 6) and to the Colossians (chapter 3); and it is not only in 1 Timothy 3 and Titus 1 that we find precise rules of conduct in the Pastoral Epistles. They appear also in 1 Timothy 5:10 (for widows), 6:18 (for rich men), 1 Timothy 4:12ff and 2 Timothy 2:21ff (for Timothy) and Titus 2:1-9 and 3:1,2,9 (for all in the ecclesia, regardless of age, sex or social status).

In modern times there has been a reaction in the ecclesias against the use of a catechism and the learning of lists or even of verses of Scripture by rote, on the ground that it does not guarantee a true knowledge of God or of the principles of the faith, and that there is a grave danger of believing that the Truth can be reduced to a series of propositions. Far better, it is said, to ensure a sound grasp of esssential principles in the broad sweep of Scripture and leave the pursuit of accurate or precise knowledge of detail till later.

On this point let it be said, in defence of the old practice, that the memorising of Scripture passages has Biblical precedent, for ready access to expensive written copies was by no means so widespread a privilege in the first century or earlier. Further, when the Scriptures were in separate scrolls they were difficult to manipulate to find a reference. Remembering what had been read or heard, therefore, was an important aspect of spiritual education. Moreover, Israel in the wilderness, who certainly had no personal copies of Scripture to which they could refer, were given songs to "put in their mouths", with the intention that by this means they should be in their hearts as well (Deuteronomy 31:19; see also Deuteronomy 6:6-9).

Secondly, abuse of a practice is not a condemnation of the practice but of those who pervert it. And thirdly, there is no evidence that there is a deeper understanding or greater literacy in the Scriptures today than in the past century, or a firmer grasp of what the Truth is, in spite of the wider range of education and the abundant attempts to translate the Scriptures themselves into everyday speech more comprehensible to "the man in the street".

The fact is that, now as then, it should be the practice to impart a sound, comprehensive grasp of Scripture teaching, including its practical or moral implications, of which the "proof text", the question and answer of the "catechism", the list of ecclesial rules of behaviour, or the pocket edition of *The Commandments of Christ*, provide convenient summaries, permitting of accurate recall in time of need. The Lord's own use of the Scriptural quotation provides an excellent example both of the method and the value of the method. The readily remembered "text", such as the three he used in the wilderness of the temptations, or those which clinched the discussions with disciples or Pharisees, facilitated a recall of the whole situation it represented and the principles of which it was the essence, as a careful reading of, say, Deuteronomy 6-8 in the light of Matthew 4 or Luke 4 reveals.

ESSAY 11

"The husband of one wife"

EMPHASIS is laid upon the quality of family life of those who have to do with the quality of ecclesial life (see 1 Timothy 3:1-5). Much discussion has centred around the precise meaning of "the husband of one wife" (verse 2), but it is naturally suggested to Paul's mind as a prime illustration of "blamelessness". We can dismiss the idea that an overseer *must* be a married man, since it is contrary to Paul's own teaching, and, as far as we know, his own example. There may well be occasions or particular circumstances in which it is better to remain unmarried; the celibate condition is certainly no reproach (1 Corinthians 7, especially verses 7 and 26), but this passage alone is sufficient to invalidate the opposite theories, the Roman Catholic that all clergy, and the Greek Orthodox that all bishops, must be celibate.

The addition of the words "at a time", to imply that we have here a prohibition against polygamy is unjustified. Polygamy was never countenanced among the early disciples. Its practice was never sufficiently widespread among the Jews of the first century (though it was not entirely unknown, according to Josephus), nor probably in a pagan society where divorce was a common practice, for a special prohibition to be made in the case of bishops and deacons alone. In any case, the practice of a woman having more than one husband at a time (polyandry) was rare if not completely unknown in either Jewish or Hellenistic culture, yet the expression we are considering has its exact counterpart and grammatical equivalent in the injunction that an enrolled widow must have been "the wife of one man" (1 Timothy 5:9).

So the interpretation "having been married only once" must be considered. This has considerable support, especially if we

ESSAY 12

A Pillar and Stay of the Truth

OF the passage in 1 Timothy 3:14-16 one commentator has written: "This section has been well described as the *caesura* of the letter, i.e. the dividing point which gives it significance. Not only does it form the bridge between the first part, with its instructions about prayer and the ministry, but by highlighting the true functions of a church it provides the theological basis for the rules and regulations, as well as for the onslaught on false teaching, which make up the body of the letter" (Kelly, *The Pastoral Epistles*). Verse 16 demands a short study all to itself (see Essay 13, page 116), but we are immediately concerned with the characteristics of the true ecclesia as *"the pillar and ground of the truth"*.

In spite of the architectural allusions in verse 15, the words "the house of God" are clearly not a reference to a literal building, but to that "building fitly framed together" of Ephesians 2:19-22, the household or family made into a unity by its upward growth into him who is the head, even Christ. It is from the living God whose dwelling-place is in this household that the whole idea of fatherhood and family is derived (Ephesians 3:14-15; 4:5). Indeed, the Apostle pursues this thought further in 1 Timothy 5, when he uses the family metaphor in his instructions about the right approach to different age-groups in the ecclesia.

The Gate of Heaven

The first mention in Scripture of the house of God is in Genesis 28, from which comes also the first reference to a pillar in it. It was *"the* place", according to the margin of verse 11 in the Revised Version. It was a place to which Jacob had been guided, although from his own point of view he had "lighted upon" it. It was of great significance in the life of the family, for Abraham

113

had encountered God there previously. Because the LORD God was there beside Jacob (verse 11, RV margin), and the covenant was then made with him, it became for Jacob "none other but the house of God, and this is the gate of heaven" (verse 17).

The stone, anointed with oil, was set up for a pillar to mark this house of the living God, the place where He who dwells in the high and holy place and inhabits eternity dwells also with him who is of a humble and a contrite heart (Isaiah 57:15). Such is the ecclesia, where the anointed stone is the head of the corner, a Son over his Father's house, and men like Timothy who know how to conduct themselves in it, are as Moses, "*faithful in all his house*" (Hebrews 3:2). To speak especially of the church of *the living God* was appropriate in Ephesus, for it was the seat of the art and culture centred around the temple of Diana where was housed the meteorite which had fallen down from heaven (Acts 19).

It is the ecclesia, then, which is described as the pillar and stay of the truth. The Authorised Version "ground" gives the wrong sense, since it implies "foundation" and it is not upon the ecclesia but upon Christ that the truth is founded. In any case the word *edraipōma* is a "oncer", but comparison with a related word in 1 Corinthians 7:37 and 15:58 ("stedfast") and Colossians 1:23 ("settled") suggest "stay" or "buttress" as the best meaning.

A Living Witness

In the days described in the Acts the rôle of the ecclesia was plain. In its external preaching and its inner life it was a living witness to the truth of the Gospel of Christ—that God was in Christ, reconciling the world unto Himself and that He was taking out a people for His Name. The preaching proclaimed the resurrection of Christ and heralded the coming Kingdom; their life of fellowship in unity was, according to the Lord's own words, "that the world may believe that thou hast sent me, and hast loved them as thou hast loved me" (John 17:20-23). Individual men were described as "pillars" of the church (Galatians 2:9; see also Revelation 3:12), and a man like Paul was "set for the defence of the gospel" (Philippians 1:17). He was able to say to the Philippian ecclesia as a whole: "I have you in my heart; inasmuch as both in my bonds and in the defence and confirmation of the gospel, ye are all partakers of my grace" (1:7).

The impetus given to the development of the Christian communities by the apostolic preaching had enabled them to withstand both opposition from without and irregularities within. Now the new situation revealed at Ephesus and Crete demanded a recall to an understanding of the nature and function of the ecclesia, which the Pastorals were designed to give. The local congregation could only discharge its function and responsibility to safeguard the true teaching and maintain its continuous witness after the death of the apostles, if men like Timothy and Titus knew how they ought to behave themselves in the ecclesia. It was equally vital that they should commit the things they had heard of Paul among many witnesses to faithful men able to teach others also, that the ecclesia itself might be properly run (2 Timothy 2:2).

Although most versions describe the ecclesia as *the* pillar and *the* stay of the truth and Catholic theologians naturally prefer this rendering to enhance the authority of *the Church*, the definite article does not appear in the Greek. On the other hand, the article is frequently omitted in the Pastoral Letters where the English seems to demand its inclusion, so the question of translation revolves around a fine point of style and grammar. There is no need, however, for the point to be settled for us to see the value of the passage in its setting for ourselves.

If we feel that, because the problems within threaten our unity and distract our attention from the continuous witness we should present to those without, some of the impetus in our Brotherhood is being lost, then the Pastoral Epistles speak directly to our situation. The remedy is for us to rekindle a lively sense that our own ecclesia and the ecclesias knit together in an active fellowship throughout the world are a pillar and stay of the Truth—and we can use a capital "T" here, because in these Letters "the truth" stands for the full revelation of God in Christ as defined in 1 Timothy 3:16—and that in learning how we ought to behave ourselves in it we are strengthening and safeguarding the community as a whole and helping it to maintain its faithful distinctive witness.

115

ESSAY 13

"Great is the mystery of godliness"

AS Paul wrote the words *"Great is the mystery of godliness"* (1 Timothy 3:16), his mind probably went back to the day when he stood in the wings of the theatre in Ephesus, while the crowd chanted "all with one voice about the space of two hours, *Great is Diana of the Ephesians"* (Acts 19:23-41). This insistent cry of those who were temple-keepers (verse 35, RV) of the great Diana and of the image which fell down from the sky, repeated by a confused, violent assembly stirred up by men with a vested interest in paganism, is re-echoed in various forms throughout all the world today, and reveals the values, threats and insidious conditioning of attitudes which put pressure upon the Ecclesia of God. Today it must still be opposed by the cry, "Great is the mystery of godliness!", for far more wonderful than the temple of Diana with its magnificent colonnades, copied in miniature for profit by Demetrius and his fellow craftsmen, is the House of God, the Ecclesia of the Living God, the Pillar and Stay of the Truth, a pattern for communities everywhere of men and women whose bodies are "the temple of the living God" (2 Corinthians 6:16) and for whom "godliness with contentment is great gain" (1 Timothy 6:6).

A Triumphant Cry

Appropriate as the apostolic phrase was, and is for us in an age when the cry is heard on every hand that this thing or that person is "Great!", its origins were of olden time: "Great is the LORD, and greatly to be praised in the city of our God"; "Great is the LORD ... and his greatness is unsearchable"; "Great is the Holy One of Israel in the midst of thee" (Psalm 48:1; 145:3; Isaiah 12:6). In fact the whole series of lines is plainly part of a hymn of which the rhythmic parallelism of *flesh . . . spirit, angels . . . nations, world . . . glory* shows its affinity with Hebrew poetry.

If the Greek poets could write odes to be chanted at the festival of a goddess represented by a shapeless meteorite fallen from heaven, "whom all Asia and the world worshippeth", yet whose mysteries were dimly perceived only by initiates, then an inspired Christian hymn-writer could rise to greater heights of majesty and beauty in praise of the mystery *manifest, seen, preached, believed on, received up* into glory. A God not made with hands who manifested His grace and lovingkindness by sending forth His Son, in the likeness of sinful flesh, yet born of the Spirit, could inspire a sense of worship and devotion unknown to the initiates into a mystery surrounding a piece of stone.

There is a twofold testimony (Ephesians 5 and Colossians 3) to the fact that the early ecclesias instructed and exhorted one another in "psalms and hymns and spiritual songs", and there are fragments and quotations from these in the Epistles, including the Pastorals. We shall consider one later when we come to the fourth "Faithful Saying" (Essay 32, page 289), and it will interest us to note the way in which the hymn-writer set into metrical verse phrases and ideas from one of Paul's own epistles. In the hymn we are now considering there is a close parallel with the last chapter in the Gospel record of Mark which, according to tradition, was the first to be written and so would antedate the Pastoral Letters by several years. It is worth comparing the phrases from 1 Timothy 3:16 with the following verses from Mark 16. The details of the Timothy passage are considered below.

Justified in the Spirit	— verse 6
Seen of angels	— verse 5
Preached unto the Gentiles	— verses 15,20
Believed on in the world	— verse 16
Received up into glory	— verse 19

The Divine Mystery

The word "mystery" was familiar in the Ancient World. It was the term applied to the secret rites of many religions, notably from the Near East, which offered those initiated an inner knowledge, an "experience" of divine things by which they could gain forgiveness, release and some hope, however shadowy, of immortality. With its mysticism and sense of privileged communion the mystery religion attracted many who found no satisfaction in the more conventional aspects of pagan worship. Such religions, particularly Isis worship from Egypt, gained a considerable following in the first century, as many inscriptions and the fully developed system discovered in Pompeii testify. Wall paintings depict the rites of Isis and others in a way that leaves little doubt that the worshippers were either deceived by the cunning craftiness and the sleight of men (almost "illusionists", Ephesians 4:14), or degraded by a painful and humiliating ceremony of initiation which revealed that the basis of the cult was a fertility rite.

So although the Gospel was, or contained, a mystery, it was of a vastly different order and with an entirely distinct origin from any of those which rivalled it in Ephesus, Rome or elsewhere. It was something which God had *revealed*, whereas the others were kept hidden by men. It was a manifestation of the great Creator, in contrast to the obscure ritual centred on things created. It was honour, glory, holiness and life, where all else was shame, degradation, filthiness and death. The knowledge of it was not the special privilege of the few but freely proclaimed to all, hidden only to those who, with eyes that would not see and ears that refused to hear, had no wish to seek out all the treasures of wisdom and knowledge that were in Christ. So Paul uses "mystery" not as a conventional term denoting what is beyond human knowledge, but what being once hidden is now revealed to those with true spiritual discernment.

The Mystery of the Gospel

"The secret things belong unto the LORD our God: but those things which are revealed belong unto us and to our children for ever, that we may do all the words of this law" (Deuteronomy 29:29). These words of Moses were spoken at the time of the renewing of the covenant "in the land of Moab, *beside* the covenant which he made with them *in Horeb*" (verse 1). This covenant, therefore, looked forward to the new covenant in Christ's blood, and to the time when the Gentiles would glorify God for His mercy (Deuteronomy 32:43; Romans 15:8-10). The future details were hidden, to be unfolded as "dark sayings" in the words of psalmist and prophet (Psalm 78:2) and in the parabolic mysteries of the Kingdom (Matthew 13:11; Mark 4:11; Luke 8:10).

118

In the Gospel the mystery was made known, as Paul declared to the Romans in 16:25-27:

"Now to him that is of power to stablish you according to my gospel, and the preaching of Jesus Christ, *according to the revelation of the mystery*, which was kept secret since the world began, but now is made manifest, and by the scriptures of the prophets, according to the commandment of the everlasting God, made known to all nations for the obedience of faith: to God only wise, be glory through Jesus Christ for ever. Amen."

It was the Lord's "good will toward men" (Luke 2:14), "the mystery of his will according to his *good pleasure* which he hath purposed in himself" (Ephesians 1:9). This purpose was associated with "redemption through his blood, the forgiveness of sins, according to the riches of his grace" (verse 7), the "mystery of Christ" (3:4), "the mystery of the gospel" (6:19). It is "the mystery which hath been hid from ages and from generations, but now is made manifest in his saints: to whom God would make known what is the riches of the glory of this mystery among the Gentiles; which is Christ in you, the hope of glory" (Colossians 1:26-27). It is associated with that other great mystery: "We shall not all sleep, but we shall all be changed, in a moment, in the twinkling of an eye, at the last trump" (1 Corinthians 15:51,52).

We have already written in some detail about the word "godliness" (*eusebeia*), that worship based on a response to a revealed purpose on which men set their faith and hope; that revelation in the person of "the man whom he hath ordained, whereof he hath given assurance unto all men in that he hath raised him from the dead" (Acts 17:31, see page 58). Many texts of the passage now before us read "Who" instead of "God" (the difference in Greek is between *hos* and *theos*), as though there was some grammatical antecedent to "who" in the hymn from which Paul is apparently quoting, which those familiar with it would readily have understood. In any case it is plain enough that the "mystery of godliness manifested" is the Lord Jesus Christ himself.

The fragment of the hymn is not so much in praise of the person of Christ as of the purpose of God in the Word made flesh. It is nevertheless interesting to speculate whether this is the hymn referred to by Pliny in his letter to the Emperor Trajan, about the Christians who were wont to "sing a hymn unto Christ as unto a God" (see *Eureka*, Vol. 1, page 254, original edition). In its Greek form the verses contain at least one example of "poetic licence" being taken with Greek grammar, in the verb for "believed on", in order to make it fit into the rhythmic pattern chosen. (So the problems of hymn writers and Hymn Book compilers are not modern ones!)

The theme is the manifestation of the grace of God in Christ at his first coming, and the sphere of his operation and of belief in him is in this world. If the lines are set out in parallel we can see the balance and progression of ideas:

(He) Who was manifested in the *flesh*	Was justified in the *Spirit*
Who was seen of *angels*	Was preached unto the *nations*
Who was believed on in the *world*	Was received up into *glory*

The First Letter to Timothy

CHAPTER 4

Timothy's Duty in the Face of Coming Difficulties

4:1-6—Dangers to be Faced in the Future

Verse 1: *"Now the Spirit speaketh expressly":* it is natural for the Apostle now to turn to the way in which the other-teaching against which he has been warning Timothy would develop. He has counselled him concerning the organisation of the ecclesia on a sound basis and has defined the true nature of the Church of God. The Revised Version is correct when it gives "But" instead of "Now" as the opening word, since Paul is really referring back to 3:15 to declare that even in the midst of the community which is the pillar and stay of the truth, with all its privileges and responsibilities, error can arise. The Spirit through Moses had likewise spoken expressly concerning the children of Israel, when he said, "For I know that after my death ye will utterly corrupt yourselves, and turn aside from the way which I have commanded: and evil will befall you in the latter days" (Deuteronomy 31:29).

The Spirit had spoken expressly through Paul, when he had said to the elders of the Ephesian ecclesia, "For I know this, that after my departing shall grievous wolves enter in among you, not sparing the flock. Also of your own selves shall men arise, speaking perverse things to draw away disciples after them" (Acts 20:29,30). To that situation he was addressing himself in these Epistles, speaking now of *"the latter times"*, that is of times future to him but not so far distant as to be "the last days" of 2 Timothy 3:1.

"Some shall depart from the faith": already some had "swerved" and "turned aside unto vain jangling" (see 1:6 and notes on

121

page 21), but now some more radical departure from the faith was in view—apostasy, a condition in which other-teaching had become false teaching with important moral and practical effects. The verb "to fall away" is used in Luke 8:13 of those who "for a while believe", but whose faith does not survive a time of testing. In Hebrews 3:12 it is a "departing from the living God" on account of "an evil heart of unbelief". The noun describes the "falling away" which precedes the manifestation of the "man of sin" in 2 Thessalonians 2:3.

"Giving heed to seducing spirits and doctrines of devils": those who hold a doctrine of Satan and his angels which makes them into immortal agents of evil see confirmation of it in these words. "They are the *ultimate*, the false teachers of the next verse being the *proximate*, cause of the errors about to appear in the Church", as one writer put it. John, however, distinguishes between *the* spirit of truth and *the* spirit of error, as representing those people who are of God and those who are not. One class "heareth us" and the other "heareth not us" (1 John 4:6). This is consistent with the rest of Scripture, that it is all that is in the world—"the lust of the flesh, the lust of the eyes, and the pride of life" (1 John 2:15,16)—that is hostile to God, and is therefore the spirit of error or wickedness. "Spirit" here means in effect "the very essence of". "We wrestle not against flesh and blood" in actual physical combat, but against fleshly ideas that war against the things of God, "against spiritual wickedness in high places" (Ephesians 6:12).

The other-teachers already at work (see page 41 and 1 Timothy 1:3ff) are apostles, but false; workers, but deceitful, and therefore the more dangerous. A fully developed process would ultimately see the rise of "false Christs, and false prophets" who shall "shew great signs and wonders; insomuch that if it were possible, they shall deceive the very elect" (Matthew 24:24). In fact, only those who successfully resist such wiles can be described as "the elect". The "doctrines of demons" are the equivalent of the wisdom that manifests itself in bitterness, envying and unwise use of the tongue; "it descendeth not from above, but is earthly, sensual, *devilish*" (James 3:15). So in opposition to the true teaching, the *didaskalia* of 1:10 (see page 46), there is an unsound teaching that becomes downright false.

Verse 2: *"Speaking lies in hypocrisy":* the Revised Version has "through the hypocrisy of men that speak lies", showing that we are dealing with actual human agents of error and not "spirits". *Pseudologos*, a 'lie-speaker', is another of those expressive words like 'other-teacher'—*mataiologos*, an 'empty-speaker'; *logomachia*, 'word-battle'—which Paul seems to have coined himself to give pithy expression to his thought in these Letters.

"Having their conscience seared with a hot iron": Again the reference can only be to men and not to spirits, and there are two possible explanations of Paul's figure of speech. Either the metaphor comes from the branding of slaves, as a penalty for crime, and refers to the very mark of sin burnt into the soul of those who have yielded themselves as slaves to it; or we have another of those medical metaphors like "sound", "sick" or "doting" about questions, and "canker", which Paul adopted for describing the health of the corporate body. This seems a preferable explanation, since to have one's conscience *cauterised* is to be devoid of moral sensitivity and, unlike those who have their senses exercised by reason of use, to become unable to distinguish between good and evil: they are reprobates (Hebrews 5:12-14; Romans 1:28). Paul lays especial emphasis on the conscience in these Letters (see page 44), and the original text here says that it is the other-teachers' *own* conscience which is seared. The second interpretation accords better with what follows.

Verse 3: *"Forbidding to marry, and commanding to abstain from meats":* A false asceticism or any extreme attitude is in Scripture the mark of the reprobate, which means "devoid of spiritual judgement". That there was a tendency for such an attitude to prevail is suggested by the reminder to the Hebrews in what is possibly a contemporary document, that "Marriage is honourable in all, and the bed undefiled" (Hebrews 13:4). Likewise there had been discussion about "meats", especially those offered to idols, and Paul had given his balanced judgement on the question, on the basis not of commandment but of consideration for others (1 Corinthians 8). The incipient tendency to make commandments of these things, which was already manifest in Colossae, he had steadfastly resisted (2:20-23). It formed a feature of the later Gnosticism, which separated God from the world He had made and regarded as unclean things which He had *"created to be received with thanksgiving"*.

Verse 4: *"For every creature of God is good"*: Paul uses the word *ktisma*, a common Septuagint word, in place of his more usual word *ktisis* for "creature", possibly to emphasise that he is referring specifically to God's handiwork. God fashioned it and therefore it must be *kalon*, or intrinsically good, not simply good for the purpose intended. The reference is back to Genesis 1, where God saw all that He had made, and behold "it was very good". The same applied to the trees of the garden, which were pleasant to the eyes and good for food. The tree of the knowledge of good and evil was no exception (Genesis 2:9), and it was to be avoided only because of God's commandment. The attitude of *"them which believe and know the truth"* is therefore an all-important element in the choice of things that satisfy.

For there is *"nothing to be refused, if it be received with thanksgiving"*: found nowhere else in the whole Greek Bible, *apoblētos*, 'refused' or 'rejected', can almost carry the idea of 'taboo', something to be avoided at all costs for cultic or philosophical reasons. Compare "Touch not, taste not, handle not" in Colossians 2:21, all "ordinances" which Paul rejects. It is important to note, however, that Paul applies a limiting condition to the believer's use of all God's gifts, which he emphasises by repetition from verse 3: *"if it be received with thanksgiving."*

Too great an emphasis cannot be laid upon the spirit of thankfulness in God's saints. Of this we have already written with respect to 2:1 (pages 54, 55). It betokens an attitude of mind sensitive to all God's benefits and requirements and therefore ensures that what God has created intrinsically "good", to be received by His people, is "good" to them because they use it aright. It is impossible to do otherwise if the thanksgiving be sincere, from the heart and out of a good conscience.

Verse 5: *"For it is sanctified by the word of God and prayer"*: the meaning is not simply that we understand from the word of God (as for example in Genesis 1:4,10,12,14,21,25,31) that created things have been declared good; or that they are good because created by the Word of God (Psalm 33:6). What we receive is sanctified, set apart with God's blessing, when we utter a "word of God" in prayer.

There is abundant evidence in Scripture that the saying of "grace before meat" has always been the common practice amongst God's children. We have the example of the Lord himself (e.g. Matthew 14:19; 15:36; 26:26) and the words of Paul in Romans 14:6 and 1 Corinthians 10:30. In this second passage Paul clearly infers that even meats which had been offered to idols could be sanctified to the use of the believer by his giving of thanks, subject of course to a consideration of the conscience of the weak brother "for whom Christ died"; and even then, not because he might be critical of Paul's conduct but because he might be led to imitate it but not "out of a pure heart, and a good conscience, and faith unfeigned" (1 Timothy 1:5, RV).

It has been suggested with some force, that a portion of the Word of God, especially a Psalm or other Old Testament passage, might have been used as part of an appropriate "grace", thus explaining the use of the phrase "the word of God and prayer" in this connection. Compare Psalm 145:15,16—"The eyes of all wait upon thee; and thou givest them their meat in due season. Thou openest thine hand and satisfieth the desire of every living thing." Certain it is that language at least suggested by the Word of God often forms the basis of our prayers and praises.

For our own times we have a valuable guide when we seek to "use this world, as not abusing it" (1 Corinthians 7:31). There are many things which are not "unclean of themselves" (Romans 14:14), many apparently innocent pastimes and pursuits which can provide a sometimes needed recreation. The question of what things should engage our time or use up our energies, where it is legitimate to go and what should be avoided at all costs, is not decided by any question of taboo, but by a more spiritual approach. Does it lead us into an "appearance of evil"? Is the pursuit of it likely to have a good or bad influence on our brethren who might be disposed to do likewise? And above all, can we genuinely and with thankfulness mention it in our prayers?

4:6-10—Dealing with False Asceticism

Verse 6: *"If thou put the brethren in remembrance of these things, thou shalt be a good minister of Jesus Christ":* Timothy's duty as a *diakonos* was not denunciation but exposition and exhortation. He had the duty of laying before his hearers a positive answer to negative doctrine. If only we as a community had kept this concept more clearly before our eyes we might well have been spared many of the "strifes about words" which have arisen from attempts to confute rather than to educate and win over. The positive setting forth of truth in a world of error is controversy enough in itself, without seeking the controversial spirit which is sometimes wrongly equated with faithfulness and zeal.

The essential quality of such a good minister was that he be *"nourished in the words of the faith, and of the good doctrine which thou hast followed until now"* (RV).

Verse 7: *"But refuse profane and old wives' fables":* Timothy had *to avoid and eliminate entirely from his teaching* those fables (see on 1:4 and Essay 2) which were the complete antithesis of the words of the faith and the good doctrine. The other-teachers succumbed to the temptation to give themselves up completely to the study of the sayings of the Rabbis or to the improper use of Scripture (specially of the genealogies and the Law), which had no spiritual content and were therefore "profane", the opposite of "holy" and "godly". Such teaching would lead to the false asceticism of "the latter days" which called in question the very goodness and power of the Creator Himself.

The word "refuse" is a strong one, the sense of which can be gauged from Acts 25:11 (*"refuse* not to die") and Hebrews 12:25 (*"refuse* not him that speaketh"). See also 1 Timothy 5:11; 2 Timothy 2:23 and Titus 3:10; the last passage involves the *rejection* of the one who persists in foolish questions and contentions as well as of the questions themselves.

"Old wives' fables" is an ironic term, no doubt referring to the spiritual quality—or rather lack of it—and ultimate value of the rhymes and fables upon which a young Greek child might be brought up at home, before he moved on to learning with a more serious content. Timothy's own experience had been vastly different, for what he had learned at his mother's knee and from his grandmother was both sacred and instructive. Once again, we in our community and in our ecclesias would have avoided—and could even now avoid—much controversy and word-fighting if we learned to distinguish the wholesome words of the faith from the "unhygienic" and the "cankerous".

"And exercise thyself unto godliness": Turning from the things to avoid, the Apostle emphasises the need for perseverance in things spiritual. The standard of godliness is that which was manifested in Christ (3:16), who is both the ideal and the end in view of all spiritual studies and devotions. *Gumnazō* appears in the New Testament only here in the Pastoral Epistles and in those other possibly contemporary documents, Hebrews and 2 Peter. Evil men practise iniquity—"an heart they have *exercised* with covetous practices" (2 Peter 2:14)—and the children of God bring forth "the peaceable fruit of righteousness" when they are *exercised* by the discipline of the Lord (Hebrews 12:11). Moreover the athlete devotes all his time and energy—he is "dedicated", to use the modern sportsman's jargon—to excelling in his chosen skill. And dedication, in the truly Scriptural sense, is required of all those who seek to attain unto "the prize of the high calling of God in Christ Jesus" (Philippians 3:14) (see Essay 14, "The Education and Discipline of the Man of God", page 138).

Verse 8: *"For bodily exercise profiteth for a little":* The RV is surely correct even although the profiting is of relatively short duration, limited by the inherent weakness of the body itself. It has been argued that Paul is making use of the Cynic philosophers' critical aphorism against the athleticism of the day, which they despised. If so, he uses it only to reject it. Perhaps also implicit in the Apostle's thought is bodily discipline of the extravagant form practised by the ascetics; in fact, a "severity to the body . . . not of any value against the indulgence of the flesh" (Colossians 2:23, RV).

In view of the fact that the contrast here is not between *bodily* and *spiritual* exercise but between *bodily exercise* and *godliness*, it is even possible that Paul is saying that the true discipline of the body is a proper attitude to its functions and use, based not upon a false concept of its impurity but upon a desire for true holy living. At any rate, *"godliness is profitable unto all things"*. It produces "the whole man", who lives a full spiritual life, the *"life that now is"*, in which all things work together for good, and it has promise of *"that which is to come"*, the eternal life "which God, that cannot lie, promised before the world began" (Titus 1:2).

Verse 9: *"This is a faithful saying":* The third of the "statements of the faith" (page 49) is like the first, *"worthy of all acceptation"*. There has been some discussion as to whether the formula refers to what precedes or follows it. Certainly verse 8 seems to conform more to the terse statement or pithy saying of a *pistos logos*. On the other hand, verse 10 takes up and extends the thought, giving it a more "doctrinal" content. It is probably best to take "Godliness is profitable unto all things" as the memorable statement of a great truth to be universally received; verse 10 then describes the practical effect for Paul and Timothy in the teaching of it.

Verse 10: *"For to this end we labour and strive"* (RV): The end is "godliness" and the metaphor is being continued. The labouring implies weariness and fatigue, toil to the point of exhaustion such as comes over the athlete or the husbandman. So we have in Matthew 11:28, "all ye that *labour* and are heavy laden"; in John 4:6, "Jesus being *wearied* with his journey"; and 2 Timothy 2:6, "the husbandman that *laboureth*"; and they who *"labour* in the word and doctrine"(1 Timothy 5:17). The textual evidence for *strive* instead of *suffer reproach* is strong, the former containing the idea of *agōna*, or athletic contests which best suits the context. (The actual difference in words is between *agōnizometha* and *oneidizometha*.) In Philippians 2:16 'running' and 'labouring' are linked in parallel ideas. Either way the verse expresses the end Paul and Timothy had in view when they laboured together. Note the change in person from "exercise *thyself*" (verse 7) to "*we* labour".

We have, moreover, the great example of the Lord himself, "godliness manifest in the flesh", who both laboured and suffered reproach, and emerged victorious from the contest (the *agony*) which caused him to sweat "as it were great drops of blood falling down to the ground" (Luke 22:44). He did it for the honour and glory of his Father who would glorify him with His own self: Paul and Timothy so laboured because *"we have our hope set on the living God"* (RV), and having set their hope they continued in it. For a discussion on *"the Saviour of all men, specially of those that believe"*, see notes on 1:1 (page 15) and 2:4 (pages 60, 61).

4:11-16—The Importance of Timothy's Personal Example

Verse 11: *"These things command and teach"*: Timothy was not only to repudiate completely the other-teaching with its dangerous tendencies: he was to counteract it by setting forth "these things", the doctrine and practice of true godliness. "Teach" meant set forth the Scriptural principle upon which the rules of the everyday life of the man of God are based; "command" referred to the putting into practice of that teaching.

As we have already noted, "command" is a strong word. It is the "charge" of 1:3, with clear military overtones. The time had come for Timothy to assert the authority vested in him by the Apostle who in his turn had received it from the Lord himself. Some have argued that Timothy was of a timid disposition and would naturally shrink from any kind of confrontation, particularly with his brethren. Certainly he was a highly sensitive man, capable of being moved to tears under the influence of great emotion (2 Timothy 1:4) and, Paul felt, he needed the constant exhortations to be strong (2:1). Probably, and understandably, he had been filled earlier with apprehension as he approached Corinth, bearing the First Letter to that ecclesia, with contents which caused even its writer to await with anxiety the news of how it had been received. There was in it a special commendation of Timothy, to ease his reception: "Now if Timotheus come, see that he may be with you without fear; for he worketh the work of the Lord, as I also do" (1 Corinthians 16:10).

Fatherly Concern

In spite of this natural fatherly concern, however, the Apostle knew the quality of his "own son in the faith", and had chosen for the delicate and difficult task in Ephesus a man who would respond to the exhortations and rise above himself in a true spirit of service. In his own town of Lystra Timothy had already witnessed the kind of affliction that awaited a servant of the Lord Jesus, but had nevertheless resolved to take up his own cross and follow (Acts 14:19; 16:1-3; 2 Timothy 3:10-12). Now, reinforced with a sound knowledge of "these things" and reposing in the Apostle's confidence in him, he would be able to carry out the "charge".

Verse 12: "Let no man despise thy youth": this was, no doubt, more of an exhortation for Timothy than an instruction for the ecclesia, although the semi-official nature of the letter to him meant that all would be aware of its contents. All true men of God have felt that sense of personal inadequacy which makes them exclaim within themselves, when faced with the realities of their responsibility: "And who is sufficient for these things?" (2 Corinthians

2:16). Compare Jeremiah at the time of his call: "Then said I, Ah, Lord God! behold, I cannot speak: for I am a child." (Jeremiah 1:6).

We cannot be sure of the exact age of Timothy. Paul uses the word "youth" only here in all his writings, although in his defence before Agrippa he speaks of "My manner of life from *my youth*" (Acts 26:4), which from its context refers to an age of responsibility to the Pharisees' code. The young man of great possessions who came to Jesus had observed the commandments "from *my youth* up". And Paul, as "a young man", was a consenting witness to the death of Stephen. The word for "youth" was common enough in the Greek Old Testament, as in the expression "the wife of thy youth" (Proverbs 5:18; Malachi 2:14). It can cover, therefore, the years of early manhood, and in Roman times its equivalent (*iuvenis, iuventus*) was applicable to the ages of 18 to 40, or the period of active military service.

We shall probably be correct in assessing Timothy's age as "in the thirties", which certainly made him young to have authority over "elders" in the ecclesia, whether the term "youth" be taken in its chronological or ecclesiastical sense. Some of the implications of this will be discussed at the beginning of the notes on chapter 5. For the moment we consider Paul's comforting admonition to Timothy, with its positive advice on how to forestall any possible criticism of his youth; or to show up the unreasonableness of such a criticism if it did arise (see Essay 15, "Timothy's Age and the Date of the Letters", page 140).

"But be thou an example of the believers": Timothy had been selected by Paul for his task on sound principles: he was no "favourite", even if he were a "son in the faith". There had been "prophecies which went before" on him, and the exhortation was not to become but to continue to be a model disciple, who displayed all the spiritual qualities of which the ecclesia was falling short. Like Titus he was not setting himself up as an example *to* the rest, but exercising himself in all the disciplines required and being a *"pattern* of good works". It was the Apostle's own way (Philippians 3:17; 2 Thessalonians 3:9) and none of his converts ever suffered the disillusionment of having the ideals created in him by the knowledge of the Truth shattered by the behaviour of

his teacher. It was also the way of the Master, who left us an example that we should follow his steps (1 Peter 2:21).

"In word, in conversation": These were the outward signs, expressed in daily conduct, of the maturity of the man of God, whatever his years. "Word" is to be taken here as ordinary speech or conversation, than which there is nothing more revealing about the quality of a man's mind. His public speaking, an essential part of Timothy's work, will be touched on in the next verse. "Conversation" is the whole way of life, as in Galatians 1:13—"For ye have heard of my *conversation* in time past in the Jews' religion, how that beyond measure I persecuted the church of God, and wasted it"; in Ephesians 4:22—"The former *conversation,* the old man, which is corrupt according to the deceitful lusts"; 1 Peter 1:15,18—"Holy in all manner of *conversation* . . . your vain conversation". See also Hebrews 13:5,7; James 3:13; 1 Peter 2:12; 3:1,2,16; 2 Peter 2:7; 3:11. In Philippians 1:27 and 3:20 the word translated "conversation" means 'citizenship'.

"In charity, in faith, in purity": The Authorised Version "in spirit" is omitted from the best manuscripts. The three qualities are of the character or inward disposition, which will find their expression in word and way of life. They have been described as "graces which may be said to cover respectively our duty to man, to God and to ourselves", and form the response to "the grace of God that bringeth salvation . . . teaching us that, denying ungodliness and worldly lusts, we should live soberly, righteously, and godly, in this present world" (Titus 2:11,12)—with a sense of the *responsibility* of our calling (pages 163-164). Love and faith are two of the abiding spiritual qualities (1 Corinthians 13), coupled together eight times in these Letters, notably in 1 Timothy 1:5, where Paul's whole purpose in writing his First Epistle, "the end of the charge", is described as "love out of a pure heart and a good conscience and faith unfeigned". See the extended comment on this verse on page 20.

"Faith", here without the definite article, probably has the sense of 'faithfulness', 'fidelity', the active quality of the man full of the spirit of *the* faith, a necessary attribute of every man of God whether in a position of ecclesial responsibility or not, and one aspect of the fruit of the Spirit (Galatians 5:22).

"Purity" *(agneia)* occurs as a noun in this form here and in 5:2 only (in the New Testament), although its related forms are more common. It includes the idea of 'chastity', but is more comprehensive of life and motive than that word, which is the outward manifestation of the quality in one particular sphere of conduct. This enlarged concept we shall be able to carry over into our consideration of 5:2, where Timothy is exhorted to treat "the younger women as sisters, with all purity", a necessary admonition in a context where the cultivation of a family atmosphere in the ecclesia is being advocated; a young man has also to "flee youthful lusts, but follow righteousness, faith, charity, peace with them that call on the Lord out of a pure heart" (2 Timothy 2:22).

It is plain that in this verse under immediate consideration Paul is ensuring that the relative youthfulness of Timothy is outweighed by the maturity of his disposition and conduct. No doubt Timothy, like all of us, would earnestly pray: "Shew me thy ways, O LORD; teach me thy paths ... Remember not the sins of my youth, nor my transgressions: according to thy mercy remember thou me for thy goodness' sake, O LORD" (Psalm 25:4-7). And praying thus, he would remember those in the ecclesia who were also but flesh, and set about his task with firmness, love and compassion.

Verse 13: *"Till I come, give heed to reading, to exhortation, to teaching"* (RV): Paul had already declared his intention to visit Ephesus (3:14) and had given Timothy a clear understanding of the doctrinal basis, or the "theory", of the ecclesia, so that he would know how he ought to conduct himself in the interim. Now the Apostle gives a brief but instructive list of the practical duties of a true shepherd and overseer to which Timothy must *devote his wholehearted attention.* See 3:8 above for the verb *prosechō*: God's servants must *be given* not to wine, but to His service.

The list, each item of which is introduced in the original by the definite article, covers the three main departments of Timothy's work. "The reading" is not the private study of the Scriptures, although such is a necessary preliminary, but the public reading of it, as in the synagogue from which the practice was carried over into the ecclesia (Luke 4:16; Acts 13:15; 15:21; 2 Corinthians 3:14). In addition to the portions from the Old Testament, Paul's own letters, also classed as Scriptures by Peter (2 Peter 3:15-16), were read aloud according to apostolic instruction (Colossians 4:16; 1 Thessalonians 5:27). Under the Law it was a priestly duty to read aloud to the congregation, and was to be approached with reverence, since one was handling the Word of God; and on at least one occasion all the people stood as a mark of respect while it was being done (Nehemiah 8:5).

Christadelphians have always followed the practice of having the Scripture read aloud at all meetings. In Dr. Thomas's "Royal Association of Believers", in 1853, four portions were read at the Breaking of Bread (see *The Christadelphian*, 1977, pages 403-404). Recently there has been a return to the practice of public readings, with no more than linking comment, as part of a preaching effort. Perhaps we would do well to redress the balance from "a short reading to introduce our speaker's address" in favour of a brief elucidation of a longer passage read, since the power lies not in the address but in the Word itself.

Much depends upon the reader, however, and this is precisely why Paul calls upon Timothy to give himself to this aspect of the work. There is a great deal to be said for giving a reader some prior notice of the passage to be read in the ecclesia, especially if he be a novice or of a nervous disposition. But familiarity with the text and an understanding of the meaning acquired by diligent private study is the best preparation for both reader and hearer alike.

The Exhortation

From Acts 13:15 we learn that "the exhortation" was based upon the reading (modern exhorting brethren please note!). *Paraklēsis* in this connection is both 'comfort', or 'strengthening', and 'appeal' (but compare *paraklētos* in the sense of 'advocate' or 'intercessor' in 1 John 2:1), and the apostolic form is set out for our example. Both "the law and the prophets" had been read, and at the invitation of the ruler of the synagogue Paul briefly reviewed the historical background, linked the prophecies with events in the life of the Lord Jesus, applied the message to his audience and appealed to them to accept it: for in it was life.

"The exhortation", therefore, was closely linked with "the teaching", "as the *appeal* to the heart and conscience ultimately rests upon the *instruction* provided for the intellect" (J. H. Bernard, *The Pastoral Epistles*, Cambridge Greek Bible for Schools and

Colleges.) The *dedicated* servant is one who has presented himself "a living sacrifice, holy, acceptable unto God" and is therefore prepared as a teacher to "wait on teaching" and as an exhorter to "wait on exhortation" (Romans 12:1,7,8). "These things teach and exhort" (1 Timothy 6:2) should be our guide today, when it is necessary to preserve the balance between exposition which stops short of appealing to the conscience or speaking to the heart and the offering of consolation which has no solid basis in the things which God has done in Christ.

Verse 14: *"Neglect not the gift that is in thee":* For a full discussion of the New Testament usage of the word *charisma* see the chapter on "The Best Gifts" in the author's *The Spirit of God* or the relevant article in *The Christadelphian*, 1975, page 148. Here it is plainly the special gift passed on by Paul to Timothy when he called him to be his minister and fellow-labourer (Acts 16:1-3; 19:22). The apostolic exhortation is interesting in the light it throws upon the nature and use of the gift: *its effectiveness was dependent upon the willingness of the recipient to use it.* It was no magical power that operated of itself without the co-operation of its possessor, and in this it was like the grace of God itself, the *charis* which was bestowed more widely than the *charismata*. A man could "fail of the grace of God" by neglecting it, or spurning what God had so freely offered. "The spirits of the prophets are subject to the prophets", Paul reminded the Corinthians (1 Corinthians 14:32), and to misuse the gift was to speak against the LORD (Deuteronomy 13:1-5; 18:20-22). A similar control could be exercised over the other gifts, it appears; they could be either "neglected" or "kindled into flame" (2 Timothy 1:6).

"Which was given thee by prophecy": The phrase is equivalent to "according to the prophecies which went before on thee" in 1:18, where we have already commented (page 37). So when Paul returned to Lystra it was not by chance that he came across Timothy and saw in him a useful helper whom he decided to enlist for the work. The language of Acts 16:1 is explicit: "And behold *a certain* disciple was there, named Timotheus." "Certain" is used here in its true meaning of someone already known and named, rather than as when the word is used to conceal identity or other more precise information. Paul looked for Timothy, and there he was, a "chosen vessel" like Paul

himself, but in need of comfort and exhortation for all that.

"With the laying on of the hands of the presbytery": It is tempting at first sight to equate this with 2 Timothy 1:6, "the gift of God, which is in thee by the putting on of my hands". The difference in the prepositions used should caution us against this. "By" or "through" (*dia*) is not the same as "with" or "accompanied by" (*meta*) and Paul was not "the presbytery". *Presbuterion*, the eldership, is the word used in Luke 22:66 and Acts 22:5 for the Sanhedrin, "all the *estate of the elders*". With the reference in Timothy these are the only occasions where the more usual *presbuteroi* (elders) is replaced by the corporate term. The eldership of the early ecclesias followed the pattern set in the wilderness, where the (usually) senior members of a tribe shared with Moses the task of shepherding the flock. They were to be men of certain qualities, selected by Moses with God confirming the appointment (Numbers 11:24-30; Deuteronomy 1:9-18). The first mention of elders in the church is in Acts 11:30, and could well refer there to the apostles themselves, but from Acts 14:23 it is clear that local ecclesias had an eldership established by Paul and Barnabas— Lystra, Timothy's home ecclesia, is included in the list here—and Titus had the task of "setting in order the things that are wanting in every city in Crete", including no doubt the ordaining of "elders in every city, as I had appointed thee" (Titus 1:5).

There were two different purposes for the laying on of hands as presented in Scripture, which we discuss in Essay 16 (page 141).

Verse 15: *"Meditate upon these things; give thyself wholly to them"*: The word "meditate" occurs only once more in the New Testament, in Acts 4:25, RV. (In Luke 21:14 it is, strictly, *pre*meditate.) The Acts passage quotes Psalm 2:1, where "the people *imagine* a vain thing". The same word is in Psalm 1:2, however, where the sense is brought out clearly for us: "But his delight is in the law of the LORD: and in his law doth he *meditate day and night.*" Evidently one cannot spend day and night in "meditation" according to the common meaning of the word in English, although to ponder deeply until one becomes thoroughly immersed in thought is an essential adjunct to a full understanding of the Scripture and its relevance to life and conduct.

The word has a practical meaning as well as a contemplative one, however, reinforced by the second injunction, *"give thyself wholly to"* these things. The man always disciplined by the law of the Lord is indeed the Lord's man day and night: he *is* what the Law says he should be. The literal translation of the second phrase is *"Be* in these things"—let these things, the things outlined in verses 12-14, be your whole life—a spirit of dedication which we need to preserve, if not to recapture, in our own days.

It is a brief, pithy saying equivalent to "Thou shalt love the LORD thy God with all thine heart, and with all thy soul, and with all thy might . . . and shalt talk of them (these words which shall be in thine heart) when thou sittest in thine house, and when thou walkest by the way, and when thou liest down, and when thou risest up" (Deuteronomy 6:5-7). In a delightful Hebrew idiom David said: "I (am) prayer" (Psalm 109:4); the intervening words in the Authorised Version are italicised, showing they were not in the original.

"That thy profiting may appear to all": Whether in the manner in which he carried out his duties or in his character (the two are inseparable really) Timothy must *progress* or mature if he followed out the apostolic exhortation, as the Philippians would *progress* in joy and faith if Paul continued among them; indeed, as the Gospel itself made *progress* because of Paul's witness in his bonds (Philippians 1:25,12, RV). In spiritual affairs nothing is static. One either matures in the faith, or *increases* "unto more ungodliness", or *"waxes* worse and worse" (2 Timothy 2:16; 3:13)—all uses of this same idea. On the idea of progress in spiritual education and discipline see Essay 14, page 138.

Verse 16: *"Take heed unto thyself, and unto the doctrine":* This exhortation comes straight from Deuteronomy, where it appears in both the singular and the plural form, according to whether Moses is addressing the nation as individuals or as a corporate entity: for example Deuteronomy 2:4; 4:9,15,23; 11:16; 12:13,19,30; 24:8, besides many equivalents like "observe", "remember", "beware lest thou forget". For Timothy the exhortation is personal, consistent with the setting of a personal example to all the ecclesia. There was a special urgency about this appeal in Ephesus, which matched that made on the borders of the Land. The age of Moses, like the apostolic age, was about to give place to a new era, in which the successors both of the apostles and of many of the elders they had chosen, would be taking up the burden of the ecclesias.

The special responsibility of Timothy had arisen precisely because Paul's warning to the elders some eight years previously had gone unheeded. *"Take heed therefore unto yourselves"*, he had pleaded, "and to all the flock, over the which the Holy Spirit hath made you overseers, to feed the church of God, which he hath purchased with his own blood" (Acts 20:28). A similar exhortation fell from the lips of Peter at about the same time, because "your adversary the devil as a roaring lion, walketh about, seeking whom he may devour" (1 Peter 5:1-9).

"For in doing this thou shalt both save thyself, and them that hear thee": This is an important word of warning and of comfort for the servant of the Lord in any age. The relationship between him and his Lord is a personal one, and by his faith and obedience under the grace of God he is saved. This personal responsibility has its effect upon others, especially if one is in a position of leadership of any kind—and to exercise voice or pen is to assume leadership, however momentarily—and if this be wrongly exercised then one is involved in the transgression of others. If it be rightly done, however, and if the counsel or example then be not followed, whether in the local ecclesia or the ecclesia "which is in every place", that is a matter of profound regret but not of personal condemnation.

There is evidence that Timothy discharged his responsibility faithfully, since the later ecclesia in Ephesus was commended for its work, labour and patience and its treatment of the other-teachers—the deceitful and false workers of Revelation 2:1-3. Whether they had seen clearly that "the end of the charge is love" (1 Timothy 1:5, RV), for all Timothy's own gentle and patient exercise of his duty, seems questionable from the reading of verse 4.

Let us then follow the Lord himself who in striving to be holy as his Father in heaven is holy, thus setting himself apart in dedication to his Father's honour and glory, could say of his disciples, *"For their sakes* I sanctify myself, that they also might be sanctified through the truth" (John 17:19).

ESSAY 14

The Discipline of the Man of God

WE have already noticed especially in these Letters that Paul had the skill and insight to express his teaching in terms familiar to and readily understood by his readers, notably in metaphors taken from contemporary everyday life. He could scarcely avoid allusion to athletics and the gymnasium, since these pursuits played such an essential part in the education of young men. The Greek boy began his education in the bosom of the family, no doubt hearing some of the "old wives' tales" (1 Timothy 4:7), perhaps the equivalent of our nursery rhyme or fairy tale. Then he was accompanied to school by the pedagogue, the slave responsible for his early training (the "schoolmaster" of Galatians 3:24). At the age of about fourteen he was sent to the gymnasium, there to have his body developed and fitted for the later participation in the competitive athletics which, in conjunction with a moral and intellectual training, would help to produce the "whole man" who was the Greek ideal.

There was considered to be a close relationship between gymnastics and morality, and the exercises had a powerful educative force, inasmuch as they were designed to make him useful in both the political and military spheres

The bodily discipline, therefore, unlike the mere asceticism which mortified the flesh but achieved no other useful purpose, was profitable even if only "for a little while" (verse 8). The youth exercised himself unto some purpose, and even though it were for his own benefit to be victorious in the contest and upon himself lay the ultimate responsibility for success or failure in the games, the whole community also gained an advantage in the reputation of one of their young citizens.

Mens Sana in Corpore Sano

The concept of "a healthy mind in a healthy body", as our Latin tag has it, brought together in harmonious relation body, soul and spirit, and although in a pagan society it could never achieve the ideal because of the "mind of the flesh" and the corruptible nature of the body, the theory is borne out by Scripture teaching. For "mortification of the flesh" means bringing under control the natural thoughts and impulses, that the "deeds done in the body" may be deeds worthy of an immortal body. Moreover, such degree of physical fitness to which we can attain and the right use of physical resources constitute a proper care of the body given us by God for us to live out our spiritual probation.

Transferred to the spiritual sphere, the concept of "wholeness" in development is exactly represented in Paul's use of the *gymnastic* metaphor. The *aim* of spiritual exercise is godliness (see pages 58,59) and it is achieved by those who love the Lord their God with all their heart, soul, strength and mind and who reach full age, after having had by reason of use "their senses exercised (*gumnazō*) to discern both good and evil" (Hebrews 5:14).

We can now see the force of the Apostle's "nourished up in the words of the faith and of the good doctrine" (verse 6). From a child Timothy had known the holy Scriptures, the perfect basis for the upbringing of the man of God to maturity, furnishing basic teaching, correction, restraint and the discipline which is righteousness (2 Timothy 3:15,16, RV with margin). The word "nourished up", another "oncer" in the Greek Bible, is in a participial form which means a *continual* nourishment and training, and therefore sums up in itself the progress of the disciple from being a newborn babe, desiring the sincere milk of the Word, to the mature age which can take strong meat but which nevertheless needs constant spiritual exercise to maintain its health. Teaching based upon Scripture played its part also, as is evident from the phrase "the words of the faith and of the good *doctrine* (or, teaching)". Such phrases, together with the "Sayings of the Faith" are part of the evidence for the existence of formal doctrinal statements, in which Timothy had been instructed and which are now to form the basis of his own teaching. Here was an appeal to true orthodoxy, the balanced faith, which Timothy had "followed until now" (verse 6, RV).

ESSAY 15

Timothy's Age and the Date of the Letters

THE following, culled from Conybeare and Howson, *The Life and Epistles of Saint Paul*, provides additional confirmation of the conclusions on page 130, and offers some internal evidence for the dating of the Pastoral Epistles as given on page 14:

"The preceding ... might lead us to place the Pastoral Epistles at any point after AD 66 ... i.e. in the last thirty-three years of the first century. But we have a limit assigned to us in this direction, by a fact mentioned in the Epistles to Timothy, viz. that Timotheus was still a young man (1 Timothy 4:12; 2 Timothy 2:22) when they were written. We must of course understand this statement relatively to the circumstances under which it was used: Timotheus was young for the authority entrusted to him; he was young to exercise supreme jurisdiction over all the Presbyters (many of them old men) of the Churches of Asia.

According even to modern notions (and much more according to the feelings of antiquity upon the subject), he would still have been very young for such a position at the age of thirty-five. Now Timotheus was ... a youth still living with his parents when Paul first took him in AD 51 (Acts 16:1-3) as his companion. From the way in which he is then mentioned (Acts 16:1-3; compare 2 Timothy 1:5) we cannot imagine him to have been more than seventeen or eighteen at the most. Nor, again, could he be much younger than this, considering the part he soon afterwards took in the conversion of Macedonia (2 Corinthians 1:19). Hence we may suppose him to have been eighteen years old in AD 51. Consequently, in 68 (the last year of Nero), he would be thirty-five years old."

ESSAY 16

The Laying on of Hands

THE laying on of the Apostle's hands, was the occasion of the bestowal of the *charisma* on Timothy (*"through* ... my hands"*, 2 Timothy 1:6) and the elders' part was to associate themselves with this act (*"with* ... the hands of the presbytery"*, 1 Timothy 4:14). The distinction between two purposes for the laying on of hands is well attested in both Old and New Testament. It was performed as an act of patriarchal blessing, as described in some detail in Genesis 48:9-22, where the gift, though deeply *spiritual* in its true import, conveyed no abstract power with it. It was, for example, the recognition of the inheritance of Ephraim and Manasseh within the context of the covenant. Even where no specific mention is made of the imposition of the hands of the patriarch, it is reasonable to infer this, from such passages as Genesis 27:16, where the care taken by Rebekah to ensure that the smooth of Jacob's neck was covered with hair indicates that she expected Isaac to touch his son on the head.

It was, moreover, "on the head of Joseph, and on the crown of the head of him that was separate from his brethren" that there came "all the blessings of (Jacob's) progenitors unto the utmost bound of the everlasting hills" (Genesis 49:25-26). The laying on of Aaron's hands, or of those of the worshipper under the Law, upon the head of the offering was likewise a symbol of identification, pointing forward to the association of the believer with the death of the Lamb of God. There was also another, more terrible act of laying on of hands, where a witness associated himself with the judgement of the Law against one who had departed from God (Deuteronomy 17:7).

On the other hand, the act of the laying of Moses' hands upon

Joshua was for the express purpose of putting "some of thine honour upon him, that all the congregation of Israel may be obedient ... And he laid his hands upon him, and gave him a charge, as the LORD commanded" (Numbers 27:18-23). "And Joshua was full of the spirit of wisdom; for Moses had laid his hands upon him: and the children of Israel hearkened unto him" (Deuteronomy 34:9). The parallels between this case and that of Paul with Timothy scarcely need stressing, but the distinction between "the giving of a charge", with the bestowing or renewal of a charismatic gift, and the stressing of solidarity with the one appointed should be borne in mind.

The Right Hand of Fellowship

There are two incidents which further illuminate this point, and are an exhortation for ourselves. When Paul and Barnabas set out on what is known as "The First Missionary Journey", it was the Lord himself through the Holy Spirit who had called them to the work. Nevertheless it was the ecclesia, "when they had fasted and prayed, and *laid their hands on them*", that sent them away, although they were "sent forth by the Holy Spirit" (Acts 13:1-4). Even in the absence of such definite guidance, for us today there is still a command for us to go forth and preach. Would that we all, especially if we are not going ourselves, would so willingly associate ourselves with the work that we could feel that by our prayers, support and fellowship *our* ecclesia had sent forth preachers wherever they may go, and that we would take so keen an interest in their return "to rehearse (for us) all that God had done with them" (Acts 14:27; see also verse 26).

"Giving the right hand of fellowship" is a simple ceremony whereby we welcome into the local family and the whole household of faith a new disciple, usually with exhortations to faithfulness and a promise of mutual support. It is right that we should follow this form, which turns our conventional greeting in a handshake into a spiritual act. We should perhaps note, however, that the handshake itself is not specifically referred to in the New Testament and that when the apostles "gave to me and Barnabas the *right hands of fellowship* (note the plural)" it was probably the laying on of hands in the same spirit as in Acts 13, "that we should go unto the heathen, and they unto the circumcision" (Galatians 2:9).

142

The First Letter to Timothy

CHAPTER 5

Privileges and Responsibilities in the Ecclesia

NOTHING reveals more clearly the spiritual quality of the shepherd of the ecclesial flock than the insight he displays in dealing with the various members, with their differences in age, sex and personal needs. They were all comprehended in the "them that hear thee" of 4:16 (page 137), whom Timothy would save by his personal example and his teaching. Although he had been entrusted with some delicate missions in the past, there had been none more so than the charge now committed to his trust, involving as it did patience, entreaty and even rebuke.

There were members senior to Timothy by many years; there were his equals in years who might well be even more resentful of his authority; there were widows, whose care had ever been a matter of Divine concern but which involved a proper use of ecclesial resources; there were rich men and poor, bond and free, representing widely separated strata of society in the world outside, who were to be united in a fellowship in the church of the Ephesians "which is in God the Father, and in the Lord Jesus Christ". And in the exercise of his charge Timothy must not "put a foot wrong".

Sensitive to all the needs of his "own son in the faith", Paul enters into some detail, basing his advice on sound principles adapted to the situation but already enshrined in the unchanging principles enunciated of old.

5:1-2—The Ecclesia as a Family

Verse 1: "Rebuke not an elder, but intreat him as a father": It is plain from the context (older women, younger men, younger women)

143

that it is not the ecclesial office of an elder which is in view. Timothy's attitude to them in certain circumstances is discussed later. The injunction here must be coupled with 4:12: Timothy must not be diffident on account of his relative youth, but there was still a proper way of setting about his necessary task. "Rebuke" is a strong word, a "oncer" in the Greek Bible, and implies greater forcefulness even than the word in 2 Timothy 4:2, which is the more usual New Testament word. This word has a relation to the word "striker" in 3:3, an instinctive reaction which an "overseer" must resist whatever the provocation. Even the more common word implies the severity with which one rebukes a junior, or even a malevolent force of some kind, and there was absolutely no room for such a display of indignation whatever the older man's offence might have been.

Respect for elders is specifically enjoined in the Fifth Commandment. True, it could be argued that the injunction there was based upon a relationship deeper than an age-difference. Under God, parents are the givers of life and have the responsibility of "gently sustaining" that which they have brought into being. A child's duty to God, therefore, is his duty to his parents until the age of responsibility brings him into a relationship with his Creator. Even then the principle of the commandment retains its force, and no man could plead, on any pretext, that he could withhold the due honour and respect. The only possible exception is where a parental command counters an obligation to God— a dilemma faced today by many a young convert from outside circles. Even so, the recompense of honour and respect paid, perhaps increased in such circumstances, though a God-dishonouring commandment is to be resisted, can sometimes bring parents to recognise and respect the higher principles which now motivate their children.

Over and beyond the sense of family responsibility which had its origin in God, "from whom the whole (idea of) family in heaven and earth is named" (Ephesians 3:15; "family" in the Greek is "fatherhood"), the idea extended to the nation. As we have seen, it was from the literal fact of seniority that the concept of eldership was developed and in ancient Israel it was impressed upon them that they were the fathers of the people, exercising an authority which had no other sanction than that it was God-given:

therefore their code of behaviour and of justice was God's alone. That older men were not always worthy of such respect in no way invalidated the principle, as Paul illustrated when, though feeling justified in calling the chief priest "a whited wall" while ignorant of his identity, he later retracted his statement with the remark, "For it is written, Thou shalt not speak evil of the ruler of thy people" (Acts 23:5, based on Exodus 22:28).

But so far we have written as though "elder" in the passage under consideration is, after all, a reference to an elder of the ecclesia. Under the Law, however, respect for the aged went beyond the limitation of official status. "Thou shalt rise up before the hoary head, and honour the face of the old man, and fear thy God: I am the LORD" was the commandment in Leviticus 19:32. "I am the LORD" should have been reason enough: it was in the Divine arrangement that seniority had its privileges in respect, for "The glory of young men is their strength: and the beauty of old men is the grey head" and "The hoary head is a crown of glory, *if it be found in the way of righteousness*" (Proverbs 20:29; 16:31).

Respect for Age

In other words, there is an honouring of the Lord Himself in showing respect for age, on the same principle as that enunciated by John: "If a man say, I love God, and hateth his brother, he is a liar: for he that loveth not his brother whom he hath seen, how can he love God whom he hath not seen?" (1 John 4:20). Similarly, disrespect or thoughtless egalitarianism can lead us into a spirit of disrespect for principles far deeper than those of mere courtesy.

If we have dwelt at some length upon this one half verse it is a measure of what appears to us its importance in the present day. Experience and Scripture teach us that elders are not always worthy of respect; sometimes the reverse. That brings its own responsibilities for them: the hoary head is a crown of glory only "if it be found in the way of righteousness", and both Timothy and Titus were to bring home that responsibility very firmly, as for example in Titus 2:2. It is also true that God is impartial in His dealings with men and women: *who* they are is of no importance, though *what* they are, young or old, is everything.

"Equals" in Scripture usually refers to equality in age (see Galatians 1:14), and from a Divine point of view does not span

145

the generations. But it is a characteristic of our time that respect for others according to their seniority is fast disappearing and it is no longer a mark of close friendship, or some other close link in association, or of valued privilege, to be invited to drop formality with older people: the most venerable can be Tom, Dick or Harry to the merest babe in Christ. The habits of our time might well make a mere ostentatious formality of the old habit of rising up before the hoary head to honour the face of the old man, but surely in the family of God the *principle* should not be lost, by whatever means we display it in action?

Supposing, however, there be the need to correct an error or, as in Timothy's case, to regulate disorder for which an older man might justifiably be held responsible? Paul's advice was clear: *"Exhort him as a father"*. *Parakaleō* has meanings ranging from "comfort" to "beseech" and "entreat", sometimes "for love's sake", and is the ordinary word for exhortation. Its use here suggests an affectionate entreaty, as befits a son with the father, which is in fact the nuance implied throughout the following verses.

"The younger men as brethren": This phrase, indeed the whole tenor of the section, suggests, although it does not prove, that Timothy was a younger man than Titus, to whom Paul gives similar advice unqualified by the emphasis on family relationship. At least, that is the view of some commentators; but even if it be so, there is ample evidence from the whole of Scripture that the ecclesia like the nation of Israel was to be regarded as a family. Of the numerous passages which might be quoted, Israel is referred to specifically in Amos 3:1 as a "whole family" brought out of Egypt, and throughout the Book of Deuteronomy particularly the wholeness of the nation and the fact that they were *brethren* is emphasised.

Another point may well be noted in passing. When writing the *Ecclesial Guide* (which no arranging brother determined to carry out his duties in a spiritual way should fail to read), Brother Robert Roberts was at pains to insist that the title of "brother" or "sister" be prefixed to the description of ecclesial offices, to help retain the family atmosphere of the ecclesia. It has been a sound Christadelphian practice ever since and can often help us over the problems of "familiarity with respect"; although it is noticeable that as we have become more "organised" as a community we have more "secretaries", "treasurers", "presidents" and "arranging committees" (rather than the offices of Recording Brother, Finance Brother etc.) in ecclesial life than before. But whatever the titles used and in whatever manner we display our sense of spiritual relationship with one another, the overriding principle of *parakaleō*—'entreat', 'comfort', 'exhort'—must govern our dealings, especially on the part of pastors of the flock.

Verse 2: *"The elder women as mothers":* Mothers in Israel were treated with the greatest respect, and in most of the injunctions about honour and obedience are linked with the father. There was the special influence of the mother over the child in the matter of early education, but above all Scripture recognises the deep love and affection which the true mother has for "the son of her womb". The Proverbs especially warn against forsaking the law of the mother, despising her, neglecting her when she is old or bringing her to shame. To mothers-to-be angels appeared and in the bearing of sons to play special parts in the Divine purpose the choice of the mother was all important. Here in this verse Paul concentrates all his own feelings of gentleness, courtesy and loving kindness which he felt for aged women, such as the lady commended in Romans 16:13 as Rufus' mother "and mine".

"The younger as sisters, with all purity": As noted before (page 131), this word for "purity" occurs twice in the New Testament, both with reference to Timothy's personal example (4:12). There were sound reasons for this. He was to be in a position of authority, even exercising discipline and offering instruction, and if for no other reason his character and demeanour must be above reproach. But one had also to be realistic, as the Lord himself was when taking the Seventh Commandment deeper than the overt act to the very thought and glance. There was, and is, a family relationship in the ecclesia, and men and women, young and old, are brought together in ties of love and affection which go deep because they are spiritually based. Even so, there are degrees of familiarity (with no intentional play upon the word "family", though even that may not be inappropriate), and *perfect propriety* was to be the hallmark of the Timothy or the Titus, the latter being commended to leave the instruction of the younger women to the older ones (Titus 2:3-4; see pages 387, 388).

There was an added reason why the demeanour of all members of the ecclesia should be beyond reproach, in this as in any other matter affecting relationship between the sexes. The ecclesia at Ephesus was as much subject to the pressures of the world around it and open to the scrutiny of ill-wishers who eagerly searched for something to criticise in a community which professed holiness, as any other ecclesia then or now. And whatever the evil *practices* of the world might be, in theory at least there was less freedom of association beween men and women (this was also true in Jewry) than fellowship in Christ allowed, in whom there was neither male nor female, bond nor free. All the more important was it, therefore, that "the bishops and deacons", to say nothing of the rest of us to whom Paul speaks through Timothy, "should have a good report of them that are without" and be "found blameless" in this as in any other matter.

5:3-16—Regulations about Widows

Verse 3: *"Honour widows that are widows indeed":* The essence of true religion, according to James 1:27, included care of the fatherless and the widows. Widows were to receive the special protection of the Law at the hand of the appointed judges. It was a characteristic of God Himself that "he doth execute the judgment of the fatherless and widow, and loveth the stranger in giving him food and raiment" (Deuteronomy 10:18, also 24:17; Psalm 68:5). Amongst the grounds of condemnation for the princes of Israel was that the cause of the widow did not come unto them.

From the very beginning the first century ecclesia singled out widows for special care and attention. They above all were examples of those in destitution, a point which is brought out vividly by the Lord's comment that when a certain poor widow had cast into the treasury "two mites which make a farthing", she had cast in all her living.

It becomes evident as we read through the present section of the Pastoral Letters that Paul is not simply reminding Timothy that widows need special respect, as though he were merely enlarging upon the instructions of verses 1 and 2. Nor would it be consistent to draw the inference that no respect need be paid to one who was not a widow indeed.

4

Bro. J. Steam   8-9-91

Letter to Timothy
& Titus   £9.00

The section on widows is surprisingly long and detailed and gives a valuable insight into some of the conditions in the Ephesian Ecclesia, if not in the apostolic ecclesias in general. For "honour" seems here to mean "officially recognise", or enrol in the order of widows, provided the conditions of entry be fulfilled. Prohibitions against women of some types being "taken into the number" are given in some detail, together with certain duties attached to enrolment which are at least implied.

It is interesting to note that *timaō*, honour, and the noun *timē*, can carry the technical sense of a financial payment (compare the word *honorarium*), which is possibly the sense to be taken in verse 17 below. For example, in Matthew 27:9 the verb is twice used for the *valuation* of 30 pieces of silver, and in Acts 5:2,3 the noun is the *price* of the land; while in 1 Corinthians 6:20 and 7:23 it is the *price* with which we are bought. Moreover, the Lord's reference to *Corban* in Mark 7:11 shows plainly that the dishonouring of the Fifth Commandment which the practice involved was more than disrespect for parents: "Ye suffer him *no more to do ought* for his father or his mother".

The Apostle is therefore charging Timothy personally (the verb is singular) to see that the practice Paul himself followed and had indeed enjoined upon the elders of the very same church, who may well have neglected it as they had so much else of their duties, was now carried out: "Yea, ye yourselves know that these hands have ministered unto my necessities, and *to them that were with me*. I have shewed you all things, how that so labouring *ye ought to support the weak* . . ." (Acts 20:34-35).

Welfare work is part of ecclesial life, but the slender resources of the community must be used wisely and with restraint: the widows must be *widows indeed*. The definition of a "widow indeed" is given us in verse 5, but first in a parenthesis Paul reminds Timothy—and ourselves, since the principle is equally valid in the ecclesia of today—of the relative obligations of the ecclesia and the family.

Family Responsibility

Verse 4: *"But if any widow have children or nephews, let them learn first to shew piety at home":* "Nephews" are in fact "grandchildren", as the Revised Version tells us, and the responsibility for the maintenance of a widowed mother or grandmother rests upon the nearest descendant. With exorbitant costs, a state service, limited ecclesial resources and certain centralised services amongst us to which we can contribute on a country-wide rather than a local basis, some may say that the individual family responsibility is much diminished. The principle remains, however, particularly in those aspects of care and concern which money does not actually touch. "Showing piety" is literally 'practising their religion', the verb from which comes *eusebeia*, true godliness (see page 58). In itself it sums up the Fifth Commandment, which makes of man's earliest and closest social contact the practical expression of the worship of God Himself.

"And to requite their parents": Literally, 'to return *recompenses*'; the expression employs another Biblical "oncer". Is the Apostle delicately avoiding, as he so often does, the actual discussion of financial affairs in detail, lifting the entire matter to the level of that which is spiritual? The whole subject is one of *eusebeia*, as of course are the collections which we take up for various causes. We may not like to talk about funds and expenses; we may even (this author believes without justification) banish the collection bags from the Breaking of Bread service altogether; but the right use and distribution of money is still a part of worship according to the Scripture.

A marginal reference directs us to the outstanding example of Joseph whose deep affection for and close affinity with his father survived both the long years of separation and his own promotion to the highest rank in Pharaoh's court: "Haste ye, and go up to my father, and say unto him, Thus saith thy son Joseph, God hath made me Lord of all Egypt: come down unto me, tarry not . . . and there I will nourish thee; for there are yet five years of famine; lest thou, and thy household, and all that thou hast, come to poverty" (Genesis 45:9-11).

"For that is good and acceptable before God": The words scarcely need comment, except to remind ourselves that *apodektos*, 'acceptable', occurs elsewhere only in 2:3 (see notes on page 60), and thus is "piety at home" linked in spiritual importance with the first of Paul's exhortations in this Letter, that there should be prayers, supplications, intercessions and giving of thanks for all men (2:1-3).

Verse 5: *"Now she that is a widow indeed, and desolate, trusteth in God":* The genuine widow in Paul's definition is, in effect, alone in the world. (We must remember that "genuine" is here in the context of the discussion of ecclesial enrolment, whatever that involved.) Again, a common Greek word, *monousthai*, 'to be absolutely on one's own', is a New Testament "oncer". Such a widow has no resource but God, and He ministers to her needs through the ecclesia, for "a father of the fatherless, and a judge of the widows, is God in his holy habitation. God setteth the solitary in families" (Psalm 68:5-6). Such a widow "hath her hope set on God", as the Revised Version puts it, and the use of the perfect tense indicates a resolve taken and adhered to. In her widowhood she has dedicated herself to God's service and abides "in supplications and prayers night and day".

The great example of such devotion was the prophetess Anna (Luke 2) who had been a widow even for 84 years (see Revised Version) and "departed not from the temple, but served God with fastings and prayers night and day". Her thankful spirit responded instantly to the sight of the infant Jesus in the temple and she bore witness to him "to all them that looked for redemption in Jerusalem". The duties of the enrolled widows will be discussed in the later section. It is worth noting here, in passing, that the order of words, "night and day", is the usual one in Scripture, and has its origin no doubt in the fact that from the beginning of Creation it was "the evening and the morning" that constituted God's days. Man's day begins in the light and ends with the darkness. It is not so with God's purpose, for His day brings us forward into light.

Verse 6: *"But she that liveth in pleasure is dead while she liveth":* Paul will have something to say about younger widows and their emotional needs in verse 11, but from this verse it seems that the spectacle of the rich widow consuming her time by rejoicing in her freedom, or perhaps more tragically seeking consolation in giving herself to pleasure rather than to the Lord, was not unknown even in apostolic times. To be dead while still alive is a spiritual metaphor common enough in Scripture (see John 5:25; Ephesians 2:1,5 etc.), but perhaps the closest parallel with this verse is to be found in Revelation 3:1, where a whole ecclesia had "a name that thou livest, and art dead".

Again, *spatalan*, 'to live in pleasure, be wanton' (James 5:5), is a rare New Testament word, but in the Septuagint which Paul no doubt has in mind as he writes, it is the word for the "prosperous ease" of the city of Sodom with whom Jerusalem, the city that should have served God night and day, was being compared by the prophet Ezekiel (16:49, see RV).

Verse 7: *"And these things give in charge"*: The "also" of the Revised Version takes us back to 4:11. To all that Timothy must command and teach in this, the practical section of the Letter for regulating the affairs of the ecclesia, he must add the criteria of genuine widowhood for the reasons we have already stated and also *"that they* (that is, the order of widows themselves) *may be without reproach"* (RV).

Verse 8: *"But if any provide not for his own"*: Paul returns to the point made in verse 4. If true worship and religion are to requite one's parents, then neglect of that duty is an act of faithlessness, or worse: *"he hath denied the faith, and is worse than an unbeliever"* (RV). The principle of the last clause is not new. It appears in the Old Testament, where for many acts of disobedience or failure to comply with Divine principles the penalty was to be "cut off from among his people"—not necessarily by death, though that was sometimes the case, but by exclusion from the camp as though one were no longer a member of God's people, or at any rate not considered so by God Himself. The principle applied to the whole of the northern kingdom in Hosea's day: they were "Lo-ammi: for ye are not my people, and I will not be your God" (1:9). The same idea appears in Matthew 18:17, where the man who refused to assent to a certain procedure was to be regarded "as an heathen man and a publican".

The negligent relative was in fact "worse than an unbeliever" in two ways: first, because family loyalty and mutual care was, and still is, a highly developed principle among many peoples ignorant of God's way; and second, because it was always considered better never to have known the way of life than, having known it, to ignore its obligations (compare Hebrews 6:4-6; 10:26 etc.). Of the commandment to love one another and to bear one another's burdens (Galatians 6:2) the community at Ephesus must have been well aware.

Isaiah 58 is worthy of careful study here. To give added point to the word of the Lord as he lifted up his voice "like a trumpet (to) shew my people their transgression" (verse 1), the prophet uses the ceremonial of the Day of Atonement when the solemn note of the trumpet proclaimed that God was coming nigh in judgement (Numbers 29:1-7). The people's sin was not in failing to keep the fast, but in neglecting the true spirit of it: it was not "an *acceptable* day to the LORD". "Is not this the fast that I have chosen? . . . Is it not to deal thy bread to the hungry, and that thou bring the poor that are cast out to thy house? when thou seest the naked, that thou cover him; and *that thou hide not thyself from thine own flesh?*" (Isaiah 58:1,5-7). The spirit of all this, the true glory of the Lord (verse 8), lies in this comment of Paul to Timothy, which is so important that its principle is stated for the third time in 1 Timothy 5:16 below.

5:9-10—The Enrolment of Widows

Verse 9: *"Let not a widow be taken into the number under threescore years old":* "Widows indeed", however, were to be the special charge of the ecclesia, but it is obvious from what follows that we have here no simple "welfare service"; we have to consider a class of women of honourable status with *a positive function* in the ecclesia. Although we may have no strict parallel today with this system of enrolment, or "taking into the number" (the verb *katalegō*, compare "catalogue", is a New Testament "oncer"), there are many things which we can learn from a careful study of what follows. We turn, as one commentator (Hendriksen) has well put it, "from widows and their *need* to widows and their *work*".

What then is this "list" and for what purpose were widows put on it? It cannot be the ordinary list of "serving sisters", since they and their qualifications have already been considered in 3:11 (see page 99) where no age limit was mentioned. Moreover, the question of which widows should receive help and which should not has already been discussed by Paul, and it would be entirely inconsistent with the principles of the ecclesia as a family to say that a woman under 60 with no relatives, or a young widow with small children, should receive no support from the ecclesia. In any case verse 10 suggests either that the widows who qualified for "the list" had at some time been comparatively well-to-do, or that their experience was a qualification for their new function.

153

"Having been the wife of one man": That we are here dealing with some kind of ecclesial "office" is further suggested by this rule, which corresponds to that for overseers, deacons and elders (3:2,12; Titus 1:6), who were to be "the husband of one wife". The implications of this were discussed in connection with the overseers (see page 88; also Essay 11, page 110; Essay 43, page 375), but not entirely resolved, at least not on the question of the precedent for today. The logic (and the Scripture) behind the concept of permanent widowhood after a single marriage as a demand upon those seeking enrolment is clear enough against the first century background of the ideal cherished even amongst pagans as well as Jews. Anna in Luke 2 is an outstanding example.

On the other hand, Paul counsels younger women to remarry, a point to be considered when we come to their case (verse 14). The implication of "waxing wanton against Christ" in verse 11, however, is that enrolled widows now dedicate their entire lives to their service in the ecclesia, "as unto the Lord" himself. What then was that service? It was obviously based upon their personal qualities and qualifications.

The Widow's Qualifications for Service

Verse 10: *"Well reported of for good works"*: See the note on 2:10 (page 72). What was intellectually understood about God is revealed in practice in charitable acts and other deeds. In the case of widows these are now further defined.

"If she have brought up children": Although the verb (a "oncer") means 'to bring up children', usually one's own, there is no suggestion that childless widows with an aptitude for looking after children are to be excluded. It could even be that the ecclesia's care for orphans, equally with widows the object of God's provision in the Law, was committed to the trust of women of experience or natural aptitude, no longer burdened with the care of their own families. Such a woman would also be able to give guidance and counsel to others—a point to which we shall return.

"If she have lodged strangers": Another "oncer", the verb 'to practise hospitality' describes a familiar Scriptural principle, and its link with 3:2 (pages 89,90) in the list of qualifications for an overseer confirms that the widows' duty was to assist in that

important aspect of ecclesial daily life and its spiritual links with those who travelled in service—preachers, messengers and also brethren and sisters simply on a journey.

"If she have washed the saints' feet": This, in many ways the most important if also the most lowly of all service to travellers and guests alike, was an expression of love which might well come under the supervision of those who had long practised it as a rule of daily life in their homes.

"If she have relieved the afflicted": covers a wide range of tasks in a community which then, as now, should commit itself to those who have committed their life to it—a devotion which in the first century involved persecution and much distress and is not without its practical problems even now. See 1 Thessalonians, for example, or the Letter to Philippi, a town where the truth came to the household of a man who washed the Apostles' wounds.

"If she have diligently followed every good work": This is either a summary of what has gone before or, more probably, the emphasis is upon "diligently". It is not sufficient to have a reputation for good works: the reputation must have been well-deserved! The word "diligently" is in the compound verb "to follow", and has a similar sense to that of the English "pursue earnestly": we are to *follow* his steps, the example of the Lord Jesus himself.

To sum up, then, the enrolled widows themselves looked after the welfare of the community in many of its aspects, and as the parallels with the work of the overseer suggest, helped with the particular branches of that work which needed the specifically feminine touch. It is interesting to note that the word "honour" is applied both to "widows indeed" and to "elders that rule well" (verse 17). There is one aspect of that work to which we have already alluded (page 147), but it was of such importance in the first century and is so worthy of careful attention today, that we refer again to it here.

In Titus 2 the aged women are named specifically as the teachers of the young women, in all that concerned a responsible approach to spiritual life in family matters (pages 387-388). It was more than "the feminine touch"; it was the passing on of mature experience, a fact which will become even plainer if we follow the word "sober" (*sōphrōn*) or 'having a sense of responsibility', and its related verb and adverbs through verses 1-6 (see page 386 especially), where it is variously translated "sober", discreet", "temperate", "be sober-minded" (see also pages 71,78,89). There is experience which only women can share; there are matters in which it is proper that only women be involved; there are tasks which it is preferable that women should undertake: such instruction as Paul has in mind when he advised Titus, for example, and probably the instruction of women for baptism as well.

If this be so in the twentieth century, how much more so in the first. Again Hendriksen (*1 & 2 Timothy and Titus*, in the New Testament Commentary series) sums it up well for us: "If even today ... older women are at times consulted and sent on missions in which *they* excel, and which may be too delicate for others to perform, it is readily understandable that *in Bible lands* (and particularly *at that time*, but to a degree even today), with their social and psychological barriers between men and women, there would be much work which these widows would be able to do with greater effectiveness than anyone else (especially work *among women*)." In this matter, as in all the others, Paul urged ecclesial organisation upon sound principles as the true basis of community life.

5:11-16—The Position of Younger Widows

Verse 11: *"But the younger widows refuse":* The next two verses, at first sight, seem brusque and forbidding, with expressions like "refuse", "wax wanton", "condemnation" and "casting off their first faith". In fact the reverse is the case. The Apostle Paul is being both realistic and sensitive to the emotional needs of others in a way he is rarely given credit for, but which is his usual way. Sound ecclesial organisation demands, as he wrote to the Corinthians, that "all things be done decently and in order" (1 Corinthians 14:40). There is a right way and a wrong way to set about anything, including all ecclesial affairs, or confusion and laxity will result. But when he says to those same Corinthians, "Let all *your* things be done with charity" (1 Corinthians 16:14), he is striking the true balance, for ecclesial management is for the purpose of creating the atmosphere in which we have *fellowship* or *partake in common*, or *communicate*, in suffering or in consolation (see 2 Corinthians 1:3-7).

The exclusion of younger widows from the list was *for their own sake* as well as that of the ecclesia. The ecclesia was best served in a certain sphere by women dedicated with single-minded devotion to that service. Many a woman, in the first shock of bereavement, might well desire to give herself to the work, finding it difficult to envisage the prospect of another marriage. But as Paul elsewhere declared on this very matter, every one has his or her "proper gift of God, one after this manner and another after that" (1 Corinthians 7:7); or as the Lord put it, when discussing with his disciples the difficulties surrounding the ideals of marriage, "All men cannot receive this saying, save they to whom it is given" (Matthew 19:11).

It is important to realise that Paul is not condemning widows who remarry: indeed, his positive advice for the younger is that they should. He is simply bearing in mind their emotional needs and ensuring that they *do not enter into a covenant which they may be unable later to keep.* Only such a view explains his very strong words, *"wax wanton against Christ".* Whatever enrolment as a widow entailed, it was the equivalent of a compact with the heavenly Bridegroom, and Paul's "oncer" is a strong version of the verb which occurs in Revelation 18:7,9, 'to live luxuriously, or deliciously'. While we contemplate this emphatic language, it is well to remind ourselves that similar terms are applied by God to Israel and by the apostles to any of us, who abandon our covenant relationship with the Lord.

Verse 12: The condemnation of the younger widows, if they were enrolled and then remarried, would not be because they *"cast off their first faith"* by becoming apostate; nor does it mean that they had broken faith with their first husband by marrying another after his death. The "faith" would be the pledge they undertook when they enrolled in an important work requiring whole-hearted devotion. Although we have no such specific "office" for widows, the general principles remain. For whatever our status, whether we are young or old, married, widowed or single, we should not seek to serve in any capacity and then not be prepared to see it through in the same spirit of dedication. For so would we be also amongst those *"having damnation".*

Verse 13: *"And withal they learn to be idle":* There have been many discussions about the exactness of the translation of the Greek of this clause, but more research has confirmed the accuracy of the Authorised Version, since the grammatical construction of "learning to be" conforms to the idiom for 'learning a profession'. This is in effect what the younger widows, who were ready to leave their profession of devotion to Christ, with its corresponding dedicated service, and "take up idleness" instead, were doing.

We have already written, when considering the deacons and their wives, about the special dangers to which any who take up service or follow a calling are exposed (3:8-13, page 96). The visiting of the sick and the needy, or similar work of the enrolled widow would entail a great deal of social contact. Once the true purpose of this house-to-house visiting was lost, then the practice of it conformed more to the life of the society lady, who in Ephesus as elsewhere in the Ancient World whiled away the hours of leisure (and boredom) in various pursuits— *"wandering about from house to house"*, as our present verse has it.

"And not only idle, but tattlers also": A rich variety of unusual New Testament words abounds in this verse. "Idle", although it is common enough in the Septuagint is found elsewhere in Titus 1:12 (*"slow* bellies" in the quotation from a Cretan poet); in Matthew it refers to the *idle* word which provides a ground of judgement at the last day and also to the unhired labourers in the parable, and it is translated as *barren* in 2 Peter 1:8. *Tattlers* is a "oncer" (its verb-form is "prating" in 3 John 10), and signifies both aimless chatter as well as the more malicious gossip or slander into which it can so easily develop.

"Busybodies, speaking things which they ought not": The work-shy members of the ecclesia in Thessalonica who became *busybodies* (it is a verb-form in 2 Thessalonians 3:11) came under heavy censure to the point of ecclesial withdrawal. This particular form of vice—'taking needless trouble' over other people's affairs—is therefore by no means confined to younger women or to any particular ecclesial office, but is one to which all can fall victim. It is just possible, however, that something more sinister may be intended, particularly in Ephesus.

Periergoi as a noun is found nowhere else, either in the Old or New Greek Testaments, except in its neuter form in Acts 19:19, where it refers to the magic arts put away in such dramatic form by the believers in Ephesus. Could Paul be referring to the charms, magical spells or other formulae to which the irresponsible young widow might resort when dealing with the sick? If so, then "saying things which they ought not" refers, not to the mischief-making of the gossip or the slanderer, but to the spells which they used. The same expression in Titus 1:10,11 could be a similar allusion to the practices of the "deceivers . . . who subvert whole houses". The fact that they of Crete were "of the circumcision" accords well with what is known of the "strolling Jews, exorcists" who turned up also at Ephesus (Acts 19:13, RV).

Verse 14: *"I will, therefore, that the younger women* (widows, RV) *marry":* The phrase "I will, therefore", is identical with what Paul said about the duty of the men in public prayer (2:8). He is exercising his apostolic authority, not expressing his personal desire. "Therefore" sums up all the reasons he has given for not enrolling younger women on the ecclesial list of widows. Marriage for them was the sensible course—advice which sets in perspective all Paul has to say in 1 Corinthians 7, and teaches us how to balance the ideal with the practical. There is little doubt that Paul found himself freer for the mission to which he had been called because he remained unmarried; moreover, on balance he sets forth the principle of no second marriages—certainly for the enrolled widow, if not for the overseer and deacon. But, having regard to the peculiar temptations to which different classes of people are exposed, he approaches the matter with realism.

The fulfilment of having a husband, and proceeding to *"marry, bear children, rule the household"* (RV) was better for widows in the prime of life than a hasty self-dedication upon which they might feel it necessary later to go back. The further justification was that thus they would *"give none occasion to the adversary to speak reproachfully".* Consistent with what we have already seen (chapter 3, page 96), the Apostle is concerned for the reputations of the ecclesia in the world, which could easily be marred by inconsistency in life and conduct of its members, especially those in office.

Verse 15: *"For some are already turned aside after Satan":* Past experience reinforces Paul's argument. This suggests that he is not innovating here at this time in Ephesus and that the system of enrolled widows had been functioning for some time. Although not necessarily so, since a short period would have sufficed to reveal the strains put on the system by those who were not wholly part of it, it was obviously something that needed Timothy's earnest attention in an ecclesia under pressure. The word "turned aside" was the subject of comment in the note on 1:6 (page 21). The women, like the other-teachers, were once in the right way, but did not keep to it.

The expression "turned aside *after Satan*" is parallelled in 1 Corinthians 7:5-7, where the Apostle, with his own "proper gift of God", recognises the strengths and weaknesses of others, and gives the best spiritual advice whereby disciples may refrain from falling into sin. The whole chapter is worth studying in the context of the advice in the passage we are now considering. It is sobering to reflect also on the implication of "Get thee behind me, Satan" in the sequence of thought in Matthew 16:21-28, in which the disciple, learning of the complete dedication of the Master even unto the death on the cross, is reminded that he too must deny himself and take up his cross if he wished to follow.

It is just possible that, if the suggestion concerning the magical arts discussed above has any validity, the "turning aside after Satan" may refer to the evil practices from which some of the converts in Ephesus had previously turned away.

Verse 16: *"But if any man or woman that believeth hath widows, let them relieve them"*: At first sight Paul repeats the instructions of verses 4 and 8. The Revised Version, however, on good manuscript evidence has "if any *woman* that believeth", and many translations follow this reading. If this is correct, then we have here no sudden return to a point that has already been dealt with, but an amplification of it in the light of what has just been said. "Hath widows" suggests something different from the ties of close relationship envisaged in the previous verses. A *familia* or "household", as in the case of the Philippian gaoler, comprised all its dependants, including slaves. Compare the "house" of Abraham, presided over by the faithful Eliezer of Damascus who, in the absence of a son, would have been the patriarch's heir (Genesis 15:2-3).

Widows among such dependants were to be the responsibility of the woman who "guided the house", whether she were married, widowed or single, so that no strain should be placed upon the resources of the ecclesia whose concern was with *widows indeed*. And why not impose such a responsibility upon a believing man?

"The reason . . . should be obvious. If such a man were unmarried or a widower, it would be most unsuitable for him to take over responsibility for a group of widows; whereas if he were married, the responsibility in all its practical aspects would devolve naturally upon his wife" (Kelly, *A Commentary on the Pastoral Epistles*).

5:17-20—Directions about Elders in the Ecclesia

Verse 17: *"Let the elders who rule well . . . especially they who labour in the word and doctrine"*: Several issues are raised in this verse, not only of interpretation of the passage but of its application to ecclesial life today. It is the first time elders, as distinct from an elder (or older man), have been mentioned in this Epistle. This seems at first sight surprising in view of the importance Paul attaches to the qualities and responsibilities of ecclesial officers in chapter 3. The parallels between that chapter and the list of qualifications for elders in Titus (pages 358-360) suggest that overseers were the same as elders, the one word describing their function and the other their status; or that the overseer was the chief administrator, the senior elder as it were. In the latter case some explanation would have to be offered as to why there were *bishops* (plural) in Philippi with no mention of elders at all. It is evident that a brief survey of the whole question of "office" and leadership in the early ecclesias is now necessary: see Essay 17, "Eldership and Rule in the First Century Ecclesia", page 170.

"Well" is *kalōs*, the adverb from the adjective *kalos*, upon which we have already commented as describing the good work which is an index of right belief (page 72; compare also chapter 3:4,12,13 and notes). It was not that some put greater effort ("labour") into their work than others. Such toil, amounting almost to athletic discipline and its resultant fatigue (1 Timothy 4:10 and note) was a characteristic of the elders' responsibility (Acts 20:35; Galatians 4:11 and elsewhere), but to add to administrative burdens the essential work of instruction certainly increased the toil, from the task of preparation to the work of delivery. Perhaps the best translation of "in the word and doctrine" would be "in the preaching and teaching".

"Worthy of double honour": The superficial explanation that a double task was doubly estimable need not detain us: it is a point Paul is not likely to make nor is it consistent with "in honour

preferring one another'' (Romans 12:10), although ''honour to whom honour is due'' is also a principle (13:7). What we must consider is the sense of ''honour'' here, coming as it does after the section on honouring widows who are truly desolate. It is difficult to escape the conclusion that some form of support or remuneration is in view, perhaps with ''honour'' carrying the meaning of ''honorarium''. The next verse seems to justify this view.

Verse 18: *''For the scripture saith, Thou shalt not muzzle the ox . . . ''*: Paul has often been unjustly criticised as being indifferent to the needs of oxen, in applying the statement from Deuteronomy 25:4 to men rather than to the ox for which it was originally intended. He is in fact following his usual practice of showing the true spirit behind the practice of the law, in order to validate a practice in the ecclesia. If a man cannot eat unless he works, then if he works something to eat is his due (see 2 Thessalonians 3:10).

The point has sometimes been obscured for us by the fact that Paul himself never exercised the privilege, though it was granted by the Lord himself (Luke 10:7), in the very words used later in this verse 18: *''the labourer is worthy of his reward''*. It should not be overlooked that in the same passage (1 Corinthians 9:4-11) in which Paul explains his own reasons for working with his hands to minister to his own necessities, he emphasises the principle of ''Have we not power (authority) to eat and drink? . . . If we have sown unto you spiritual things, is it a great thing if we shall reap your carnal things?'' The decision to ''use none of these things'' was Paul's own, for the sake of the example of complete dedication he could then offer, particularly in answer to his critics.

It could be argued that by the analogy of the ox receiving a mouthful or so while actually engaged in treading corn, the elder had some other regular means of livelihood but received emoluments, or in our parlance ''expenses'', while engaged in ecclesial duties. To what extent these would occupy him, or what other resources of time or money a capable elder might possess we have insufficient information. It is plain, however, that Paul is envisaging adequate recompense, which is what ''double'' implies, not simply ''twice as much''. The simple fact was, that where ecclesial work demanded a great deal of time which could not then be spent in remunerative employment, it had to be paid for by someone—either by the community, by a rich brother or sister whose contributions Paul valued (see for example Philippians 4:15), or by the worker himself, who then had to spend of his own substance as well as of his time and energy.

There were practical problems raised by the system, which could be abused. Hence the necessity for choosing men of integrity, "not greedy of filthy lucre", or like the other-teachers, "supposing that gain is godliness" (1 Timothy 3:3; 6:5). The temptations for a poor man were greater than for rich brethren, for whom the charge was "that they do good . . . (be) ready to distribute, willing to communicate" (6:17,18). The reasons why the Christadelphian Brotherhood has from the beginning eschewed the system of a paid ministry were, and still are, excellent, especially in view of the manifest abuses which prevailed in the era of its inception. Two things should be remembered, however: while there are many sound practical considerations in favour of our method, there seems to be no Scriptural principle involved; and no one should be *expected* (irrespective of what he *chooses*) to "war a warfare at his own charges" (1 Corinthians 9:7). Moreover, we should never confuse *expenses* with the *hire* of the labourer.

"For the scripture saith": For the formula, compare Romans 9:17; 10:11. It is important to note that the two passages upon which Paul bases his injunction, from Deuteronomy and a saying of Jesus, are equally classed as "scripture". The passage from the Law appears in a different order of words from his original use of it in 1 Corinthians 9:9, which follows the Septuagint order. The second raises the question of whether the saying of the Lord was already written down or not. Critics who deny that Paul wrote the Pastoral Epistles see one more evidence here of their later date. We prefer to think that irrespective of whether there existed a written collection of the words of the Lord Jesus—and at least one of his sayings is known to us only through Paul's reference to it in Acts 20:35—the Apostle learned of these two at least from his close companion Luke, the beloved physician, from whom he assimilated many other phrases, including his medical metaphors in these Letters (page 47).

Verse 19: *"Against an elder receive not an accusation":* This instruction is a natural corollary of what has just been written, for, given

163

their status and function, elders were naturally exposed to criticism and even rumour and gossip. We saw in Chapter 3 of this book that their blameless character and experience were essential qualifications for their appointment in the first place, lest "they that are without", to say nothing of "those that are within", might have occasion to speak reproachfully.

The respect due to an elder, a sense not to be excluded from the word "honour" even if it bears the meaning outlined above, was underlined by this protection from malicious rumour. Any Israelite was safeguarded by the Law against indictment and sentence unless two or three reliable witnesses could testify to his guilt (Numbers 35:30; Deuteronomy 17:6; 19:15, the last being the passage most relevant to the case under discussion). Timothy, however, must not even receive, or take up, a charge against an elder, *"but before* (literally, upon) *two or three witnesses".* Presumably the charge could cover inadequacies in the performance of ecclesial duties as well as misdemeanours. The principle is similar to that prescribed by the Lord for the treatment of private offences in Matthew 18:15-17.

Verse 20: "Them that sin rebuke before all": Commensurate with the status of the elders was the degree of their accountability. They were in the public eye, and it is evident that charges were investigated in public also. Although the investigation would never have begun if there had not been a degree of certainty about the charge, if it were in fact unfounded then it would be disposed of openly and finally. Some apply the verse to any of the congregation that sinned, but the change of topic would be too abrupt, since the whole section is about the treatment of elders.

"Before all" may refer to all the elders, but after the analogy of the public judgement of those who sought to lead Israel astray it means more probably the whole ecclesia. *"That (the) others also may fear"*, however, probably means the rest of the elders. The allusion is to Deuteronomy 13:11—"And all Israel shall hear, and fear, and shall do no more any such wickedness as this among you." No greater emphasis could be laid upon the importance of leadership and its solemn obligations. After all, the responsibility of "watching for souls", one's own or other people's, is great indeed, and this is underlined for us in the Apostle's solemn command to Timothy which now follows.

5:21-25—Timothy's Personal Conduct

Verse 21: *"I charge thee before God, and the Lord Jesus Christ, and the elect angels":* This is not the same as the overall "charge" (*parangellia*) of the Epistle itself (1:3,5) but a formal testifying (*diamarturomai*), always in these Letters before God and the Lord (2 Timothy 2:14; 4:1), to the Divine responsibility of Timothy's work. In this verse "the elect angels" are called to witness also. No distinction between "elect" and "fallen" angels is intended here, nor have we, of necessity, a reference to specific "guardian angels", for they are "*all* ministering spirits", concerned with the whole process of man's salvation, individually and collectively. The more usual adjective for angels is "holy", which accords well with the scene conjured up by this verse. For Timothy acts as the representative upon earth of those who will come to judge the quality of every man's discipleship—the Lord with all his holy angels (Matthew 25:31; Mark 8:38; Luke 9:26; Revelation 14:10).

"Observe these things": The "things" are all that has just been set before Timothy in the treatment of elders, which might well have caused the younger man much heart-searching, especially in view of the specific cases confronting him in Ephesus. For it was among the elders that the other-teachers were numbered (Acts 20:30), and there must have been faction in the ecclesia if the process of "drawing away disciples after them" had progressed very far.

The subtle allusion to Korah, Dathan and Abiram in 2 Timothy 2:19 ("The Lord knoweth them that are his"; compare Numbers 16:4-7,20-27) suggests that this was so. The command to act *"without preferring one before another, doing nothing by partiality"* is based upon the oneness and justice of God Himself, in whose Name and upon whose principles the elders of Israel were expected to act. The word *prokrima*, 'preference' or 'prejudice', is a New Testament "oncer" and implies prejudice against as much as favouritism towards an individual.

Verse 22: *"Lay hands suddenly on no man":* For the note on the practice of the laying on of hands, see page 141. There is no New Testament record which confirms the view that Paul is here dealing with the re-admission to the ecclesia of penitent offenders, even if they were the elders that sinned, as the sequence of thought would demand if that interpretation were followed. It is true that there would seem to be something appropriate in the gesture of giving "the right hand of fellowship" when a brother is welcomed back—do we always make them *feel* welcome?—but the solemn charge of the previous verse that "these things" (the instructions from verses 17-21 inclusive) be observed must surely suggest the warning to take great care and thought in the appointment of elders in the first place.

"Neither be partaker of other men's sins": The word "partaker" is the verb 'to fellowship', but we have here no precedent for "instant excommunication". We follow the actual words of J. H. Bernard (*The Pastoral Epistles*, Cambridge Greek Testament for Schools and Colleges), who has expressed the sequence of thought clearly and concisely in a manner upon which we cannot improve:

> "Do not lightly entertain accusations against a presbyter (verse 19); Do not spare rebuke if he fall into sinful habits (verse 20); Do not be partial (verse 21); Do not admit him to the presbyterate without due enquiry (verse 22a); If you do, you accept responsibility for his sins, which, in a manner, you have made your own (verse 22b). And this last grave thought leads on to the personal warning *keep thyself pure*; that is, pure in the first instance as not being *koinōnos* ('partaker') of other men's sins, and in a more general sense as well."

The advice is consistent with the whole Epistle: a sense of responsibility in the leadership of the ecclesia is the major factor in its spiritual health and vigour. The reader is referred back once more to the whole of Chapter 3, with its detailed exposition of what that sense of responsibility implies, which leads up to the definition of the nature and function of the ecclesia itself (page 85). In the absence of such an overseer as Timothy or Paul himself, and given the democratic principle, all the members of the modern ecclesia bear their own responsibility in the selection of their leaders.

"Pure" *(hagnos)* and "purity" *(hagneia,* 1 Timothy 4:12 and 5:2 only) are important words in this context. The noun describes a characteristic already considered—the *purity* of the way of life of a young man who must be an example of the believers, especially in his treatment of the younger women. The adjective describes things to think upon (Philippians 4:8), the chastity of the virgin (compare Revelation 14:4 for the idea, though not the word), the purity of the young wife (Titus 2:5), of the bride of Christ (2 Corinthians 11:2) and of the condition of an ecclesia which has faced up to its obligations in the disciplining—and redemption—of one of its members ("clear" in 2 Corinthians 7:11). Above all it describes the way of life of one of the sons of God who hopes to be like his Lord when he "sees him as he is". "And every man that hath this hope in him purifieth himself, even as he is pure" (1 John 3:2-3).

To the best of his ability Timothy must strive to *keep himself* pure, even as "he that is begotten of God *keepeth himself*" (1 John 5:18), and even as God's commandments must be *kept*. This verb *tereō*, frequent in the Revelation, where the visions of the Lord's judgements are linked with strong exhortation to His people to observe His statutes, is the same as that for *preserve* or *reserve* in all those passages which speak of the faithfulness of God in exercising mercy or judgement upon His people: for example 1 Peter 1:4 and 2 Peter throughout.

Verse 23: *"Drink no longer water, but use a little wine for . . . thine often infirmities":* This verse is to be regarded as a surprising interpolation only if the spiritual implications of the foregoing against the background of "the charge" contained in the whole Epistle be missed. To dismiss it as a proof against inspiration or as an example of a supposed characteristic of Paul's to interject irrelevant material into his arguments, is an attitude of the hostile critic, but not of the devoted student of the Word. To understand the message of the verse may help us in an approach to some of our modern problems of use and abuse.

It is a question of "purity" and "keeping oneself" with the help of Him to whom the Lord prayed, "Holy Father . . . I pray not that thou shouldest take them out of the world, but that thou shouldest *keep them* from the evil" (John 17:11-15). In view of the obvious need in Ephesus to guard against being *"given to wine"* (note the implication of excess) and to be careful over this very matter in the choice of a bishop (3:3,8; see also Titus 1:7; 2:3; Romans 13:13; Galatians 5:21, and notes on pages 91, 92, 97, 359), Timothy may well have already decided on total abstinence, in order to be an example of the believers in all purity. The verb *hydropotein* (a "oncer" in the Bible, but common enough in everyday life) means habitual "water-drinking", as opposed to *oinopotein*, wine-bibbing.

There is the possibility that the water in Ephesus affected Timothy's stomach and contributed to his *often infirmities*. But the Apostle is really declaring that to persist in water-bibbing was not the purity to which he referred. Such an attitude had more of law than grace in it, and could even, as it did in the other-teachers, tend towards the kind of asceticism which commanded to "abstain from meats". The Scripturally-informed conscience is sensitive, not seared as with a hot iron, and can distinguish between use and abuse, between what can be received with thanksgiving and be sanctified by the Word of God and prayer and what cannot (see 4:1-7 and notes, pages 121-126).

So Timothy was not to exchange water-bibbing for wine-bibbing. He was—and the words were carefully chosen—to "use a *little* wine". His purity would be assured by his attitude of mind and the self-discipline which it produced in him. Would that we could all so educate ourselves in Divine things and be governed by the principles of purity and responsibility instead of rules in which we may boast and condemn others. Intolerance, criticism, self-righteousness and a false asceticism are in themselves "impurity" according to the Scriptures.

Verse 24: *"Some men's sins are open beforehand":* The theme of careful selection of elders is now resumed and evidently the secret of sound choice lay in caution and detailed investigation. To obtain a true estimate of character it was not sufficient to consider the notorious failures of the obvious sinner, which are referred to as *"going before to judgment"*. *Whose* judgement it is not quite clear. Timothy should have no difficulty in exercising his own, in the case of the kind of men who were "enemies of the cross of Christ" (Philippians 3:18). The future judgement of God is equally certain in such a case. But in such a delicate issue as the choice of elders, extreme caution must be exercised. Timothy dare not rest satisfied with negative evidence about those upon whom he lays hands, since serious character defects will reveal themselves or *"follow after"* a careful and detailed enquiry.

Verse 25: *"Likewise also the good works of some are manifest beforehand":* The corollary to verse 24 is plain enough. Care and scrupulous impartiality should reveal the good as well as the bad, and hasty judgements are to be avoided either way. If sins can be *prodēlos*, 'manifest beforehand' (the only other occurrence of this word is in Hebrews 7:14, with reference to Christ's descent from Judah), so can works of righteousness and good. Some *kala erga*, 'good works', however, being of less public character are not immediately apparent, but if genuine *"cannot be hid"*.

The whole passage, verses 17-25, emphasising so clearly the importance of eldership to the ecclesia, is a revelation of spiritual values to which enough attention had evidently not been paid, at least not in Ephesus. Timothy was left in no doubt about the course that should be followed: neither are we.

ESSAY 17

Eldership and Rule
in the First Century Ecclesia

WE have already referred to J. B. Norris's work on *The First Century Ecclesia*. In these days of reappraisal and attempted "reformation" of the Christadelphian community this useful book should be regarded as required reading. We may well have assumed too readily that because the first century ecclesia had an apostolically appointed, spirit-guided eldership and we have not, there is less guidance for us in the Word than we should like. Indeed, we may in some instances have gone even further, and thought that our necessary democratic procedure gave a political rather than a spiritual character to our organisations. If so, then we have not penetrated deeply enough into the spirit of the apostolic age, nor grasped the Scriptural principles underlying our *Ecclesial Guide*. To the chapters on "Elders—Their Standing and Responsibilities" and "First Century Bishops" in *The First Century Ecclesia* we are indebted for some of the material on which this note is based.

The Principle of Leadership

God has always dealt with His people upon the principle of leadership. He chose men capable of guiding, or in the Hebrew idiom of "feeding", and gave them the responsibility of working together with Him in the task of building up what was in effect a family relationship with the Father, "From whom every family in heaven and in earth is named". It seems that rarely did the people of themselves incur God's anger or rebuke directly: they bore their own iniquity, but the heaviest censure was reserved for those who had misled them.

170

A similar system was Divinely ordained in the first century ecclesia. The eldership of the Jerusalem Ecclesia was based upon the Lord's own chosen apostles, and others like James whose authority was evidently Divinely recognised. When Paul and Barnabas carried the message of the Gospel throughout the world of Asia Minor and the eastern European mainland, they "ordained them elders in every church" with prayer and fasting and "commended them to the Lord, on whom they believed" (Acts 14:23). Where, as in Crete, this process had not been carried out for one reason or another, it became essential for the spiritual health of the ecclesias there to remedy that situation and "set in order the things that are wanting" (Titus 1:5).

As we have already seen, the prelude to reformation in Ephesus as well as Crete was to give close attention to the qualifications of the leaders, especially since in the former case the problems had arisen through the failure of the elders to take heed unto themselves. Remarkably, elders are not mentioned in any of Paul's epistles prior to the Pastorals, but we can gain a glimpse of their responsibilities if not their specific duties by putting together several passages, including some that we have already reviewed in this book.

Elders had to exercise "rulership" as 1 Timothy 5:17 indicates; they were "over the ecclesia" in the Lord "to admonish" and the brethren were exhorted to "know them" or appreciate their worth (1 Thessalonians 5:12); the bishop had to be able to rule well his own house as a necessary qualification for exercising his function in the ecclesia (1 Timothy 3:4-5); according to Romans 12:8, "he that ruleth" had to do it "with diligence" or with the "earnest care" (2 Corinthians 8:16) that characterises the man attending to his own "business" (Romans 12:11), or with the sense of urgency with which Mary went "with haste" (Luke 1:39) to see Elisabeth after the angel Gabriel's visit to her.

In Hebrews the exhortation is more emphatic: "Remember them which have the rule over you, who have spoken unto you the word of God . . . Obey them that have the rule over you, and submit yourselves: for they watch for your souls, as they that must give account . . . Salute all them that have the rule over you" (Hebrews 13:7,17,24). It is noteworthy that the whole chapter deals with the expression in practical terms for the believers individually and collectively of the life of faith in "the Apostle and High Priest of your profession" (3:1), "the captain of our salvation" (2:10).

The Implications of "Rulership"

A brief consideration of the two words for "rule" in the original of the foregoing will help us here. In all but the Hebrews passage the word is from *proistēmi*, 'to set before' or 'over', or in its intransitive sense, 'to stand before'. The stronger word in Hebrews means 'to lead', 'to be chief', besides having meanings related to 'esteem' and 'judging'. The idea of some necessary prominence is implicit, then, in what we know about eldership from the New Testament. The matter is put into perspective when we balance the responsibilities with the authority, after the Hebrew style which makes "rule" and "feed" the same word. For authority in Scripture is based entirely upon the capacity to benefit those over whom it is exercised, whether it be a good shepherd with his flock or a King David chosen to exercise similar qualities over "my people Israel". It is the way of God Himself: "I am God Almighty (*Ail Shaddai*), Creator and Sustainer; walk before me, and be thou perfect" (see Genesis 17:1).

The faithful elders in the ecclesias had "*addicted themselves*" to their service (1 Corinthians 16:15); they "*laboured* in the word and in the teaching"; they "spoke the word of God"; they "*watched over your souls, as they that must give account*"; they "fed the flock of God" and took "the oversight thereof, not by constraint, but willingly ... of a ready mind". This last quotation, from 1 Peter 5:2, implies that the responsibilities might well induce a sense of reluctance to respond to the call or invitation to serve. It also makes plain that there was no *essential* difference between elders and bishops. Bishops were almost certainly elders, in both senses of the word, and the elders exercised oversight (*episkopeō*) which was the proper function of a bishop (*episkopos*).

The elders, therefore, while exercising some authority, were not "as being lords over God's heritage, but being ensamples to the flock", bearing well in mind the Lord's own advice to the twelve, as he gently chided them for their strife amongst themselves as to "which of them should be accounted the greatest. And he said unto them, The kings of the Gentiles exercise lordship over them ... But ye shall not be so: but he that is greatest among you, let him be as the younger (a nice touch when we are considering 'elders'!); and he that is chief, as he that doth serve ... I am among you as he that serveth'' (Luke 22:24-27).

No Divine Sanction

It may well be objected that the concept of leadership and authority we have been considering had a Divine sanction: there is no parallel today. The contrary is the case, if the principles be understood and followed. In a democracy there is a *delegation* of authority, since it is impossible, or at least impracticable, for a whole assembly to act unless it be very small. Even in the so-called "direct democracy" of Athens, where the whole "ecclesia" (the actual word used for the body of citizens) assembled in the open air to exercise its vote and voice in the affairs of state and to receive the account of their leaders' stewardship, the procedure was based upon the fact that the generals had been elected to command and the *archons* to rule. Otherwise nothing could be done, and indeed, when the elected leadership was weak or its authority resisted nothing effective was done and disaster followed.

Now, a presiding brother by definition "sits before" the meeting, with authority and leadership to exercise within the framework of his defined duties. If due attention to his spiritual qualities was paid at the time of his election, then the ecclesia will have more than an executant, an announcer of items in a constitutionally defined programme of service: it will have guidance and there will be an atmosphere to the meeting which even an indifferent speaker will be unable to spoil completely (see article on "An Appeal to Presiding Brethren", *The Christadelphian*, December 1977).

So with arranging brethren. Their appointment should rest on something more than skill with the finances or administration, which is part of the routine of a well-founded ecclesia anyway. The question to be asked is, Who will best "watch for our souls"? To whom can we safely entrust the decisions which must be theirs and will be binding upon us, until we have the opportunity to confirm or deny in a properly convened assembly of the whole ecclesia?

If ecclesial appointments were made with attention to the Word of God and prayer, and if the servants for the year, or whatever period, were committed unto God for His guidance and blessing at a special meeting for the purpose, then there might be less murmuring or criticism when a difficult and unenviable task is carried out by our brethren, partakers of flesh and blood like ourselves.

The Right Spirit

J. B. Norris's conclusion is worth reproducing in full:

> "From these testimonies, it is evident that there is no room among true brethren for either the autocratic type of mind on the one hand, or the shop-steward type on the other, for lovers of power, or opponents of the authority which comes from Christian character and experience. The true elder, being a true servant of the Lord and of his fellow disciples, is entitled to respect and submission. It is right that the decisions of the ecclesia should be subject to the confirmation of the ecclesia, of whom, after all, they are the servants. Ultimate authority, humanly speaking, rests in the ecclesia as a whole. But the decisions of elders and explanatory words of elders in connection with those decisions should be treated with deference. The spirit of modern political democracy with its insistence upon rights and its readiness to complain or resent, should not be allowed to infest our business meetings or any other sphere of ecclesial activity" (*The First Century Ecclesia*, page 59).

Where the right spirit prevails, the elders can "watch for our souls . . . with joy and not with grief".

The First Letter to Timothy

CHAPTER 6

Concluding Exhortations, Warnings and Advice

THE second part of this First Epistle has been dealing with practical exhortation concerning the administration of the ecclesia and relationships between its members. The influence of social status in the world outside affected these relationships, and as in all his letters Paul is at pains to emphasise the true spiritual approach.

The question of slavery was a difficult one: it troubled the consciences of many pagans and the whole system cut across the concept of brotherhood in the ecclesia. Although in the Pastoral Epistles attention is concentrated on the demeanour of Christian *slaves*, Paul had already written elsewhere of the duties of masters. It will be helpful to remind ourselves of the nature of the system of slavery so that we may set his words in context: see Essay 18, "Masters and Slaves in the Ancient World", page 204.

6:1-2—The Duty of Christian Slaves

Verse 1: *"Let as many servants as are under the yoke"*: The order of the Greek words yields the better sense: "under the yoke as slaves", emphasising the complete subjugation described above. The yoke is a frequent figure for servitude in both Old and New Testaments, especially in Jeremiah, where the people were to be brought under the dominion of the Babylonians and, incidentally, could have showed their willing obedience to their true overlord, God Himself, by submitting to Nebuchadnezzar without rebellion. For servitude can be mitigated and burdens lightened by the yoke, especially if it fits easily upon the shoulder (Matthew 11:28-30).

"Count their own masters worthy of all honour": At this point no distinction is made between believing and unbelieving masters. We must not minimise the demand made upon the disciple or underrate the spiritual insight called for to show honour *on principle rather than according to desert*. Mutual respect amounting even to affection was not unknown between pagan master and man, but the character and disposition of them both played a major part in such a relationship. In this verse, however, it is the *status* and not the *worth* of the master that demands respect, "as unto the Lord". See the discussion on the principle involved in the notes on 5:1, pages 143-146. It was a principle to be followed by all God's people in their relationship with the powers that be, whether in the shape of a Nebuchadnezzar, a Nero or the Lord's anointed. "Honour" bears the double sense we have been considering earlier—both respect and material benefit, in this case service of high quality.

The usual word for "master" is *kurios*, 'lord', but here it is *despotēs*, a word more expressive of complete ownership. The New Testament use of the word, especially here, is sufficiently remarkable to justify an extended comment: see Essay 19, "O Lord, our Lord, how excellent is thy name", page 207.

The fact that *despotēs* came later into the New Testament vocabulary to signify a human slave-master (the Pastoral Epistles and 1 Peter 2:18) may be an influence from the world outside. But surely it is more than coincidence that the Apostles use it always with reference to the obedience of believing slaves to their earthly masters as an expression of their full submission to the *Despotēs* "holy and true" (Revelation 6:10). This view is reinforced by the words Paul uses next.

"That the name of God and his doctrine be not blasphemed": The behaviour of His people has always been an occasion for the glorifying or the dishonouring of God's Name. Paul here quotes Isaiah 52:5, but Ezekiel 36:20 is also much to the point: "And when they entered unto the heathen, whither they went, they profaned my holy name, when they said to them, These are the people of the LORD, and are gone forth out of his land." See also Romans 2:24.

For if God's people *profess* to be wholly His, then the pagans will charge Him with their subversive and anti-social activities.

Hence the insistence of all the Apostles in their writings that the disciple is a better servant, a better citizen even (within the limited possibilities of that word for a disciple) because of his service to the Lord. In the Acts, Luke makes it clear that there was nothing done contrary to the law of the land in all the apostolic activity. If the disciples suffered, they suffered as Christians and not as evil-doers.

Verse 2: *"And they that have believing masters, let them not despise them":* It is a sad commentary on human nature that the spirit of egalitarianism should render necessary such an exhortation! Why should masters be despised *because they are brethren?* The answer can only be because men are concerned more with rights than responsibilities, and while pride, arrogance, tyranny and snobbery on the part of masters can have no excuse, neither can that "inverted snobbery" which makes the poor despise the rich, the uneducated pour scorn on education, and the slave long to "take it out of" his master. Both tendencies are alike carnal, and have nothing to do with him who, though he was rich, for our sakes became poor; and though he was Lord of all, condescended to men of low estate; and though being in the form of God, was content to glorify His Father by taking the form of a slave (cf. Philippians 2:7-9; Romans 12:16).

When the slaves *"do them service"* because such a Christ-like spirit between master and man prevails that they are mutually *"faithful and beloved"*, they are both *"partakers of the benefit"*.

There can be no subjective approach to this matter, no shades of opinion: *"These things teach and exhort."*

6:3-10—Dangers of False Teaching

Verse 3: *"If any man teach otherwise":* The words which close verse 2 not only sum up the practical instructions just given but introduce "the conclusion of the whole matter". The word *heterodidaskalein,* 'other-teach', occurs here and in 1:3 and its meaning was discussed at some length in the notes on that verse (page 41). The setting out of parallel verses from chapter 1 and chapter 6 will show clearly how Paul now returns to his original "charge" to Timothy, by way of résumé of the whole Epistle in which he has given advice on how to carry that charge into effect: there was a sharp contrast between sound doctrine and other-teaching, seen not merely in its content but in the *moral effects it produced*:

Chapter 1	*Chapter 6*
verse 3: certain men (RV) other-teach	verse 3: any man other-teach
verse 4: questionings	verse 4: questions
verse 7: understanding not	verse 4: knowing nothing
verse 10: sound doctrine	verse 5: sound word

"Consent not to wholesome words": Of the word "sound" or "wholesome" much has been written already (pages 46-48). The use of the word "consent" here is unique in the New Testament. Paul does not use it again, and elsewhere it signifies literal movement of the body rather than an assent of the mind in coming over to a point of view. The usage was common enough in later Greek, and its origin can be seen in a similar, much earlier, Latin phrase meaning to vote for or support a motion in the Senate. *Pedibus in sententiam ire*, "to walk over to an opinion", meant quite literally to walk across the floor of the chamber and stand with the speaker proposing the motion—"to vote with one's feet".

Although the primary sense in this verse is that an other-teacher cannot easily be won over to sound teaching, for reasons that will become apparent below, it has an exhortational sense for us as well. How much consenting to the sound teaching is being done in our ecclesias in the active sense, that of support for the work to which we are theoretically committed? It would be irony indeed if we voted for the ecclesial programme of preaching and study in committee and omitted to vote for it with our feet, or other form of conveyance!

"Even the words of our Lord Jesus Christ": This definition of sound teaching, and by contrast of the other-teaching which does not conform to it, raises an interesting and important point. The knowledge of what those words are is pre-supposed, as is also the fact that Timothy, like Paul, could know them for certain. So could the other-teachers if they chose, otherwise there is no point in the definition. It could be that they were enshrined still in the minds of those who could accurately recall them, through the Comforter who will "bring all things to your remembrance, whatsoever I have said unto you" (John 14:26).

The earliest preaching was a witness to the things seen and heard, confirmed by the Lord with signs following. Moreover,

Paul in Ephesus had not shunned to declare the whole counsel of God, including some of the "words of the Lord Jesus" which are positively known to us only because of his use of them (Acts 20:35). The situation in Ephesus, however, and the concern Paul reveals for the ecclesia's future, foreshadows the ending of the apostolic age proper, and there is no evidence that so close and able a lieutenant as Timothy had the gift of accurate recall, particularly of words he had not heard at first hand. If it be objected that it is not the actual words of the Lord Jesus Christ which are meant here but those consistent with his teaching, we are still left with the point that the teaching must have been as readily accessible in some form, apart from Timothy's own duty to speak forth words which become sound doctrine.

An Early Written Gospel?

The existence of a body of Faithful Sayings (see page 49) and the hints in other places such as the Letters of Peter, point to the probability that a collection of sayings of Jesus, or even at least one of the Gospels was already in circulation, and that the early church was better supported with a written basis for their faith in addition to the Old Testament than was at one time thought. The coincidence of some of the vocabulary of the Pastoral Epistles and their use of medical metaphors give some credence to the idea that the Gospel of Luke was already in circulation.

"The doctrine which is according to godliness": The phrase is the equivalent of the preceding expressions, for Christ is "the mystery of godliness" in open manifestation, and both his words and his work were the basis of the life of the disciple individually and ecclesially. Unsound or "unhygienic" teaching cannot feed the flock, nor promote their holy living, for its characteristic is that it sets itself apart from—refuses to come over to the side of— the wholesome. A more emphatic statement of the relationship between doctrine and living cannot be imagined.

Verse 4: *"He is proud, knowing nothing"*: But if the words of the Lord Jesus are so readily available, how can one refuse to know them or consent to them, and dare to put forward ideas claiming to be based on them which are so opposed to them in content and effect? The answer is, he is blinded by pride in his own under-standing. The word for 'is proud' is *tetuphōtai* (see 3:6 and 2 Timothy 3:4, with reference to the novice and the characteristics

179

of some of the men of the "perilous times" to come), the root meaning of which comes from the word for 'smoke'. "Pride goes to the head, like smoke which blinds and confuses, and in a head so filled, sureness of judgement and the standards of wise oversight can no longer be guaranteed" (see page 95).

The remarkable thing is the tenacity with which men can cling to a speculation or a "way-out" interpretation, until it becomes a hobby-horse to be ridden on all conceivable occasions. It is easy to consider oneself a specialist on a theme, and claim to "know" where others are unlearned. If one wanders from the truth the reason is not always ignorance or a failure to understand of itself. It can be a *moral* defect, a reluctance to consider other than one's own viewpoint: one has the knowledge which "puffeth up" (1 Corinthians 8:1) but in reality is devoid of understanding—the logical result of not knowing the Lord Jesus Christ and him crucified, with insight into what that means.

"But doting about questions and strifes of words": "Doting" is really 'sick' (*nosōn*, a "oncer"), the effect of unwholesome spiritual fare. The malady takes a definite form—a morbid preoccupation with endless speculations and wordy battles. The "questions" or "searchings out" to which the Apostle refers in three other places in these Letters (1:4; 2 Timothy 2:23; Titus 3:9) and in a related word in 1 Corinthians 1:20, is always connected with strife or faction; it is the characteristic of the philosophical rather than the spiritual mind: "The Greeks *seek after* wisdom", the product of pure intellectual curiosity. We are familiar with the way in which the Word of God is often handled even today, when it is treated as a kind of cryptogram, whose meaning lies not in its words but in some hidden symbolism or allegory which obscures the plain message. The use of words as weapons, which is the force of Paul's unique word *logomachia* ('battle *of*—not *over*—words': also in 2 Timothy 2:14), was not confined to the other-teachers of Ephesus.

"Whereof cometh envy, strife, railings, evil surmisings": The list of bitter fruits of controversy is long and forthright. "Envy" is a natural result of intellectual strife. If it was present amongst the disciples as they strove together as to "which of them should be the greatest", we cannot expect such strife to be absent from the kind of debate which displays more of verbal skill than of spiritual

understanding. "Envy" and "strife" are listed amongst those things to which men are "given up" when God is not "retained in their knowledge" (Romans 1:28).

The poorer the case the more bitter the strife and "railings" which result from it. The Greek word is *blasphēmiai*, which the translators are correct in not limiting to the usual English under-standing of blasphemy as abusive language only with respect to God or things divine (see also Ephesians 4:31 and Colossians 3:8). It is a well known ploy to direct attention away from a weak case by using scornful or insolent language about an opponent. One of the sad effects of controversy is the development of the moral weakness that can never see good in the "other side", and motives as well as overt acts are suspect.

Verse 5: "Perverse disputings of men of corrupt minds": The Apostle can find no language strong enough to emphasise his point, so here coins yet another word to be found nowhere else in the Bible or the Greek language—*diaparatribai* or 'perpetual, violent friction'. This constant 'rubbing together', in which some have seen an allusion to the spreading of skin disease amongst sheep by con-tagion, is a familiar enough concept. Since all that Paul has been saying has its lessons for us today, we would do well to remember that we can as easily fall a prey to the moral failures of the Ephesian ecclesia if we fail to "take heed" to ourselves.

For the opposite of "sound" is "unsound", of "healthy", "unhealthy" and of "wholesome", "unwholesome". Paul is blunt enough to say "men of corrupt minds": there comes a point when the other-teachers have definitely lost all possibility of sound thinking. The effect of being puffed up with pride or deficient in spiritual health is cumulative.

"Destitute of the truth": This is perhaps the most terrifying phrase of all. It is possible, through want of right motive or sound method to be like the "silly women", characteristic of the last days, who fell under the spell of false teachers, "ever learning and never able to come to the knowledge of the truth". Or those in Crete for whom nothing was pure, since "even their mind and conscience is defiled" (Titus 1:15; cf. 2 Timothy 3:8). By their actions the other-teachers *defraud themselves of the truth*, which is the force of *apostereō* in its other usages (Mark 10:19; 1 Corinthians 6:7,8; 7:5; James 5:4).

"Supposing that gain is godliness": The sense of this phrase is not so clear in the Authorised Version as in the Revised Version, which has "that godliness is a way of gain". *Porismos*, a 'gainful trade', is used only in this passage in the New Testament, although the idea of "teaching things which they ought not, for filthy lucre's sake" is spelled out in Titus 1:11. One of the qualifications for both overseer and deacon was their aversion to "filthy lucre" (3:3,8 and notes, see pages 93,97), so evidently pecuniary advantage is in view here, as the immediate sequel confirms.

Given the background of the society of the day, when the sophists gave their philosophical lectures for money and an honorarium was normal for ecclesial servants (see page 162), it was an easy transition from a morbid desire for the prestige and influence that intellectual superiority was thought to bring to the making of a trade of spiritual things. No true service can be rendered if the "What's in it for me?" attitude prevails: although, as we have remarked before, while such lack of concern for material things should motivate the servant, the beneficiaries should concern themselves with the welfare of those who give all they have in service.

"From such withdraw thyself": The textual evidence for this clause is slender: the Revised Version omits it and commentators for the most part ignore it. The instruction that Timothy should have nothing to do with such men is clear enough (as in verse 11), however, and while "withdraw" may not have the same formal overtones as it has in our use of the word today, its practical effect was the same in view of Timothy's authority. It is the equivalent of Titus 3:10—"A man that is an heretick after the first and second admonition reject", where "heretic" is the 'leader of a faction' (see page 416).

The Contentment of the Godly Man

Verse 6: *"But godliness with contentment is great gain"*: With skill and a fine irony Paul plays on the word "gain" to declare the fruitfulness of the true spiritual life—the *eusebeia* (see page 58) revealed in the life of Christ, which godly women profess (2:10) and unto which Timothy should exercise himself (4:7,8). It has "promise of the life that now is, and of that which is to come" and is worth all—the pearl of great price. It is a great gain, for it gives a true sense of value, a proper object to seek after, a pursuit which delivers from anxious concern for what to eat, to drink or to wear: "Seek ye first the kingdom of God, and his righteousness; and all these things shall be added unto you" (Matthew 6:25-33).

"With contentment" is not meant to imply here that there can be any other kind of godliness, *without* contentment, for example. True godliness is inseparable from contentment, just as covetousness is idolatry: a godly man learns (though it may be a steady process, as suggested by Paul's "I *have* learned") in whatsoever state he is, therewith to be content (Philippians 4:11). Contentment (*autarkia*, translated "sufficiency" in 2 Corinthians 9:8) is further commented on in verses 7-10 below.

Verse 7: *"For we brought nothing into this world":* Nothing can more dramatically illustrate the worthless nature of worldly goods amassed with great effort and much anxiety than the parable of the rich man and his barns (Luke 12):

"He heaps up treasures mixed with woe;
He dies, and leaves them all behind."

Or, in the powerful words of Job: "Naked came I out of my mother's womb, and naked shall I return thither: the LORD gave, and the LORD hath taken away; blessed be the name of the LORD" (1:21).

It is interesting to note that in one of the two uses of the verb form of *eusebeia* (*eusebeō*, 'to worship'), Paul reminds the philosophers who had missed the true point of the worship of God, that it is He who "giveth to all life, and breath, and *all things*" (Acts 17:23,25). In his complete dependence upon God, his joyful use of what God gives and his humble submission to deprivation, the man of God is "instructed both to be full and to be hungry, both to abound and to suffer need" (Philippians 4:12). *"And it is certain that we can carry nothing out"* of this world, so he sets his hope upon God who will include amongst the "all things" the life which is to come.

Verse 8: *"And having food and raiment let us be therewith content":* This much God has promised to provide, as we recognise from the Lord's Prayer: all our salvation and all our desire is for the hallowing of the Father's Name, the coming of His Kingdom, the doing of His will. He will:

"Our daily bread supply,
While by Thy word we live."

This verse 8 is rich in "oncers", *diatrophē* and *skepasma* being
literally 'nourishment' and 'covering', which could be shelter as
well as clothing; although by the analogy of Matthew 6:25 the
Authorised Version translation is justified. Most languages have
similar expressions for the basic necessities of life. The Roman
was outlawed by being "cut off from fire and water". Paul's
words, like the Lord's own teaching about the Father, are Old
Testament based, connected closely with the covenant name of
"the LORD your God is God of gods, and Lord of lords, a great
God, a mighty, and a terrible, which regardeth not persons, nor
taketh reward: he doth execute the judgment of the fatherless and
widow, and loveth the stranger, in giving him *food and raiment*"
(Deuteronomy 10:17-18). The whole section, about older people,
widows, elders, bondservants and Timothy's impartiality is based
upon the Apostle's thoughts as enriched by the Word of God.

6:9-10—Advice for the Rich

Verse 9: *"But they that will be rich fall into temptation":* There is no
condemnation here of the rich, and certainly not of those who
recognise that God has blessed them. We have good cause to be
grateful for all those in our community who recognise and share
their blessings, and upon whom, if the tale could be told, many
of our ecclesias and organisations depend to an extent undreamed
of by most of us. Paul's emphasis is upon *will*, the same word as
in *"I will* therefore" (2:8; 5:14). It is a natural development of
thought to go from the cupidity of the other-teachers of Ephesus
to the question of the single-minded pursuit of wealth for its own
sake. There is an interesting parallel with the Lord's Prayer, in
that "Give us this day our daily bread" is there too followed by
"And lead us not into temptation", which includes thoughts not
necessarily limited to those temptations arising from discontent
with mere daily bread. Is Paul also making a play upon the words
peirasmos ('temptation') and *prosimos* ('gain')?

"Accursed hunger for gold," cried a pagan poet, "to what do
you not compel our mortal hearts?" The answer throughout the
ages has always been "to injustice, extortion, deceit, theft and
even murder: at the least to the worship of mammon and to
covetousness". To continue with this verse, men *"fall"* and are

"snared" as the evil effects of their conduct come suddenly upon them. The insatiable desires (*"lusts"*) are *"many"* and *"foolish"* (compare "Thou fool", said to the rich man in Luke 12:20) and *"hurtful"*. Another New Testament "oncer", *blaberos* really means 'deadly'.

Verse 10: *"For the love of money is the root of all evil"*: This notoriously misquoted saying (*"Money* is the root of all evil") takes up the preceding thoughts in a more direct if less picturesque form. *Philarguria,* 'love of silver', is a "oncer", but the adjective is translated "covetous" in both Luke 16:14 and 2 Timothy 3:2. The spiritual effects of covetousness are clearly seen in the Gospel passage, since it led the Pharisees to deride the Lord's teaching about faithful stewardship and single-minded worship of God, for *philarguria* can deflect a man. The command "Thou shalt not covet" is important enough to be listed amongst the Ten Commandments, the basic principles of keeping covenant with God. Jude is also explicit on the relationship between covetousness, rebellion, leading a faction and even murder, when he links together "the way of Cain ... the error of Balaam ... the gainsaying of Core" (verse 11).

"They have erred from the faith": Taking up the thought in chapter 1 that the other-teachers have "swerved, have turned aside", Paul says that those who follow the way of covetousness (*followed after*) have taken a wrong turning in their life in the Truth, or have been *seduced* by their pursuit as even the elect would be (if that were not a contradiction in terms!) by following false Christs and false prophets: note the link with the "last days" in both Mark 13:22 and 2 Timothy 3:2.

"Have pierced themselves through with many sorrows": "Pierced" (a "oncer") as with thorns and briers, the wanderer from the path of a good conscience suffers the pangs of remorse, a "continual" sorrow akin to Paul's in Romans 9:2 for a different cause. The whole passage, unique in many of its forms of expression though dealing with a common Scriptural theme, has a message for the ecclesias today. Even a doctrinal orthodoxy has no value if it is not expressed in dedicated living. The whole spirit of our age, as never before, is given over to "reaching after more" (or *pleonexia,* the word for "covetousness"); the pursuit of wealth and the acquisition of it make greater and greater inroads upon family

and ecclesial life. People labour to "make ends meet"' where ends are no longer food and raiment but "cieled houses" and every provision for leisure and enjoyment.

6:11-14—Positive Qualities of the Man of God

Verse 11: *"But thou, O man of God, flee these things":* There can scarcely be a more emphatic opening to the sentence in which Paul contrasts the behaviour of the other-teachers with what Timothy's own attitude should be. It has been suggested that Timothy needed personally the warning against covetousness which immediately precedes this verse. That he was neither perfect nor infallible, and that he needed all the exhortation he could get, goes without saying. It is difficult to believe, however, that Paul had so far mistaken his "own son in the faith" (1:2), of whom he had written, "Ye know the proof of him, that, as a son with the father, he hath served with me in the gospel" (Philippians 2:20-22), as to place him in danger to which he was liable to succumb. For a consideration of the expression "Man of God", see Essay 20, page 209.

True, the hazards of the missionary journeys had been replaced by a settled period in an ecclesia, and faith is stimulated more in adversity than in prosperity, but "supposing that gain is godliness" seems hardly likely to have been Timothy's weak point. "These things" refers much more probably to the whole, subtle propaganda of the other-teachers, which Timothy was to shun, especially in view of their consequences, which were so destructive of all that he had been commissioned to achieve in the life of the ecclesia at Ephesus. "Flee" is expressive: "these things" were to be escaped from as from any other dangerous situation, such as "youthful lusts" for example (2 Timothy 2:22).

"And follow after righteousness, godliness, faith, love, patience, meekness": The clause is parallel to that in 2 Timothy 2:22; there also "flee" is balanced by "pursue"—the positive action ensures that the avoidance of evil does not create a spiritual vacuum into which "seven unclean spirits worse than the first" can enter. The vigorous nature of the pursuit is apparent when we realise that the word is also the usual one for "persecute".

To acquire spiritual qualities demands all our energies, an idea common enough in the New Testament, especially in Paul; this is one more pointer to the fact that he was the author of the Pastoral Epistles. For example, *"Follow after* the things which make for peace, and the things wherewith one may edify another"* (Romans 14:19). *"Follow after* charity, and desire spiritual gifts"* (1 Corinthians 14:1). "I *follow after,* if I may apprehend that for which also I am apprehended of Christ Jesus ... I *press toward* the mark for the prize of the high calling" (Philippians 3:12,14). "Ever *follow* that which is good, both among yourselves, and to all men" (1 Thessalonians 5:15). There was good Old Testament precedent for the use of the phrase, for example in Proverbs 15:9—"The way of the wicked is an abomination unto the LORD: but he loveth him that *followeth after* righteousness."

The qualities to be pursued are set before us in pairs: of "righteousness" and "godliness", the second is our word *eusebeia,* so frequent in these Letters for the devout worship of the ecclesia as a whole and of its members in particular (see page 58). The other is common in Paul's writings, above all in the Letter to the Romans, and is especially appropriate here, since its root meaning is 'justice' or 'impartiality'. Such conduct is required of a man of God like Timothy in his relations with the community, since he speaks for God to them. He will find a similar response in "all them that call upon the Lord out of a pure heart" (2 Timothy 2:22).

The Fruit of the Spirit

"Faith" and "love" are "fruit of the Spirit" (Galatians 5:22), two of the three abiding things which are not natural to man but have to be cultivated. They are linked with patience in Titus 2:2 and 1 Thessalonians 1:3. "Patience" (or "steadfastness") and "meekness" (or "gentleness") are equally necessary qualities for a defender of the faith, since they indicate that he has a confidence in God, constancy under trial of all sorts, and the capacity to endure rebuff, attack and ingratitude without personal rancour or bitterness. Patience "worketh experience", and so can be described as the essential quality for the exercise of all the other moral virtues. "For ye have need of patience, that, after ye have done the will of God, ye might receive the promise" (Hebrews 10:36). So "let patience have her perfect work, that ye may be perfect and entire, wanting nothing" (James 1:4).

The word for "meekness" is a "oncer"; it is a synonym for another word for meekness in 2 Timothy 2:25, which "the servant of the Lord" must possess if he is to exercise his duty to rebuke and instruct. Otherwise he will raise his voice and engage in *logomachiai* ('word-battles') like the other-teachers. No one ever convinced a gainsayer by shouting at him or storming out of a meeting. "Take my yoke upon you, and learn of me; for I am *meek* and lowly in heart" (Matthew 11:29). "Behold my servant, whom I have chosen; my beloved, in whom my soul is well pleased: I will put my spirit upon him . . . He shall not strive, nor cry; neither shall any man hear his voice in the streets" (Matthew 12:17-19; Isaiah 42:1-2).

Verse 12: *"Fight the good fight of faith":* We are in the realm not of the military contest but of the athletic. The reader is referred to Essay 14 on "The Discipline of the Man of God" (see page 138) for a discussion of the background to the "exercise thyself rather unto godliness" of 1 Timothy 4:7, a metaphor taken from the *gymnasium*. For the purpose of providing background to the present verse, we turn to the more sporting metaphor of *agōnizesthai*, 'to contend or strive in the athletic games': see Essay 21, "Paul and the Spiritual Athlete", page 210 .

"Lay hold on eternal life": There can be only one justification for dealing in Greek or Hebrew words and tenses, and that is for the sake of greater clarity and understanding. The two imperative verbs (commands) in this verse have different tenses in Greek and conveyed distinctive meanings to Timothy. "Fight" (*agōnizou*) is present tense, and indicates that the struggle would be long, even continuous. "Lay hold", however, an aorist command, implies a once-for-all action. Timothy is therefore to reach out for the crown. It is not immortality that is in question: that is ultimately the gift of God. It is more John's concept of eternal life, the new life which begins at baptism, or when those dead in trespasses and sins have been *quickened* through God's grace (Ephesians 2:1-7).

The actual crown, of course, or as its name in English suggests, the final consummation, will be bestowed when we shall be changed into immortality and incorruptibility. Until then we have to hold fast what we have, "that no man take (deprive us of) our crown" (see Revelation 2:10; 3:11).

There is no contradiction between this and Paul's teaching elsewhere. In Romans 6:22 he speaks of "your fruit unto holiness, and *the end* everlasting life"; in Galatians 6:8 everlasting life is something to be reaped eventually. Yet he also speaks of "newness of life" as something in which we must walk now (Romans 6:4), or as the life of the risen Lord which must be made manifest in our mortal flesh (2 Corinthians 4:10-11); Christ is already our life, and when he "shall appear, then shall ye also appear with him in glory" (Colossians 3:1-3). We could say therefore that Timothy had to lay hold upon the eternal life which he would be granted in its fulness as a reward of faithful following.

"Whereunto thou art also called": Here is one good reason why Timothy should strive to attain to eternal life: he had been "called" to it. He who hath saved us hath also *"called us with an holy calling* ... according to his own purpose and grace ... now made manifest by the appearing of our Saviour Jesus Christ, who hath abolished death, and hath brought life and immortality to light through the gospel" (2 Timothy 1:9-10). Paul was an apostle by the will of God according to the promise of "eternal life, which God that cannot lie, promised before the world began" (Titus 1:2).

There is a second reason why Timothy should lay hold on eternal life: he had already *"professed a good confession before many witnesses".* Much discussion has centred around the precise reference of these words. Was it a brave confession of Christ before some legal authority, as for example when Timothy was imprisoned (Hebrews 13:23)? Or was it when he stood before "the presbytery" who assessed his suitability for the task to which he had been called? The former explanation is considered to have some support from the example of Christ referred to in verse 13, on the assumption that Timothy's profession was being compared with the Lord's own witness to his kingship and ministry when he stood before Pilate.

The best explanation is that Timothy is being reminded of the occasion of his baptism, when he "witnessed a good confession"; that is, professed his faith in the Lord Jesus Christ, his death and resurrection and the forgiveness of sins. For the context is not Timothy's call to the ministry but to eternal life, which surely refers to the occasion of his becoming a disciple. The very use of the word *homologia* for ''confession'' implies ''language agreeing'' to what is happening: ''If thou believest with all thine heart, thou mayest (be baptized)''. This was the occasion above all when Timothy responded to the call to eternal life.

The verb *homologeō,* also in this verse, is common enough in the New Testament, especially in the Gospels, for confessing Christ, and being confessed by him before the Father (Matthew 7:23; 10:32; Luke 12:8; John 1:20; 9:22; 12:42). Its use in Romans 10:9,10 is especially interesting: ''If thou shalt *confess with thy mouth* the Lord Jesus, and shalt believe in thine heart that God hath raised him from the dead, thou shalt be saved. For with the heart man believeth unto righteousness; and with the mouth confession is made unto salvation.''

The noun *homologia*, on the other hand, appears in the verse we are considering, in Hebrews 3:1; 4:14; 10:23 and in 2 Corinthians 9:13 only. In these it clearly bears the meaning we have suggested above—''the obedience of your confession into the gospel of Christ'', ''the High Priest of our profession'', ''let us hold fast the profession of our faith''. The fact that it was frequent in a later epistle like Hebrews suggests that it had by that time become the recognised, almost ''technical'' term, for the public witness, perhaps even ''the interview'', in the presence of the ecclesia (''many witnesses''), before baptism. In which case the use of the adverb *homologoumenōs*, 'without controversy', in 1 Timothy 3:16 becomes even plainer in its meaning. It is ''as we all believe'', as we publicly confess—''God was manifest in the flesh'' (see Essay 13, ''Great is the Mystery of Godliness'', page 116).

Verse 13: *''I give thee charge in the sight of God'':* There can be no more solemn reminder to us as well as to Timothy of the seriousness of the call to eternal life and of the importance of the ecclesia's witness to the ''good confession''. The ecclesia is the earthly witness to that which is done before God in heaven. (It is worth noting, in passing, that for God's children the same is true in the case of marriage: the law of the land demands, and it was evidently the Scriptural custom, that a man and a woman take each other in the presence of witness, but *the Lord is present to witness also*.) So in this last formal exhortation, Paul not only gathers up the whole Epistle but links it with the theme of Timothy's own call and profession.

The sphere of Timothy's activity as he fought the good fight, was at that time Ephesus: his own keeping of the covenant he had made was crucial to the effective carrying out of his duties to that ecclesia. He had been deputed by the Apostle to "*charge* some not to other-teach" (1:3); he was to *charge* and teach the things which would counter the effect of the "old wives' fables" (4:11); and the regulations about elders and widows he was to "*give in charge*" (5:7; verse 21 is a different word); and now he himself was *charged* by the Apostle in the sight of two heavenly witnesses to keep the commandment he had received.

"*Who quickeneth all things*": The particular word for "quicken" (*zoōgoneō*) is applied to God in this verse only. It is used twice more in the New Testament, in the sense of '*preserve* alive', in Luke 17:33 and Acts 7:19. The more usual word, *zoōpoieō*, means literally 'to *make* alive', as in John 5:21; Romans 4:17; 8:11; 1 Corinthians 15:22,36,45; 2 Corinthians 3:6; Galatians 3:21; 1 Peter 3:18, and refers both to the quickening into the new life of the baptized disciple and the resurrection of the dead.

In the Greek Old Testament, Paul's word, *zoōgoneō*, has usually the sense of 'save alive', as in Exodus 1:17,22; Judges 8:10; 1 Samuel 27:9,11 and 2 Kings 7:4. When the term is applied to God, however, it applies equally to the giving of life as to its preservation, and in view of the solemn tone of this passage and its overtones of witness and judgement we may well consider Paul to have in mind a passage from Deuteronomy 32:

> "For the LORD shall judge his people, and repent himself for his servants, when he seeth that their power is gone, and there is none shut up, or left ... See now that I, even I, am he, and there is no god with me: *I kill, and I make alive*; I wound, and I heal: neither is there any that can deliver out of my hand. For I lift up my hand to heaven, and say, I live for ever."
>
> (verses 36,39,40)

At his baptism, after his good profession, Timothy had been quickened into newness of life. The God who quickened him would also preserve him while he fought the good fight of faith and strove to lay hold upon that eternal life to which he had been called. The same God would assess the quality of his discipleship and grant him immortality.

"And before Jesus Christ": There was a second heavenly witness to Timothy's good profession and the manner of his fulfilment of what he had covenanted to do: Jesus Christ, the Author and Perfecter of our faith (Hebrews 12:2). By virtue of his own faithfulness unto death and the redemption through his blood, the Saviour has been appointed judge. It was his example that Timothy was to follow.

"Who before Pontius Pilate witnessed the good confession" (RV): The concept of the Lord Jesus as a witness to God's truth is well established in Scripture, for "in him all the promises of God are yea, and in him Amen" (2 Corinthians 1:20). In the presence of Pontius Pilate he himself made the declaration: "To this end was I born, and for this cause came I into the world, that I should bear witness unto the truth" (John 18:37). The fact that the Lord was on trial for his life gives added significance to the word for "witness", *martureō*: he witnessed unto the death, as did many of his followers, and from this fact has developed the special meaning of the English word "martyr". Christ was "the faithful and true witness" (Revelation 1:5; 3:14) and he appears finally in the Scripture as "he that beareth witness to these things", since by his death he had shown himself worthy to open the sealed book and show unto his servants the things which must shortly come to pass.

"Suffered under Pontius Pilate"

But in what sense is it best to understand the expression "before Pontius Pilate"? *Epi* can mean either 'in the presence of' or 'in the time of' as in Mark 2:26, where *epi Abiathar archierōs* can only mean *"in the days of* Abiathar the high priest". It is true that there is a parallel being drawn between Timothy's oral confession in the presence of witnesses and the Lord's own profession. It is also true that the Lord's oral testimony before Pontius Pilate was that he was the Messiah and was born to witness to the truth that makes men free. As we have seen, the word *homologia*, 'profession', in the New Testament, with the exception of Hebrews 10:23—"profession of our faith", is always used for a profession of faith in the Gospel of the Lord Jesus Christ, as in 2 Corinthians 9:13; Hebrews 3:1; 4:14.

This confession of faith, however, although summed up in the declaration that Jesus is the Christ, the Son of the living God (the latter clause was also implied in the testimony before Pilate in John 19:7,9-11) included the belief that the Lord had suffered for sin, had been raised from the dead and would come again. So the Lord's "good profession" went beyond his oral witness to his Father's commandment and purpose. It comprised the whole of his ministry—"all that Jesus began both *to do* and *to teach*", including his submission to death and his resurrection, "until the day in which he was taken up" (Acts 1:1,2). All this happened *in the time of* Pontius Pilate, and belief in these things subsequently formed the subject of every good profession of the faith.

The more one considers this sequence of verses in 1 Timothy 6:12-16, the stronger becomes the impression that there existed in the early ecclesias a "statement of the faith" to which each new disciple assented as he embraced the hope and accepted the call of Christ. There may even have been a first century precedent for that which in later times became known as "The Apostles' Creed" which referred to Christ as having "suffered under Pontius Pilate".

Verse 14: *"That thou keep the commandment, without spot, without reproach":* It is not possible to determine exactly from the grammar of this phrase whether it is the commandment or Timothy himself that is to be kept pure. The balance of probability is all in favour of the first interpretation, since the final exhortation in verse 20 is to keep the "good deposit" of the faith, and the whole tenor of the epistle is that only through sound teaching and by faith unfeigned can Timothy keep himself unreproachable in conduct, and so influence his brethren.

Again, the sequence of thought demands that "the commandment" be taken as that which was laid upon him at his baptism, rather than the immediate instructions of the earlier verses in this section or even the specific "charge" of the whole letter. "Commandment" in the singular in the New Testament usually, if not invariably, refers to a particular ordinance of God—either one commandment out of the Old Law, for example (Mark 7:8,9; Romans 13:9), or the New (John 13:34; 15:12), or all the Law (Romans 7:8,12,13), or else a revelation (John 12:50), or commission (14:31) which Christ received from his Father.

The Pure Commandment

"The commandment of the Lord is pure" (Psalm 19:8) and must be kept so by all who, like Timothy, professed at the moment of making covenant at their baptism, "All that the LORD hath spoken will we do, and be obedient". The two adjectives in verse 14 are quite explicit. The principal use of *apsilos*, 'without spot', is in its reference to Christ in 1 Peter 1:19, and fits beautifully into the harmony of this section of 1 Timothy. For the Lord's precious blood was "as of a lamb without blemish and *without spot*; who verily was foreordained before the foundation of the world, but was manifest in these last times *for you, who by him do believe in God, that raised him up from the dead, and gave him glory*; that your faith and hope might be in God". So those who await the Lord's coming again in judgement must be "diligent that ye may be found of him in peace, *without spot*, and blameless" (2 Peter 3:14).

True to the pastoral charge given to Timothy is James' declaration that "pure religion and undefiled . . . is this, To visit the fatherless and widows in their affliction (compare 1 Timothy 5:3-16), and to keep himself *unspotted* from the world" (James 1:27). These are the only occurrences of this word in the New Testament, and the only time Paul uses it is in this verse. He does, however, use the expression "not having spot (*splios*)" in his exposition of the mystery of human marriage and the church: for the spotless Lamb of God gave himself for his Bride that he might present her "to himself a glorious church, *not having spot*, or wrinkle, or any such thing; but that it should be holy and without blemish" (Ephesians 5:27). The other word, *anepilēmptos*, 'unrebukeable' or 'without reproach', is one we have already considered in the qualifications for overseers (3:2 and note on page 87.)

The emphasis in verse 14, as it is in James 1:27, is on the word "keep" (*tereō*: see note on 5:22, page 166). In Revelation the accent is on "*keep* those things that are written" (1:3). "And he that overcometh and *keepeth* my works unto the end . . ." (2:26); "hold fast (literally, *keep*) and repent" (3:3); "thou hast . . . *kept* my word . . . because thou hast *kept* the word of my patience, I also will *keep* thee from the hour of temptation" (3:8,10). The saints are they who "*keep* the commandments of God, and hold the testimony of Jesus Christ" (12:17, RV), that watch and *keep* their garments (16:15) and that have the blessedness of those which *keep* the sayings of this book (22:7,9) along with their fellowservants and their brethren the prophets, whose honour it was to receive the word and pass it on intact. For "the faith", "the good confession" and "the commandment" are almost synonyms for the truth as it is in Jesus, of which the ecclesia is the guardian and indeed the stay (1 Timothy 3:15) in this world.

Our passage then stands out as possibly the most vigorous appeal for orthodoxy, in the true Scriptural sense, going far beyond any exhortation about Timothy's personal conduct to a charge to guard the faith once committed to the saints as a sacred trust (see note on verse 20 below). Without it, in its purity, all is lost, since there can be no blameless conduct or irreproachable life in the sight of God, if by other-teaching we "swerve" and "turn aside" from the "end of the commandment . . . (which is) charity out of a pure heart and of a good conscience, and of faith unfeigned" (1:5,6).

The Judgement of the Last Day

"Until the appearing of our Lord Jesus Christ": The labour and the strife are not that of one day: they are until the coming of the Lord, the consummation of "our faith which is our hope in God". The expression is also a reminder that the Lord will judge his servants "at his appearing and his kingdom" (see Essay 22, page 213). It is clearly stated in Scripture that the judgement committed by the Father to the Son will be exercised at the last day: there is no room for the concept that the responsible are in some sense judged during their lifetime and so need not appear before the dread tribunal of Christ. It may well be that the circumstances of their life, as was the case with Adam, reflect the consequences of their actions; but as with Adam there is to be a formal process of assessment which brings home to them the results of their life lived "in the body", and the sentence of condemnation or acquittal pronounced. The following passages all emphasise this future aspect of judgement:

"It shall be more tolerable . . . *in the day of judgment.*"
(Matthew 10:15; also 11:22,24; Mark 6:11)

"For the Son of man shall come in *the glory of his Father* with his angels; and *then* shall he reward every man according to his works."
(Matthew 16:27)

195

"The word that I have spoken, the same shall judge him *in the last day.*" (John 12:48)

"It is he who was *ordained of God to be the Judge* of quick and dead." (Acts 10:42)

"*He hath appointed a day,* in the which he will judge the world in righteousness." (Acts 17:31)

"*In the day* when God shall judge the secrets of men by Jesus Christ." (Romans 2:16)

"The Lord Jesus Christ, who shall judge the quick and the dead *at his appearing and his kingdom.*" (2 Timothy 4:1)

"Who shall give account to him that is ready to judge the quick and the dead." (1 Peter 4:5)

"The Lord knoweth how . . . to reserve the unjust unto the *day of judgment.*" (2 Peter 2:9; also 3:7)

The word "appearing", *epiphania*, is almost exclusive to the Pastoral Epistles: the exceptions are in Luke 1:79—"to give light", Acts 27:20 and 2 Thessalonians 2:8. The absence of the more usual New Testament word *parousia* has been counted as important evidence against the genuineness of these Letters, which have been attributed to the Second Century.

Verses 15,16: *"Which in his times he shall shew":* If Paul gave the Thessalonians the impression, in one of his earliest letters, that the coming of the Lord was imminent, he clearly corrected it in the Second Letter. There he leaves indefinite the time when God will reveal on earth the glory and power of the Risen Lord; it will be in His *own* time, as the Lord had said to his disciples prior to his ascension: the times and the seasons the Father "hath put in his own power" (Acts 1:7); see also note 2:6 (page 64) and Essay 40, "In Due Times" (page 369).

"Who is the blessed and only Potentate . . . to whom be honour and power everlasting": The Apostle's contemplation of the Lord's first coming into the world to save sinners had led him to burst forth in a hymn of praise to "the King eternal, immortal, invisible, the only wise God" who is in very truth our Saviour (1:17). The meditation on the Second Coming moves him likewise to pen a doxology, in which the same ideas are more fully expressed (6:15-16), see Essay 23, "A Hymn of Praise", page 215.

6:17-19— Advice to the Rich

Verse 17: *"Charge them that are rich in this world"*: There are many remarkable features in this passage. First it seems a great anti-climax to the lofty theme set forth in the preceding doxology, so much so that some have seen the hymn of praise as an inter-polation or a misplacement in the text. They point out that the "charge" takes up the theme of verses 9 onwards, leading to positive recommendations to balance the negative warning of verse 10 particularly. It is plain, however, that the anti-climax is intentional. Nothing can throw into sharper relief the folly of trusting in the wealth of this world, nor of being haughty or puffed up by riches, than to see such behaviour against the revela-tion of that which is eternal and glorious in the world to come: it is both a solemn warning and a forceful exhortation.

Secondly, this is the only time Paul uses the word *plousios*, 'rich', in its proper sense of wealthy (the word in verse 9 is a verb, as in verse 18). His other uses refer to the riches of Christ, which certainly did not consist of this world's goods (2 Corinthians 8:9), and the richness of God's mercy (Ephesians 2:4). There is thus a fine play upon words between "the rich", with their "uncertain riches", and that which God gives men "richly to enjoy" which stimulates them to be "rich in good works".

Apparently preoccupation with wealth constituted a significant problem in the Ephesian ecclesia, since Paul found it necessary to be so emphatic on the subject, though his exhortation is to avoid being ensnared by riches rather than against the possession of them. This is consistent with his theme throughout the Epistle, that unsound teaching with all its dire consequences can be related to covetousness—"supposing that gain is godliness"—a vice from which the leaders of an ecclesia must be entirely free (1 Timothy 3:3,8; 6:3-6; see also 2 Timothy 4:3-4; 1 Peter 5:2 and especially Titus 1:7,11; page 364).

"In this world" is also an interesting phrase, meaning literally 'in the age now', and it is distinctive in these Letters. Paul's more usual expression is literally "in *this* world (age)", as in Romans 12:2, 1 Corinthians 2:6, Ephesians 1:21 and other places. Here it contrasts with that which is to be revealed "in his times" (verse 15). The expression occurs also in 2 Timothy 4:10 ("Demas ... loved the *world of now*") and Titus 2:12-13, where the thought is

197

similarly connected with "the glorious appearing of the great God and our Saviour Jesus Christ".

"That they be not highminded": In Romans 12:16 Paul uses the expression *"Mind* not *high* things", but here as in Romans 11:20, "Be not *highminded"*, he has made a single verb out of the two elements, rather like his use of the word "other-teach" for "teach other than what is sound". "Highmindedness" for Paul corresponds to John's *"pride* of life" or *"boasting"* (1 John 2:16) which is linked with covetousness in 2 Timothy 3:2. The thought of our verse 17 comes from Jeremiah 9:23-24: "Thus saith the LORD, Let not the wise man glory in his wisdom, neither let the mighty man glory in his might, let not the rich man glory in his riches; but let him that glorieth glory in this, that he understandeth and knoweth me." Pride of purse, therefore, is sinful in God's sight.

"Nor have their hope set on the uncertainty of riches", as the Revised Version has it, is much more forceful and literal a translation, and echoes the sentiment of Proverbs 23:4,5: "Weary not thyself to be rich: cease from thine own wisdom. Wilt thou set thine eyes upon that which is not? for riches certainly make themselves wings, like an eagle that flieth toward heaven" (Revised Version). Essay 24, page 220, considers "The Uncertainty of Riches".

"(God) giveth us richly all things to enjoy": As already remarked in the note on 4:3-5 (pages 123-125), asceticism for its own sake plays no part in the worship of God. In our present passage the warning is against *confidence* in wealth, not the *enjoyment* of it. On the contrary, riches amongst other things are given by God *especially to be enjoyed,* and the expression must be given its full force. The word for "enjoy" is a strong one, used again only in Hebrews 11:25, where its sense of wrongful enjoyment comes only from its association with "the pleasures of sin": in Timothy it is more akin to the "whatsoever thy soul lusteth after" of Deuteronomy 14:26, as Israel ate, drank and rejoiced *before the Lord.* God gives richly, and this is one of the signs that He is a living God, as Paul proclaimed at Lystra:

"Ye should turn ... unto the living God which made heaven, and earth, and the sea, and all things that are therein ... he left not himself without witness, in that he did good, and gave

us rain from heaven, and fruitful seasons, filling our hearts
with *food and gladness.*" (Acts 14:15-17)

Thus did the Apostle strike the balance between the excesses of
the other-teachers in the direction of either immorality or
asceticism by defining the proper use of all God's gifts. The
thought of the Father's generosity leads on to an exposition of the
wealthy man's duty if he is to display true godliness.

Verse 18: *"That they do good, that they be rich in good works":* The
verse is full of "oncers" of which *agathoergeō,* 'do good', is one.
It replaces the *agathopoieō* of Acts 14 above, and if there is any
difference in meaning intended, it is probably that while God is
the source of all good, the rich should be doers of good works, or
separate acts of kindness, as ministers of His good. In any case,
the disciple's life and conduct are a conscious response to what
the Father has revealed Himself to be. He is open-handed and
generous, and so must His children be.

Israel were constantly reminded that as the Lord their God had
shown His care for the fatherless and the widow, the stranger and
the bondman, they would keep His Law by doing the same. As
we have already seen (2:10; 5:10 and notes on page 72, also Titus
2:14; 3:1,8), the Pastoral Epistles lay great stress upon the practical expression of faith in God by their constant exhortation that
men should be in effect "followers (Greek, *imitators*) of God as
dear children" (Ephesians 5:1).

"Ready to distribute, willing to communicate": These phrases contain two "oncers", and it is difficult to distinguish between their
meanings; *koinōnikos,* the second of them, seems to have a wider
meaning than *eumetadotos,* which is concerned with the giving or
sharing of worldly goods: *communicate* suggests a kind heart as well
as a generous hand, and all the sympathy and feeling that make
up true fellowship. *Koinōnia,* or 'fellowship', is directly connected
with good works in Hebrews 13:16—"But to do good and to communicate forget not: for with such sacrifices God is well-pleased."

Verse 19: *"Laying up in store for themselves a good foundation against
the time to come":* From the strictly literary point of view we seem
to have a mixed metaphor here, especially when it is realised that
"laying up in store" is literally "laying up as treasure". The
idea of "treasure in heaven" is expounded by the Lord himself,

particularly in Matthew 6:19-21. In Luke 18:22 also, the distribution of goods to the poor provides a treasure in heaven; while Luke 16:11, the Parable of the Unjust Steward, treats of the right use of money in view of rewards to come. Incidentally, verse 12 of this passage, "that *which is your own*", illustrates the Apostle's use of *for themselves* in the verse we are considering: the heavenly riches become personal property, "reserved in heaven", of those who disposed of their earthly wealth aright.

But the apparent mixed metaphor is really a compression of thought. For the Lord's teaching in the Sermon on the Mount ends with the assurance that those who have both heard and done what he said, including the teaching about treasure in heaven, will be found in *the time to come* to have laid a sure foundation. Further, *themelion*, 'a foundation', can also be the word for a *fund*, and a "good foundation" is therefore an assurance against a banking failure: so the metaphor is not so mixed as it appears.

"That they may lay hold on eternal life": For the expression see the note on verse 12 (page 188). The nature of the true riches is thus defined. They are nothing less than eternal life—not just immortality as a gift from Him "who only hath immortality", but the very fulness of the life of God, a *quality* of life and not merely an expression of its *duration*.

6:20-21—The Final Exhortation

The last two verses have been described as "the most perfect conclusion imaginable for this Epistle", since they contain, in effect, the two main themes of the letter which are closely connected with each other:

1. An exhortation to Timothy to guard carefully the faith entrusted to him;
2. An exhortation to be vigilant against the other-teaching which was then developing and threatening the life of the ecclesia.

The very conciseness of these exhortations betrays the anxiety which Paul has already expressed several times with respect to the difficulties and dangers he foresaw for the future. The truth of the Gospel had been established and the ecclesias organised: all that was left to do was remain faithful in the face of all who would oppose themselves. The final wish (verse 21) commits all such faithful continuance into the hands of a gracious God.

Verse 20: *"O Timothy, keep that which is committed to thy trust"*:
As in 1:18 the Apostle calls upon Timothy by name, not only as
an expression of tender affection but as an urgent exhortation to
which (as in 6:1) the "O" gives added point. The "charge" is
now committed firmly to the younger man, who is to take the
oversight of the ecclesia, "the pillar and ground of the truth", in
the capital city of the province of Asia, the very seat of art, culture
and pagan worship. In a single word (in the Greek), employed for
the very first time by him, Paul "sums up all his feelings, the final
prayer and all the very spirit of his letter" (Spicq, *Les Epîtres
Pastorales*): *"Guard the deposit."* See Essay 25, page 221.

What had been committed to Timothy's trust? There was
first that which is committed to all disciples, ourselves included,
at baptism: it is to keep the "commandment without spot,
unrebukeable, until the appearing of our Lord Jesus" (verse 14).
But more suited both to the immediate context and to the Letter
as a whole, is that the good deposit is here all that is contained
in this Epistle, of which not only Timothy but the whole church
is the true guardian: the wholesome doctrine, the truth about
salvation, "the mystery of godliness". Timothy's special charge
is that he will preserve all this in the special conditions of Ephesus,
according to the specific instructions he has been given.

For Timothy, as for us all, emphasis is upon patient continuance, the aorist imperative of the verb yielding the sense of
"Guard to the very end". The "deposit" of the faith has been
committed to us, and we are provisional keepers of a treasure
which is not our own. We must keep it with scrupulous care,
adding nothing to it and taking nothing away, and with a loyalty
rendered even more necessary as pressures to degrade or corrupt
it increase.

"Avoiding profane and vain babblings": The vigilance in practical
form consists in turning away from discussions devoid of spiritual
content, or even sense. "Vain babblings" is literally "empty
sounds, or voices", expressed in one word, *kenophōnia*. The other-
teachers were alas! not actually voiceless but vociferous: for all
that they *said nothing*. For *bebēlos*, meaning 'profane', see on 1:7,
page 24. The whole expression is repeated in 2 Timothy 2:16, in
the exhortation about "rightly dividing the word of truth" as the
positive counter to the destructive teaching which would "eat

as doth a canker''. Of the word for ''turning aside'' we have already written, when it appeared in the opening verses, and it is worth re-reading the section on ''Missing the Mark'' (page 21). Timothy was as forcefully to *avoid* or ''turn aside'' from the other-teachers as they had from the sound doctrine.

''And oppositions of science falsely so called'': The adjective ''profane'' qualifies these *antithesēs* also. The Revised Version is better here, in translating as ''the *knowledge* which is falsely so called'', since *gnōsis* is not ''science'' in the modern sense, nor is it strictly philosophy either. The word *gnōsis*, which is the ordinary word for 'knowledge', became attached later to the Gnostic heresy, whose adherents claimed a special insight by virtue of their superior knowledge and philosophical skill. Undoubtedly the tendencies were beginning to manifest themselves at this time, as these Letters and Colossians and the Epistles of John give evidence. Gnosticism as a developed heresy, however, was related more to the early second century than the first, and we do better to limit the meaning of *gnōsis* in verse 20 to the immediate context of the Epistle. See also Essay 26, ''Knowledge'', page 223.

Verse 21: *''(This knowledge) some professing have erred concerning the faith''*: So the Epistle comes almost full circle with the use of the word ''erred'' as in 1:6 (and 2 Timothy 2:18). The other-teachers ''missed the mark'' completely in all that concerned the faith, for want of true understanding and sound method. By exalting their speculations and methods of reasoning into a system of teaching, or doctrine, they had undermined their own faith and were threatening the healthy life of the community.

The lessons for ourselves, in both positive and negative form, are obvious. Upon most of them we have dwelt when considering the Epistle in its detail—matters of faith, methods of organisation. It is worth reminding ourselves once more, however, of the dangers of imbalance even in dealing with Scripture and the use of our own jargon. Perhaps we can justifiably claim to be clear in this matter as far as the first two definitions of jargon according to the *Concise Oxford Dictionary* are concerned: 'Unintelligible words, gibberish; barbarous or debased language.' But when it comes to controversial non-Scriptural phrases, or even to the ''shorthand'' terminology in which we have frequently summarised or discussed our faith, we have often come close to the third definition of a 'mode of speech full of unfamiliar terms'.

For the faith, though conveniently expressed in propositions, can never be reduced to a skeleton with no spirit in it; and brethren have been kept apart more by the traditional phrase than by the plain discussion of the Scriptural meaning we think is attached to it. The "good deposit" committed to our trust is that which was committed to Paul and Timothy—"faithful men able to teach others also". It was "the words of the faith" and not any particular traditional phraseology.

"Grace be with you. Amen": With this prayer the Letter does indeed come full circle. "Grace" opened the greeting (1:2) and "grace" is the concluding wish. The ordinary conclusion of a private letter of the period was "Farewell" (Acts 15:29), but all Paul's letters end with the word "grace", with or without the name of the Lord attached. This was no doubt "the salutation of Paul with mine own hand, which is the token in every epistle: so I write" (2 Thessalonians 3:17). It is possible that the Revised Version's use of the plural "you" is correct, and that the final blessing was for all the ecclesia. Certainly Paul has them in his heart. The versions disagree as to whether the "Amen" is in the original, but who, on reading the Letter and taking its message, so necessary, so urgent, so practical, could refrain from saying *Amen* in his own heart?

ESSAY 18

Masters and Slaves in the Ancient World

SLAVES ("servants" in 1 Timothy 6:1), sometimes referred to by the Greeks as "bodies" (see Revelation 18:13 margin) and "live possessions", had no civil or religious rights whatsoever and were debarred from participation in the city's assemblies for public worship. The expression "under the yoke" implies a status, sometimes an actual function, similar to that of beasts of burden, the yoke-animals, over whom the power of the master was absolute.

Men became slaves as prisoners of war, as men condemned for crimes committed, after being kidnapped or when sold for their debts, or even when sold in infancy by their parents. In addition they could be born into slavery or, ultimate degradation, they might actually be the slaves of a slave. By no means all were desperadoes or unintelligent. In Roman society physicians, schoolmasters, poets and theatrical producers were often Greek slaves. They could be forced into hard labour, chained, beaten and branded: a "three-letter man" had the letters FUR (thief) branded on his forehead. The penalty for a recaptured runaway was usually death, often by crucifixion.

Aspects of this system are reflected in the pages of the Old Testament; the more brutal aspects of it were practised in the heathen world and the higher the degree of "civilisation" the more refined the cruelty, a tendency also exemplified in the world of the first century. The Law of Moses sought to transform the system by its legislation, which included the commandment that the Israelites should treat their slaves with the compassion which the LORD had shown to them (see Deuteronomy 5:14,15 and elsewhere).

But what of the system in the society where master was to slave and slave to master as "the brother for whom Christ died"? Where there was "neither bond nor free" and the very sign of their fellowship was to partake of one cup and one loaf at the same table? The problem was especially acute in Ephesus, in the very area where the word *doulos* ('bondservant') had come into the Greek language (it is unknown in Homer), and where the slaves in the ecclesia as in the city formed a large proportion of the population.

A Radical Reform

One answer would have been to overthrow the system altogether which, if the Christian Gospel had in fact been concerned with the existing social order, with the bodies rather than the souls of men, it should logically have done. Instead it envisaged a more radical reform than any revolution at that time could have produced, a redemption not from bondage to any overlord: the promise of God was nothing less than a liberation from sin, a redemption from death, and a new order of society that could only be compared to a new heaven and a new earth.

Surely within the ecclesia, however, since it was a reflection in miniature of the coming Kingdom of which the principles were already at work in the young community, all was different? Different, indeed. And therefore there was no longer any need to maintain the old distinctions between master and man? There were new rights, new privileges, in which deference and respect were no longer necessary? Such an attitude could only arise from a complete failure of spiritual understanding, and may well have been one of the by-products of the other-teaching in Ephesus, although the Cretan ecclesias may not have been entirely unaffected.

For it is noteworthy that in the Pastoral Epistles there is no exhortation for masters, but a two-fold one for slaves only: for those who had non-believing masters and for those whose masters were also brethren. That Paul was concerned for slaves cannot be in doubt. The whole Letter to Philemon is a plea for compassion and a recognition of the brotherly relationship on the part of the master of a runaway. It is a piece of delicate, understanding exposition of spiritual considerations in a human situation, which took account of all the master's rights and the proprieties of the case, and breathed a spirit of trust which Onesimus himself must also have caught when he yielded to the Apostle's command to throw himself on his master's mercy.

In Ephesians 5 and Colossians 3 the appeal to masters is on the basis of "knowing that your Master is also in heaven". Believing masters were Christ's slaves, or bondservants, a title in which the Apostle himself rejoiced (Romans 1:1; 1 Corinthians 7:22; Galatians 1:10; Philippians 1:1; Titus 1:1; the last is a significant salutation—see page 352); and the exercise of their own lordship should be consistent with that of Christ over them, "forbearing threatening", giving unto their servants "that which is just and equal". For slaves, the exercise of their daily duties in humility and obedience was their reasonable service. Their pattern was the one who took upon himself the form of a slave, girding himself with humility. In fact they served Christ by serving their masters and their attitude to them was considered to be their attitude to him. Thus they could even "adorn the doctrine of God our Saviour in all things", since this exemplary behaviour could only be the fruit of a higher obedience: it was spiritual not carnal.

It would be carnal, however, to exploit one's freedom, to insist upon rights to the abandonment of duties, a spirit which it has sadly to be confessed is not entirely lacking in some of the twentieth century ecclesias either. In 1 Timothy 6:1-2 (see pages 175-177) we are exhorted, or commanded, by Paul in unmistakable terms.

ESSAY 19

"O Lord, our Lord, how excellent
is thy name"

THE word *despotēs* in the New Testament, when applied to God
or Christ, is the equivalent of *Adon* in the Old. It carries the idea
of complete sovereignty, in the case of God because He is the
Creator and Sustainer, and therefore those to whom He has given
"life, and breath, and all things . . . live, and move, and have
(their) being" entirely in Him (Acts 17:25,28). The title is given
to Christ by the Father by virtue of the function he exercises in
the Father's Name. In His special relationship with the people He
redeemed, God was known by the Name of *Yahweh*, He who
would be their God in mercy, compassion and judgement, and in
final redemption in Christ.

The name and the title together (spelled out in English versions
as Lord GOD) appear together very rarely, and then usually in
invocations, when in full recognition of Divine sovereignty and
absolute authority, appeal is made to His covenant-love for
forgiveness or favour. Moses, for example, twice addresses prayer
to *Adonai Yahweh* (Deuteronomy 3:24 and 9:26) and David uses
the same form of address, in awe, at the terms of the covenant
(2 Samuel 7:18,19). Jeremiah 32:17ff is particularly expressive:
"Ah Lord GOD! behold, thou hast made the heaven and the
earth by thy great power and stretched out arm . . . Thou shewest
loving kindness unto thousands, and recompensest the iniquity of
the fathers . . . the Great, the Mighty God, the LORD of hosts is
his name, great in counsel, and mighty in work."

The title *Adon* is alluded to by the Lord Jesus in his reference
to Psalm 8, "O *Yahweh* our *Adon*", in Matthew 11:25: "I thank

thee, O *Father, Lord of heaven and earth*". (The sequence of thought here, culminating in "Take *my yoke* upon you", should not be ignored.) The title is translated into the Greek *despotēs* in certain passages in which complete sovereignty or ownership is expressed. Simeon says, "*Despotēs*, now lettest thou *thy servant* depart in peace, according to thy word" (Luke 2:29), although there is nothing of tyranny or servility in the relationship between the Lord and his servant.

In Acts 4:24-30 the disciples, having suffered at the hands of the kings and rulers of the earth, express their complete confidence in their true *Despotēs* who is "God, which hast made heaven, and earth, and the sea, and all that in them is", who spake by the mouth of his servant (*pais*) David about his holy child (*pais*, 'servant') Jesus, "for to do whatsoever thy hand and thy counsel determined before to be done".

The occurrences in the Pastoral Epistles are in 1 Timothy 6:1; 2 Timothy 2:21 and Titus 2:9. In 2 Peter 2:1 the *Despotēs* is he "that bought them", that is, their Redeemer and Saviour as well as their possessor in both body and soul. The saints who suffered death at the hands of the ruling powers of the earth "for the word of God, and for the testimony" (Revelation 1:9) which they held, called upon their own "*Despotēs*, holy and true" (Revelation 6:10) to judge and avenge their blood. For overlordship has always implied responsibility in God's society ("to rule" is 'to feed' in Hebrew) and though the time appointed was long, God's servants did not appeal to Him in vain. For a more extended treatment of the theme, see the author's *The Name that is Above Every Name*, published by The Christadelphian Office, 1983.

ESSAY 20

The Man of God

THE title *"man of God"* occurs only in 1 Timothy 6:11 and in 2 Timothy 3:17. Its use is sufficient indication that far from this being a purely private and personal section of the letter upon which we have now entered, it is still part of the authoritative document which Timothy is to use in his ecclesial task. In the Old Testament, "man of God" is the regular expression for a prophet, a leader or anyone in God's service, and it was applied here to Timothy deliberately. Moses was the "man of God" to Israel as their prophet, lawgiver, mediator and bestower of blessings (Deuteronomy 33:1; Joshua 14:6). So also were David, in his capacity as organiser of the Temple music (2 Chronicles 8:14; Nehemiah 12:24,36), and Samuel as seer or prophet of God (1 Samuel 9:6-10). Both Elijah and Elisha were so addressed (1 Kings 17:18; 2 Kings 4:7) and the title was granted to more obscure or even anonymous men who had a message from the LORD for the leaders, for the people, or even for a prophet himself (1 Samuel 2:27; 1 Kings 12:22; 13:1; Jeremiah 35:4).

While we accept, of course, that all can profit and be "throughly furnished unto all good works" by diligent attention to the inspired Scriptures, the context of 2 Timothy 3:17 makes it clear that it is in the discharge of the responsibility laid upon him by Paul, that Timothy is to show himself the "man of God". He must teach, reprove, correct and instruct in righteousness as well as accept the discipline for himself: for all this the Scriptures he had known from his youth were essential. We should bear in mind this emphasis on the authority of Scripture and its all-sufficiency as we prayerfully re-examine our own ecclesial affairs and the quality of our leadership.

ESSAY 21

Paul and the Spiritual Athlete

IT is clear that success in sport, particularly in athletics, depended as much in the Ancient World as in the modern upon the rigorous training and preparation of the athlete. Before professionalism ruined the Greek ideal as it has the present-day sporting scene, the honour and glory of winning the *stephanos*, or 'crown', were considered more than ample reward for the concentrated effort of preparation which is in the modern jargon known as the "dedication" of the sportsman. It is true that more material advantages might have been offered by the city which welcomed home its victor—tax concessions, citizen's privileges, perhaps even a pension. But the principal prize was renown, symbolised by the coronal wreath of leaves, the composition of which varied according to which of the four great games had seen the victory. At Corinth the Isthmian Games attracted the crowds from all over Greece, while the greatest festival of all was the Olympian, in honour of Zeus.

The "race for eternal life" is a well-understood figure, elaborated by Paul in 1 Corinthians 9:24-25—"Know ye not that they which run in a race run all, but one receiveth the prize. So run that ye may obtain. And every man that striveth for the mastery (RV, in the games, or the *agōna*) is temperate in all things. Now they do it to obtain a corruptible crown, but we an incorruptible." There is powerful exhortation here: the rewards for faithful striving are a "crown of rejoicing" (1 Thessalonians 2:19), a "crown of righteousness" (2 Timothy 4:8), a "crown of life" (James 1:12) and a "crown of glory" (1 Peter 5:4)—not in fact four different crowns but one, the one that "fadeth not away".

If men will so "dedicate" themselves that they eschew the pleasures of life and its society throughout their period of training for a reward of leaves, which begin to fade as soon as they are cut from the tree, what ought to be the discipline of the spiritual athlete who hopes to join the throng before the throne of God, and cast his golden *stephanos* down in honour of the greatest of God's Victors (Revelation 4:4-11)?

"I therefore run, not as uncertainly; so box I (changing the figure), not as a 'shadow-boxer': but I keep under my body, and bring it into subjection: lest by any means, when I have preached to others ('heralded', like the trumpeter who summons competitors to the contests), I myself should not stand up to the test" (1 Corinthians 9:26-27, freely rendered). "And if also a man contend in the games, he is not crowned except he have contended lawfully" (that is, according to the rules: 2 Timothy 2:5, RV). The final verdict on himself, Paul was content to leave to the ultimate authority of "the Lord, the righteous judge", confident that his assessment of the contest, the race he had run to the end, would be fair and that the quality of his struggle would be attested by the award from the Lord's own hands of the *stephanos* of righteousness (2 Timothy 4:7,8).

Often the crown was literally "laid up", attached to the finishing post towards which the athletes ran. We can therefore "look unto Jesus", the object of our faith "from start to finish", while all the noble victors of the past, who wrought great things by faith, assemble like a cloud to witness our struggle in our day of toil, urging us on to greater efforts by their example (Hebrews 12:1-2). We must, however, run free of the encumbrance of the sin which, like the garment that should be laid aside as athletes strip for action, would otherwise cling to us and hamper the free movement of our limbs.

The Lord's Own Strife

When the Lord himself was "in an agony", it was not so much that he was in physical pain, although the testimony that "his sweat was as it were great drops of blood falling down to the ground" indicates that the experience overwhelmed him body, soul and spirit. It was the *agōna*, the contest with himself which issued in the "gentle resignation" with which "he yielded to his Father's will" (Luke 22:39-46).

To complete this short study, mention should be made of the chariot race. The *biga*, or light two-wheeled chariot, was drawn by two horses, and it needed all the driver's skill and concentration to avoid disaster. One had never to look back, but keep his eye steadfastly on the goal, the forward-leaning stance helping to maintain the balance and control. So said Paul, ''I *press on*, if so be that I may apprehend (lay hold on) that for which also I was apprehended by Christ Jesus ... but this one thing I do, forgetting the things which are behind, and *stretching forward* to the things which are before, I *press on toward the goal* unto the *prize* of the high calling of God in Christ Jesus'' (Philippians 3:12-14, RV).

Inspired and instructed by such an example, as well as that of the Lord himself, Timothy too could be encouraged to ''fight the good fight of faith'' (1 Timothy 6:12). It was truly described as ''good'' (*kalon*, pages 72, 86), because it was quite unlike the striving of the other-teachers, which was about words to no profit. Timothy's goal was a sound mature faith and its reward eternal life.

ESSAY 22

Paul's Expressions Descriptive of the Second Coming

IN connection with the phrase in 1 Timothy 6:14, it is worth a brief consideration of Paul's terms for Christ's Second Coming to show that he made use of such a variety of expressions that the absence of any one of them from the Pastoral Epistles is an objection without any solid foundation.

1. One of his characteristic phrases is "the day of the Lord". In 1 Thessalonians 5:2 it "cometh as a thief" and in 2 Thessalonians 2:2 it is also known as "the day of Christ". Paul affirms that the Corinthians who are "waiting for the coming of the Lord Jesus Christ" may be "blameless in *the day of our Lord Jesus Christ*" (1 Corinthians 1:7,8). "The spirit may be saved in *the day of the Lord Jesus*" (5:5) and Paul will share a rejoicing with them "in *the day of the Lord Jesus*" (2 Corinthians 1:14), which is also "the day of salvation" (6:2), the "day of redemption" (Ephesians 4:30). Consistent with the exhortation to Timothy to keep the commandment pure until the Lord appear, Paul assured the Philippians that "he which hath begun a good work in you will perform it *until the day of Jesus Christ*" (1:6), provided they remain "sincere and without offence *till the day of Christ*" (1:10).

2. There was also "the revelation (or apocalypse) of our Lord Jesus", coupled with "the day of our Lord Jesus Christ" (1 Corinthians 1:7,8 again). The apostles were aware that the Lord was with them, as indeed we believe that he is with us, especially where two or three are gathered together in his name. But before our faith is turned into sight we have to await the apocalypse of Christ, "when the Lord Jesus shall be *revealed* from heaven with his mighty angels" (2 Thessalonians 1:7).

3. The *parousia* is literally the 'presence of the Lord', but it is frequently translated as "the coming" because of its obviously future meaning. It is the word for *the coming* of the Son of man in Matthew 24:3,27,37,39 and in 1 Corinthians 15:23 it refers to the future coming when those who are Christ's will be made alive. The Letters to Thessalonica contain the word in five of the eight chapters, all directing the believers to the day for which they were waiting: for they had "turned to God from idols to serve the living and true God; and to wait for his Son from heaven" (1 Thessalonians 1:9,10). They would rejoice together "in the presence of our Lord Jesus Christ *at his coming*" (2:19), and their hearts would be established "unblameable in holiness before God, even our Father, *at the coming of our Lord Jesus Christ* with all his saints" (3:13). And there would be glad reunion between those who were alive and remained "*unto the coming of the Lord*" and those who had fallen asleep in him (4:15); and until that *coming*, they could be preserved blameless in their "whole spirit and soul and body" (5:23).

4. Then there is "the appearing of his coming"—the *epiphania* of his *parousia* (2 Thessalonians 2:8)—translated as "the brightness of his coming", with true understanding of the meaning of *epiphania*. It is the sense given to the word in Luke 1:78,79, and reminds us that *epiphania* is frequently used in the Septuagint of the manifestation of God's glory: "The dayspring from on high hath visited us, to give light (*epiphanō*) to them that sit in darkness and in the shadow of death."

5. So in Titus 2:13 we read of "the *epiphania* of the glory of the great God and our Saviour Jesus Christ" (see page 395).

There is, therefore, sufficient variety of expression, and indeed combination of expression in single passages, in Paul's writing to enable us to discount the statement that the use of *epiphania* is in any way uncharacteristic of his style. The contrary is in fact the case when we think of the manifestation of the Lord who sits at the right hand of him who dwelleth in the light and who is to come in the glory of the Father.

ESSAY 23

A Hymn of Praise

IN the doxology of 1 Timothy 6:15,16, Paul is possibly drawing on words used in synagogue services, or even repeating one of those "hymns and spiritual songs" which the early ecclesias had made their own. Certainly every phrase had its Old Testament origins, as we shall see more clearly by setting them out in parallel.

1 Timothy 6:15-16	*Old Testament Parallels*
"The blessed and only potentate"	"The LORD our God is one LORD" (Deuteronomy 6:4)
	"Blessed be the LORD God of Israel from everlasting, and to everlasting" (Psalm 41:13)
	"All nations before him are as nothing . . . To whom then will ye liken God?" (Isaiah 40:12-31)
	"The Most High . . . that liveth for ever, whose dominion is an everlasting dominion" (Daniel 4:34)
"The King of kings and Lord of Lords"	"For the LORD your God is God of gods, and Lord of lords, a great God, a mighty, and a terrible" (Deuteronomy 10:17)
	"O give thanks to the Lord of lords" (Psalm 136:3)

215

"Who only hath immortality"

"For with thee is the fountain of life" (Psalm 36:9)

"The everlasting God, the Lord ... fainteth not, neither is weary" (Isaiah 40:28)

"The Most High ... that liveth for ever" (Daniel 4:34)

"Dwelling in the light which no man can approach unto"

"And the sight of the glory of the Lord was like a devouring fire" (Exodus 24:17; see also 34:29-35)

"Who coverest thyself with light as with a garment" (Psalm 104:2)

"Whom no man hath seen nor can see"

"Thou canst not see my face: for there shall no man see me, and live" (Exodus 33:20)

"Ye heard the voice of the words, but saw no similitude" (Deuteronomy 4:12)

"Woe is me! for I am undone ... for mine eyes have seen the King, the Lord of hosts" (Isaiah 6:5)

"To whom be honour and power everlasting. Amen"

"And Ezra blessed the LORD, the great God. And all the people answered, Amen, Amen" (Nehemiah 8:6; Psalm 41:13)

"And blessed be his glorious name for ever: and let the whole earth be filled with his glory; Amen and Amen" (Psalm 72:19)

"Blessed be the LORD for evermore. Amen, and Amen" (Psalm 89:52)

The seven terms descriptive of God stress His incomparable greatness. *Dynastēs*, 'potentate' or 'sovereign', unique to Paul here, but applied elsewhere to human rulers (Luke 1:52; Acts 8:27, "of great authority") is probably introduced here in contrast to Pontius Pilate, who could have had no power at all against Christ had it not been given him from above (John 19:11). For God is not only sovereign: He is the only Sovereign, by whom all the powers that be are ordained (Romans 13:1-6; 1 Peter 2:13-14). Compare what was said of God's Wisdom: "By me kings reign, and princes decree justice. By me princes rule, and nobles, even all the judges of the earth" (Proverbs 8:15-16).

The title "King of kings and Lord of lords" is granted by the Father to Christ (Revelation 17:14), whom God established as "both Lord and Christ by the resurrection from the dead". The unique version of the phrase in this Hymn is in literal translation "King of those who reign as king and Lord of those who lord it". It is a direct denial of the power and authority of those kings and rulers who claimed divinity by reason of their status. In His supremacy, acknowledged even by the Son—a great blow to those who hold the doctrine of the Trinity (John 20:17; 1 Corinthians 15:27-28)—God had reserved until "his own times" the moment of revelation of Christ's exaltation.

The phrase "Who only hath immortality" takes us far beyond the simple adjective "immortal" of 1 Timothy 1:17. That word describes the incorruptible nature which the saints will be privileged to share—the incorruptible crown, the inheritance incorruptible as in Romans 2:7, 1 Corinthians 15 throughout and 1 Peter 1:4,23; 3:4. *Athanasia*, 'deathlessness', is also something which "this mortal must put on" (1 Corinthians 15:53), but this verse is declaring that it is the essential property of God alone: there is no such thing as *inherent* deathlessness: it is uniquely in the gift of God who alone has it.

God is also "dwelling in the light which no man can approach unto". From the beginning of creation it has been evident that God *is* light. He separated it from the darkness and it became symbolic of all that is of Him, while the world of men is darkness. So no man can approach Him, and in manifestations of Him His brightness has nearly always been veiled, in cloud or smoke for example.

The very first mention in Scripture of "the glory of the Lord" indicates that the brightness was discernible behind the cloud, but that men, even His people Israel, by virtue of their sin came short of it (Exodus 16:6-10; Romans 3:23). The thought behind Paul's hymn of praise is Exodus 33:18-23 and is especially appropriate when he is treating of the *epiphania* of the Lord Jesus, when "the glory of the LORD shall be revealed, and all flesh shall see it together" (Isaiah 40:5). The theme also follows that of John 1, concerning the life which was the light of men, which the darkness could not overcome. The Apostle John's commentary on the Exodus passage is, in effect:

> "No man hath seen God at any time; the only begotten Son which is in the bosom of the Father, he hath declared him"
>
> (verse 18)

In the ascription "To whom be honour and power everlasting", instead of the more usual "honour and glory" the word "power" is consistent with the general theme of the doxology, which stresses the supreme eternal power of God. The responsibility of being "a man of God" cannot be more clearly demonstrated than in such ascriptions of praise, which for the apostles are frequently called forth by their contemplation of the works of God, and by the realisation of the wonder and solemnity of being part of His purpose. Compare Peter's exhortation to all who would be "good stewards of the manifold grace of God":

> "If any man speak, let him speak *as the oracles of God*; if any man minister, let him do it as of *the ability which God giveth*: that God in all things may be glorified through Jesus Christ, *to whom be praise and dominion* for ever and ever. Amen."
>
> (1 Peter 4:11)

And again in 5:10-11:

> "But the God of all grace, who hath called us unto his eternal glory by Christ Jesus, after that ye have suffered a while (as in 1 Timothy 6:12), make you perfect, stablish, strengthen, settle you. To him be glory and dominion for ever and ever. Amen."

See also Romans 11:33-36; Galatians 1:3-5; Jude 25; and especially Revelation 5:12-13:

"Blessing, and honour, and glory, and power, be unto him that sitteth upon the throne, and unto the Lamb for ever and ever."

How powerful are these ascriptions of praise, springing from the heart of those whose intelligent understanding and appreciation of the manifold works of God and of the privilege of working together with Him, both now and for ever, stirred their emotions, to love Him with all their heart, with all their soul, with all their strength and with all their mind! May we never be so bemused by arid theological speculation or so trapped in phraseology of our own devising that our faith no longer allows us to be "lost in wonder, love and praise".

ESSAY 24

The Uncertainty of Riches

THE reminder about the instability of any trust in wealth is as necessary today as it was for Timothy (1 Timothy 6:17). The misconception that wealth brings security and happiness is widespread in the world and many a brother has brought bitterness to his home and shipwreck to his faith through the pursuit of a career or salary with more singlemindedness than in his devotion to the Lord's service. In a footnote to their chapter on "Language" in *The Riddle of the New Testament* (Hoskyns and Davey) the authors make an interesting point which further illustrates both the Apostle's thought and the Lord's teaching that the disciple cannot serve both God and mammon (Matthew 6:24). Writing about the use of the word "truth" (compare "the God of truth", *amēn*, in Isaiah 65:16) they say on page 28:

"The Hebrew root *'MN* is preserved in English in the liturgical *amen*, in which the confidence that God will hear the prayers of His faithful people is formally expressed, and also, curiously enough, in the word *mammon*, meaning that in which the men of the world falsely trust (usually riches, of course), and implying a contrast with the living God who alone is the proper object of confidence."

The negative aspect of the charge may be summed up in the words of Psalm 52:7:

"Lo, this is the man that made not God his strength, but trusted in the abundance of his riches, and strengthened himself in his wickedness."

ESSAY 25

The Good Deposit

THE word *parathēkē* confirms us in the impression that "foundation" in verse 19 is a banker's term (page 199), for Paul introduces another in the same sequence of thought. It occurs three times in the New Testament and only in the Pastoral Epistles, here in 1 Timothy 6:20, and in 2 Timothy 1:12,14 (pages 244, 245); in two cases the Received Text has *parakatathēkē*, which does not differ substantially in meaning. In the Greek Old Testament it appears twice in Leviticus 6:2,4 where it is translated in the Revised Version as "a matter of deposit". There was thus a Divine "law of the deposit", which held a man responsible for the safe keeping of that which was formally committed to his trust, whether it was a sum of money or some other valuable possession. Failure to restore it whole constituted a "trespass against the Lord", and called for restitution of the principal with added interest and a trespass offering.

The law of the *parathēkē* was also well-known in the Greek world of Paul's day and was the ordinary term for the kind of banking transaction with which we are familair today. The verbal form *paratithēmi* is more frequent in the New Testament and helps us to understand the uses of *parathēkē*, the other two of which we study in their context. In Luke 12:48 the Lord says: "To whom men have *committed* much, of him they will ask the more"; and in 23:46: "Father, into thy hands I *commend* my spirit". In Acts 14:23 and 20:32 the disciples are *commended* to God; in 1 Timothy 1:18, "This charge I *commit* unto thee"; in 2 Timothy 2:2, what Timothy has learned he is to "*commit* to faithful men"; while in 1 Peter 4:19 the righteous are to "*commit* the keeping of their souls to him in well doing, as unto a faithful Creator".

221

Clearly, then, the idea of two-way trust is contained in this word: we can confidently commit ourselves, our very lives, to God, believing that He will render them back to us in greater fulness (see 1 Timothy 1:12, with 4:8), and He has committed to us a great trust in the Gospel, to enrich it with the increase of preaching and adorn it with our own fidelity (Titus 2:10), and above all to preserve it from all that would tarnish or destroy (see on 1 Timothy 1:11, page 26).

According to some authorities, men could lay up their treasures in the depository in the Temple at Jerusalem or even in the temple of Diana in Ephesus. How much better to lay up treasure in heaven, "a good foundation against the time to come, that (we) may lay hold on eternal life" (Matthew 6:19-21; 1 Timothy 6:19)!

ESSAY 26

Knowledge Falsely So Called

THE problem in Ephesus was the tension between true knowledge and *"knowledge falsely so called"* (1 Timothy 6:20). The Christian hope and discipleship are based upon knowledge:

> "This is life eternal, that they should *know thee* the only true God, and him whom thou didst send, even Jesus Christ."
> (John 17:3, RV)

> "But thanks be unto God, which . . . maketh manifest through us the *savour of his knowledge* in every place."
> (2 Corinthians 2:14, RV)

> "For God . . . hath shined in our hearts, to give *the light of the knowledge* of the glory of God in the face of Jesus Christ."
> (4:6)

> "I count all things but loss for the excellency of *the knowledge* of Christ Jesus my Lord." (Philippians 3:8)

> "In whom are hid all the treasures of wisdom and *knowledge*."
> (Colossians 2:3)

(In Colossae the tendencies which developed into the later Gnosticism were already manifesting themselves. Compare 2:2-23 with 1 Timothy 4:1-5.)

The disciples were therefore the true wise men, *those who knew*, for,

> "In everything ye are enriched by him, in all utterance, and in *all knowledge*." (1 Corinthians 1:5)

> "Therefore, as ye abound in everything, in faith, in utterance, and *knowledge* . . . see that ye abound in this grace also."
> (2 Corinthians 8:7)

223

> "And ye have an anointing from the Holy One, and ye *all know*."   (1 John 2:20, RV with margin)

All other knowledge and reasoning must be subjected to this knowledge of God:

> "We do not war according to the flesh ... casting down reasonings, and every high thing that is exalted against the *knowledge of God*, and bringing every thought into captivity to the obedience of Christ."
>
> (2 Corinthians 10:3-6, RV with margin)

But even before the era of the Pastoral Epistles it had become necessary for Paul to warn the believers that this knowledge of God was more than an intellectual achievement: being centred on the Father and His grace in salvation it was never separated from the charity that buildeth up: knowledge of the wrong kind "puffeth up", as became only too evident later in Ephesus (see 1 Corinthians 8:1 and note on "proud" in 1 Timothy 6:4, page 179). Indeed, knowledge of the most penetrating kind is nothing without charity (1 Corinthians 13:2), a point which Paul emphasised in this First Epistle to Timothy from the very first (1:5). The Apostle would no doubt have heartily agreed with the later writer who said: "Where there is no faith, there is no knowledge. When something is born of personal speculation, that is not knowledge."

So in 1:7 Paul had declared that those in Ephesus who desired to be teachers of the law understood "neither what they say, nor whereof they affirm". They were, like their knowledge, *pseudonymous* (another "oncer"). Their *antithesēs*, therefore, were not strictly opposition to Timothy and his work, although that was necessarily involved. He had in meekness to instruct "them that oppose themselves" (2 Timothy 2:25), and the "themselves" is significant: it was a *personality* problem as much as an ideological one. But *antithesis* (a "oncer") is a more precise word than *logomachia* ('strifes of words', 6:4 and notes), being a technical word for a certain style of argument, described as "the endless contrasts of decisions founded on endless distinctions, which played so large a part in the casuistry of the Scribes as interpreters of the Law" (Bernard). To apply this method to the Gospel and make it a subject of philosophical discussions as abstruse as they are devoid of true meaning is to misconstrue it entirely: the Gospel is not a proposition for disputation but "a good deposit".

The Second Letter to Timothy

INTRODUCTION

ALTHOUGH the Second Epistle was the last of the Pastorals to be written, it will be convenient to follow our New Testament order and deal with it next, since the same recipient is involved as in the First. Much of what has already been written as to the style, content and special vocabulary applies to this Letter, and we shall have no need to go over the ground again. The special features to be considered are the changed situation of the Apostle himself; the increased urgency of his appeals to his son in the faith to stand firm, coupled with the anxious desire to see him; and the more detailed list of names, that "panorama of judgement day", of those who had helped or hindered, adhered to or departed from the faith.

If we are right in our conjectural dating (see the "Suggested Table of the Last Years of Paul's Life", page 13), then this Second Letter is the Apostle's last, written from prison shortly before his execution. The entire atmosphere of the Letter is different from that of the First, in which he was able to make arrangements for travel as a free man. In 2 Timothy he is a prisoner (1:12,16; 2:9) and the location is Rome (1:17). He has already appeared before the emperor's tribunal (4:16,17), but although on that occasion he was "delivered out of the mouth of the lion", he is persuaded that he is approaching death (4:6-9).

A Dangerous Period

The idea that Paul was apprehended, perhaps at Nicopolis, and taken to Rome, or even arrested on his return to Rome, is by no means inconsistent with the itinerary suggested by his references to Miletus, Troas and Corinth in 2 Timothy 4:20 and Nicopolis in Titus 3:12. Why he made this journey is not clear, but that it should lead him into danger is entirely consistent with the changed

225

official attitude to the Christians after the Great Fire and the consequent Neronian persecutions of AD 64.

There is the interesting possible alternative that Paul was arrested in Ephesus itself after some incident similar to that described in Acts 19, but this time with no kindly intervention of the local magistrates, or Asiarchs, for Asia was a Roman proconsular province. At any rate, Paul had some avowed enemies in the city, who might well have denounced him to the imperial police on some pretext. In that case Timothy's tears were understandable (1:4) as the Apostle left the city under guard, possibly in the company of Luke (4:11), Demas, Crescens, Titus (4:10), Tychicus (4:12), Erastus and Trophimus (4:20), of whom one left him at Corinth, another fell sick at Miletus early in the journey, and others departed on various missions, or pretexts, leaving only Luke to accompany him all the way.

That Timothy was left in Ephesus in such circumstances is almost sufficient explanation for the content of the Second Letter. He needed comfort and the most urgent exhortation to courage and steadfastness, to stand firm in the faith and defend it against all error. For in Paul's mind the decisive moment had come when that which had been committed to his trust was to be entrusted in turn to the faithful men who would come after him. "Be not thou therefore ashamed of the testimony of our Lord" (1:8). There is also the strong appeal to Timothy to come to Rome as soon as possible in view of the Apostle's impending death: "... greatly desiring to see thee ... Do thy diligence to come before winter" (1:4; 4:9,21).

A Personal Letter

We have, therefore, a warm-hearted, personal letter, the testimony of a father to his son in the faith, full of mingled trust, hope and concern, which is yet an important document of the times in the ecclesial world, with sound advice for us personally and as a community today.

In the detailed commentary that follows points which have had a fuller treatment in the notes on the First Epistle or in the Letter to Titus will be followed by a simple reference to the appropriate page number.

The Second Letter to Timothy

CHAPTER 1

Exhortation to Courage in the Service of the Gospel

1:1-12—Address and Salutation

"Paul, an apostle of Jesus Christ by the will of God": The whole question of New Testament letters and their greetings and farewell has already been reviewed (pages 8-13). The Revised Version here gives the order "Christ Jesus", the more usual form in these Letters. Unlike the First Epistle, however, which described his apostolate as "according to the commandment of God", Paul here uses his more frequent way of defining his commission—"through the *will* of God", as in 1 Corinthians 1:1, 2 Corinthians 1:1, Ephesians 1:1 and Colossians 1:1. Even in this intensely personal letter the Apostle is making clear upon what authority he writes, especially since he is handing over his charge: He who called him is "the God whose I am, and whom I serve" (Acts 27:23).

"According to the promise of life which is in Christ Jesus": For a man under sentence of death "the promise of life" takes on an added significance. Such expressions of faith and confidence abound in this Letter, from the statement that "God hath not given us the spirit of fear" (verse 7) to the allusion to the Lord's prayer in 4:18: "And the Lord shall deliver me ... and will preserve me unto his heavenly kingdom" (page 344). He might "suffer trouble" in the Gospel (2:8-13), but it spoke of the resurrection of Christ, and gave the promise that "if we be dead with him, we shall also live with him", and that there was laid up for him a crown of righteousness which the Lord would give him when he came (4:8).

227

Eternal Life in the Purpose of God

There is, however, even more in this expression than a personal statement of faith: it was the very will of God, that life should be given to men in Christ Jesus. It is the very "hope of eternal life, which God, that cannot lie, promised before the world began; but hath in due times manifested his word through preaching . . . according to the commandment of God our Saviour" (Titus 1:2-3, pages 15 and 353).

At the time of his first imprisonment Paul had written: "For to me to live is Christ, and to die is gain" (Philippians 1:21), thus revealing his deep insight into the true nature of the Gospel message committed to him. It revealed a way of life which is wholly centred in Christ—"For ye are dead, and your life is hid with Christ in God" (Colossians 3:3)—and also the hope of ultimate salvation from death at the appearing of our Saviour Jesus Christ. For he has "abolished death, *and hath brought life and immortality to light* through the gospel" (2 Timothy 1:10). The "new life" is that which will spring up into eternal life for those who, having partaken of the divine mind, will become partakers of the divine nature" (2 Peter 1:1-4).

Verse 2: "To Timothy, my dearly beloved son: Grace, mercy and peace": For the salutation in general see page 16. Onesimus had been "begotten in my bonds" (Philemon 10) and the apostle had travailed in pain for his "little children", the Galatians (4:19). We sense an even deeper affection, however, in this final address to Timothy.

It is almost the Hebrew sense of "beloved" or "darling", meaning 'only one' (cf. Psalm 22:20, margin), since so many have parted from or abandoned Paul (1:15; 4:10-16,20), while Timothy was yearning for his lost companion and spiritual father, now writing his "last will and testament". And what greater blessing could he bestow than "Grace, mercy and peace", *"from God the Father"*, who is the source of all the blessings of salvation, and from *"Christ Jesus our Lord"*, the mediator through whom they are bestowed?

1:3-5—Thanksgiving

Verse 3: "I thank God": For the special form of this expression in the original see on 1 Timothy 1:12, page 27. Although using a conventional device of ancient letter writing (pages 8-13) in introducing at this point an expression of thanks or a blessing, or an assurance that he is offering prayers on behalf of the recipient, Paul is not merely following custom, but expressing all that is in his heart. In 1 Timothy 1:12 the thanksgiving is delayed until he has stated the purpose of the letter. In Ephesians and 2 Corinthians he ascribes blessing to God, the Father of the Lord Jesus Christ; otherwise all his letters except Galatians and Titus express a genuine feeling of gratitude, as he remembers those to whom he is writing.

So he thanks God for the faith of the Romans, the grace given to the Corinthians, the fellowship in the Gospel of the Philippians, the faith and love of the Colossians, the work of faith, labour of love and patience of hope of the Thessalonians, the love and faith of Philemon, and the unfeigned faith of Timothy.

Nothing could express more clearly the "motivation" of the Apostle: those amongst whom he laboured were his joy; indeed, his hope and crown of rejoicing would be to stand approved with them in the presence of the Lord Jesus at his coming (1 Thessalonians 2:19).

"Whom I serve from my forefathers": The word *latreuō*, 'to serve', bears the double meaning, like the word "ministry", of acts of service and a religious service, like the Breaking of Bread or the "services" in the Temple. For the Apostle, there was no distinction, since his whole life was ministry or worship. The Law taught this, when it made clear that one honoured the Lord by "rising up before the hoary head" or avoiding the unjust balance and the unjust weight, as well as by coming before Him with sacrifice and offering.

In fact, the worship of the man who neglected the observance of its spirit in daily life was unacceptable. What Paul had been taught to observe from his childhood, therefore, he pursued with a zeal made even greater by his knowledge of its relationship to the faith in Christ. For him the Law was *fulfilled* not superseded, and nowhere does he speak of its observance with disrespect. His clashes with the Judaisers arose because of their insistence that salvation came by the works of the Law and not by faith in the covenants of promise.

229

A Sense of Gratitude

Paul's sense of gratitude for his upbringing and his feelings for his kinsmen are frequently expressed, as for example in Romans 9:3-5 and Philippians 3:4-6. Even there, however, he recognises the much greater privilege of having the knowledge of God in Christ—the glory that excelleth, beside which even the glory of the Law seems dim. For him there was a continuity of service. His apostleship ministered to the same God, was based upon the same hope of the resurrection, and was a worshipping of "the God of my fathers, believing all things which are written in the law and in the prophets" (Acts 24:14), although his kinsmen believed it to be a sectarian ministry.

"With pure conscience": It was a great comfort for a man on a criminal charge to be able honestly to make that claim. It was a claim to which Paul attached great importance, as for example when arraigned before the Sanhedrin: "Men and brethren, I have lived in all good conscience before God until this day" (Acts 23:1); and before Felix: "And herein do I exercise myself, to have always a conscience void of offence toward God, and toward men" (24:16; see also 2 Corinthians 1:12; 4:2).

As we have already noted, many passages in the Pastoral Epistles refer to the importance of a pure conscience, that is, of a Scripturally informed conscience, able to distinguish right from wrong and rightly divide the word of truth in practice as well as theory (page 44; also Titus 1:15, page 365).

There is a deeper meaning behind the word, therefore, than the mere idea of knowing nothing against oneself, for "I am not hereby justified: but he that judgeth me is the Lord" (1 Corinthians 4:4). True worship and service depends upon a pure conscience, since the Lord offers forgiveness of sins that He may be feared, and we are able to serve the living God with a conscience purged from dead works (Hebrews 9:14). So although Paul, in his zeal for the Lord God, had been in fact "a blasphemer, and a persecutor and injurious", he had "obtained mercy because I did it ignorantly in unbelief" (1 Timothy 1:13; pages 29-30), and was "put into the ministry" of his apostleship.

Remembrance in Prayer

"That without ceasing I have remembrance of thee in my prayers": Once again the conventional expression of concern for the recipient of the Letter is transformed, giving us an insight into the spirituality of an Apostle who has the capacity for taking others into his pastoral care through prayer and intercession for them (Romans 1:9; Philippians 1:3; Colossians 1:3). "Without ceasing" is applied by him to prayer, thanksgiving and remembrance in Romans 1:9 and 1 Thessalonians 1:3; 2:13; 5:17, and refers of course to a continual habit and not something which is *continuous*: we must never abandon the practice of prayer. In the Hebrew idiom of Psalm 109:4, "I—prayer", the italicised "give myself unto" has been inserted by the translators to fill up the meaning for the English reader. For the Psalmist it is as though "I" and "prayer" were the same thing. *"Night and day"* is the usual Hebrew order of words; for the beginning "the evening and the morning" marked the day in God's time (Genesis 1; see page 151).

It is evident that much more attention should be paid by the twentieth century disciple to the question of prayer on behalf of the Brotherhood in general and individuals in particular. In the discussion of this point two views usually emerge: (1) that there should be special prayer for particular purposes, in cases of sickness or other distress, or projects being planned by the ecclesia; (2) others feel that such prayers and intercessions should be part of the regular pattern of ecclesial life, the special need giving direction to the prayer of, say, the presiding brother when the ecclesia assembles for its weekly worship.

It is a great pity that there should even appear to be a conflict of view on such a matter. The important thing is not whether there should be a special "prayer meeting or not", but that the intercession should be made, if not in public then in private. Both practices have Scriptural precedent, for besides the Apostle's private devotions which we are now considering, there were occasions when "prayer was made without ceasing of the church", for Peter for example (Acts 12:5). The ministry of prayer is something in which all can engage; and many can testify to the strength, courage and increased faith that comes from the knowledge that others, individually or collectively, remember them "without ceasing" in their prayers.

A Deep Longing

Verse 4: *"Greatly desiring to see thee"*: The longing to see Timothy is expressed twice more, in the phrase "Do thy diligence to come" (4:9,21). Perhaps the request formed part of Paul's earnest supplications, and there is certainly the implication that if the young man tarries any longer he will be too late. This yearning to see again a beloved face or even to behold for the first time those who were known only by their spiritual relationship, is a frequent theme of Paul, so important to him were the persons of those in Christ.

His was no fellowship in the abstract: it had to do with sharing with people the fellowship of Christ's sufferings in joyful anticipation of the glory to follow. *Epipotheō* indicates 'strong yearning' as in the following passages:

"For I *long* to see you, that I may impart unto you some spiritual gift, to the end that ye may be established; that is, that I may be comforted together with you by the mutual faith both of you and me."
(Romans 1:11-12)

"(The saints which) by their prayer for you . . . *long* after you for the exceeding grace of God in you."
(2 Corinthians 9:14)

"For God is my record, how greatly I *long* after you all in the bowels of Jesus Christ."
(Philippians 1:8; see also 1 Thessalonians 3:6)

"Being mindful of thy tears": Some have deduced a certain weakness of character in Timothy from these words and from the strong exhortatory tone of the letter. But sensitivity of feeling is not weakness of character, and probably both men had sensed that at his arrest Paul was being parted from Timothy for the last time, as it may well have proved to be. There is no record of such emotion at any previous partings from one another, when for example Paul left Timothy at Ephesus previously (1 Timothy 1:3); but the departure of Paul from Miletus on an earlier occasion had caused a whole congregation to weep sore, "sorrowing most of all for the words which he spake, that they should see his face no more" (Acts 20:38).

"That I may be filled with joy": The words "tears" and "joy" are next to each other in the Greek, as are "suffering" and "glory"

so often in the Apostle's thought. Joy at the prospect of a reunion is in proportion to the sorrow of parting. "To fill", sometimes "to fulfil", is a characteristic word of Paul's (23 times in his epistles). If he preached the Gospel, it was fully (Romans 15:19); if he was joyful, he felt that that joy was fulfilled (Philippians 2:2), and he could wish nothing better than that his readers should be *filled* with joy and peace, as he would be *filled* with comfort (2 Corinthians 7:4) and God would *fill* (supply) all his need (Philippians 4:19). His service was nothing if not wholehearted.

Unfeigned Faith

"When I call to remembrance the unfeigned faith that is in thee": The Revised Version makes it clear that while "mindful" in verse 4 means that he has recalled something to his mind, no doubt as he remembered Timothy in his prayers, here Paul has been reminded in some way of Timothy's faith. We have no means of determining who or what had reminded him. Could it have been a letter from Timothy, or some incident that happened in Rome? Or might it have been Onesiphorus, whose household was at Ephesus (2 Timothy 4:19) and who had been a frequent, welcome visitor to Paul in his prison (1:16-18)? At all events, the reminder stimulated the desire to see the young man and to exhort him to continue in that faith.

"Which dwelt first in thy grandmother Lois, and in thy mother Eunice": It is remarkable that this should be the only reference to a grandmother in the New Testament. Both women were Jewesses, and it is probable that the words applied to the younger in Acts 16:1, "a certain woman which . . . believed", meant that she was a believer in Christ. Paul is not here indicating that the grandmother believed first and Eunice and Timothy believed afterwards, but that the women were the first of his family to become disciples. From 3:14-17 we learn that they had diligently followed the precepts of the Law and instilled into the next generation the knowledge of the Scriptures which provided the true education in righteousness. (Contrast with the "old wives' fables" which Timothy was to refuse, 1 Timothy 4:7, page 126.) In spite of the fact that Eunice had married a Gentile, the mother's influence had prevailed (or was it the influence of Lois primarily?), in accordance with the principle that emerges from the record of the Kings. For of many of them it is written: "And he did that which

233

was right (or evil) in the sight of the LORD. And his mother's name was ..." (for example see 1 Kings 15:2; 2 Chronicles 13:2, etc.).

"And I am persuaded that in thee also": The Apostle's thankfulness for his own upbringing (verse 3) and for the value of his spiritual heritage no doubt strengthened his confidence in Timothy's own grounding in Scripture as the basis of his faith in Christ and as the motive of his careful observance of its principles in practice.

Arising from the faith which dwelt in Lois and Eunice, the topic of "Believers and Faithful in the New Testament" is taken up in Essay 27, page 250.

Brought up in the Law

It is not stretching imagination too far to suggest that Lois dwelt in Eunice's house and together with her daughter saw to it that the son of the marriage with the Gentile was firmly brought up in the Law of the Lord. They were, of course, Hellenistic Jews, and for some reason had not seen to it that the boy was circumcised (Acts 16:3). The women had joined the small ecclesia which grew up as a result of the first preaching of the Gospel in Lystra, a preaching which centred around witness to the living God (a characteristic Old Testament expression), and the power Christ had given Paul to heal. The young man himself was baptized, possibly by Paul himself at the first return with Barnabas to organise the ecclesia there. On his second journey, this time with Silas, Paul chose Timothy to accompany him (to take Mark's place?) because he had already formed an estimate of his true worth.

In any event, the importance attached by Paul to a sure grounding in the Scriptures, primarily the Old Testament, and training in godly habits, clearly emerges. There are equally clear messages for us today. All concerned with the care of the young, whether children or young people, which means every ecclesia in effect, should ponder deeply how they strike the balance between instruction in righteousness and "activities" of a recreational kind. Is the balance in some cases tending to swing too much in favour of simple "togetherness" and entertainment or recreational pursuits on the grounds that young people nowadays are not attracted to us without our "sugaring the pill"? "How sweet are *thy words* unto my taste! yea, sweeter than honey to my mouth!'' (Psalm 119:103).

1:6-14—Encouragement from Experience

Verse 6: *"Wherefore I put thee in remembrance":* It is precisely because of his confidence in Timothy that the Apostle urges him to bring his full qualities and privileges fully into service and to be prepared to suffer affliction for the Gospel—affliction such as Paul was then enduring and to which Timothy would himself become more and more exposed (verse 12; 2:3-13).

There have been three different expressions for remembering in the Epistle, and more are to follow (2:8,14). It is almost as though Paul is like Moses, instructing his people of that which is to come after his death and urging them above all things to *remember*—remember what the Lord had done and what the disciple should do in defence and confirmation of the Gospel. Phrases exhorting to remembrance are characteristic of the Book of Deuteronomy. But although Paul's exhortation is urgent and follows what has gone before by one of the strongest linking expressions ("For the which cause . . .", RV) used by him only here, in verse 12 and in Titus 1:13, it is expressed in gentle terms: he *reminds* Timothy of certain things, confident that he will respond.

"That thou stir up the gift of God": The subject of the gift that Timothy received was discussed at some length in the note on 1 Timothy 4:14 (page 134). Here the gift is likened to a fire which has to be "kindled into flame", a reminder that just as "the spirits of the prophets are subject unto the prophets" (1 Corinthians 14:32), so the use of the other gifts was dependent upon the willingness of the recipient to exercise them. In the face of the determined opposition of the false teachers in Ephesus, the possible impending persecution and the probable death of Paul, Timothy could rely upon the strength he had been given if only he would exercise it.

"Which is in thee through the laying on of my hands" (RV): The topic of the laying on of hands was considered in connection with 1 Timothy 4:14; see also Essay 16, page 141.

Verse 7—The Spirit of Power, Love and Self-Discipline

"For God hath not given us the spirit of fear": The primary meaning here seems to be that the "gift of God" could certainly not have

been a *spirit of cowardice*. The Revised Version "gave us not" indicates that the gift was given once for all in the past, that is, at the time of the laying on of Paul's hands in Timothy's case. The "us" then refers to Paul and Timothy who both had received such a gift. The Apostle gently brings himself into his exhortation, since his purpose is not to rebuke the younger man, even by implication, but to encourage him and build him up. People like ourselves should not be fearful. We may boldly say, "The Lord is my helper, and I will not fear what man shall do unto me" (Hebrews 13:6). Imprisoned and under the shadow of death as he was, Paul was proclaiming his own confidence that "the Lord shall deliver me from every evil work, and will preserve me unto his heavenly kingdom" (2 Timothy 4:18).

"But of power, and of love, and of a sound mind": In place of one failing unworthy of the man of God, Paul speaks of three positive qualities with which Timothy was fully equipped: *power* to enable him to fulfil his arduous task in Ephesus and enable him to dominate any situation that might arise; *love* to enable him to give self-sacrificing service in the spirit of the true servant of the Lord who "must not strive; but be gentle unto all men, apt to teach, patient, in meekness instructing those that oppose themselves" (2:24-25); and *self-discipline*, the ability to "take heed unto thyself" (1 Timothy 4:16).

Three Positive Qualities

Power is frequently associated with the Spirit of God in action. Paul's preaching at Corinth had been "in demonstration of the Spirit and of power: that your faith should ... stand ... in the power of God" (1 Corinthians 2:4,5). The Gospel came to the Thessalonians not "in word only, but also in power, and in the Holy Spirit and in much assurance" (1 Thessalonians 1:5). It is evident that it is not a power to work miracles that is under discussion here, since there is no evidence that Timothy either could or was ever instructed to work any, as surely it would have seemed from a human standpoint advantageous to do in resisting the gainsayers. It was a moral power and a God-given authority which enabled him where necessary to reprove and rebuke (4:2; Titus 2:15, page 396).

Love is an essential quality for the shepherd (John 10:11; 15:13) if he is to feed the flock as well as protect it from the grievous wolves (Acts 20:28-29; John 21:15-17). The supreme example was that of the Shepherd and Bishop of our souls, who suffered and was kind (1 Corinthians 13).

The Pastoral Epistles strongly emphasise the need for self-discipline. *Sōphronismos* is a "oncer" in the Greek Bible, but the idea it represents appears in several related words, and is one of the key themes of the three books. Some translations call it simply *discipline*, that is, the discipline Timothy was to exercise over the ecclesia, but that misses the major point of Paul's advice to him: Take heed unto *thyself*, and the ability to influence others will follow. We have already commented on *sōphrōsunē* (1 Timothy 2:9, page 71), a word of almost identical meaning: it stood for 'a true sense of responsibility' in ecclesial servants, and communicated through them to the ecclesia as a whole. When we come to the Letter to Titus we shall see how the ecclesias in Crete were to have this sense developed in them by wholesome teaching: the aged men would become "temperate" (*sōphrōn*), the aged women likewise, so that they might teach the young women "to be sober" (*sōphrōnizein*) and "discreet" (*sōphrōn*), and the young men would be "sober-minded" (*sōphrōnein*) (see on Titus 2:2-6, pages 386-390).

The Best Gifts

It can justifiably be asked, If the spirit of power, love and self-discipline was a "charismatic" gift and the Apostle was talking of himself and Timothy, wherein is the exhortation for us today who have no such gifts? How can the ecclesias be adequately organised and led without men of such moral force and authority?

The answer is to be found in 3:15-17. The man of God is wise unto salvation, adequately equipped to reprove, correct and instruct in righteousness, in short, "throughly furnished unto all good works" by taking heed to the inspired Scriptures. Is not the Gospel itself "the power of God unto salvation to every one that believeth" (Romans 1:16)? Those who are sons of God, being led by the Spirit of God (Romans 8:14), are, and always have been, those who have absorbed the Word of God and are transformed by the renewing of their minds by diligent attention to it. They too "have not received the spirit of bondage again to fear; but ye have received the spirit of adoption, whereby we cry, Abba, Father" (Romans 8:14-16; see also the chapter on "The Best

237

Gifts'' in the author's *The Spirit of God*, or the article with the same title in *The Christadelphian*, 1975, page 148).

Verse 8: *"Be not thou therefore ashamed of the testimony of our Lord"*: The allusion to Romans 1:16 is now seen to be inescapable and confirms the view that the exhortation is equally valid for us today: the Gospel, to him that believes, can be *"the power of God unto salvation"*—*"a spirit of power, of love and of a sound mind"*. "The testimony of our Lord" is either the testimony borne by him, and the sense is then that of "the good confession" in 1 Timothy 6:12 to which Christ bore witness by his death; or to the testimony about him, which is more probable.

1 Corinthians 1 helps us here, for Paul refers to "the testimony of Christ" in this sense in verse 6, and then gives two reasons why men might feel ashamed of it. To the Jew the very idea of a crucified Christ was a stumbling-block, and the persecutions Paul and the other apostles endured, according to the Acts, were mainly at the hands of their countrymen for proclaiming the death and resurrection of their Messiah. To the most tolerant of pagans the idea that the salvation of the world would come through a man put to death by the Romans was plain nonsense.

Among the people who would respond to such a message would be "not many wise men after the flesh, not many mighty, not many noble, but ... the weak things of the world ... the base things of the world ... and things which are despised" (verses 27-28). Timothy might well recall those words since he had delivered the letter to Corinth and had probably heard it read out to the ecclesia. He would also have remembered, therefore, that "Christ crucified" was "unto them which are called, both Jews and Greeks, Christ the power of God, and the wisdom of God. Because the foolishness of God is wiser than men; and the weakness of God is stronger than men" (verses 24-25). The whole apostolic vocation was to bear witness to this (Acts 1:8; 26:16) in the knowledge that "whosoever shall be ashamed of me and of my words in this adulterous and sinful generation: of him also shall the Son of man be ashamed, when he cometh in the glory of his Father with the holy angels" (Mark 8:38).

Ashamed of the Gospel in Modern Times

In our day, when the force of the words "adulterous and sinful generation" can be even more clearly seen, the world is more used to the idea of "Christ crucified". It is *the moral implications* of the Gospel—its revelation of the righteousness and wrath of God, and the absolute standards imposed upon the disciple—upon which it pours scorn. For the tolerant age which allows a man the freedom of speech to proclaim what he likes is also the permissive society which, ironically, is intolerant of righteousness. We have need, therefore, of the same exhortation not to be ashamed of the testimony and of the encouragement to follow the apostles' example: "They spake the word with boldness." Moreover, Paul sought the prayers of the saints, "that utterance may be given unto me, that I may open my mouth boldly, to make known the mystery of the gospel, for which I am *an ambassador in bonds*: that therein I may speak boldly, as I ought to speak" (Acts 4:31; Ephesians 6:19-20).

"Nor of me his prisoner": "His" is the most important word here. For although Paul was chained like any common criminal and association with him might well be considered humiliating if not dangerous, Timothy need have no qualms: the Apostle was not Nero's prisoner, he was Christ's. It is an expression of utmost confidence in the God and the Master whose he was and whom he served. It may be well at this point to consider briefly both the whole question of Paul's imprisonment and his attitude to it, especially since this whole epistle breathes a spirit of resignation, trust and hope which the fact of his imprisonment has produced: see Essay 28, "The Lord's Prisoner", page 252.

A Fellowship of Suffering

"But be thou partaker of the afflictions of the gospel": "To suffer evil with" (*sunkakopathein*), although not a word coined by the Apostle himself, is used only by him in the Greek Bible (2:3 also), and it illustrates his use of *sun-* compounds. There is a *fellowship* in the sufferings of the Gospel in which Timothy would gladly share since they were on behalf of the same Lord whose prisoner Paul was. The translation "*of* the gospel" is deceptive; we could easily imagine that the sufferings resulting from preaching were all that is meant. "Sufferings *for* the gospel" more accurately represents the Apostle's thought here and, indeed, his whole outlook. Grammarians call this usage "the dative of advantage"; the sufferings were for the benefit of the Gospel message. Paul would have agreed:

"But I would ye should understand, brethren, that the things which happened unto me have *fallen out rather unto the furtherance* of the gospel; so that my bonds in Christ are manifest in all the palace, and in all other places." (Philippians 1:12-13)

The brethren who had witnessed Paul's earlier imprisonment "waxed confident . . . to speak the word without fear", so powerful was the witness Paul bore. Timothy should now be prepared to share more closely the affliction with equal confidence. There was another aspect to suffering for Christ's sake: it was a privilege (Acts 5:41). Moreover, "yourselves know that we are appointed thereunto" (1 Thessalonians 3:3). For Paul it was a filling up of "that which is lacking of the afflictions of Christ in my flesh for *his body's sake, which is the church"* (Colossians 1:24, RV), and therein he could rejoice.

"According to the power of God": The Gospel *is* "the power of God unto salvation" (Romans 1:16). Therefore God is able to strengthen His servants for their tasks, assuring them that no test will prove beyond their capacity to bear (1 Corinthians 10:13).

Verse 9: *"Who hath saved us":* There has been some discussion as to whether verses 9 and 10 are taken from a hymn used in the first century ecclesia. The careful balance of words and the compact nature of the summary of the character of the Gospel point to this. Evidence for the use of such hymns in worship and of the existence of extracts from them in these Letters to reinforce or familiarise a point is not lacking. We have already alluded to this in general terms (see comments on "The Faithful Sayings", page 49, and "Great is the Mystery of Godliness", page 116). A more detailed study of the question and of the reasons why this writer thinks the Apostle may himself have been the author of at least one hymn will be reserved until we come to 2 Timothy 2:11-13 (see Essay 32, page 289). Here we limit ourselves to comment on verses 9-10 in context, and for a discussion of salvation and being "saved" refer the reader to Essay 29, "God our Saviour", page 255.

"And called us with an holy calling": The grace of God is especially seen in "the calling", or the invitation to respond to and so to participate in what God has accomplished in Christ. "The gifts and calling of God are without repentance" (Romans 11:29), but we ourselves have to give diligence to make our calling and election sure (2 Peter 1:10). For "many are called, but few are

chosen'' (Matthew 22:14). In Paul's letters ''call'' denotes the *first* stage in the individual process of salvation: God who Himself is holy has called us out of the world to a life of consecration: we are ''called to be saints'' (1 Corinthians 1:2) or ''called to holiness'' (1 Thessalonians 4:7). Those whom He calls He will also justify and eventually glorify (Romans 8:30). This calling is *always* ascribed by Paul to God as Father, which is consistent with the Lord's own declaration that ''no man can come unto me except the Father which hath sent me draw him'' (John 6:44). It is God who bears us on eagles' wings and brings us unto Himself (1 Corinthians 1:9; Galatians 1:6; Romans 8:28).

''Not according to our works, but according to his own purpose and grace . . . '': The complete inadequacy of human nature with respect to all things Divine is repeatedly emphasised in Scripture, to counteract one of the greatest of all human failings—pride arising from a feeling of self-sufficiency, which is basically a denial of the supremacy of God. Israel were warned that their election and privilege were based upon God's covenants with the fathers which He kept with their children, and not upon their superiority in number or in righteousness (Deuteronomy 7:7).

The man of the highest attainments in wealth, strength or wisdom could make his boast only in his humble acceptance of the Divine ways (Jeremiah 9:23-24). In that passage which especially outlines the meaning of salvation—a deliverance from all the evil of the world and its consequence so outstanding that it could only be compared to an exchanging of death for life—it is twice declared, ''By grace ye are saved . . . for by grace are ye saved through faith; and that not of yourselves: it is the gift of God: not of works, lest any man should boast'' (Ephesians 2:5-9). Perhaps even now we are not completely delivered from the concept that somehow by our doctrinal orthodoxy alone or by our punctilious carrying out of certain acts we can earn salvation. Without adequate ideas about God we can neither know nor respond to His purpose; and when we do know and believe, our faith can be expressed only in what we do. But that response is not our righteousness, which can only be based upon faith in what God has done, ''according to the good pleasure of his will'': see Essay 30, page 256.

Verse 10: *''But is now made manifest by the appearing of our Saviour Jesus Christ'':* The purpose determined before the creation of the world was made visible in the historical facts of the life and death of "Christ Jesus" (RV: for the order of words see on 1 Timothy 1:1, page 15), who is revealed as "our Saviour" because he embodies God's purpose to save. It is noteworthy that Christ never claimed the title of Saviour for himself (see Essay 29, page 255). The concept of an everlasting purpose in historical manifestation is frequent in Scripture. Isaiah particularly links the God of Creation with the covenants with Israel (chapters 40-45; see also Psalms 135, 136, 147 etc.). The purpose in Christ is also an eternal mystery "made manifest to his saints" (1 Corinthians 1:26; Romans 3:21; also especially Romans 16:25-27). See also notes on 1 Timothy 3:16 (pages 102-105); and for the phrase "the appearing" see pages 213, 214 and on Titus 2:11-14, especially pages 393-395.

"Who hath abolished death": The saving work of Christ is now summarised, with an emphasis appropriate to a man under sentence of death but also an apostle by the will of God according to the promise of life. *Katargeō*, 'abolish', is a powerful word, as its various translations clearly show: "make of none effect", "make void", "destroy", "loose from", "deliver from" (Romans 3:3,31; 4:14; 6:6; 7:2,6); "bring to nought", "come to nought", "fail", "vanish away", "put down", "be done away", "abolish" (1 Corinthians 1:28; 2:6; 13:8,10,11; 15:24; 2 Corinthians 3:7,13) and notably "The last enemy that shall be *destroyed* is death" (1 Corinthians 15:26).

Death, with the definite article as in the verse we are considering, reigned as a tyrant (Romans 5:14), but henceforth has no power (cf. Hebrews 2:14) since Christ abolished it by his resurrection, granting the hope of resurrection to all that are his. If they are still subject to death they know that they will come forth from the grave.

"And hath brought life and immortality to light through the gospel": To reveal the true nature and reality of eternal life was to pour a flood of light over what had previously been hidden and obscure. "For God, who commanded the light to shine out of darkness, hath shined in our hearts, to give the light of the knowledge of the glory of God in the face of Jesus Christ", in whom "was life, and the life was the light of men" (2 Corinthians 4:6; John 1:4). This life is characterised by immortality, or more

correctly, *incorruptibility*, the term Paul uses regularly to describe the resurrection-body (1 Corinthians 15:42,50,53), which is a body changed from corruptibility (verse 52) and "fashioned like unto (the Lord's) glorious body" (Philippians 3:21). Incorruptibility is a gift which derives from God Himself, "who only hath immortality" (1 Timothy 6:16; Romans 2:7).

Contrary to the theory of those who think that these Letters betray ideas akin to Gnosticism, with their stress upon knowledge, "Paul affirms that this disclosure has been made *through the gospel*, by which he means not just the Christian message, but the entire revelation of God in Christ which forms its content" (Kelly, *A Commentary on the Pastoral Epistles*).

The important parenthesis of verses 9 and 10 provides the doctrinal foundation for the exhortation to Timothy which Paul now resumes. Such passages are again entirely characteristic of his writings and provide us with a good pattern for our own exhortations. They should not be mere spiritual homilies, psychological sketches or expressions of personal experience, but a solid basis of Scripture from which may be drawn both patience and comfort, that we may have hope.

Verse 11: *"Whereunto I am appointed a preacher, and an apostle, and a teacher of the Gentiles":* Paul's "whereunto" is almost triumphant: for the Lord's prisoner he might be, but for such a Gospel as this who would not gladly suffer, especially since the Word of God was not bound? No prisoner he, in reality, for he had been appointed to a great work, no less than the proclamation of the Gospel. The three offices named are referred to in 1 Timothy 2:7, on which see the note on pages 65,66. As a "preacher" (more correctly, "herald") he had to give the message the greatest possible publicity, even by his sufferings if necessary; as an "apostle" he spoke not of himself, but had to transmit faithfully what had been committed to his trust by the one who had sent him; as a "teacher" he had to guide into the way of wisdom and truth by personal example as well as by the content of his message. See Essay 4 on "Sound Doctrine", pages 46-48. The parallels between Paul's situation and commission and Timothy's would be clear enough to the young man: he too had to render a public witness, and might have similarly to endure (2:3). The exhortation begun in 1:6 thus comes full circle with the words which follow.

Verse 12: *"For the which cause I also suffer these things":* The reason for confidence, even pride, in his sufferings is that nothing can alter God's purpose. If then he suffers for this cause, he must as surely rejoice in the crown of life yet to be bestowed: "For as the sufferings of Christ abound in us, so our consolation also aboundeth by Christ" (2 Corinthians 1:5).

"Nevertheless I am not ashamed": See on verse 8. But the Apostle's confidence goes beyond not feeling ashamed because he is despised—"the filth and offscouring of all things unto this day" (1 Corinthians 4:13)—bound like any thief or cut-throat. He knows he will never be *put to shame,* "according to my earnest expectation and my hope, that in nothing I shall be ashamed" (Philippians 1:20). And why should he be, if Christ, the risen Christ, is not ashamed to call us brethren, and God is not ashamed to be called the God of men of faith (Hebrews 2:11; 11:16)? Or as the Psalmist put it: "Our fathers trusted in thee . . . and thou didst deliver them. They cried unto thee, and were delivered: they trusted in thee, and were not ashamed" (Psalm 22:4,5, RV).

"For I know whom I have believed": For the thought behind the rest of this verse, see Essay 25 on "The Good Deposit" (page 221). As God had entrusted to Paul the Gospel as a *deposit,* so Paul had entrusted his life to Him, confident that his "life was hid with Christ in God" (Colossians 3:3).

The Exhortation Resumed

Verse 13: *"Hold fast the form of sound words":* After the digression upon the testimony of the Lord and his own relationship to it, Paul resumes his exhortation to Timothy begun in verses 6-9. Timothy is to *keep as his pattern* the sound or healthful teaching he had received from Paul, his spiritual father. The only way to combat the other-teachers and faithfully to discharge his responsibility as overseer in Ephesus was to be a herald and a teacher of the Gospel as it had been committed to him.

Hupotupōsis was the artist's sketch or the author's synopsis in which the essence or the spirit of the work contemplated was exactly caught. Once it had been laid down, the detailed picture or the finished book was an exposition of it. So Paul is not here concerned with some creed or formula to be repeated but is urging Timothy to be unswervingly loyal to the teaching *"which thou hast heard of me"*. An example of such a *hupotupōsis* is given us in 2:8—"Remember that Jesus Christ of the seed of David was raised from the dead *according to my gospel"*. Any exposition of the Gospel which nullified that vital point of doctrine was a cankerous, not a healthful word (2:17,18).

Even though the doctrine that it does not matter what one believes so long as it is sincerely held finds no place in the Pastoral Epistles, the *spirit* in which one holds and proclaims the Truth is important. It must be *"in faith and love in Christ Jesus"*. Timothy had to live as well as hold the faith, manifesting all the qualities of the true believer, as in 1 Timothy 4:12, where faith and love are among the attributes which make him in his turn a *tupos*, an example, for others to follow (cf. Titus 2:7 and note, page 390). We do well to bear this exhortation in mind today, when the remedies offered for the ecclesias of the late twentieth century are either an emotional zeal which is said to render doctrine unimportant, or a rigid traditionalism to be preserved by whatever method even when the end scarcely justifies the means. To follow either is not to know what manner of spirit we are of.

Verse 14: *"That good thing which was committed unto thee"* is quite simply "the good deposit" (page 221). The Revised Version's "guard" is the more faithful rendering of the verb. Paul obviously regards Timothy as his "successor" and "legatee" (2:2), who is to preserve the Gospel safe from corruption and distortion. It was not only a matter of maintaining a historical tradition: the very life of the ecclesia depended upon it.

"Keep by the Holy Spirit which dwelleth in us": The "us" here is certainly Paul and Timothy. The young man is not to rely upon his own strength but upon that which God would give, indeed had already given if Timothy would "kindle it into flame" (1 Timothy 4:14; page 134). According to Paul in 1 Corinthians (12:4-11,28-31) there had been given to the servants of the first century ecclesia an appropriate endowment of the Spirit for the necessary tasks of grounding, settling and edifying the infant community (Ephesians 4:11-16). The interesting and vitally important fact emerges, however, that the gift was still "subject unto the prophets" or other recipient (1 Corinthians 14:32) and was no substitute for faith, hope and love (1 Corinthians 13). The sense of personal responsibility was necessary to ensure that the gift was exercised

to the edifying of the ecclesia, and some of the elders of Ephesus who had been "ordained" by Paul had not been impelled by an inescapable sense of duty toward God, but had been more concerned with "drawing away disciples after themselves" (Acts 20).

Although the "us" of this passage, therefore, probably refers to Paul and Timothy, rather than to believers in general, the exhortation can be taken to ourselves, even though the Spirit-gift of "ordination" is not for us. Paul would show the same fatherly concern for us today, that we should hold fast the form of sound words, as we have been taught of him through the power of his word. For, as with Timothy, it would have no power in us if we were not receptive; and "if any man have not the Spirit of Christ, he is none of his" (Romans 8:9). Moreover, we too have not to strive in our own might, but in that which God supplies to those who put their trust in Him.

1:15-18—Examples to Follow—and Avoid

Verse 15: *"This thou knowest, that all they which are in Asia be turned away from me"*: Many and varied are the explanations given of this sentence, from the wholesale defection of all the ecclesias in Asia to the failure of some of Paul's friends to stand with him in his trial (see 4:16). Certainly Paul is referring to something that affected him personally, but it is stretching "in Asia" too far, to imagine that it refers to some who had come "out of Asia" and were now back home, instead of staying to support the Apostle. Moreover, "this thou knowest" seems too emphatic to imply other than that Timothy knew because he, like the defectors, was in Asia at the time, rather than that Paul was now confirming what Timothy had only just gathered from the returning Asiatics.

There is no reason why "all in Asia" should not mean all those in Ephesus, the capital of the Roman province, on whom Paul had placed reliance either as personal friends or as faithful elders. As has been pointed out, *"all* are turned away" is consistent with the language of a man in prison deserted by trusted companions. "Turned away" is indeed a strong phrase, as in 4:4, Titus 1:14 and Hebrews 12:25. The personal pronoun, however, suggests that it is not the apostasy of the brethren Paul has in mind, but possibly the attitude of these brethren at the time of his arrest— a strong contrast to the tears of Timothy, of which Paul also retained a vivid and poignant recollection (1:4). It is possible, though, that Paul is referring to the "other-teachers", who had rejected his warnings and had brought such a different atmosphere into the ecclesia from that obtaining at the time of the visit described in Acts 20. *"Phygellus and Hermogenes"* are not known apart from the single reference to them here.

Verse 16: *"The Lord give mercy unto the house of Onesiphorus":* It has been inferred, probably correctly, that Onesiphorus was dead at the time Paul wrote this, since there is a two-fold reference to his house (also in 4:19), as though his family had survived him and were in some need or difficulty (but see verse 18 below). Aptly named "a bringer of benefit", Onesiphorus is also known only through these references in 2 Timothy. Unlike Phygellus and Hermogenes and the rest, he had been an active supporter of Paul's.

"For he oft refreshed me": The word for "refreshed" is a "oncer", although it is related to "the times of *refreshing"* of Acts 3:20. The Old Testament antecedents of Peter's words there show the refreshing to be a time of renewal of spirit, of springs in the desert and of comforting—all of which Onesiphorus represented for the Apostle in prison. It is salutary to realise that even a Paul can feel the need of companionship, and although we do not know in detail the form the refreshing took, we do not need much imagination to realise how much benefit was derived from the visit, the spiritual conversation, perhaps the prayers together, and the gifts of food and other things to compensate for the rigours of a prison régime. "Lord, when saw we thee . . . in prison, and came unto thee?"

"And was not ashamed of my chain": See the notes on verse 8 (pages 239,252). It could be that Onesiphorus had placed himself in some danger in his diligent searching for and frequent visits to a prisoner who had fallen foul of the Imperial authorities.

Verse 17: *"He sought me out very diligently and found me":* The record of Paul's case was almost certainly kept in the *Tabularium,* the Imperial public record office which still stands at one end of the Forum, beneath the Palazzio Senatorio or "City Hall" of modern Rome. There was no reason why the details or the whereabouts of Paul should have been widely known, however, and if Onesiphorus were a stranger in Rome he would have had difficulty in tracking down the Apostle. Important though he was to the Christians at Rome, Paul was but one of many awaiting trial, and the brethren may well have been reluctant at first to claim too accurate a knowledge to communicate to a comparative stranger. Alternatively, if Paul was still a notable prisoner as a leader of a now suspect sect (cf. Barabbas, Matthew 27:16), there was a further reason why the brethren would wish to prove Onesiphorus' credentials before giving him the information: caution ruled even if they were not afraid.

If Paul were not confined in the notorious Mamertine Prison, we must add to the foregoing the difficulty of finding one's way in a city as vast as Rome, and still suffering from the effects of the devastating fire of AD 64. At any rate, the diligence of Onesiphorus was rewarded, and Paul's statement is almost a cry of triumph: *"And he found me!"*

A Prayer for Mercy

Verse 18: *"The Lord grant unto him"*: This verse has been taken as conclusive proof that Onesiphorus was *not* dead at the time Paul wrote. If he were, the argument runs, we have the only example of a prayer for the dead in Scripture. In so far as the Catholic practice of prayers for the dead is in view, that their souls may be released from purgatory, or any other practice which envisages survival after death, one can have sympathy with the objection. But the prayer is *"that he may find mercy of the Lord in that day"*—the day of judgement, which the Apostle has constantly in view in these Letters and in expectation of which he makes his solemn exhortations and warnings (1 Timothy 6:13-16; 2 Timothy 4:1; Titus 2:11-14, and notes).

The prayer for mercy "in that day" is natural to the Apostle, therefore, and, in full cognisance of the fact that for Onesiphorus, if he were dead, the book was made up already, as it were, and the course of his life irrevocably run, Paul can still with prayer and supplication, with thanksgiving, let his request be made known unto God (Philippians 4:6).

There remains the question of the identity of the two "Lords" of this passage: the first has the definite article, the second does not. Are both words to be applied to the Lord Jesus? Certainly the judgement is committed into the hands of the Son, and the underlying idea of Matthew 25 in this passage makes this identification of "the Lord" more probable. For all Onesiphorus' many acts of kindness, being done to Paul, had been done to Jesus, and Paul requests that when the Son of Man comes in his glory, he will say unto Onesiphorus, "Come, thou blessed of my Father ... Inasmuch ...". Yet it is God who is both the source of mercy and the Judge of all the earth (Romans 2:6; 3:6; 1 Timothy 6:14-15), as His very Name declared in, for example, Exodus 34:6-7.

How remarkable, then, to discover that *Kyrios*, without the article, is in fact the Septuagint form of the Name of God, rendered in the Authorised Version of the Old Testament as LORD. When Paul writes of mercy *para Kyriou*, "from the Lord", he must surely have this in mind. No doubt also, Paul intentionally repeats the verb "find" from the previous verse: what better reward for a diligent attempt to *find* the Apostle in order to minister unto him, than that the seeker should *find* mercy of the Lord in the day of his coming?

"And in how many things he ministered unto me at Ephesus, thou knowest very well": Onesiphorus' behaviour in Rome was evidently well in keeping with his character, since he had been equally assiduous in the Apostle's service and no doubt in that of others in Ephesus. At any rate, Timothy had personal knowledge of these acts of kindness, as the verb for "know" indicates. In verse 15 it was *oidas*, the knowledge of facts: here it is *ginōskeis*, a more intimate knowledge based on experience. Perhaps the best comment on this whole section, and upon Onesiphorus, is to be found in Hebrews 6:10—"For God is not unrighteous to forget your work and labour of love, which ye have shewed toward his name, in that ye have ministered to the saints, and do minister."

ESSAY 27

Believers and Faithful in the New Testament

AS a further proof that "the faith which dwelt" in Lois and Eunice was not the belief in God which all Jews professed but the faith in Christ, Hendriksen (*1 & 2 Timothy and Titus*, New Testament Commentary, Banner of Truth Trust) makes some interesting points on which the following comments are based:

1. Eunice is introduced at the beginning of Paul's second journey as a *believing* Jewish woman.

2. "Belief" and "faith" are the same word in Greek, and it is therefore probable that the sense of Lydia's words in Acts 16:15, after the Lord had opened her heart to those things Paul was saying and she was baptized, is "If ye judge me to be *a believer in the Lord,* come into my house". Before her baptism she had been described (verse 14) as one that *worshipped God,* which is the term usually applied to *religious* proselytes (Acts 13:43), devout women (13:50) and devout Greeks (17:4) who assembled at the synagogue with the Jews and who were amongst the first to respond to the apostolic preaching (17:4 again).

3. In Acts 16:31 and 34 the Philippian gaoler is described as "*believing* in God with all his house" after his baptism.

It seems that Paul uses the term for those who had formerly trusted in the promises, whether Jew or Gentile, and then had eagerly accepted Christ as the confirmation and fulfilment of those promises. In Romans 4:12 Abraham is the father of them "who are not of the circumcision only, but who also walk in the steps of that faith of our father Abraham, which he had being yet

250

uncircumcised". "So then they which are of (the) *faith* are blessed with *faithful* Abraham"—the *believer* (Galatians 3:9). In 2 Corinthians 6:15 the *believers* are Christians, Jew or Gentile, as the parallel between *"Christ"* and *"he that believeth"* and between *"Belial"* and *"an infidel"*—he that is *"not a believer"*—indicates. Finally, in Acts 10:45, converted Jews are described as "they of the circumcision *which believed* ...".

ESSAY 28

The Lord's Prisoner

THE word for "prisoner" (*desmios*) is the usual Greek expression and always denotes that the captive was not merely in prison but *bound*, either in wooden stocks or a collar (Acts 16:24), or in chains. There is frequent reference to the use of chains in the New Testament, and on occasions in a speech Paul indicated his own fetters to emphasise his point: "For the hope of Israel I am bound with this chain" (Acts 28:20). Onesiphorus was "not ashamed of my chain" and was a frequent visitor to the Apostle's prison in Rome (2 Timothy 1:16-17). The first precaution taken by the captain of the guard in Jerusalem, when he rescued Paul from the mob, was to bind him with two chains before opening his enquiry (see Mark 5:3; Luke 8:29; Acts 12:6,7; 21:33).

Tradition and Truth

In Rome there are many traditions about Peter and Paul and relics supposedly associated with them in their sojourn there are displayed for veneration. We can dismiss the superstitious element, of course, and question the traditions, but we can sometimes learn from the objects or places themselves.

In the Church of St. Peter in Chains in Rome, the supposed fetters that bound that Apostle are on view. Whatever their true origin they are very old and at least are fashioned on the ancient model, if not themselves of the first century. They are of iron and very heavy, and would obviously chafe the limbs and weary the captive, encumbered as he was in every movement. Together with the scourgings which were freely administered as part of the process of interrogation, they expressed the brutality of the treatment meted out to all who came into conflict with the law and order of the day. Certainly such humiliation should never have been inflicted upon any ambassador, much less one who came with a message of reconciliation and peace.

Whether Paul bore his chains throughout the long journey from Caesarea to Rome for his first imprisonment is doubtful, especially in view of the high regard in which he was held by the centurion in charge. Apparently the prisoners on the wrecked ship were not in chains either, otherwise the soldiers would not have advised killing them to prevent their escape. It is probable that Paul was only loosely fettered on the march up the Appian Way until the point where the road dips down and the city opened out in full view. There was then but a short march to the gate, and so the prisoner was once more heavily secured in the manner traditional for captives being brought into the city.

Where was he then imprisoned? There are two possibilities. If the word *praitōrion* in Philippians referred to the camp of the Praetorian Guard, then Paul was incarcerated in the barracks on the northern side of the city. But in fact the transport and guarding of prisoners from the provinces was not the duty of the emperor's personal bodyguard, but of the troops stationed in the *castra peregrina*, or barracks for troops from outside the city. It is far more likely that the translation "Caesar's palace", or imperial court, is the correct one since the palace was a general head-quarters, and probably housed those who, having appealed to the emperor, were detained until sentence was formally passed which determined their fate—death, imprisonment or liberty. The evidence suggests that Paul, who had to wait the statutory two years to see if his accusers came to conduct the prosecution, as the law demanded, was taken there first and then transferred to "house arrest" in his own hired house (Acts 28:30).

A Grim Abode

The second imprisonment envisaged in 2 Timothy was, however, a vastly different affair. The arrest and prosecution were a matter of state, not of private or provincial concern; for this there was no "open" prison. Again tradition puts both Peter and Paul in the Mamertine Prison, at the foot of the Capitoline Hill. This was the scene of famous executions in Roman history and the place where the captives led in a Roman general's triumph were done to death, before the procession went on its way up to the Capitol to give thanks for victory to the supreme gods of the Roman world.

Again, there is nothing inherently improbable in such a tradition. From what is known of dungeons in the Ancient World (compare the gaol which still stands in Philippi), the Mamertine Prison is as typical as any. It is gloomy, dank and chill, even sinister in its atmosphere, the kind of place in which Paul would regard with apprehension the onset of winter and urgently request "the cloke that I left at Troas with Carpus" (2 Timothy 4:13). The present-day visitor to the lower cell can easily understand why Paul so greatly appreciated the visits of Onesiphorus, who "oft refreshed me, and was not ashamed of my chain"—truly a breath of fresh air to revive the spirit of a man who knew that the time of his departure was at hand (1:16; 4:6).

It is interesting to note, in passing, that in 2 Corinthians 2:14-16 (RV) we have a probable allusion to the ceremony of a Roman triumph, during which incense was offered as the procession passed by, the conquering general escorted by prominent citizens and his victorious army, for whom the occasion was one of joy. Accompanying them also were the mourning captives, destined either for slavery or death. The Gospel proclaimed the Lord's triumph, as "he led captivity captive", to bring life and peace to those who received it, but judgement and death to those who refused.

> "Now thanks be unto God, which always leadeth us in triumph in Christ, and maketh manifest through us the savour of his knowledge in every place. For we are a sweet savour of Christ and God, in them that are being saved, and in them that are perishing; to the one a savour from death unto death; to the other a savour from life unto life. And who is sufficient for these things?" (2 Corinthians 2:16)

Who, indeed!

254

ESSAY 29

"God our Saviour"

"SAVIOUR" as a title of God is characteristic of the Pastoral Epistles (page 34). Throughout the Old Testament God's power to save is emphasised by psalmist and prophet, who take up the theme from the Song of Moses at the Red Sea: "The LORD is my strength and song, and he is become my salvation" (Exodus 15:2; Psalm 118:14; Isaiah 12:2). Saving grace is revealed in that holy Name which expresses all His compassion and forgiveness, together with His judgement (Exodus 34:6,7). But in what sense is it true that He *hath* saved us? Some have found a matter for controversy in the question of whether salvation is a "present possession". There are those Scriptures which speak of salvation and eternal life as already granted, and those which refer the gift of both to the day of judgement and recompense.

As usual, the resolution of the problem lies in rightly dividing—holding a straight course in—the Word of God. The language which speaks of God's purpose as already fulfilled expresses the finality of all God's works from His point of view: "He spake and it was done"; they "were finished from the foundation of the world" (Psalm 33:9; Hebrews 4:3). Man's part as an individual in the work of God, however, is not so sure. Those whose names are already written in the book of life may have them blotted out; one of the twelve appointed to sit upon thrones, judging the twelve tribes of Israel, turned out to be a son of perdition. God can call things that are not as though they are, and even the dead "live unto him"; but for us victory is not certain until "the only wise God our Saviour" presents us "faultless before the presence of his glory with exceeding joy" (Philippians 4:3; Revelation 3:5; Matthew 19:28; John 17:12; Mark 12:26,27; Jude 24,25).

255

ESSAY 30

The Good Pleasure of His Will

"GOOD WILL", "good pleasure", "be well pleased" are all translations of either the verb *eudokeō* or the noun *eudokia*. The Old Testament equivalent is *ratzon* translated "good will" in Deuteronomy 33:16. The theme we have been considering can be summed up beautifully in a brief consideration of the "good pleasure which he hath purposed in himself". The expressions mentioned above occur in Luke 2:14, Ephesians 1:5,9, Philippians 2:13, and 2 Thessalonians 1:11. The contexts are the birth of Christ, the predestination of the saints to adoption as God's children by Jesus Christ, the revelation of the mystery of God's will, a prayer that God "may fulfil all the good pleasure of his goodness, and the work of faith with power". In Matthew 11:26 the phrase, "for so it seemed good (*eudokia*) in thy sight", figures in the Lord's comment upon Psalm 8, which is eloquent of the purpose of God in the manifestation of His Name.

The verb occurs especially with reference to God's acknowledgement of His beloved Son at his baptism (Matthew 3:17; Mark 1:11; Luke 3:22) and at the Transfiguration (Matthew 17:5; 2 Peter 1:17). Its Old Testament roots are seen in Isaiah 42:1 (quoted in Matthew 12:18) and in Psalms 51:18 and 103:21.

The passages in the Psalms are closely related to the forgiveness of sins; the creation of a clean heart and the renewal of a right spirit, that a man may be enabled to worship rightly; the redemption of our life which is, apart from God's mercy, as a flower of the field; and the praise of His glory by the works of His hands, His angels and ministers alike (see Essay 51, "For We are His Workmanship", page 423).

In Deuteronomy 33:16, which refers to "the good will of him

256

who dwelt in the bush'', God's purpose in the manifestation of Himself and the glorifying of His Name was enunciated, a purpose to be unfolded with power and compassion. Israel, alas, did not respond and so, said Paul, ''with many of them he was *not well pleased*'' (1 Corinthians 10:5) and so could not accomplish His purpose in them.

The Second Letter to Timothy

CHAPTER 2

The Self-Discipline of the Man of God

2:1-13—The Need for Steadfastness and Dedication

Verse 1: *"Thou therefore, my son, be strong":* The link with the preceding verses in chapter 1 is made by the very strong *therefore*. In view of the example of men like Onesiphorus on the one hand and all them "of Asia" on the other, and of the precious nature of "the deposit" entrusted to him, Timothy had a clear and unmistakable duty. Perhaps the translation, "it is for *you* then", comes near the meaning. The power and sharpness of the exhortation is, in a manner characteristic of Paul, softened by the term of endearment. For the expression "my son", see notes on 1 Timothy 1:2 and 2 Timothy 1:2 (pages 16, 228).

"Be strong" is literally "be strengthened (continually)", a favourite idea of the Apostle Paul's. Abraham "waxed strong through faith" (Romans 4:20, RV) and the Ephesians were exhorted to "be made powerful in the Lord, and in the power of his might" (Ephesians 6:10, margin).

"In the grace that is in Christ Jesus": It is this phrase, however, which helps us to penetrate more deeply into Paul's meaning. It is not that Timothy is to acquire greater grace, if that were possible, but that through the grace given him in Christ he will have the necessary strength to do the work which is his responsibility as a servant of the Lord Jesus. As Paul put it in 1 Timothy 1:12, he that had counted him faithful, putting him into the ministry, also "enabled me", or "gave me the strength", using the same verb as here.

Perhaps the most powerful commentary of all, however, is in 2 Corinthians 12:9. Afflicted by some thorn in the flesh, Paul earnestly besought the Lord to remove it, thinking no doubt that his work would be better, his ministry more effective, if he were free from this burden. Strength and power do not find their source in freedom from pain, from problems or any of the other things to which the flesh is heir: *"My grace is sufficient for thee: for my strength is made perfect in weakness."* And "the power of Christ" would "rest upon" him (Gk. 'overshadow', like the cloud in the wilderness), if he gloried in his infirmities (2 Corinthians 12:10).

Verse 2: *"The things that thou hast heard of me":* The Apostle is convinced that his own course is nearly run (4:6-7) and that he will no more take up the task of preaching and teaching in the ecclesias. It is possible that he feels that Timothy could also be threatened with persecution or his ministry be cut short. So the Apostle is ensuring that there is a true "apostolic succession"— not a continuous line of men ordained by the successive transmission of a gift of ordination by the laying on of hands, but a passing on of the "deposit" of sound apostolic teaching. Timothy has a sound grasp of the faith: he must not only guard it, be strong in it, but also pass it on.

It is not so much general instruction in the Christian faith which is in question here. "What you have heard of me" is the apostolic Gospel itself, one important element of which is recalled to Timothy's attention in verse 8. There had been numerous attempts to vary this Gospel, notably in Galatia, in Corinth and in Ephesus itself. Paul had guarded it jealously: Timothy and his successors must do the same.

The Witness

"Among many witnesses": It has been pointed out that there are six ways of interpreting the original Greek phrase *dia pollōn marturōn*, according to whether one understands *dia* to mean 'by', or 'in the presence of', or whether "witnesses" can include such things as the miracles by which the the Lord "confirmed the word with signs following".

Four of these interpretations need not detain us here. It is tempting, however, to link this passage with 1 Timothy 6:12, where Timothy is described as having made his public confession "before many witnesses", and assume that Paul had previously instructed him in a similarly public way. This view seems strengthened by the references to the witness "of the prophecies which went before on thee" and "the presbytery", or eldership of Ephesus in 1 Timothy 1:18 and 4:14, where see notes (pages 36, 37, 134, 135).

This author's preference, however, is for the view that gives the meaning of *dia* as 'with the attestation of'. Paul is reminding Timothy of the fact that his Gospel could always be checked by the independent testimony of other authorities—the Scripture, the Lord's own disciples, or perhaps Timothy's own mother and grandmother, for example—so that not only the accuracy of his words but the interpretation of his teaching could be verified. For Paul was not preaching the gospel of "experience", although his experiences were all true to the nature of the Gospel message and its outworking in the believer. He proclaimed the historical facts about the Lord, set against the background of the prophetic testimony of the Old Testament, and witnessed personally by "above five hundred brethren at once; of whom the greater part remain unto this present, but some are fallen asleep" (1 Corinthians 15:3-7). Neither Paul nor an angel from heaven, and certainly not the other-teachers of Ephesus, had the right to make the Gospel into anything different (2 Corinthians 11:4; Galatians 1:6-9; 1 Timothy 6:3).

"The same commit thou to faithful men": The foregoing is seen to be doubly relevant in the light of this commandment to pass on what had been preserved. The noun for the "good deposit" (pages 201, 221, 245) comes from the same root as the verb "commit". The whole question of "succession" and the preservation of the Truth as a sacred trust is based upon a sound Scriptural principle.

God did speak directly to His people in a voice from heaven at Sinai and there were generations who heard the authoritative voice of the prophets, usually calling them to repentance. But throughout most of Israel's long history the spiritual education of successive generations should have been carried on by those who had "these words which I command thee . . . in thine heart: and thou shalt teach them diligently (the Hebrew word means 'to whet' or 'keep sharp') unto thy children . . . and when thy son asketh thee in time to come, saying, What mean the testimonies, and the statutes, and the judgments, which the LORD our God hath commanded you? Then thou shalt say unto thy son . . . the LORD commanded us . . . and it shall be our righteousness, if we observe to do all these commandments before the LORD our God" (Deuteronomy 6).

It cannot be too strongly emphasised today, especially in view of the growing tendency to attempt to base discipleship upon "an experience" and make the Gospel something purely subjective, that Divine teaching is a solemn charge to keep, with its own power to stimulate our obedience and deepen our reverence. If the Word makes no impact upon our hearts, we should be in no better case though we did hear the voice direct from heaven.

"Who shall be able to teach others also": The importance of faithfulness in those to whom the Word is committed is seen to be paramount. It is one of the main themes of these Letters, as we see in 1 Timothy 3 and Titus 1. The spiritual health of the ecclesia, today as then, will depend greatly upon the fact that there are in it those "apt to teach". The manner of their teaching could be as important as the content: both the Word and the pupil should be "in their heart". Or, as Paul put it in 1 Corinthians 4:14-17 (the reference to Timothy's rôle should not be overlooked):

"For though ye have *ten thousand instructors* in Christ, yet have ye *not may fathers:* for in Christ Jesus I have begotten you through the gospel. Wherefore I beseech you, be ye followers of me. For this cause have I sent unto you Timotheus, who is *my beloved son,* and *faithful* in the Lord, who shall bring you into remembrance of *my ways which be in Christ,* as I teach every where in every church."

The Good Soldier

Verse 3: "Thou therefore endure hardness as a good soldier of Jesus Christ": The soldier's calling demands great personal courage and endurance, but he is *not alone.* He is but rarely called upon to fight in isolation, for his individual actions are part of a battle or campaign to be viewed as a whole. So he must have a sense of *esprit de corps,* that sense of community, in which the service of a captain and honour of a cause transcend all personal feeling or ambition.

This sense is clearly brought out here in Paul's second use of the verb *sunkakopathein*, discussed in the note on 2 Timothy 1:8 (page 239): Timothy was *to take his share* of the rough treatment and hardships which are a minister's lot, and of which Paul's current plight was a good example. But there were two sides even to the question of hardship: to take one's share in it was also to receive great comfort and encouragement, to be part of a brotherhood in which the fellowship of suffering was the prelude to a fellowship of glory and rejoicing (1 Thessalonians 2:19; 2 Corinthians 1:5, etc.).

It may come as a surprise to discover that this verse is the only one in the whole of his writings in which Paul uses the word "soldier". His metaphors taken from the soldier's life and service are frequent, however, and it will be convenient to give separate consideration to them for the light they cast upon the discipline Timothy is being urged to accept: see Essay 31, "Paul's Use of Military Metaphor", page 286.

Verse 4: *"No man that warreth entangleth himself with the affairs of this life":* The disciple, then, like the soldier, has already in effect made the sacrifice of his life. He is wholly concerned with exercising himself unto godliness to the limit of his capacity (Romans 12:6-8). Also, like the soldier, he has neither the need nor the desire to be entangled in the things the Gentiles seek after, "for your heavenly Father knoweth that ye have need of all these things" (Matthew 6:31-33). The verb "entangled" is used once more in Scripture, again with reference to worldly things which defile (2 Peter 2:20).

"That he may please him who enrolled him as a soldier" (RV): To abstain from worldly pursuits is now seen to be no negative attitude—an asceticism which is an end in itself, sometimes called in modern parlance "the hair-shirt mentality", that leads a man to make himself uncomfortable for the sake of it. The soldier's life was in itself a career, appropriately known as being "in the Services", with the positive aim of his being a *good* soldier. His allegiance was not to some faceless corporate body but directly to his commanding officer, to whom had often been committed the task of raising a legion for a specific campaign. So Timothy was "a good soldier of Jesus Christ", who was "the captain of (his) salvation" (Hebrews 2:10).

The Spiritual Athlete

Verse 5: *"And if a man also strive for masteries"*: The "masteries" were the athletic games (RV) which were a prominent feature of Greek city life. For a more detailed note on Paul's use of the athletic metaphor, see on 1 Timothy 4:8 and 6:12 and Essay 21 (pages 127, 210). In introducing this theme here the Apostle is not merely offering another example of the kind of self-discipline which the Lord's servant must be prepared to exercise: he is adding a further dimension to it, as will become apparent from the second half of the verse. It is true that by the first century, following a trend similar to that observed in modern Olympics and other sporting events, there were "professional" sportsmen as well as those amateurs who had been the ideal of the earlier Greek city-state. However, the general principle Paul cites would be applicable to either class of athlete.

"Yet is he not crowned, except he strive lawfully": The soldier committed himself to a certain way of life upon enrolment; the athlete had to keep to a certain code of practice throughout the whole of his training and competition. There were similarities between the soldier's discipline and the athlete's self-denial during his training period, and the competitor in the major games, at Olympia, Corinth or Delphi for example, had to take an oath that he had conducted himself well throughout the long months of preparation before he was allowed to compete on the appointed day.

Then he had to run, wrestle or display his skill strictly according to the rules and might even be disqualified after victory if subsequent enquiry revealed some irregularity. There was a spirit of fair play to be cultivated and shortcomings were treated as acts of disloyalty to the athlete's code. Certain tricks, stratagems and the taking of mean advantage were completely barred. So Timothy is being exhorted to faithfulness and loyalty during the exercise of his ministry, above all in his careful handling both of the Gospel committed to him and of "those that oppose themselves" (see 2:25). Otherwise he would "run in vain" (Galatians 2:2; cf. Matthew 7:21-23).

The message has relevance to us today. No plea of "the service of the truth" can be entered as a justification for sharp practice, flouting of authority, evasion of just dues or taxes, plagiarism

263

of another's work, discourtesy or any other works of the flesh by which the world seeks to advance its own causes.

The Spiritual Husbandman

Verse 6: *"The husbandman that laboureth must be first partaker of the fruits"*: So the figure changes once again. "Husbandman" is a "oncer", though its related word, "husbandry", is used in 1 Corinthians 3:9 for the preacher's work of labouring together with God. The emphasis here is on *laboureth*. The idle, lazy farmer who is afraid of hard work can never expect a harvest. The diligent, on the other hand, has above all else and beyond everyone else, an incontestable right to enjoy the fruit of his labour. The labourer in the Gospel will be blessed of God and is entitled to some recompense in respect (and perhaps in the first century, at least, some measure of support) from those for whom he works. See Romans 1:13, Philippians 1:22 and 1 Timothy 5:17,18, with notes, pages 161, 162.

So, says Spicq (*Les Epîtres Pastorales*), "there is a progression to be observed in service and reward: first there is renunciation (as when one dedicates himself to the noble career of military service); keeping the rules laid down (like the athlete); perseverance in the work (with the characteristic zeal of the farmer); secondly, in this way, when one pleases God, he will be crowned by Him, and will be among the first to share the benefits of His Kingdom".

Verse 7: *"Consider what I say"*: Perhaps "Think out my meaning" conveys the best sense. Paul has given only a brief outline, although the principles are clear enough. There are deeper implications, and applications of the principles in practice, which could prove difficult or delicate, and these Timothy must work out for himself.

"For the Lord shall give thee understanding in all things" (RV): This encouragement confirms the interpretation just given above. "Understanding" is in fact right judgement, and we may compare its use here with Colossians 1:9-11:

"(We) do not cease to pray for you, and to desire that ye might be filled with the knowledge of his will in all wisdom and *spiritual understanding*: that ye might walk worthy of the Lord unto all pleasing, being fruitful in every good work, and increasing in the knowledge of God; strengthened with all might, according to his glorious power, unto all patience and longsuffering with joyfulness.''

2:8-13—The Exhortation Continued

Verse 8: *"Remember Jesus Christ, risen from the dead, of the seed of David"* (RV): Verse 7 was in effect an aside, after which Paul resumes his exhortation: Timothy is to take as his inspiration and example the Lord himself, supreme pattern of faithful service, endurance (Hebrews 12:2) and suffering, and the first to enter into the great reward: God raised him from the dead. The historical event, which is the heart of the Gospel, is the source of strength and endurance as well as of comfort (1 Thessalonians 4:14-18) for all who follow his steps. The order of words—*Jesus* before *Christ*—appears nowhere else in this epistle, and this is probably because the whole phrase, "Jesus Christ, risen from the dead, of the seed of David", is a brief statement of faith, quoted from some early catechism (Essay 5, page 49), in which the Davidic descent and Divine Sonship of the Lord Jesus were set out.

This was *"according to my gospel"* (see also Romans 2:16; 16:25; 1 Timothy 1:11), since Paul was always at pains to "persuade them concerning Jesus, both out of the Law of Moses, and out of the prophets" (Acts 28:23). The theme of our verse is well expressed in Romans 1:1-5:

"The gospel of God (which he had promised afore by his prophets in the holy scriptures), concerning his Son *Jesus Christ* our Lord, which was made *of the seed of David* according to the flesh, and declared to be the Son of God with power, according to the spirit of holiness, *by the resurrection from the dead*: by whom *we have received grace and apostleship ...*"

So once again we are reminded that "morality" and the Christian life, that is, the life of the disciple, are based upon fundamental doctrines about the purpose of God in Christ, doctrines which are expressed in easily remembered phrases to be kept in mind at all times.

Verse 9: *"Wherein I suffer trouble, as an evil doer, even unto bonds":* The foregoing statement, indeed the whole of Paul's exhortation, is now reinforced by this reference to his own case. It was for the preaching of the facts about Christ's nature and resurrection (which is the significance of his "wherein" here) and for no other reason that he was suffering "even unto bonds". The two words for "suffer trouble" and "evil doer" are "oncers" for the Apostle.

The play upon words of *kakopatheō* ('evil-suffer') with *kakourgos* ('evil-doer') brings out the humiliation Paul endured by being condemned as a common criminal, a pestilent, seditious fellow (Acts 24:5), because he preached righteousness and peace. He bore it bravely and never allowed himself to be deflected from his purpose; but that does not mean that he did not feel it keenly, as we can gather from such passages like 1 Corinthians 4:13:

> "Being defamed, we entreat: we are made as the filth of the world, and are the offscouring (*peripsēma*) of all things unto this day."

The *peripsēma* was the dirt scraped from an athlete's body after he had been massaged with olive oil!

Again, Paul was following his Master, who "endured the cross, despising the shame" (Hebrews 12:2). The only other use in Scripture of the word *kakourgos* ('evil-doer') is in Luke 23:32,33,39. The Lord was "numbered among the transgressors", being crucified between two *"malefactors*, one on the right hand, and the other on the left".

"But the word of God is not bound": This is almost a cry of triumph; for the spirit of it see that earlier letter written from prison, Philippians 1:12-14 and pages 239, 252.

Suffering and Fellowship

Verse 10: *"Therefore I endure all things for the elect's sakes":* We are now given a deeper insight into the heart and mind of the Apostle. From the time when he heard with a sense of shock the voice of Jesus declare, "I am Jesus whom thou persecutest" (Acts 9:5), Paul had realised that the service of Christ was the service of his brethren also, and that in imparting to them "not the gospel of God only, but *also our own souls, because ye were dear unto us"* (1 Thessalonians 2:8), he was fulfilling his ministry. He travailed in birth again, "until Christ be formed" in them (Galatians 4:19), and was gentle amongst them "as a nurse cherisheth her children" (1 Thessalonians 2:7). His joy and hope, his crown of rejoicing, would be to stand side by side with them "in the presence of our Lord Jesus Christ at his coming. For ye are our glory and joy" (verses 19,20). All this lies behind this profession in 2 Timothy 2:10.

But is there something more? There is a distinct impression to be gained from the Scriptures that there is a *certain measure* of tribulation for the saints to endure before the Lord comes. It is as though the "sufferings of Christ" are something more than that which Jesus himself endured: the "body of Christ", which is the church, fellowships the sufferings, or takes its share of them, as they will fellowship the glory to be revealed. It is clearly stated that there is a "time appointed", and that for the elect's sake the days will be shortened; otherwise "there should no flesh be saved" (Matthew 24:22). In the Revelation, the cry of the souls under the altar—"How long, O Lord, holy and true ... ?"—is answered by the command that they should rest "until their fellowservants also and their brethren, that should be killed as they were, *should be fulfilled*" (6:9-11). A similar thought is expressed in Colossians 1:23-24:

> "I Paul am made a minister; who now rejoice in my sufferings for you, and *fill up that which is behind* (RV, lacking) *of the afflictions of Christ* in my flesh *for his body's sake, which is the church.*"

Is Paul then saying here (2 Timothy 2:10) that just as the Lord was conscious (especially in Gethsemane) that the weight of responsibility for the salvation of his disciples rested upon his shoulders, so Paul realises that *"the salvation which is in Christ Jesus with eternal glory"* is somehow brought nearer for the elect as he faithfully endures? If so, then that alternative translation of 2 Peter 3:12 (RV margin) may well be correct, which declares that by our earnest desire and prayer we can somehow "hasten the coming of the day of God".

2:11-13—A Faithful Saying

Verses 11-13 constitute the fourth "Faithful Saying" of the Pastoral Epistles. For a general statement on this characteristic of the Letters see Essay 5, pages 49-51. This saying we shall discuss separately in Essay 32, pages 289-292.

2:14-21—Opposing False Teachers

Verse 14: "Of these things put them in remembrance": Paul now turns to the practical aspect of the foregoing exhortations in the then contemporary ecclesial situation in Ephesus. Like Moses in Deuteronomy he is constantly urging the necessity of keeping certain things in remembrance, if spiritual disaster is to be avoided. So Timothy is to *keep on remembering* (the verb is a continuous command). Often we avoid repetition of necessary exhortation, on the ground that it has been said (or written!) once before, but the whole tenor of Scripture in the Law, the prophets and the apostles is against us. Against us too is the example of the Lord himself who, remembering our frame, gave us a weekly memorial feast "until he come". Such exhortation was to be Timothy's regular practice also.

"These things" are the positive doctrinal statements of "my gospel" which Paul has just set forth. The sound method of them he now describes both positively and negatively. The importance of method is emphasised by the solemn *"charging them before* (RV, in the sight of) *the Lord"* (pages 17-19, 41). As we have already seen, it was partly through lack of sound method that the other-teachers corrupted the faith, "missing the mark" (page 21).

"That they strive not about words to no profit": For *logomachiai*, 'word-battles', see 1 Timothy 6:4 (page 180). The other-teachers *indulged* in controversy, and the man of God had to guard against getting involved in that kind of theological discussion which is in the end purely verbal, and has little or nothing to do with Scriptural truth. *No good comes of it:* indeed, it can produce positive evil—*"to the subverting of them that hear"* (RV).

The word for "subverting" is the noun *katastrophē*, which scarcely needs translating! It is a "oncer" for Paul, and possibly in the New Testament, although some manuscripts give it as the original word in 2 Peter 2:6: Sodom and Gomorrah were condemned "with *an overthrow"*. In Matthew 21:12 and Mark 11:15 the verb *katastrepheō* is applied to the overthrow of the money-changers' tables. We can see the force of the word: it is the exact opposite of *edifying*, or building up, for the effect of controversy is—*catastrophic!*

This constant warning needs to be kept before the Brotherhood today as much as throughout the first century. It is a sad fact that in some controversies or schisms the issues have centred on the use or avoidance of certain words or phrases, or of "additional clauses" to an original statement of belief. In attempts to resolve the difficulties sometimes a simple positive statement of belief has proved acceptable only if it could be translated back into the traditional ambiguities it was seeking to avoid. All this can have, and has been proved to have, a demoralising effect upon ecclesial work and worship. It is not often that we find words of the Latin Fathers to be appropriate sources of quotation, but those of Augustine are so apposite here that they should not be missed: "To strive with words is to take thought not for the way in which error is to be conquered by truth but for the way your own speech can be preferred to that of your opponent."

Approved of God

Verse 15: *"Study to shew thyself approved unto God":* Happily there is now, as there was in Ephesus, a remedy, if we are willing to apply it to ourselves. The exhortation of this verse is a personal one, since all reformation begins with leaders whose example is worthy of being followed: *"Take heed to thyself and to thy teaching."* "Continue in these things" was the message, "for in doing this thou shalt save both thyself and them that hear thee" (1 Timothy 4:16, RV).

Bible study is, of course, a basic necessity for the servant of the Lord. It is right that we should bring to it all the skills and aptitudes which any student would bring to an intellectual pursuit. Even so, it is not the depth of academic knowledge of the Word which counts, although we may profit from the labours of those whose capacity is in these things. It is the quality of one's *meditation* that produces spiritual insight and understanding, and this is not the province solely of the academic or the intellectual. All who "love thy law" can make it their "study all the day" (Psalm 119:97).

But the exhortation of verse 15 is not so much concerned with knowledge as with effort, as is evident from all other uses of the verb *spoudazō*: "I also was *forward* to do" (Galatians 2:10; 2 Corinthians 8:17); *"endeavouring* to keep the unity of the spirit" (Ephesians 4:3; also 1 Thessalonians 2:17 and 2 Peter 1:15); *"Do thy diligence* to come shortly" (2 Timothy 4:9,21; also Titus 3:12; 2 Peter 1:10; 3:14; 2 Corinthians 8:22); and "Let us *labour* therefore to enter into that rest" (Hebrews 4:11).

"Shew thyself" is literally 'Stand before'; Timothy was to "appear in the presence of God", as when the infant Jesus was *presented before* the Lord (Luke 2:22) or the saints are *presented* "holy and unblameable and unreproveable in his sight" by the blood of Christ (Colossians 1:22; also verse 28).

There is here, as in the "charge before the Lord", the idea of a keen sense of responsibility in the full knowledge of the judgement to come, when the quality of discipleship will be righteously assessed. "Approved", or *dokimos*, implies testing and trying (James 1:12) and therefore "acceptable"—"acceptable to God and *approved* of men" (Romans 14:18). The negative of the word is *adokimos*, 'a reprobate', like one who could even preach to others yet be himself found "a *castaway*", not able to endure the searching scrutiny of Him in whose service he had claimed to be labouring (1 Corinthians 9:27); the figure is actually taken from the idea of a herald summoning athletes to a race to which he was not himself equal. See also Matthew 7:21-23.

"A workman that needeth not to be ashamed, rightly dividing the word of truth": The "workman" is in fact an agricultural labourer, and so the thought of verse 6 is taken up with a slightly different emphasis. The use of "labourer" in the sense of preacher and teacher of the Gospel comes from Luke 10:7—"For the labourer is worthy of his hire." See also 1 Timothy 5:18 (pages 162, 163). It is not merely that the "workman" has no need to be ashamed of his calling, that is of the Gospel (Romans 1:16); he will have no need to blush with shame at the poor quality or deficiency of his work, like the servant who hid his talent in the ground (Matthew 25:26). Although the former sense has many parallels in the New Testament besides Romans 1:16—such as 2 Timothy 1:8; Hebrews 2:11; 11:16, and seems to be almost a direct reference to Luke 9:26, "Whosoever shall be ashamed of me and of my words"—it is the second sense which best fits our context.

Verse 16: *"But shun profane and vain babblings":* The Apostle shows the sharp contrast between "the word of truth" of verse 15 and the "empty voices" of the other-teachers. See the note on this and the word "profane" on pages 24, 201.

"For they will increase unto more ungodliness": Timothy is to shun rather than debate with the empty talkers; for controversy develops controversy and they would "progress" only in the direction of ungodliness—*asebeia*, the opposite of *eusebeia*, which is

the mark of the true believer (page 58). There is a deliberate irony in Paul's words, since the other-teachers claimed to be progressives, but the end of their progress was ungodliness! A parallel idea is found in 2 John 9: "Whosoever *goeth onward* and abideth not in the teaching of Christ hath not God (RV)."

The Cancerous Word

Verse 17: *"And their word will eat as doth a canker":* Consistent with the medical metaphor for the "soundness" of the body of Christ and of the doctrine which keeps it so (page 46), false teaching is said to be like a malignant disease. We have already noted the passage in 1 Timothy 6:4-5 (page 180), where one who consents not to wholesome words is described as sick about questions and strifes about words. Here, however, the erroneous teaching is described as having taken hold and there is grievous danger that it will spread. The Biblical "oncer", *gangraina*, has been translated as "cancer", but the Revised Version "gangrene" is not only nearer the sound but also the sense of what Paul wrote. It will eat or "find *pasture*" in all directions. The only other New Testament use of the word *nomē* is for the pasturing of sheep in John 10:9, but in ordinary Greek it was a common medical term for "the consuming progress of mortifying disease", as well as for "the devastating progress of fire".

Most of the medical expressions attached by Paul to the teaching of error are equally strong; for example, cauterisation in 1 Timothy 4:2 (page 123) and defilement and infection in Titus 1:15 (page 365). From the vigour with which Paul pursues his theme in all three epistles we can gauge both the danger to which the ecclesias in Ephesus and Crete were exposed and the urgency with which the Apostle sought to promote their spiritual health.

Once again there are lessons for us. True Scriptural teaching has both a moral and a saving power. The dangers of error are likewise twofold: it can easily spread, carrying moral consequences, and it can destroy a vigorous corporate spiritual life. This sound teaching never does, and we may well ask ourselves, in these days of innovation and reaction, whether present trends in either direction promote the health of the *whole* community or not. For Paul has yet more to say on this and related topics in what follows.

"Of whom is Hymenaeus and Philetus": Of Philetus nothing is known except what is recorded in these verses. Hymenaeus was probably the ringleader, since he had been cast out by Paul (1 Timothy 1:20), but appeared to be continuing his activities with damaging effect. Had Alexander, associated with him earlier, returned to the fold? The situation in Ephesus at this time was evidently very critical indeed.

The Path of Error

Verse 18: *"Who concerning the truth have erred"*: The Revised Version, "men who (*hoitines*, 'the kind of people who')", brings out the point that Paul is citing these two men as examples of the behaviour he has in mind, and underlines an important truth already discussed (page 21), but worth repeating here.

From a Scriptural point of view, error is not always that which stands out as an obvious denial of the truth, although it may eventually lead to it and is in any case the same in principle. It quite frequently contains *some* truth, but not *all* truth—"the truth, the whole truth and nothing but the truth"—and, to use Paul's words, "misses the mark" (*astocheō*), or fails to get the point of what God has said. Hence the very strong "swerved aside" and "turned aside" of 1 Timothy 1:6. It is like the serpent reasoning of Genesis 3: it begins with "Hath God said?" (verse 3), replies with a blend of what God actually did say, toned down a little, and some additional words based upon human opinion, and is eventually prepared to accept the exact opposite of the Divine Word (verses 3-4).

"Saying that the resurrection is past already": At first, no doubt, the teaching of Hymenaeus and Philetus seemed plausible, or even setting forth a "higher" view of the life in Christ. After all, Paul himself had taught that at baptism there is a resurrection to newness of life in the moral sense, and that one begins to live fully and in the spirit for the first time:

"... that like as Christ was *raised up from the dead* ... even so we also should walk *in newness of life.*"   (Romans 6:1-11)

"Even when we were dead in sins (God) hath *quickened us* together with Christ ... and hath *raised us up together.*"
(Ephesians 2:5-6)

"Wherefore he saith, Awake thou that sleepest . . . and Christ shall give thee light. See then that ye walk circumspectly . . ."
(Ephesians 5:14-15)

"And ye are complete in him . . . buried with him in *baptism, wherein also ye are risen with him* through the faith of the operation of God, who *hath raised him from the dead.*"
(Colossians 2:10-13)

"If ye then be *risen with Christ*, seek those things which are above." (Colossians 3:1)

The list of Scriptures on this topic, even in brief selection, is impressive: of course one cannot deny that the focal point of the Christian hope lies in the resurrection. If one leaves it at that, then, it could be that the resurrection is indeed past already. Moreover, it might be argued with great force in the first century (as indeed today), such a doctrine is much more palatable for religious contemporaries—it was even, to use one of the twentieth century "in words", *relevant* to the thinking of the day.

For intellectual culture was the religion ("a form of godliness") of the thinking people, who felt themselves liberated from the crudities of pagan ritual. For them the material world was essentially evil, and the progressive liberation of the spirit from the body was the highest ideal, to be pursued until the happy consummation when the immortal soul was set free from the body altogether. Further, with such a teaching the ecclesia could win over some of the Hellenistic Jews as well, followers of the teachings of Philo of Alexandria, for example. He considered that the translation of Enoch (Genesis 5:24; Hebrews 11:5) was the equivalent of an ascent to a higher degree of moral existence, a doctrine which found widespread acceptance among the Gnostics of the second century.

"Not knowing the Scriptures . . ."

It was all so logical and consistent, even "Scriptural", and one could neatly fit "the coming of the Lord" into the scheme—had not he himself promised, "If any man love me, he will keep my words . . . and we will *come* unto him" (John 14:23)—and the Kingdom of God as well. And further—if the resurrection from sin to holiness, from ignorance to knowledge has already past, why concern oneself with sin any more (Romans 6:1)? Or on the other hand, being "in the resurrection" (Matthew 22:30), perhaps one should forbid to marry? Or command to abstain from meats (1 Timothy 4:3; 2 Timothy 3:1-5)?

How greatly did they err, "not knowing the scriptures, nor the power of God" (Matthew 22:29)! The Apostle Paul did not fear the ridicule he excited by proclaiming the resurrection of the dead to the "masters of them that know", the intellectual and cultured court of the Areopagites (Acts 17:32), to whom for all their knowledge, the living God of purpose and of judgement remained *unknown*. Their knowledge was no saving knowledge in which the righteousness and power of God was revealed. They lived in "the times of this ignorance" (verse 30).

There can be no doubt as to what Martha and Mary understood by the resurrection of the dead, when they declared of their brother Lazarus, already four days in the tomb: "I know that he shall rise again in the resurrection *at the last day*". Nor was the sign that Jesus did before the open tomb intended to symbolise a purely moral resurrection. Equally there was no confusion in Paul's mind when he declared:.

> "Now if Christ be preached that he rose from the dead, how say some among you that there is no resurrection of the dead? But if there be no resurrection of the dead, then is Christ not risen ... your faith is vain; *ye are yet in your sins*."
> (1 Corinthians 15:12-17)

And lest there should be any doubt at all as to what he understands by "resurrection", he adds,

> "Then they also which are fallen asleep in Christ are perished. If *in this life only* we have hope in Christ, we are of all men most miserable. But *now* is Christ risen from the dead ... *afterward* they that are Christ's at his coming". (verses 18-23)

It is true that some in Corinth and Thessalonica may not have grasped the full implication of the preaching of the resurrection at first. But after such forthright explanation, or the "I would not have you to be ignorant" of 1 Thessalonians 4:13, there was no longer any cause for uncertainty. There was certainly no excuse for *proclaiming* (for the *logos* and the *legontes* of 2 Timothy 2:17-18 indicate that the new doctrine was being actively promulgated) such a pernicious teaching which *"overthrew the faith of some"*.

274

Confidence and Reassurance

Verse 19: *"Nevertheless the foundation of God standeth sure"*: Immediately Paul sounds a note of confident assurance with a most emphatic "nevertheless", the only time in his writings he ever uses this particular Greek word. In the Ephesian ecclesia, as in the Brotherhood today, when it became necessary to point to dangerous trends, or seek to recall to fundamentals which have either been lost sight of or become submerged beneath the weight of practical problems, brethren and sisters became discouraged. How can the Brotherhood survive, if its distinctive character is being lost or it is splitting itself into factions as every man does that which is right in his own eyes?

Some well-meaning brethren and sisters urge us not to comment on problems of morality, unsound teaching, strifes and tension in the Brotherhood, even in an attempt to help, improve or edify. No doubt many in Ephesus thought the same, and Timothy may well have been overwhelmed at times at the magnitude of the problems confronting him, had the Apostle's words been all warning, without balancing exhortations of the most positive kind. We today need his confident "Nevertheless".

For as in the "faithful saying" of verses 11-13 (RV):

> "If we are faithless,
> He abideth faithful:
> For he cannot deny himself."

Paul emphasises that the consummation of God's purpose does not depend upon the quality of the believers' lives, as was seen in the case of Israel: the LORD God of hosts always left a remnant, and there were 7,000 men in Israel who had not bowed the knee to Baal (1 Kings 19:14-18; Isaiah 1:2-9).

The mention of the foundation shows that what is under consideration is "the house of God, which is the church of the living God, the pillar and ground (margin, stay) of the truth" (1 Timothy 3:15). The Apostle's use of this metaphor is nearly always in connection with the ecclesia itself. Even where it is applied to Christ, it is always concerned with activity in the house of God. Thus, "ye are God's building ... for other foundation can no man lay than that is laid, which is Jesus Christ" (1 Corinthians 3:9-11); "Now therefore ye are ... of the household of

God; and are built upon the foundation of the apostles and prophets, Jesus Christ himself being the chief corner stone . . . . in whom ye also are builded together for an habitation of God through the Spirit" (Ephesians 2:19-22). It is the Divine character of the work which gives it stability in contrast to the unstable views of the other-teachers. As Isaiah says regarding the stable foundation:

> "Therefore thus saith the Lord GOD, Behold I lay in Zion for a foundation a stone, a tried stone, a precious corner stone, *a sure foundation*: he that believeth shall not make haste (or be put to shame)."   (Isaiah 28:16)

The word for "laid", 'established', is placed in the most emphatic position in Paul's statement, offering a strong contrast to the *katastrophē*, the subversive work of the errorists (verse 14).

"Having this seal": There is a double seal or inscription on the Lord's foundation, a device used to mark both ownership and authenticity. There was a seal set upon Christ's tomb for the former purpose (Matthew 27:66) and there are frequent references to the second in the New Testament:

> "Now he which stablisheth us with you in Christ . . . is God, who hath also *sealed us*."   (2 Corinthians 1:21-22)

> "And he received the sign of circumcision, a *seal* of the righteousness of the faith."   (Romans 4:11)

> "For the *seal* of mine apostleship are ye in the Lord."
> (1 Corinthians 9:2)

Seals, foundations and inscriptions are linked together in the Apocalypse, for "the wall of the city had twelve foundations, and in them the names of the twelve apostles of the Lamb" (21:14).

"The Lord knoweth them that are his": With this skilful citation, taken with only the change from "God" to "the Lord" from the Septuagint version of Numbers 16:5, Paul illuminates his whole thesis about the false teachers. They were murmurers and disputers, they sought to draw away disciples after them and to overthrow what God had established. They were, therefore, like Korah, Dathan and Abiram, "gainsayers" who became the very Scriptural types of the heretical or schismatic teachers (see the Epistle of Jude). The ultimate "catastrophe", however, was not the frustration of God's purpose with Israel, but that in which

276

they themselves suffered. They were "sinners against their own souls" (Numbers 16:38), and in their judgement, which was the Lord's and not man's, the Lord revealed those "who are his, and who is holy; and will cause him to come near unto him: even him whom he hath chosen will he cause to come near unto him" (16:5).

Departing from Iniquity

"Let every one that nameth the name of the Lord (RV) *depart from iniquity":* The second "seal" further extends the reference to Korah, Dathan and Abiram. "Naming the name" is an Old Testament expression for professing allegiance to someone, as in Joshua 23:7,8:

"Neither make mention of the name of their gods, nor cause to swear by them, neither serve them, nor bow down yourselves unto them: but cleave unto the LORD your God";

and Isaiah 26:13:

"O LORD our God, other lords beside thee have had dominion over us: but by thee only will we make mention of thy name."

To use the Name lightly was contrary to a fundamental commandment of the Lord's covenant, and was punishable by death (Leviticus 24:16).

In the New Testament to "call upon the name of the Lord" is synonymous with belonging to the church of the living God, as a survey of the usage of the Acts alone would show. Paul himself had been converted while in the very act of persecuting "them which called upon this name" (Acts 9:14,21), to be himself baptized and wash away his sins, "calling on the name of the Lord" (22:16; see also 7:59). The world-wide brotherhood were those "that in every place call upon the name of Jesus Christ our Lord" (1 Corinthians 1:2).

To depart from iniquity, to come out and be separate, were constant exhortations for the believers in Christ as for the people of God in older times. The renunciation of sin in all its forms had on occasion to be marked by a physical separation from the rebellious sinner, of the kind seen in the incident from which Paul is now drawing his exhortation. The Lord revealed those who were His: they were those who had obeyed the words of Moses to the congregation: "Depart, I pray you, from the tents of these wicked men, and touch nothing of theirs, lest ye be consumed in all their sins" (Numbers 16:26,27). Thus, with what had evidently become a proverbial saying (compare with Matthew 7:23 and Luke 13:27), Paul reinforces his instruction as to what Timothy should shun and to what he should pay earnest heed in order to discharge the responsibility of his office.

We too can take our lessons and our comfort: to deny a fundamental principle of the faith is closely linked Scripturally with sin; the faithful believer, however, rests upon the foundation laid by God Himself, and bears the Divine seal upon his teaching and the uprightness of his life.

Verse 20: *"But in a great house there are not only vessels of gold and of silver, but also of wood and of earth"*: The "but" introduces a possible objection to the full acceptance of the foregoing. If the house of God is so well-founded, with a doctrinal and moral stability, how can there be in it those who fall into error and sin? The Apostle's answer is in the form of a parable.

The *human* aspect of the church of God is like a great house which contains all kinds of utensils, of varying quality and different uses. The simile has to be of a *great house*, since few everyday dwellings contained vessels of gold and silver. Like all parables, one must not press the analogy too far: the point lies in the general drift and not in the detail. For this parable has not the same intent as the simile with the body (1 Corinthians 12:14-27), since the body has an organic unity, and the apparently trivial or less honourable "member" is still a vital, integral part without which the whole cannot function.

"Some to honour, and some to dishonour": The thought in this verse is nearer to that of Romans 9:21-23, which distinguishes between "vessels of wrath, fitted to destruction", or "vessels unto dishonour", and "vessels of mercy ... unto honour"; though even here the theme is God's prerogative of mercy and judgement and not an explanation of the presence of good and evil in one community (see Lamentations 4:2). In short, this passage in Timothy is the only occasion where Paul directly expresses the thought that the ecclesia embraces bad members as well as good, as part of the necessary discipline of the corporate life. It is a different version of the Lord's parable of the Gospel net which brought in both good and bad fish, which would not be finally

separated out until the day of judgement (Matthew 13:47-50: compare also the parable of the wheat and the tares, verses 24-30).

Holy Vessels

Verse 21: *"If a man therefore purge himself from these":* At first sight Paul is counselling Timothy simply to keep clear of the vessels for dishonourable use. While it might indeed be a stern duty to cast out men like Hymenaeus and Philetus, as Paul himself had done (1 Timothy 1:20), the topic of this verse is rather what one must do to be a vessel unto honour, which is to avoid taking the path trodden by the other-teachers. So we are taken back to verse 16: "Shun profane and vain babblings" which lead in the direction of ungodliness; and to verse 19: "Depart from iniquity", that is, in the context of Numbers 16, depart from men like Korah, Dathan and Abiram *and* from all their works. "Purge" (*ekkathairō*) is used once more by Paul in the same sense, in 1 Corinthians 5:5-7. See also Isaiah 52:11:

> "Depart ye, depart ye, go ye out from thence, touch no unclean thing; go ye out of the midst of her; be ye clean, *ye that bear the vessels of the LORD.*"

"He shall be a vessel unto honour": The quality of such a vessel is threefold:

(1) It is *"sanctified"*, a holy vessel set apart, like the vessels in the tabernacle, exclusively for the service of the Lord as was the Master himself: "And for their sakes I sanctify myself, that they also might be sanctified through the truth" (John 17:19);

(2) It is *"meet for the master's use"*, a typically Pauline expression, since in the New Testament it is he alone who uses the word *euchrēstos*. Mark was *"profitable* to me for the ministry" (4:11), and Onesimus was *profitable* to both Philemon and Paul (Philemon 11), while the words of the false teachers were to no profit;

(3) The vessel was also *"prepared unto every good work"*. So the true servant has the duty to equip himself for his task by self-discipline and application of the gifts which God has given him.

Verse 22: *"Flee also youthful lusts":* Abandoning imagery the Apostle takes up the thought from verse 15, combining it with those of 1 Timothy 4:12 ("Let no man despise thy youth ...")

and 6:11 ("Flee . . . follow after . . ."). It was the Psalmist's plea that the Lord should "remember not the sins of my youth" (25:7), but we must be careful not to assume from the word "lusts" here that Paul is referring to weaknesses and passion in a general sense, with the added assumption that old age is free from them. It is *the* youthful lusts to which he alludes, passions to which a younger man might easily yield in the situation in which Timothy found himself.

It was no time for giving way to impulse or ill-considered action, for displaying impatience, engaging in disputes, following after novelty or showing the wrong kind of ambition for leadership. All these are opposed to what he should *"follow after"* (RV)—*"righteousness"*, in the broadest Old Testament meaning of that which is right in God's eyes; *"faith"*, implying both faithfulness and adherence to the faith; *"charity"*, with all the overtones of 1 Corinthians 13—patience, humility and judgement—and *"peace"*, which is the ideal state produced by all the other virtues. The "youthful lusts" only lead to the "strifes" of verse 23.

Verse 23: *"But foolish and unlearned questions avoid"*: See pages 180, 181. We today are not free from the tendency to discuss, and sometimes insist upon answers to, questions to which there is no final Scriptural solution, or which do nothing to further our understanding of the great and fundamental truths of our calling.

2:24-26—The Servant of the Lord

Verse 24: *"And the servant of the Lord must not strive"*: The Lord's servant (*doulos*, 'bondman') has indeed a struggle to maintain; the good soldier of Jesus Christ has to war a warfare; but it is against error and not against people. Uncompromising as his attitude must be towards false doctrine, his aim is not to vanquish but to restore those who have been deceived by it. Remarkably, as experience shows, this attitude is extraordinarily difficult to maintain, human nature being what it is. "Zeal for the Truth" seems often to be accompanied by a spirit of harshness and intolerance on the part of those who claim to have it. A consideration of the Scriptural basis of Paul's instruction to Timothy on this matter will, therefore, be an important guide for our own conduct.

Our Pattern

Our pattern is, of course, "the meekness and gentleness of Christ", as is suggested by the title Paul ascribes to Timothy in this passage. For although he frequently describes himself and his associates as "servants of God", or "servants of the Lord Jesus Christ", the expression "the servant *of the Lord*" is surely intended to take Timothy, and us, back to the prophet Isaiah and his sequence of passages about the Lord's Servant:

"Behold my servant, whom I uphold; mine elect in whom my soul delighteth; I have put my spirit upon him: he shall bring forth judgment to the Gentiles. He shall not cry (*strive* nor cry, according to Matthew 12:18), nor lift up, nor cause his voice to be heard in the street. A bruised reed shall he not break, and the smoking flax shall he not quench; he shall bring forth judgment unto truth." (42:1-3)

"He shall see of the travail of his soul, and shall be satisfied: by his knowledge shall my righteous servant justify many; for he shall bear their iniquities." (53:11)

The work of the Lord Jesus Christ being the *salvation* and not the destruction of men, his life of redemptive love culminated in a redemptive sacrifice of himself.

"But be gentle unto all men": The gentleness here referred to is not merely descriptive of the demeanour of the Lord's servant: it suggests also the calming effect which he has upon those who are the objects of his care. Paul could have exercised his apostolic authority with asperity and brusqueness, but preferred an entirely different approach: "But we were *gentle* among you, even as a nurse cherisheth her children ... As ye know how we exhorted and comforted and charged every one of you, as a father doth his children" (1 Thessalonians 2:7-11).

An Important Qualification

The qualification "unto all men" reminds us once more of "the spirit of ... a sound mind (self-control)" (2 Timothy 1:7) that is so difficult to acquire, yet it is the part of all true disciples to exercise in their relations with others: "If ye love them which love you, what reward have ye? do not even the publicans the same? And if ye salute your brethren only, what do ye more than others? do not even the publicans so?" (Matthew 5:46-47). Moreover, it is evident that "strifes" and "word-battles" cannot develop far unless there are two parties willing to enter into dispute.

"Apt to teach, patient": As we have already seen, patience and the ability to teach others were important qualifications for Timothy and for all who aspired to eldership (1 Timothy 3:2,3; pages 87-91). The word for "apt to teach", *didaktikos*, gives us the English word 'didactic', which usually bears the meaning of 'having the manner of a teacher', with slight overtones of 'authoritarian' rather than of 'skilful in his art'. No such nuance lies in the Greek word (unique in Scripture to the Letters), for the knowledge to be imparted is about a way of life—*doctrine* in the sense already discussed (page 46). Such a teacher is not so much "ready to teach out of his profound knowledge as skilled in the art of Christian teaching, which makes no use of sarcasm, but seeks every means of making the truth he is setting out acceptable, without despising the ignorant, or becoming impatient with those who fail to understand" (Spicq, *Les Epîtres Pastorales*).

The *patience* here referred to goes beyond ordinary forebearance: it is literally 'ready to suffer wrong', and so, in this context, 'when the argument waxes violent and tempers are becoming frayed, able to listen patiently without answering back heatedly'.

Verse 25: *"In meekness instructing those that oppose themselves"*: Meekness is an inward disposition which gives rise to the outward demeanour of the Lord's servant, and it is worth considering in some detail the emphasis laid on it in the New Testament, especially in times like ours when faction and strife threaten our unity (see Essay 33, "The Meekness of the True Disciple", page 293).

"Those that oppose themselves" is a form of the verb which indicates that the opponents were constantly placing themselves in opposition to Timothy. It is important to realise this, since he was dealing not with the weak brother or with the occasional lapse in conduct or failure in understanding, but with the habitual opponent always coming up with ignorant enquiries as a means of self expression. Such behaviour serves to highlight the meekness and gentleness of the Lord's servant: "patient continuance in well-doing" is not easy. Instructing the (willingly) uninstructed, informing the uninformed, to reproduce a little of Paul's play upon words here, can be a wearisome task.

"If God peradventure will give them repentance to the acknowledging of the truth": Timothy is now reminded once more of the purpose of his opposition to the other-teachers: it goes beyond the preservation of the ecclesia to the possible salvation of the heretics themselves. This idea is consistently set forth in the New Testament, including these Letters, although this passage contains the fullest statement of it. See for example, "That they may *learn* not to blaspheme" (1 Timothy 1:20, page 39), and 1 Corinthians 5:3-5 with 2 Corinthians 2:4-11 (RV), noting especially the words, "lest by any means such a one should be swallowed up with his overmuch sorrow". Note also the danger of persistent refusal to acknowledge true repentance in others, revealed in the words of verses 10,11: "For your sakes have I forgiven it in the person of Christ; that no advantage may be gained over us by Satan" (RV).

This goes closely with what follows in the Timothy passage we are considering.

A Clear Message

For the obvious message of these passages to us is that "in giving the Truth the benefit of the doubt" in difficult cases, we have a duty to speak plainly about the issues involved, but with sympathy and understanding—"considering thyself, lest thou also be tempted" (Galatians 6:1)—in an effort to restore. Such restoration God will effect if it is His will. After all, the whole process of salvation is a gift of God's grace and we should do our utmost to see that we place no barrier in the way of others receiving what we stand so desperately in need of ourselves.

The attitude of some in the first century towards the Gentiles was that none of them could be saved: yet the apostles rejoiced over them with the words: "Then hath God also to the Gentiles *granted repentance* unto life" (Acts 11:18). And even now, while the world is sinking deeper into the evil which merits the judgements of God, He "is longsuffering to us-ward, not willing that any should perish, but that *all should come to repentance*" (2 Peter 3:9). We must beware, therefore, of writing off those whom God may in fact receive: the final judgement depends upon "the acknowledging of the truth". We must indeed exercise ecclesial discipline (we reserve Titus 3:10-11 for more detailed consideration, see page 417), but the restoration of the offender or the

283

opponent is the principal aim. They, however, have their own necessary part to play in the process.

For a further discussion of "The Acknowledging of the Truth", see Essay 34, page 296.

Restoration to Life

Verse 26: *"And that they may recover themselves out of the snare of the devil"*: The Revised Version margin gives "return to soberness" as the literal Greek for "recover themselves". Although it is a New Testament "oncer", the root idea appears in 4:5—"Watch thou", or "Be thou sober"—and in 1 Thessalonians 5:6-8 and especially 1 Corinthians 15:34: "Awake to righteousness" or (RV margin) "Awake out of drunkenness righteously". Faction and strife are therefore seen to be *moral* not intellectual problems. Hence the apostolic emphasis upon the moral qualities of the teacher who has to work for the rehabilitation of the other-teachers. They have to be encouraged to come to their senses.

"The snare of the devil" is of course the desperate state into which man falls when he follows the mind of the flesh rather than of the spirit. As we see from 2 Corinthians 10, our warfare is against "imaginations" opposed to God, and what has to be brought "into captivity to the obedience of Christ" is "every thought". If sin gains the ascendancy, it takes its captives until "even their mind and conscience is defiled. They profess that they know God; but in works they deny him, being abominable, and disobedient, and unto every good work reprobate" (Titus 1:15-16).

The metaphor of the snare is a consistent one, especially in the New Testament, and refers to the deceitfulness of the sin in which a man suddenly finds himself embroiled, or the judgements of God which come upon men heedless of their departure from God, and for the evil devices of the wicked against the man of God. The "snare of the devil" occurs twice in these Letters, here and in 1 Timothy 3:6 (page 96), there significantly enough in the context of the qualifications for eldership, though with a different emphasis.

"Taken captive by him at his will": The Authorised Version translation suggests that both "him" and "his" apply to the devil, and it is just possible to interpret the grammar in that way. The difficulty then becomes a Scriptural one. The vivid, forceful

verb for "take captive" is literally 'take alive', a "oncer" in the New Testament except for Luke 5:10—"And Jesus said unto Simon, Fear not; from henceforth thou shall *catch* men"—a reference of course to the saving power of the apostolic preaching which brought to life those who were "taken" by it. Even allowing for strong personification and interpreting the devil's will as being "the will of the flesh", the metaphor of "taking men alive" would be entirely inappropriate with such a context. But when we consider the whole thrust of the argument here—Paul is not writing in Classical Greek anyway—we see that he is in effect saying that those who repent and acknowledge the truth have their thoughts once more brought into captivity to the obedience of Christ. It is they who are "taken alive" by the Lord's servant unto the will of God. The "acknowledging of the truth" and "the will of God" are then seen as parallel ideas, and the former opponents come to accept both.

ESSAY 31

Paul's Use of Military Metaphor

IN 1 Corinthians 9:7 and 2 Corinthians 10:3, Paul likens his apostolic ministry to a warfare, or more strictly, a period of active service. It is the word also used for "soldiers" in Luke 3:14, thereby revealing to us that it was *soldiers on active service* who brought their query to John the Baptist. He told them that their "works meet for repentance" consisted in avoiding "their calling's snare"—excessive violence and grumbling at the pay for which they had contracted their service.

The first Corinthians passage indicates that the soldier's every need was the responsibility of the enrolling officer, and therefore he had no need to concern himself with the things of everyday civilian life. On the other hand, as we learn from the second passage, the parallel between the soldier's and the apostle's service ends there: Paul's service may be in the world, but worldly methods are not as his disposal. The "good soldier" does not entangle himself with the affairs of this life (2 Timothy 2:3,4); he must "war a *good* warfare" (1 Timothy 1:18) in faith and a good conscience.

For this task he is equipped with the "whole armour of God", shunning "the weapons of unrighteousness unto sin" and using his "members as weapons of righteousness unto God" (Romans 6:13, RV margin), "the armour of light" (Romans 13:12; also 2 Corinthians 6:7; 10:4). This "panoply of God" is described in detail in Ephesians 6:11-17. The separate parts of this spiritual armour have been the subject of many an article and address and readers are no doubt aware of the aptness of the simile which each presents. It is worth adding that the disciple, like the soldier on active service, was issued with his equipment but the care and maintenance of it was his personal responsibility. The unoiled leather shield would crack and become useless, the loose-fitting shoe-strap could hinder a man, even if he had "done all", from standing or keeping his foothold (verses 13-14), and so make him vulnerable. The spiritual parallels can be easily followed through, especially when it be remembered that his feet were to have shoes "prepared by the gospel of peace".

Shouldering One's Own Pack

The "burden" of Galatians 6:5 which every man must bear for himself was the *phortion*, the soldier's pack or kit-bag. In it he carried the regulation issue of a cloak which served as both garment and blanket; digging tools with which he dug his allotted portion of the trench and corresponding mound *every night* before camping on the march; one stake for the palisade which surrounded the camp, no detail of which was omitted lest the camp be surprised in the night; a small grinding-mill and a daily ration of corn, with which to make the evening meal after settling in camp; and any additional items he chose to carry, bearing in mind that they rested upon his own shoulder and a march was anything up to 20 miles a day—more if they were proceeding by forced marches in an emergency.

It is still true that "every man must shoulder his own pack" in the spiritual life. With how many unnecessary things or anxieties of our own devising do we diminish our spiritual fitness? And how often do we give someone else a hand with the *barē*, 'weights' ("burdens" in Galatians 6:2), and so fulfil the law of Christ?

A soldier's pay was usually a meagre affair, since it was in reality a supplement to the necessities of life which were provided, and there was always in prospect a share of the plunder which became his *peculium* or private possession (see page 392 for the slave's *peculium*). He did not therefore serve at his own expense (cf. the "charges" of 1 Corinthians 9:7 and the "wages" of Romans 6:23). It will be seen from this that the "service" of sin or righteousness is more closely related in this passage to the metaphors of military service than of bond service.

Keeping watch is an essential part of a soldier's duty, and severe penalties attached to failure or neglect. The reason is obvious: not only the life of the sentry but those of the whole company depend upon the alertness of those who keep vigil. The

Greek words, like our word "vigil", carry the idea of *keeping awake*. Frequent exhortations to watch are found in the New Testament, and in Paul's writings particularly in 1 Corinthians 16:13: "Watch ye, stand fast in the faith, quit you like men, be strong"; and Colossians 4:2: "Continue in prayer, and watch in the same with thanksgiving."

An interesting passage in 1 Thessalonians 5:3-10 develops the military metaphor, including keeping the watch, in a way which shows that for Paul the whole life in Christ should be watching, or keeping awake (verse 10, RV margin), and that the only sleepers were the dead in Christ. The special responsibilities of elders in the ecclesia are emphasised in the expression in Hebrews 13:17: "They *watch for your souls*, as they that must give account."

The citadel and the taking of captives appear in 2 Corinthians 10:4-5. The constant necessity of looking to the defences is an important Scriptural theme, and no doubt Paul is drawing as much, if not more, upon his Old Testament knowledge as upon his everyday experience of the Roman military system, close to it though he was. For him the Lord was his refuge and his strength: "The name of the LORD is a strong tower; the righteous runneth into it and is safe" (Proverbs 18:10).

Captivity was something inseparable from warfare, bringing the vanquished completely under the power of the victor. How powerful, then, is the image of "casting down imaginations (RV margin, reasonings) ... and bringing every thought into captivity to the obedience of Christ"! Liberty and thought and freedom of action become completely assimilated to the mind and will of the Lord. This thought is worth meditating upon deeply, in an age where the subjective opinion is paramount and "every man does that which is right in his own eyes"—a trend which has developed within the Brotherhood as well as in the world at large.

It should be *Christ* who leads us in *his* triumphal procession (2 Corinthians 2:14-16; see the note on 1:8, page 254).

ESSAY 32

The Fourth Faithful Saying

THE use of "psalms and hymns and spiritual songs" as a medium of teaching and exhortation in worship was an established practice in the synagogues, to be followed by the first century ecclesias from their inception. The evidence for this provided by the Pastoral Epistles alone is worth a study in itself.

The spiritual songs no doubt followed a pattern familiar to us today—paraphrases in metrical form and "anthems in the words of Scripture"—and the faithful saying now under consideration is an example of such an early Christian hymn (see also 1 Timothy 3:16 and Essay 13, page 116).

It is rendered all the more interesting when we consider that the use the Apostle is making of it is in many respects similar to our own use of poetry and hymns in our speaking and writing. We often quote them because they express in concise or figurative language, with the added qualities of metre and rhythm, thoughts which we have laboured to express in prose, and so help us to remember them or impress them on others the better. Sometimes we allude to the words of a hymn with no attempt to reproduce the metre, with added comment of our own, and end by quoting a line or two verbatim. It would seem that that is what Paul is doing here.

Songs at Midnight

From the record of his night in the Philippian gaol, we know that it was Paul's habit in joy and adversity to express himself in the singing of praises to God (Acts 16:25), a habit which was ingrained in all the people of God who felt it a good thing to give thanks unto the Lord, "to show forth thy lovingkindness in the morning, and thy faithfulness every night" (Psalm 92:1-2).

289

The passage under consideration was written in a Roman gaol, from which he knew there could be no release except in death. He did not spend his time in morbid preoccupation with his own miseries, however, but meditated upon the faithfulness of God and the promise of life in Christ Jesus. This promise and the need for personal faithfulness he commends to his "dearly beloved son in the faith", Timothy.

The theme of the third faithful saying, the Godly exercise and the hope on which the apostolic preaching was based, together with the suffering and the consolation it brought (1 Timothy 4:8-10, pages 127, 128), has been repeated under different figures—the striving of the athlete, the discipline of the soldier and the labour of the farmer (2 Timothy 2:1-6). Then the man under the shadow of death referred to what could well be the opening theme of the hymn: "Jesus Christ of the seed of David was raised from the dead" (verse 8). He draws his comfort from the assurance of life which the Gospel brings, and also from the fact that his endurance under trial would help the elect who believed through his preaching to gain salvation in Christ Jesus.

The actual "faithful saying" which follows is in metrical Greek and is obviously direct quotation:

"For if we be dead with him, we shall also live with him:
If we suffer, we shall also reign with him:
If we deny him, he also will deny us:
If we believe not, yet he abideth faithful"—

with an added comment of Paul's own, "He cannot deny himself".

Dying with Christ

How exactly this suits his mood and the burden of his exhortation! The allusion to dying with Christ is no reference to Paul's impending execution but to an event which had already taken place. The tense indicates completed action and the idea is that of Romans 6:8, "Now if we be dead (have died) with Christ, we believe that we shall also live with him", for in faithful continuance after baptism the life in Christ becomes eternal life in him. Jesus Christ of the seed of David was born to reign, and those who suffer with him, as the Apostle was suffering then, and for the same cause, will share the glory of his kingdom. Again there is allusion to Romans, this time 8:17—"... *joint-heirs* with Christ (cf. "then are ye *Abraham's seed,* and *heirs*", Galatians 3:26-29); if so be that we suffer with him, that we may be glorified together."

An Early Collection of Sayings

The reference to denial of Christ and its consequences is another evidence of the early existence of a written collection of sayings of Jesus, if not a full Gospel record. Certain it is that very many of the Master's words were known and understood, such as the saying: "Whosoever shall deny me before men, him will I also deny before my Father which is in heaven" (Matthew 10:33). But the hymn ends on a note of confidence in the abiding mercy of God. The fulfilment of the promises and the gift do not depend upon human reliability. The Apostle was well aware of his personal weaknesses and failures, and the expression, "If we believe not", does not refer to unbelief of the Gospel or apostasy, but to the possibility of our failure to respond or to overcome.

The strict parallelism of the hymn would seem to require, "If we are unfaithful, he will be unfaithful too". But this is unthinkable, for God is one "that cannot lie" (Titus 1:2—the word for "that cannot lie" occurs here only in all the New Testament; see page 354 and Hebrews 6:18), and His faithfulness toward us is beyond question. He is unable, as Paul himself comments, to deny His own nature. In this phrase, as in the Pastoral Epistles generally, the contrast between man's faithlessness toward God and His Word with which he has been put in trust, and God's faithfulness to man, is sharply drawn. Again there is an allusion to the Letter to the Romans: "Shall their unbelief make the faith of God without effect?" (Romans 3:3; see also Numbers 23:19).

An Ecclesial Poet?

Who was the author of this hymn which is so accurate a summary of the words of the faith? Could it have been Paul himself, with his gift for a turn of phrase and the capacity to meditate deeply on the things of the Spirit? Or did some spiritually-minded poet of the Roman ecclesia, with deep insight into the letter Paul had written to his brethren, turn some of the Apostle's own phrases into metrical verse and present it to him when he visited them? We can only speculate.

One thing is certain: the words which Paul had used to comfort and instruct others as he went amongst them as an apostle and servant of the Lord Jesus Christ now returned to him for his own comfort and exhortation in the hour of crisis, much as the words of the Lord's prayer, no doubt ever present in his mind, lie behind his closing expression of confidence in God in 2 Timothy 4:18. This is what made his preaching so powerful and effective, and caused him to stand out as one of the few fathers among ten thousand instructors in Christ—his preaching was effective for himself and his exhortations proved valid in his own experience.

For convenience we set out the hymn and the Scriptures upon which it appears to be based in parallel:

THE HYMN	THE SCRIPTURAL BASIS
For if we be dead with him, We shall also live with him:	Now if we be dead with Christ, we believe that we shall also live with him.'' (Romans 6:8)
If we suffer (endure, RV), We shall also reign with him:	If so be that we suffer with him (Christ), that we may be also glorified together. (Romans 8:17)
If we deny him, He also will deny us:	But whosoever shall deny me before men, him will I also deny before my Father which is in heaven. (Matthew 10:33)
If we believe not, Yet he abideth faithful:	For what if some did not believe? Shall their unbelief make the faith of God without effect? (Romans 3:3)
He cannot deny himself.	God is not a man, that he should lie; neither the son of man, that he should repent. (Numbers 23:19)

ESSAY 33

The Meekness of the True Disciple

"TAKE my yoke upon you, and learn of me; for I am *meek* and lowly in heart: and ye shall find rest to your souls. For my yoke is easy, and my burden is light" (Matthew 11:29-30). So the Master himself (*Didaskalos*, or Teacher, as the disciples regularly called him in the days of his flesh) is as always the great exemplar of the characteristics to be developed by his servants.

For Timothy was, in effect, being called upon (2 Timothy 2:25) to display a quality with which he was already familiar from the time he had been Paul's ambassador to Corinth: "For this cause have I sent unto you Timotheus, who is my beloved son, and faithful in the Lord, who shall bring you into remembrance of my ways which be in Christ, as I teach everywhere in every church . . . For the kingdom of God is not in word, but in power. What will ye? Shall I come unto you with a rod, or in love, or in the spirit of *meekness?*" (1 Corinthians 4:17,20-21).

As it was, the Apostle was greatly troubled at the possible effect of his letter on the Corinthians, although as it turned out he had been guided to use the right blend of plain speaking in the matters at stake with such an obvious display of affection and concern that his words had the desired effect: "I write not these things to shame you, but as my beloved sons I warn you. For though ye have ten thousand instructors in Christ, yet have ye not many fathers" (verses 14,15).

Meekness and Gentleness

He had besought them "by the *meekness* and gentleness of Christ" (2 Corinthians 10:1). "Admittedly I live in this world, but that does not mean I fight my battles with worldly weapons. The

293

weapons I use for fighting are not of this world; but they are powerful in God's hands for the demolition of strongholds. With them I overthrow lofty imaginations and everything that is high and lifted up against the knowledge of God; with them I take prisoner the minds of all and force them to render allegiance to Christ" (2 Corinthians 10:3-5, F. F. Bruce, *An Expanded Paraphrase of the Epistles of Paul*).

Such meekness is one aspect of "the fruit of the Spirit" (Galatians 5:23). When we follow Paul into his discussion of some of the practical expressions of these qualities, we have a perfect illustration of both the attitude of the teacher and the source of his own wisdom and knowledge: "Brethren, if a man be overtaken in a fault, ye which are spiritual, restore such an one in the spirit of *meekness*; considering thyself, lest thou also be tempted. Bear ye one another's burdens, and so fulfil the law of Christ. For if a man thinketh himself to be something when he is nothing, he deceiveth himself ... Let him that is taught in the word communicate unto him that teacheth unto all good things" (Galatians 6:1-6).

This is to "walk worthy of the vocation wherewith ye are called, with all lowliness and *meekness*, with longsuffering, forbearing one another in love", and is a major contribution towards "keeping the unity of the Spirit in the bond of peace", as befits members of "one body ... called in one hope of your calling" (Ephesians 4:2-4). Such meekness is the mark of those who are risen with Christ. Having put on Christ, they must see to it also that they "put on therefore, as the elect of God, holy and beloved, bowels of mercies, kindness, humbleness of mind, *meekness*, longsuffering; forbearing one another ... and let the peace of God rule in your hearts, to the which also ye are called in one body" (Colossians 3:1,12-13,15).

The spiritual teacher must be a man endowed with wisdom and knowledge which, when combined with charity, builds up rather than puffs up. His teaching, therefore, must not be "academic" in the modern—but, alas, sadly misused—sense of that word. For to be scholarly in the sense of being devoted to learning and scrupulously honest and diligent in the sifting of facts and applying them, is perhaps more important in an approach to the Scriptures than to any other form of knowledge. Academic *disciplines*, as they are called, can be rightly applied to the Word of God *provided* that the advice of James be followed:

> "Who is a wise man and endued with knowledge among you? Let him show out of a good conversation ('way of life') his works with *meekness* of wisdom. But if ye have bitter envying and strife in your hearts, glory not, and lie not against the truth. This wisdom descendeth not from above, but is earthly, sensual, devilish. For where envying and strife is, there is confusion and every evil work. But the wisdom that is from above is first pure, then peaceable, gentle, and easy to be entreated, full of mercy and good fruits, without partiality, and without hypocrisy." (James 3:13-17)

We must beware of interpreting "*first* pure" in a way that nullifies the meaning of what follows. The phrase means 'above all unmixed with false motives or double standards', and is related to the preceding metaphor of the fountain which can only run with one kind of water. If we receive with *meekness* the engrafted word (James 1:21), it is able to save our souls, and in so saving ourselves we shall also save them that hear us (1 Timothy 4:16).*

Perhaps the whole approach of the Lord's servant to those within and without the Brotherhood, but especially to his opponents, can best be summed up by the quotation which contains the last occurrence of the word "meekness" in Scripture:

> "But sanctify in your hearts Christ as Lord: being ready always to give answer to every man that asketh you a reason concerning the hope that is in you, yet with *meekness* and fear (margin, reverence): having a good conscience (another word characteristic of the Pastoral Epistles, see page 44); that, wherein ye are spoken against, they may be put to shame who revile your good manner of life in Christ." (1 Peter 3:15-16, RV)

These words and the attitude they represent ought to be pondered, then practised by every disciple and especially by those who labour in the Word and in the doctrine.

---

*For a fuller discussion of "first pure, then peaceable" see *The Christadelphian*, 1976, page 161.

ESSAY 34

The Acknowledging of the Truth

THE rendering "acknowledging of the truth" (2 Timothy 2:25) is an attempt by the translators of the Authorised Version to give the full meaning of the words used by the Apostle—*epignōsis tēs alētheias*. In earlier letters Paul had used both *gnōsis* and *epignōsis* and the verbs *ginōskein* and *epiginōskein* without any apparent distinction in the shade of meaning. In the Pastoral Epistles, however, it is the second pair, the compound words, which are preferred. Indeed, *gnōsis* is used only once, and then in a hostile sense as "*science* falsely so-called" (1 Timothy 6:20). Of the three uses of *ginōskein*, two refer to factual knowledge and the third is a quotation from the Old Testament: "The Lord *knoweth* them that are his" (2 Timothy 2:19; Numbers 16:5).

As we have seen (pages 202, 223, 224), Paul is careful to distinguish between factual knowledge and the knowledge or understanding of the ways of God, which constitutes "the faith" or "the truth", and which is "salvation". His use of *epignōsis* seems to emphasise that distinction in 1 Timothy 2:4; 2 Timothy 2:25; 3:7 and Titus 1:1. The object of such knowledge is God, its content clearly to be understood (1 Timothy 2:4,5; John 17:3) and its source is also God, who has revealed it to His servants that they may proclaim it to others.

The knowledge which saves, therefore, is not gained by research or initiation, as into the mystery religions. It comes from the *acknowledging* of what God has revealed, and the *acceptance* of it into a good and honest heart. It is therefore closely linked with *metanoia*, 'a change of heart' or '*repentance*'. So the truth of God is "worthy of all acceptation", that is, something which all men ought to receive (page 34), but their acceptance depends upon whether they be men of good will or not. In the Pastoral Epistles, "the acknowledging of the truth" means intimate knowledge and perception, close acquaintance and understanding, based upon humble acceptance and submission to the will of God. Remarkably Paul's expression is always used with a preposition implying motion towards: such saving knowledge and close communion with God is not a matter of instant intellectual comprehension—you *come unto it*.

The Second Letter to Timothy

CHAPTER 3

Facing the Perils to Come

IN this chapter the perils of the last times, particularly for the ecclesias, are specifically described.

Verse 1: *"This know also":* This phrase appears to be not so much a reminder of what Timothy already knew as a command to be on the look-out for the developments of which Paul had already warned him. For when he saw the things described taking shape, he would know that the end was nigh.

"In the last days perilous times shall come": In 1 Timothy 4:1 the Apostle had spoken of "the latter times" (page 121). Like that of Moses in a similar warning (Deuteronomy 31:29), the time referred to was in an indefinite future when the full effects of what was already at work would be manifest. "The last days", however, relate particularly to that time long foretold when the consummation of men's evil works would herald the coming of the Lord. There is a sense in which the first coming of the Lord had brought the beginning of "the last time"—the age when the command to repent had gone forth, since the days of "this ignorance" were over. But *now* hath God commanded "all men everywhere to repent: because he hath appointed a day, in the which he will judge the world in righteousness ..." (Acts 17:30,31). It is more in this sense that John writes in 1 John 2:18 and Paul in Hebrews 1:2.

But the phrase "last day" or "last days" in John 6:39,40,44,54; 11:24; 12:48; 2 Peter 3:3 and Jude 18 is clearly taken as the era of resurrection and judgement (see also Isaiah 2:2). That these days should be characterised by a sharp decline in standards of morality and faith was well understood in the first century ecclesias (Luke 18:8; 21:34,35; 2 Thessalonians 3:6,11). It gives some idea of the force of the word, to know that "perilous" here, or 'difficult' as it means literally, should appear only twice in the New Testament, here and in Matthew 8:28 with reference to the demoniac, who was "exceeding *fierce*, so that no man might pass by that way". A *difficult* customer indeed!

Verse 2: *"For men shall be lovers of their own selves, covetous"*: It has sometimes been objected that every period of history has seen rampant in the earth the kind of wickedness Paul describes here, and that the times have always been bad. Each generation has looked back nostalgically upon the former days and proclaimed that things are not as they used to be. There is a measure of truth in this objection, and Scripture warns against allowing such an attitude to dominate one's thinking (Ecclesiastes 7:10). It is even more dangerous to allow the thought that "all things continue as they were from the beginning of creation" (2 Peter 3:4) to blunt one's perception that the end is near. The Scriptural truth is that "an end, the end is come" (Ezekiel 7:2) upon different periods of human history and in each case its approach has been signalled by a filling up of a measure of iniquity in some outstandingly characteristic fashion. We need mention only the days of Noah, the destruction of Sodom and Gomorrah, the destruction of Jerusalem and the end of the commonwealth of Israel.

The Keyword of the Permissive Society

The opening word in the Apostle's present list is *philautoi*, 'lovers of self'. The passage does not mean, "There will be men who are ...", but "Men in general will be ..." self-centred to a degree that will result in the throwing off of all social, to say nothing of moral, constraint. *Philautoi* is the keyword in a permissive society, and all the other vices are expressions of it in some form.

We shall discuss the Scriptural use in general of "Catalogues of Vices" in Essay 35, page 313, but will deal here with the items in the catalogue before us. It is possible to group them in pairs, a stylistic device whereby the Apostle rendered them easier to remember. The grouping sometimes depends upon assonance— the similarity of sounds in the Greek—but even where the force of this is lost on the English reader we can trace the link in meaning.

Thus *philautoi*, 'self-lovers', is obviously connected with *philarguroi*, 'money-lovers', or 'covetous'. It is surprising, since the first of these is basic to the human heart, to learn that it is a Biblical "oncer", while the second occurs elsewhere only in Luke 16:14, where the Pharisees derided the Lord for his warnings against covetousness. As we have seen, *philarguria*, 'the love of money', is "the root of all evil", being one of the most obvious practical manifestations of selfishness, such as characterises our own inflationary times. The important thing nowadays is not whether one has sufficient for one's own need so much as whether someone else has more (see notes on 1 Timothy 6:8-10,17-19, pages 183-185, 197-199; also Essay 24).

"Boasters, proud": One of the three things that place men at enmity with God, *alazoneia*, "pride of life" in 1 John 2:16, springs from self-centredness, and "boasters" (*alazones*) give expression to it by their words and gestures. Their inward attitude is best described by the word *hyperēphanoi*, 'haughty', of whom it is recorded that God resisteth them (James 4:6; 1 Peter 5:5) or *"scattered* ... in the imagination of their hearts" (Luke 1:51).

"Blasphemers, disobedient to parents": Though the English word usually carries the sense of evil-speaking about God, *blasphēmoi* and its kindred words, especially in these Letters, can equally well refer to abuse of men. So Paul, who would never have taken the name of God in vain or spoken an irreverent word, described himself as a blasphemer (1 Timothy 1:13) by virtue of his "breathing out threatenings and slaughter" against the disciples and thus persecuting Jesus of Nazareth himself. The translation "railings", "railing accusation" in 1 Timothy 6:4; 2 Peter 2:11 and Jude 9 gives the basic sense (see also Titus 3:2). It is linked therefore with disobedience to parents, since both sins are forms of unnatural or ungodly conduct towards others.

"Neither were they thankful"

"Unthankful, unholy": The supreme ingratitude of denying one's parents marks a man out as one of the *acharistoi*, who refuses to consider himself beholden to anyone, not even to God; he is therefore also *anosios*, since to him nothing is sacred (see note on "unholy and profane", page 24).

Verse 3: *"Without natural affection, trucebreakers":* The words *astorgoi* and *aspondoi* appear together in Romans 1:31. They describe those whose hearts are so hardened by their attitudes—a kind of progressive degeneration can be discerned in the order of vices listed by Paul in these verses—that they become incapable of kindly or affectionate feelings. It is not so much that they are truce*breakers*, although such men are unlikely to keep covenant with God or man (see "traitors" below); they are *truceless* (an author's "oncer"!), incapable of forming attachments to others of any kind at all.

"False accusers, incontinent": That such men should violate one of the great commandments of the Lord—"Thou shalt not bear false witness"—is no surprise. From gossip, which is an exaggeration of the truth about others, to downright falsehood about them, false witness is roundly condemned in the Pastoral Epistles, and it is significant that the word used to describe both forms of it is also the basic word for what is worst in human nature. No servant of the Lord, male or female, should give way to this weakness and become a *diabolos*, and we should take note that it is a vice especially characteristic of the last times. See 1 Timothy 3:11 (page 100) and Titus 2:3; also Revelation 12, where there is an interesting connection of thought between verse 10, "the *accuser* of our brethren is cast down", and verse 12, "Woe . . . for the *diabolos* is come down to you, having great wrath, because he knoweth that he hath but a short time"; that is, the last days are upon him.

The other word in the pair, *akratēs*, is a "oncer", but its meaning is not difficult: without control over their passions and giving free rein to their basic impulses, men become 'powerless over themselves'.

"Fierce, despisers of those that are good": The dreadful combination of *anēmeroi, aphilagathoi* (both "oncers" in the whole of Scripture) paints a picture of men who are 'savage', yet whose animal instinct retains sufficient concept of what is good to hate it. *Aphilagathos* is the opposite of the *philagathos* of Titus 1:8 (page 360).

Verse 4: *"Traitors, heady":* The first word is to be taken quite literally. Judas Iscariot stands out as the classic example of a man in whom love of money culminated in an act of betrayal. Love of self can lead a man to do the same. There were no doubt those in the first century ecclesias who were prepared to betray their brethren to the pagan authorities, either for the sake of gain or in the hope of saving their own skin in time of persecution.

It is frightening to contemplate the possibility of such times recurring, but treachery and betrayal on the part of those within and without are to be acknowledged as characteristic of the time of the "beginning of sorrows" which is the prelude to the Lord's return. When the despisers of those that are good begin to hate them as well, "for my name's sake", then "shall many stumble and shall betray one another, and hate one another" (Matthew 24:8-10; also Mark 13:12; Luke 21:16; Micah 7:5,6). Men will be not only *prodotai*, 'traitors', but also *propeteis*, "rash" (Acts 19:36), stopping at nothing to attain their ends.

"High-minded, lovers of pleasures more than lovers of God": The first word we have met before in 1 Timothy 3:6 and 6:4 (pages 95, 179). Pride, like smoke, goes to the head, to puff up and confuse; men are blinded by their own self-sufficiency. Therefore since they do not love God they are described, with masterly understatement, as *philēdonoi* rather than *philotheoi*. Many an earnest brother or sister has pondered these words, interpreting "pleasures" in the restricted sense of recreation or entertainment. It is true that modern entertainments, like the shows in the first century theatre or amphitheatre, tend to minister to the baser instincts—and men, "knowing the judgment of God, that they which commit such things are worthy of death, not only do the same, but have pleasure in (RV, consent with) them that do them" (Romans 1:32). But it is not healthy relaxation or recreation and enjoyment, of the kind envisaged in 1 Timothy 4:4-5 (pages 124, 125), which is here in question. In such enjoyment God can be honoured; He cannot be in that which is indulged in purely for *self-satisfaction* in ways that go beyond what God intended or permits. So the list has come full circle from "lovers of their own selves" in verse 2. But not quite . . .

The Outward Show

Verse 5: *"Having a form of godliness, but denying the power thereof"*: The vices are compounded by the greatest evil of all—hypocrisy. That wickedness should masquerade as goodness is bad enough:

but that it should pretend to godliness, *eusebeia*, the true worship of God, is indefensible (see on "godliness", page 58). True godliness has a power in it, and those who embrace it yield their wills to the moral and spiritual influence of the Divine Word. But mere outward form, like the outside of the cup or the whited sepulchre, is no guide as to what is within.

It is with a sense of shock that we now realise that these things which we recognise as signs of the times are not necessarily *outside* the ecclesia. Indeed, even where they are, it is evident from Paul's words that the ecclesia could resist their influence only by the most diligent watchfulness and sound leadership. Although the Apostle is manifestly talking of "the last days", these things were at least in embryo already in the church at Ephesus, as our reference back to other parts of these Epistles should have taught us. And insofar as we recognise the characteristics of our own day we must be prepared to identify and resist the trends which will cause them to develop in our midst. The advice to Timothy for the guidance of his contemporaries is equally valid for us today: *"from such turn away"*. The word he uses is an even stronger form of that translated "avoiding" in 1 Timothy 6:20 (pages 21, 201): Timothy was to turn away from men who displayed such character in the ecclesia even more emphatically than they had turned from the truth. For further discussion of "Catalogues of Vices" in the writings of Paul, see Essay 35, page 313.

May God grant us the wisdom to hold a straight course in His Word in these perilous times.

3:6-9—Perils amongst False Brethren

Verse 6: *"For of this sort are they which creep into houses"*: The command to "turn away" from the false teachers who depart from the truth intellectually as well as morally is reinforced by the verse following, linked to the preceding by the emphatic "For". The heretics in Ephesus were keen propagandists for their point of view, and it was vital that Timothy should dissociate himself from them and campaign actively for the truth, if he was to discharge his responsibility to the ecclesia. The word for "creep" is yet another Biblical "oncer", although the furtive manner it describes is matched by a related word in Jude 4, which also describes the activities of perverters of the faith: "For there are certain men *crept in unawares* ..."

Paul accurately describes the psychology of this kind of subversion—the "heretic", which Scripturally means the leader of a faction (Essay 52, page 426), uses every means, legitimate and illegitimate, to win converts to his point of view, often proclaiming that the end justifies the means. There was nothing wrong in "house meetings" of themselves. Indeed the records of the Acts describes many a meeting for private discussion which supplemented or in some cases replaced the formal public proclamation of the Gospel. The examples of Cornelius and Lydia spring to mind. In neither case was there any question of "extraecclesial activity". The parties concerned in fact often became the nucleus of the ecclesia that was to be in their district. To "creep in", however, suggests some realisation on the part of the false teacher that stealth is his only hope of achieving his end: "He that is such is subverted, and sinneth, being condemned of himself" (Titus 3:11).

The Influence of Women in Things Spiritual

"And lead captive silly women": The phrase means 'to conquer and take captive', 'to enslave completely and bring the victim under thrall'. The vital influence of women in things moral and spiritual is referred to more than once in these Letters, and indeed figures prominently in other parts of Scripture. Not only is woman considered to be more susceptible and more easily led than man, but she has a great power to captivate in her turn. Her influence can be powerful for good or ill, as the oft repeated phrase attached to the assessment of Israel's kings suggests: "And his mother's name was . . ." is introduced almost by way of explanation for the monarch's conduct.

The honourable women of Berea are given priority of mention amongst those who searched the Scriptures diligently (Acts 17:12), whereas the stirring up of the devout and honourable women by the Jews in Pisidian Antioch was evidently considered such a serious setback to the work of the Apostle there that he could only shake the dust of the city off his feet (Acts 13:50-51). He was, however, always quick to acknowledge the service of those who had been "succourers of many", "his mother and mine", and "helpers in the Lord".

The women referred to in our present passage by the contemptuous diminutive *gynakaria* were those whose influence would prove nothing but pernicious, once they were under the control of the "evil men and seducers". Being unable to speak in the ecclesia and probably spending their days alone in the house, they would easily fall prey to the deceivers, as Eve had to the beguiling serpent in the absence of Adam.

"Laden with sins": It is important to realise that the Apostle's strictures on such women arise not from prejudice but from a righteous assessment of their characters. They were weak, their sins heaped up as it were on their consciences. So they eagerly grasped at novelty in the hope of finding release from their guilt in a new knowledge, a fresh experience, instead of casting their burden upon the Lord who would truly give them rest.

"Led away with divers lusts": The impression is reinforced by this phrase—they do not know what they want and so are wide open to anything which seems to offer "satisfaction" or "fulfilment". They think it is to be found in the pursuit of "religious" knowledge, as do the other-teachers themselves, who are "sick about questions and strifes of words" (1 Timothy 6:4, page 180).

The Quest for Novelty

Verse 7: *"Ever learning, and never able to come to the knowledge of the truth"*: In this expression we cannot avoid seeing the link with Acts 17:19-21—"May we know what this new doctrine whereof thou speakest is? ... (For all the Athenians ... spent their time in *nothing else*, but either to tell, or to hear *some new thing*)." Such curiosity, when it is purely intellectual, is rarely if ever productive of sound spiritual results. To discuss all and settle nothing is no recipe for a full assurance of faith. Even allowing for the fact that the Court of the Areopagites was originally charged with the examination of religious cults before their devotees could practise freely in the city, the assembly of both Stoics and Epicureans on Mars' Hill that day indicates that for them the philosophic debate was of major importance in this confrontation with the Apostle, and the logic and spiritual force of his argument was appreciated by relatively few.

True faith demands a humility which the intellectually gifted often find difficult to display, and the Gospel message, linked as it was to a strong call to *metanoia*, a change of heart and mind, or repentance, made demands to which few were prepared to submit. They could not come to an "acknowledging of the truth".

For a detailed discussion of the full import of this characteristic phrase in these Epistles see Essay 34 (page 296): it represents the total acceptance of the saving knowledge of God by the disciple. It is evident that what is difficult for the learned of the world will be equally so for the *dilettanti*, those who love dabbling in new ideas without pursuing any line of study with the dedication of the scholar. The *gnōsis* of this world, whether it be in the deep or shallow mind, is still foolishness with God.

Verse 8: *"Now as Jannes and Jambres withstood Moses, so do these also resist the truth":* It seems beyond doubt that the reference is to the Egyptian magicians of Exodus 7:11-14,22; 8:7, although there is no other Scriptural record of their names. The phenomenon of the magicians and the appropriateness of the comparison Paul makes with the other-teachers of Ephesus is discussed in Essay 36, "Magic, Miracles and Mighty Works", page 317.

Here we simply point out that their power to deceive lay in the counterfeiting of the true: the illusion created by the magicians had its parallel in those who preached a gospel that was "another". They were apostles, but "false"; workers, but "deceitful", and even the Jesus they preached was not he in whom the saving grace had been revealed. Such a preaching of the truth was in fact a resistance to it—a solemn thought for our day when the many attempts to redefine the fundamentals of our faith are weaning folk away from us in favour of a wider fellowship or a different "experience".

One cannot doubt the sincerity of those who seek a genuine understanding or a sense of commitment: our concern is lest they "miss the mark" by "swerving aside" (1 Timothy 1:6, page 21). The dangers are clearly indicated by Paul when he describes the extreme case of those who were deliberately pursuing a policy of subversion, and the language he uses shows that he is not dealing with attacks from without the Ephesian ecclesia, but from those who from within were turning others away from the apostolic faith.

"Men of corrupt minds, reprobate concerning the faith": This is the only occasion when the emphatic word meaning 'utterly corrupt' is used in the New Testament, so Paul evidently feels very strongly indeed about the activities of the false teachers. Reprobate, *adokimos*, is a favourite word of Paul's as a description of those who are void of judgement in Divine things, or who run the grave risk of being *castaway* (1 Corinthians 9:27) or *rejected* (Hebrews 6:8) because they do not stand the test of true discipleship. "The faith" here means the true faith as in 1 Timothy 1:19 (page 38).

The End of the Matter

This section of the Epistle ends on a positive note:

Verse 9: *"But they shall proceed no further: for their folly shall be manifest unto all men, as theirs also was"*: There are surely lessons for us here. Even if our case is not exactly similar, the effects of current trends can be the same and the principles for teaching what is sound or healthful (*hugiēs*, page 46) to the body of Christ are identical. In our own day we suffer from two opposing trends: that which leads in the direction of the evangelicals, with the tendency to minimise the importance of fundamental doctrine in fellowship; and the other extreme, which leads brethren to be exclusive in practice while remaining theoretically committed to our fellowship.

In either case we have the phenomenon of the group within the group, or the "cell of strength" as it is sometimes known, which endeavours to swing the whole ecclesia to its own way of thinking. Where it fails, then a "breakaway" ecclesia may be set up, though still not belonging officially to another "fellowship".

The effect on an ecclesia can be very disturbing, since it has members in it but not of it—not praying the same kind of prayers, nor using the same form of address to the Father, not supporting all the meetings of the ecclesia, but holding private meetings among the members of the inner group, for study or for "devotional purposes". This kind of "separate assembly" within the ecclesia has no sanction in Scripture and militates against the spiritual life of the body as a whole, whether the local ecclesia or the Brotherhood at large be considered.

Our Conviction

It is our firm conviction that it *is* possible to come to a full assurance of faith, and that not only does that faith form the basis of Christadelphian life and worship, but that it imposes a separation in fellowship from those who hold doctrines with no Scriptural basis. Were it not so, there would be no need for the existence of the Christadelphian community at all, or for its magazines and organisations, or for the labours of those who serve it.

3:10-17—The Man of God and the Word of God

Verse 10: "But thou hast fully known my doctrine, manner of life, purpose, faith": With what profound thankfulness the Apostle, with an emphatic "But thou", was able to recall the faith and loyalty of Timothy in sharp contrast to the other-teachers. The verb is in effect "to follow closely", as a disciple, and is related in 1 Timothy 4:6 to the words of the faith and the good doctrine. Luke refers to himself as "having had perfect understanding" of the things most surely believed (1:3). There was no egotism in Paul when he urged others to be followers of him: he exercised himself always to have a conscience void of offence toward God in his Christ-centred life and was therefore simply offering a practical example of what he was urging others to undertake. So to his teaching he adds "manner of life", "purpose" and "faith" to the list of things Timothy has learned of him.

Agoge, another New Testament "oncer", means simply 'conduct', or 'behaviour', but one cannot escape the link here with the previous word "teaching" (RV), which adds to it the sense of the whole method of preaching, organising ecclesias, and giving an example of the life in Christ, which Timothy had observed in his close relationship with Paul and would now himself employ in his difficult assignment in Ephesus. So it is joined with *prothesis*, 'purpose', a word which is used elsewhere by Paul exclusively with reference to the purpose of God— "called according to his purpose", "the purpose ... according to election", "the eternal purpose" (Romans 8.28; 9:11; Ephesians 3:11). Although the word can be used in a secular sense (Acts 27:13), for Paul the purpose of God and his own were the same thing: it was the basis both for the confidence of his way of life and of his *faith*.

"Longsuffering, charity, patience": "Longsuffering" is a quality of God Himself—"The longsuffering of our Lord is salvation", as Peter puts it (2 Peter 3:15)—and certainly Timothy had had ample evidence of this quality in the Apostle, as he observed him in his dealings with the ecclesias, notably Corinth to which Timothy had brought Paul's letters. "Patience" too was an essential quality for the first century disciple particularly, as for the man of God at any time (see 1 Timothy 6:11, page 186), since there were great afflictions to be endured, as Paul is reminded by the reference to longsuffering, which was one aspect of the fruit of the Spirit.

Verse 11: *"Persecutions, afflictions, which came unto me at Antioch, at Iconium, at Lystra"*: These were aspects of discipleship which Timothy had also seen manifested in the Apostle's experience, and indeed he had himself shared some of them with him. Those which Paul selects for special mention here, however, he had endured before the conversion of the young man. Opponents of the belief that Paul wrote these Letters make much of this, as an evidence that we have here the work of an imitator not fully conversant with all the details of the author he is striving to copy.

In fact the reverse is the case, since the forger would be less likely to introduce any detail which the reader might find surprising. There were innumerable persecutions to which the Apostle could have referred, including those of Acts 16-17 in which Timothy had shared; see also 2 Corinthians 11:22-33. Those at Antioch and Iconium, however, would have become well-known in Lystra, where Timothy witnessed the stoning of Paul almost to death (Acts 14:19), *and yet became a disciple*. He had truly "fully known" the cost of discipleship, therefore, but had also seen how *"out of them all the Lord delivered me"*.

The Apostle's sense of gratitude to the Lord for his deliverance is as prominent a feature of his character as the humble acceptance of the persecutions his ministry brought upon him. He too had "fully known" that they were inevitable, for from the moment of his conversion the Lord had shown unto him "how great things he must suffer for my name's sake", as he bore that name "before the Gentiles, and kings, and the children of Israel" (Acts 9:15-16).

Verse 12: *"Yea, and all that will live godly in Christ Jesus shall suffer persecution":* Paul's constant exhortation to the brethren who witnessed his persecutions—"that we must through much tribulation (*thlipsis*, 'pressure') enter into the kingdom of God" (Acts 14:22)—is here repeated for Timothy's benefit. There is neither mistake nor failure in God's purpose that there should be heresy to combat and persecution to endure: such things play an integral part in service to the Lord. As one commentator has put it: "Every life fully consecrated to the service of God and of Christ crucified must bear the mark of the cross."

Verse 13: *"But evil men and seducers shall wax worse and worse":* This verse takes up the thought of verses 1-9 above. The seducers are in fact *wizards* (a Biblical "oncer"), adept at the "sleight of men, and cunning craftiness" which produce the "winds of doctrine" described in Ephesians 4:14. We are not to see here any contradiction with verse 9, since the reference is to the intensity and not to the extent of the false teachers' "progress". They will indeed "advance" but it will be from bad to worse! See 2 Timothy 2:16 and note on pages 270, 271. Because deception is part of the other-teachers' method it recoils upon themselves—they come to believe wholeheartedly in their own teaching, and so are at once *"deceiving, and being deceived"*.

Verse 14: *"But continue thou in the things which thou hast learned":* Paul resumes the exhortation of verse 10, and indeed of the whole section of the epistle from 2:1 onwards. The essential attitude of the man of God was to *remain* in the things he had learned (possibly with the implied contrast to the *movement away* of the false teachers).

Timothy was to need spiritual strength, courage and self-discipline, with all of which he had been equipped from the beginning. It was now a question of continuance in those things which were a part of the God-provided heritage of the man the Lord had set aside for himself. He had received the faith through the early work of his mother and grandmother (1:5) and of the Apostle Paul himself—sure and reliable witnesses. He had not received these things half-heartedly, for he had *"been assured of* (them), *knowing of whom* (or, of what people) *thou hast learned them"*.

Verse 15: *"And that from a child thou hast known the holy scriptures,* *which are able to make thee wise . . . ":* In Timothy the end in view in Deuteronomy 6:6-7 had been achieved:

> "And these words, which I command thee this day, shall be in thine heart: and thou shalt teach them diligently unto thy children, and shalt talk of them when thou sittest in thine house, and when thou walkest by the way, and when thou liest down, and when thou risest up."

There is no other way provided by God for the acquisition of the wisdom that brings salvation than that revealed through the Scriptures. This cannot be too strongly emphasised in these troubled days, when there are so many voices clamouring for attention.

Personal study of "the things which are most surely believed among us" (Luke 1:1) is greatly to be commended. It is a rewarding exercise to list for oneself, and then carefully to consider, *all* the Scriptural passages which bear upon the first principles of the faith, not overlooking passages which may appear "awkward", and not ignoring the implications of the details of the text. Having done that, in prayer, one can conclude with a personal testimony, "I believe and am sure" of the elements of the faith and of their importance as aspects of saving truth. If controversy or dispute should arise, we can also then be in a position to speak from personal conviction based on our own Bible study. If we ask, What saith the Scripture? we shall soon discover what the doctrines of the Scripture are and their integral place in the worship of God. *"Salvation"*, said Paul, is *"through faith which is in Christ Jesus"*. What that faith consisted of, in content and in practical response, the careful study of the apostolic preaching soon reveals. See for example the details of the speech which pricked men's hearts on the day of Pentecost (Acts 2).

Verse 16: *"All scripture is given by inspiration of God":* So important is this verse that it calls for a separate study of its full meaning, especially since verses 16 and 17 have played a considerable part in controversies about inspiration.* See Essay 37, "By Inspiration of God", page 322.

---

*See also the chapter on "The Spirit that Inspires", in the context of the activity of God through His Spirit, in the author's book, *The Spirit of God* (published in 1976 by The Christadelphian Office).

"Throughly furnished"

Verses 16-17: In the light of the above, together with Essay 37, we can now see the full force of the Apostle's words which close this chapter. Since Scripture is the "written voice of God" it must be *"profitable for doctrine* (teaching), *for reproof, for correction, for instruction in righteousness"*. The primary sense of "profitable" here is "useful for the apostolic ministry", but, as we have seen, the "profiting" is for everyone who reads and obeys, since that ministry was in itself the proclamation and practice of the Word of God.

One has only to read the Lord's own words and the letters of the apostles to be aware of how they carried out their work of reproving, correcting and teaching. The title *"man of God"* was given to God's prophets, but it is equally applicable to those who are willing to be instructed in righteousness by the words which they proclaimed in the name of the Lord. The vital importance of Scripture in every aspect of our own corporate and personal lives is clearly demonstrated, and in the special context of Timothy's responsibilities in Ephesus and ours today, who have been left the same "good deposit" of Divine truth, the Apostle's exhortation is both comforting and timely.

ESSAY 35

Catalogues of Vices

THE opening verses of 2 Timothy 3 provide an outstanding example of Paul's "catalogues of evil". Each of the Pastoral Epistles contains at least one, enumerating at least 30 different evil practices. The other lists are in 1 Timothy 1:9-10 (pages 23-26), 6:4-5 (pages 180, 181) and Titus 3:2,3 (pages 410, 411), and there are a dozen examples in the passage under consideration. Spicq (*Les Epîtres Pastorales*) has identified 21 such catalogues in the New Testament, of which the following are in the writings of Paul: Romans 1:29-31; 13:13: 1 Corinthians 5:10-11; 6:9-10; 2 Corinthians 12:20-21; Galatians 5:19-21; Ephesians 4:31; 5:3-5; Colossians 3:5-8. It is possible also to enumerate corresponding catalogues of virtues, as for example the duties in the lists of qualifications for eldership (Essay 10, page 107) and the duties of young women in Titus 2:3.

Before we consider the implication of the existence of such catalogues, it is worth comparing our present list with that of Romans 1 (below). In the former passage the Apostle has clearly defined the reason why the pagan world, representing the human condition from which it needs the power of the Gospel to redeem, should be in such a degraded state. "When they did not like to retain God in their knowledge, *they glorified him not as God* . . . changed the truth of God into a lie . . . did not like to retain God in their knowledge." Doctrine, or sound teaching, therefore, is seen to be more than of intellectual value: *it is the only basis for sound living, or morality.* It follows that the work of the other-teachers in Ephesus, however well-meaning their original intent, would tend ultimately in the same direction as the pagan world, a point made continually in these Letters, which underlies the urgency of the apostolic charge to the young man responsible for the ecclesia's welfare.

2 TIMOTHY 3		ROMANS 1	
Verse 2	Boasters, proud	*Verse 30*	Proud, boasters
	Disobedient to parents		Disobedient to parents
Verse 2	Unthankful	*Verse 21*	Neither were thankful
Verse 3	Without natural	*Verse 31*	Without natural
	affection		affection
	Trucebreakers		Covenant-breakers

It is important these days, when it is no longer fashionable to learn lists, verses or texts, or recite catechisms, to consider what part could have been played by the constant repetition of such catalogues of good and evil, for it is evident that they were in common use as a basis of exhortation or reproof. We cannot deny that *mere* rote learning or repetition is no guarantee either of sound learning or good living. With this the Apostle would heartily agree. In fact, he said as much when he wrote of the "form of godliness" which had no dynamic power in it. The point has equally to be conceded, however, that at some stage facts and details have to be firmly fixed in the mind before the principles they illustrate can be recalled and applied with profit.

The proliferation of translations of Scripture has eroded the common language which makes communication (and communion) more effective. Ultimately this could mean that the Scriptural allusions upon which exhortations are based will not be universally appreciated.

The first century ecclesia, whether it were Jew or Greek, barbarian or Scythian, had no such problem. It had a vocabulary of virtue and vice, and a set of "faithful sayings", or statements of the faith, sometimes adapted to suit the problem or condition of a particular ecclesia, but all used as the basis of practical exhortation in the face of a real issue. There was also a *lingua franca*, a common tongue which ensured a wider understanding of the "basics" of the life in Christ throughout the worldwide ecclesia, no matter how much local pressures made them fall short of the ideal.

Thus, on two occasions when a list of evil practices to be shunned was set out, it related directly to the conduct of a brother and the ecclesia's reaction to it or to the whole attitude of an ecclesia to the fundamental principles of the Gospel: "Know ye not", says Paul (with the force of "Of course you are well aware"), "that the unrighteous *shall not inherit the kingdom of God.* Be not deceived: neither fornicators, nor idolaters, nor adulterers, nor effeminate, nor abusers of themselves with mankind, nor thieves, nor covetous, nor drunkards, nor revilers, nor extortioners, *shall inherit the kingdom of God"* (1 Corinthians 6:9-10).

And in Galatians 5:19-21—"Now the works of the flesh are manifest, which are these: adultery, fornication, uncleanness, lasciviousness, idolatry, witchcraft, hatred, variance, emulations, wrath, strife, seditions, heresies, envyings, murders, drunkenness, revellings, and such like: of the which I tell you before, *as I have also told you in time past,* that they which do such things *shall not inherit the kingdom of God."* If they were to walk in the Spirit it was important for them to know what that entailed, both in what they should do and what they should avoid (verse 22).

We are reminded that the Lord himself made use of such a catalogue in his teaching about the human heart, in the very context of the denunciation of hypocrisy: "But those things which proceed out of the mouth come forth from the heart; and they defile the man. For out of the heart proceed evil thoughts, murders, adulteries, fornications, thefts, false witness, blasphemies: these are the things which defile a man" (Matthew 15:18-20). Perhaps with due remembrance of the fact that by professing a form of godliness without allowing the power thereof to influence our personal conduct—the most culpable vice of all—a return to the accurate learning of detail in Divine things would be no bad thing.

Contemporary Patterns

Some have seen in these catalogues a pattern taken from contemporary Hellenistic thought, which puts them on a par with the lists of qualifications for ecclesial office, which are said to have been modelled on the lists of requirements for those eligible for political office in the small towns and cities of the Roman world. These were discussed in some detail in Essay 10 (page 107) with reference to 1 Timothy 3. It is far more likely that the catalogues were modelled on the Jewish literature written to combat idolatry and the vices which followed in the wake of the worship of false gods.

Old Testament Background

Some of this literature was written between the Testaments, and Paul would have been familiar with it. There was also the treatise of Philo the Alexandrian Jew, written earlier in the first century AD, which influenced some of the other-teachers (see on 1 Timothy 1:4, page 19). Some of the phrases used in the list in 2 Timothy 3 are almost identical with those employed in Philo's writings on the "philosophy" of the Law of Moses. But as we saw when discussing the special vocabulary of these Epistles earlier, Paul gave a unique spiritual emphasis to his words from whatever source they were drawn. The same is also true of any existing lists of virtues from which he may have drawn.

It is natural that Paul should make reference to known sayings and contemporary works where they were relevant to his argument, and many of the Biblical "oncers" can be attributed to the wide experience of five years travel in the "mission field" after his first release from the prison in Rome. The apostle's real roots, however, lay in the Old Testament Scriptures, to such an extent that even when using Greek words it was in a Hebrew idiom. For the Old Testament origins of the lists of commandments, both positive and negative, upon the keeping of which length of days and fellowship with God depended, we should not have far to seek. See for example Exodus 20, Deuteronomy 27 and 28 and many other places.

ESSAY 36

Magic, Miracles and Mighty Works

IN this Essay we consider more closely the comparison Paul has made between Jannes and Jambres and the other-teachers (1 Timothy 3:8). The Ancient World was riddled with magic and mystery. Egypt, if not the original home, was at least the principal source for the dissemination of the magical arts and the mystery cults, which also depended largely upon illusion. Isis worship had influenced the Romans from their first occupation of Egypt in 30 BC, and many a governor's daughter became a priestess of the cult which found a place even in Rome itself. One of the most important temples in Pompeii was dedicated to Isis, who numbered leading magistrates among her devotees. The wall paintings give some indication of the nature of her worship, which had features in it which the Apostle would have described as "the sleight of men, and cunning craftiness", a phrase taken appropriately enough from the Letter to the Ephesians in the context of withstanding "every wind of doctrine" (4:14).

We have New Testament evidence for recognising Ephesus itself as a centre for the practice of the "curious arts", for as a result of the mighty "growing and prevailing" of the Word of God, a whole library of books on the subject, worth 50,000 pieces of silver, was publicly burned (Acts 19:19-20). Given such an environment for the ecclesia, there was good reason for the Apostle to warn them against those other-teachers who, with all the skill of those other "illusionists", were advocating a system of thought and worship apparently similar to the Gospel, but which proved to be in fact "other" in all its fundamentals.

The magicians of Egypt opposed Moses, the representative of God, by doing the same wonders as he. The heretics of Ephesus,

317

loudly proclaiming that they were no innovators but were throwing new light upon the traditional faith, claimed to be preaching the same Gospel as the Lord's messenger and so used the same vocabulary while resisting his apostolic authority. Under the cloak of the same words the basic principles were changed. So intellectually and spiritually the other-teachers were incapable of comprehending saving truth: their understanding was *corrupt*— a New Testament "oncer" of powerful meaning.

What then are we to make of the illusions the magicians created, or indeed of all the signs and wonders done by false prophets and so-called disciples throughout the ages? It has frankly to be confessed, at least by the present author, that we have no knowledge of how the illusions were performed by the Egyptians. Equally mysterious is the basis of the extraordinary powers which some people seem to possess whereby they see, hear or do what seems beyond the average capacity.

That there *are* clairvoyants, workers of black magic, exorcists, people highly sensitive to vibrations of one kind or another, or possessed of a benign power of healing, is well enough attested, and Scripture certainly does not deny that this is so. It simply challenges the claims made by them or on their behalf. So when in response to Pharaoh's command, "Show a miracle for you", Aaron threw down his rod and it became a serpent, "the magicians of Egypt, *they did in like manner with their enchantments*". At this stage the superiority of the God of Israel was demonstrated simply by the fact that "Aaron's rod swallowed up their rods".

The magicians' secret arts were powerful enough, however, for Pharaoh to refuse to yield to the Word of God, as they were in the case of the river turning into blood and the conjuring up of the frogs. The effect produced was similar to that of Moses by the Word of the Lord, but *their basis was quite different*. That was clearly seen when it came to the plague of lice or sand flies (Exodus 8:16-19). The record says that "the dust of the land *became* lice throughout all the land of Egypt". It seems plain that it was the creation of one of the lowest forms of life that took place here, an act so fundamentally an act of God alone that "the magicians did so with their enchantments to bring forth lice, *but they could not . . .* Then the magicians said unto Pharaoh, *This is the finger of God*". There had come a point, therefore, when the basic difference between enchantment and the work of God was manifest to all, and even the magicians themselves had to admit it. The phrase "the finger of God" passed into Scripture to refer to that Divine power which can in no way be counterfeited by men.

The Finger of God

Remarkably the expression is used again in Exodus with reference to the powerful, life-giving Word of God—the permanent visible reminder of what the living Voice of God had declared. Twice is it said that the record was "written with the finger of God" (Exodus 31:18; 32:16; also 34:1; Deuteronomy 10:2). The tables of the Law were the touchstone of the Divine teaching upon which the covenant of life and inheritance was based. The prophets were the appointed spokesmen of the Lord, to declare, explain and interpret "the word of the Lord". Parallel with the responsibility of the prophet to speak only according to the Word was that of the people to hear and obey the Word alone. But how were they to distinguish between the true and the false? They were given clear and unmistakable guidance from the Word itself.

For the people, when they came into a land of false worship, including mysteries, enchantments and enticements to sin, there were two things to consider. First, in whose name did the prophet speak, that of the LORD or of other gods? For the people of the LORD that should have been a sufficient test of authenticity in itself. But if there was any uncertainty "in thine heart", there was a simple negative test to apply:

> "When a prophet speaketh in the name of the LORD, if the thing follow not, nor come to pass, that is the thing which the LORD hath not spoken, but the prophet hath spoken it presumptuously; thou shalt not be afraid of him."
>
> (Deuteronomy 18:20-22)

There was, however, the possibility of coincidence, a 50-50 chance of fulfilment. There might be more—an undoubted sign or wonder which came to pass. Upon what criterion could the people then judge the orthodoxy of the prophet and exercise their own spiritual discernment? Whatever the sign or wonder, it was to carry no conviction of itself. The assessment was to be on other grounds than that of subjective experience: the great test was, What was *the basis of the prophet's words*?

"If . . . the sign or wonder come to pass, whereof he spake unto thee, saying, Let us go after other gods, which thou hast not known, and let us serve them; *thou shalt not hearken unto the words of that prophet, or that dreamer of dreams*: for the LORD your God proveth you, to know whether ye love the LORD your God with all your heart and with all your soul."

(Deuteronomy 13:1-3)

So the principle was established, and it is valid for all generations: "When they shall say unto you, Seek unto them that have familiar spirits, and unto wizards that peep, and that mutter . . . To the law and to the testimony: *if they speak not according to this word, it is because there is no light in them*" (Isaiah 8:19,20). But surely, it may be objected, this language is too strong to be applied to those who were not dealers in magic nor did they lay claim to prophetic gifts, but simply put forward a point of view or attempted to adjust the Gospel to what they believed were true contemporary values?

According to Paul the principle is the same wherever is offered the illusion of Divine sanction for what is not according to the Divine Word. Indeed, the Lord himself emphasised that appearances were not enough. Many will say unto him "in that day, Lord, Lord, have we not prophesied in thy name? and in thy name have cast out devils? and in thy name done many wonderful works?" There was no suggestion that the words had not been spoken in his name, that devils had not in fact been cast out, nor wonderful works accomplished. The verdict was, nevertheless, "I never knew you: depart from me, *ye that work iniquity*" (Matthew 7:21-23).

A Stern Rebuke from the Lord

This solemn warning of the Lord's, that the performance of signs and wonders, and even forceful preaching in his name, is no substitute for the doing of the will of his Father, which can only be based upon the knowledge of Him as revealed in His Word, was later reinforced by a stern rebuke for Peter—"Get thee behind me, Satan!"—when the disciple allowed sentiment to deny one of the fundamental aspects of Scripture teaching, the cross of Christ. There could be no true denying of himself, no discipleship possible, if Peter failed to discern the meaning of taking up the cross to follow the Master who had taken up his.

Even for Peter, sincerity was not enough. As John put it in his Second Epistle, "Whoso *goeth on* (that is, becomes too advanced in his thinking), and abideth not in the doctrine of Christ, hath not God" (verse 9).

If we appear to have laboured this point, we believe it is with good reason. Even if the other-teachers in Ephesus lacked the more sinister qualities of a Jannes or Jambres, or a Simon Magus, and confined themselves simply to accommodating the Gospel of Christ to prevailing sentiment, the Apostle Paul had no wish to see the flock weaned away from saving truth. For him there was a "good deposit" (see page 221), "the faith which was once delivered unto the saints" (Jude 3), for which it was necessary to contend earnestly. That others should wish constantly to be redefining it concerned him deeply, both because of the divisive effect it had upon the ecclesia and because those who led the factions were in ultimate danger of losing their own salvation.

ESSAY 37

"By inspiration of God"

FIRST a brief but necessary textual comment on 2 Timothy 3:16. The Authorised Version differs in emphasis from the Revised, which reads: "Every scripture inspired of God is also profitable . . ." This has raised the question as to whether there is any other *inspired* scripture than that which is inspired of God, which can be equally profitable. If there is, then that begs the whole question of inspiration in this context and invalidates the point the Apostle is making. For it is not his point that *inspired writing*, as distinct from any other kind, is profitable for the instruction of the man of God, but that the holy *grammata*, or 'writings', to which he has just referred in verse 15, constitute Scripture because they have a special quality, and that it is that quality which makes them profitable even unto salvation.

The writings in question are those which Timothy has known from early childhood, the Old Testament Scriptures, as surely Divine as the Tables of the Decalogue which had been "written with the finger of God". The question of the New Testament Scriptures is related to that of the Old, of course, and we have already in our study of these Letters seen evidences that there was a body of New Testament writing which had the seal of an inspired Apostle's approval. Peter also confirms that Paul's own writings were to be numbered amongst "the other scriptures" (2 Peter 3:16). For a discussion of the actual Greek grammar of the verse we are considering, as additional proof of the accuracy of the Authorised Version translation, please see *The Christadelphian*, 1968, pages 359-361.

What then is this special quality described as "by inspiration of God"? The full force of the expression will be missed if our concept of inspiration is limited to the idea usually suggested by the English word. The Latin *inspirare*, the root from which our word comes, has the literal sense of 'to blow upon', 'to breathe into', and the figurative meaning 'to inspire, excite, inflame, instil, implant'. The inspiration of a poet, musician or prophet, was thought in ancient times to be the process by which his native genius was excited to creative or prophetic activity. But this idea does not convey the full force of the "by inspiration of God" of 2 Timothy 3:16 or the "moved by the Holy Spirit" of 2 Peter 1:21.

The phrase "given by inspiration of God" is represented in the Greek of our verse by a single word, *theopneustos*, meaning literally 'God-breathed'. The key to our understanding of this verse and of the Biblical doctrine of inspiration lies in the fact that the reference here is not to *inspired men* but to *God-breathed Scripture*. The meaning of *theopneustos*, used nowhere else in the Greek version of either the Old or New Testament, and rare in the Greek language itself, can be well illustrated from Scripture, and its message is profound yet simple to grasp.

"Spirit" and "Word"

In Genesis 1 it is recorded that "the Spirit of God moved upon the face of the waters. And God said, Let there be light, and there was light" (verses 1,2). Here is the first parallel drawn between the activity of God's *Spirit* and what He *said*. When we read the Psalmist's comment in Psalm 33:6-9—"By the *word* of the Lord were the heavens made; and all the host of them by the *breath of his mouth* . . . For he spake, and it was done; he commanded, and it stood fast"—we see that the movement of God's Spirit, His "breathing-out", and His Word are closely related ideas. The Hebrew and Greek words used in the original and Septuagint versions emphasise this close relationship.

The Hebrew for "spirit" (*ruach*) in Genesis 1:2 is used frequently in the Old Testament for "breath" as well, including man's breath, but usually in the special sense of the breath which God has put into the nostrils of every living thing—the life which is essentially in God's hands. The Greek word for "spirit" is *pneuma*, used frequently in the Septuagint with both senses of *ruach*, "spirit" and "breath", and the New Testament *theopneustos* is composed of the two Greek words for "God" and "spirit" or "breath". The Scripture which is God-breathed, therefore, must, like the first recorded God-breathed word, be immediately authoritative and of creative power in those that receive it.

Of the creation of man it is written, "The Lord God ... breathed into his nostrils the breath of life; and man became a living soul" (Genesis 2:7). Here the verb "to breathe" has the sense of 'to breathe out, to blow upon', as for example in Isaiah 54:16, Ezekiel 22:20,21 and Haggai 1:9, where the smith blows upon the coals, God blows upon Israel in the fire of His wrath, or blows contemptuously upon the results of the people's labour. The special sense of Genesis 2:7 is seen again in Ezekiel 37:9, where the wind, or spirit, or breath, is commanded to blow upon the dead bones of the house of Israel to give them life.

Here, then, are two instances of *theopneustia*, of 'God's breathing out', when what is exhaled is the breath of life. As man's word is produced by the exhalation of his breath, so the Spirit carries forth God's Word to the accomplishment of His purpose. But the Divine Word is life-giving as well as authoritative: "O ye dry bones, hear the *word of the LORD*" (Ezekiel 37:4). "Incline your ear ... hear, and your soul shall live ... So shall my word be that goeth forth out of my mouth ... it shall accomplish that which I please, and it shall prosper in the thing whereto I sent it" (Isaiah 55:3,11).

"It is written", says Paul in 1 Corinthians 15:45, "The first man Adam was made a living soul; the last Adam was made a quickening spirit." The first clause is a reference to Genesis 2:7, and an equally clear illustration of the meaning of the second is given in John 20:22, where the risen Lord encountered his disciples, and *breathed out* on them, and said, "Receive ye holy Spirit". John's choice of the identical expression, *enephusēsen*, used in the Septuagint for the giving of the breath of life, tells us that the Word made flesh, now become the Lord the Spirit, had the power in himself to quicken his disciples and give them life— a power which would culminate in their resurrection from the dead (see John 5:21-29).

In the description of the baptism of the church in Spirit (Acts 2:2), there is a sound from heaven as of a rushing mighty wind, to mark the oncoming of the Spirit. The word here for "wind" (*pnoë*) occurs only once more in the New Testament, in Acts 17:25, where it means the breath of life which God gives to all men. So it was a rushing mighty *breath* which filled the house, to make the church a living fellowship.

A Creative and Authoritative Force

The breathing-out of God, therefore, is associated in Scripture with creative activity, the speaking of a word, a commandment, the giving of life, and the accomplishment of God's purpose in Israel and the world. The first record of a *writing down* of the Divine Word is in Exodus, where the words which had been breathed out in Sinai in the voice of the living God Himself, were "written with the finger of God", as a permanent record for posterity of what God had said. This, and all subsequent Scripture, then, being likewise *theopneustos*, was the written record of the final, authoritative and unchanging will of God, creative and life-giving.

It is impossible to speak of degrees of inspiration, or to separate revelation from inspiration in the Scriptural sense of either word. The apostolic view recognises no distinction in the quality, or indeed in the profitable nature of any of the parts of Scripture, nor do the historical background or presumed limitations of knowledge in the writers in any way impair the value of the Scriptures as part of the all-round equipment of the man of God.

Nevertheless something must be said about the "inspiring" of the men who wrote. The Scripture term for what is often (but inadequately in English) called *inspiration* in this sense is *moved by the Holy Spirit*. The idea conveyed by the Greek words of 2 Peter 1:21 is not so much that the holy men were moved to speak, but that as they were *being borne along* by the Holy Spirit, they spoke. Again, it is the Scripture which illuminates its own meaning.

On Eagle's Wings

Having followed a sequence of thought about the Spirit or breath of God, we must return to Genesis 1:2 to consider the nature of its activity. "The Spirit of God *moved* upon the face of the waters. And God said ..." The Hebrew word for "moved" (*rachaph*, a rare word in the Bible), is most expressive of "love in creation". It is to be understood in the same sense as it is used in Deuteronomy 32:11,12—"As an eagle stirreth up her nest,

fluttereth over her young ... so the LORD alone did lead him.''
God Himself uses the same figure, though not the same word,
when He proclaims Himself as the LORD their God who had
borne Israel out of Egypt ''on eagles' wings'', to bring them unto
Himself (Exodus 19:4).

The Speaker's Commentary says: ''The Spirit of God appears
to be represented as a great quickening principle, hovering or
brooding over the earth and ocean, and breathing upon them
light and life.'' Gesenius, in the *Hebrew Lexicon*, gives cognate
words expressive of compassion and tender mercies, and says:
''The Syriac root is of more frequent use ... of birds brooding
over their young, of parents cherishing their children ... also
of a *voice descending from heaven.*'' The Creation, then, was not
merely an act of power. It was a loving, purposeful, compassionate act, which fully justified the later statement that God
so loved the world, even when it went astray, that He gave His
only begotten Son for its redemption. That beloved Son He
publicly acknowledged with the Spirit descending and a Voice
from heaven over the waters of his baptism, and again at the
Transfiguration (Luke 9:35).

The Spirit Borne from God

The Greek translation of Genesis 1:2 uses the verb *pherō*, 'to
bear', for *rachaph*: ''The Spirit of God was being borne upon the
face of the waters.'' The breath was exhaled, and carried with
it the Divine Word. The verb is the usual one for 'to bear'
or 'to carry', and though not expressive of all the meanings
of *rachaph*—for instance, it does not of itself carry the idea of
mercy and compassion—it can convey the same sense of powerful
activity. Compare its use in compounds in Acts 27:15,27—when
the mariners let the ship ride they were *borne along* by the wind,
and were *driven up and down* in Adria.

The use of the verb with the rather technical meaning of the
way in which the Spirit of God was sent forth for the accomplishment of His will is carried over into the New Testament. In Acts
2:2, the wind or breath which marked the descent of the Holy
Spirit is described as *pheromenē*—'being borne along'; and there is
no doubt that this word, translated ''rushing'' in the Authorised
Version, is one of those which the Holy Spirit itself teaches,
and that the ''rushing mighty wind'' describes the same light-

bringing, creative, authoritative and life-giving activity as in Genesis.

Power and Authority

The deep significance of Peter's statement about the holy men of God who spake (2 Peter 1:21) can now be seen in the context of the whole passage. There is a direct relationship between the way in which the voice came from heaven (verses 17,18) and the moving of the holy men. The voice of God which announced the Divine Sonship of the Lord Jesus and invested him with power and authority ("Hear ye him") was, says Peter (using the aorist passive tense of the verb *pherō*), *"borne to him* from the excellent glory", just as the Spirit of God was borne out over the waters so long before. "And this voice, *borne* from heaven (this time, the participle of *pherō*), we heard when we were with him on the holy mount." (See also the quotation from Gesenius above in this connection.) What they heard is to be compared with the word of prophecy which, like the voice from heaven itself, was God-breathed, a breath sent forth. And holy men of God, themselves caught up in that same breath, "being borne along (*pheromenoi*) by the Holy Spirit", they spake.

This, then, is the authentic first century view of the Scriptures. The words must have been "words which the Holy Spirit teacheth", and no question of degrees of inspiration enters into the discussion. The written message itself was as clearly Divine and unmistakable as the activity of the Spirit being borne over the face of the waters, or God's historical acts with Israel. True inspiration cannot be confused with mechanical dictation, since the men who spoke and wrote were themselves part of God's purpose in the process.

The Second Letter to Timothy
CHAPTER 4
The End of the Charge

4:1-5—Repetition of the Charge to Timothy

Verse 1: *"I charge thee, therefore":* This marks the final appeal to Timothy to fulfil his responsibilities with faithfulness and courage. In the First Letter the Apostle defined "the charge" Timothy was to give to the other-teachers, a duty with which he in turn had been charged by Paul. The positive and negative aspects of that charge—what Timothy was himself to do and what he was to restrain others from doing—are repeated and alluded to throughout both Letters (1 Timothy 5:21; 6:13; 2 Timothy 1:6,8,13; 2:1-3,8,14; 3:14). All is now gathered up in this, the most solemn command of all, which sums up the entire spirit and content of all that Paul has written to the younger man.

"Before God, and the Lord Jesus Christ": Once more Paul calls upon those invisible but ever-present witnesses in whose sight all things must be done. The solemnity of the charge is emphasised by the reference to the fact that Christ *"shall judge the quick and the dead":* for it is Christ at his coming who will judge the work of the other-teachers as well as how far Timothy (and *all* God's servants in *every* age) has discharged his great responsibilities.

It is salutary to remember that it is he through whom salvation came who is to be Judge (compare "the Lamb of God that taketh away the sin of the world" of John's Gospel with "the wrath of the Lamb" of the Apocalypse). In these Letters it is *God* who is set forth as the Saviour (page 15) and *Christ* before whom His servants will stand for judgement. It is probable that in the phrase "the quick and the dead" we find yet one more echo of an early creed or statement of the faith which was in use in the first century ecclesias (page 49). It certainly found its place in the first

328

preaching to the Gentiles, when Peter told Cornelius that the apostles had been "*charged* to preach unto the people, and to testify that this is he which is ordained of God to be the Judge of the quick and dead" (Acts 10:42, RV).

"*At his appearing and his kingdom*": The sentence construction is varied by the Apostle here, to suggest that it is also *by the fact of Christ's second coming* that he is appealing to Timothy—"the appearing and the kingdom" being cardinal elements of the faith and hope upon which his discipleship is based. Moreover, the young man's resolution for the task should be strengthened by the knowledge (to anticipate verse 8), that there is a reward for those "who love his appearing". For a discussion of the word "appearing" see Essay 22, page 213).

Verse 2: "*Preach the word*": The first of the five imperatives is the natural sequel to the declaration in 3:14-17 of the power and total adequacy of the Scripture for the spiritual equipment of the man of God. There could be no better apostolic advice for the last days with all their dangers for the ecclesia, and neglect of it would expose the brethren to the destructive work of those who had something "other" to proclaim. The expression is not exactly the equivalent of preaching the Gospel, although that is equally vital, as verse 5 will tell us. The command here is *kēruxon*—'proclaim', 'herald', 'sound forth the Word', while holding a straight course in it (2:15, RV margin), striking a true balance between grace and judgement, the goodness and severity of God, instead of proclaiming the words which man's wisdom teacheth (see verses 3-4 below). A fuller survey of the "Word of God" in the New Testament is undertaken in Essay 38, page 347.

"*Be instant in season, out of season*": This is not quite the same thing as "press on regardless", although the verb "be instant" has the overtones of "standing to it". The metaphor is rather that of standing to one's post, like a good sentry or watchman, and here is applied to the whole "charge" laid upon Timothy. The Greek has even more of a play upon words than our "in season, out of season", although the Apostle never used the expression *euchairōs, achairōs* elsewhere in his writings. The whole command is rather like that given to the prophet Isaiah: "Cry aloud, *spare not*, lift up thy voice like a trumpet, and shew my people their transgression, and the house of Jacob their sins" (58:1).

329

Diligent, constant attention to the sounding forth of the Word is the only way to promote healthful teaching in the ecclesias today, and we should let the very solemnity of the charge and the sense of urgency stimulated by the imminence of the Lord's return recall us as a community to our duty. Even if the expression "in season, out of season" does not exactly convey such a meaning, we are justified in using it as a call to our preparedness. So often our interest is only aroused by dramatic events to pay more earnest heed to Scripture—in times of crisis in the world, in the Brotherhood, or at some other "seasonable" time. We should be better equipped to deal with problems, however, and always ready to give an answer for the hope that is within us, if we were as devoted to the study of the Word "out of season" as well! Yet another consideration is that we should do this whether it is convenient to ourselves or not: we must "make *full proof*" of this ministry of the Word.

"Reprove, rebuke, exhort": The method, however, must vary according to circumstance and the needs of the flock. The Scripture is profitable for *elengxis*, 'reproof'. On the basis, not of his subjective opinion but of the light of the Word of God, which is "a discerner of the thoughts and intents of the heart", Timothy was to appeal to the conscience of the believers, that they might be convicted by it (*elengchō*; see John 8:9). This was also a work of the Spirit (John 16:8), which will *"reprove* the world of sin"*, and both Timothy and Titus were called upon frequently to carry out the same work, "before all" if necessary: *convincing* the gainsayer, sharply, with all authority (1 Timothy 5:20; Titus 1:9,13; 2:15; pages 164, 361, 364, 396). For "all things that are *reproved* are made manifest by the light" (Ephesians 5:13).

"Rebuke" (*epitimaō*) as a noun, however, is used only once elsewhere by Paul, in the case of the sinner at Corinth (2 Corinthians 2:6), where the word suggests a scolding or disciplinary action, which had its full effect upon the brother involved, who repented. It is a common enough word in the Gospels, and implies the act of a teacher or superior in moral force, such as when the Lord rebuked Peter or the raging sea.

"Exhort" is *parakaleō*, the usual word for exhortation or comforting by strengthening another's resolve. This also is the function of the teacher, and is more of an appeal to the good will or good sense of the hearers to stir them up to repentance. Timothy was to lose no opportunity, spare no effort, in the discharge of his duty as a shepherd of the flock.

Longsuffering and Forbearance

"With all longsuffering and doctrine": Whatever the form of the appeal, however, the manner of it was of the utmost importance. There must be no rancour, only patience (3:10, page 308), and the charity which "hopeth all things", especially for the recovery of those who have turned out of the way. For "the servant of the Lord must not strive; but be gentle unto all men, apt to teach, patient ..." (1 Corinthians 13:7; 2 Timothy 2:24, page 280). Viewed in context, it is the Word which is the effective agent, not the teacher himself, as it will be the Word by which a man is judged in the last day (John 12:48).

Verse 3: *"For the time will come when they will not endure sound doctrine":* This verse explains the urgency of Paul's final appeal, and whatever the immediate relevance to Timothy, it is accurately prophetic of the current era in the Brotherhood. We refer the reader to the detailed notes on "sound doctrine", or "healthful doctrine" (pages 46-48), and the "faithful sayings" (pages 49-51), together with the exposition of 1 Timothy 2. It will be seen that while it is true that the word "doctrine" has a strong moral significance in the New Testament, it is equally true that there is always presented a Scriptural or "doctrinal" basis (in the more limited sense of that word) for the behaviour described.

The time has now come when the idea is being freely promulgated that elements of the faith are of less importance than that of the life in Christ. The Scripture knows nothing of any such distinctions: there was something which Cornelius, for all his exemplary life, had to know and do before his *life in Christ* could begin. It is becoming increasingly difficult to convince people of the importance of doctrine, yet the only alternative to accepting it is the ultimately factious and divisive practice of every man believing that which is right in his own eyes, to be followed later by every man *doing* likewise. That too is becoming more prevalent, as it did among the Corinthians: "For if he that cometh preacheth another Jesus, which we have not preached, or if ye receive another spirit, which ye have not received, or another gospel, which ye have not accepted, *ye might well bear with him*" (2 Corinthians 11:4).

"But, having itching ears, will heap to themselves teachers after their own lusts" (RV): The Apostle reinforces with two picturesque metaphors what he had written in 3:7 (page 305). The first (in the RV) is "itching ears": it is of course "they" and not the "teachers" who have "itching ears", a "oncer" which graphically portrays the continual search for something to tickle or scratch the ears, since the sufferer can only find relief in novelty (cf. Acts 17:21). The other, also a "oncer", describes the gathering together of a 'whole heap' of teachers, a veritable 'court' or 'salon' to tell the people who chose them what they wanted to hear. Dissatisfaction with Divine arrangements has been characteristic of man from the beginning and was the undoing of Israel in the wilderness. "Our soul loatheth this light bread", they cried, for even although the manna was God-given, for them it was "no-bread" (Numbers 21:5). Paul might well have quoted Isaiah 30:9,10 to Timothy:

> "(They are) children that will not hear the law of the Lord ... (and) say to the seers, See not; and to the prophets, Prophesy not unto us right things, speak unto us smooth things, prophesy deceits (illusions)."

Verse 4: *"And they shall turn away their ears from the truth"*: Since the truth appears to them insipid, lacking the piquancy and excitement of everlasting novelty, it proves difficult to gainsayers: they will turn away—a powerful word used in Romans 11:26 and Acts 3:26 for the turning away of Israel from their iniquities, but more nearly here in the sense of 1 Timothy 1:6: "They have swerved aside unto vain jangling" (page 21). The *"fables"* or myths (*muthoi*, page 42) assumed for those who believed them all the authority of the Word of God. There may well be in this verse an allusion to a famous dictum of Socrates popularised by Latin authors, that such professed teachers "addressed themselves more to the pleasure of the ears than to the judgement of the intellect".

Verse 5: *"But watch thou in all things"*: The "but ... thou" is emphatic. Above all things Timothy had to be sober, which is the more usual translation of *nēphō*, or 'to keep his head'. It is the *vigilance* demanded of the elders in 1 Timothy 3:2 (page 88), to be compared with the *sobriety* of the man who abstains from excessive wine while others are becoming "heady" (2 Timothy 3:4, page 301; see also note on 3:8,9,13, pages 306-307,309). Certain it is that if a man like Timothy did not remain clear-headed and alert, the faith would not be preserved against the effervescent fantasies of the other-teachers. Only if such as he were *nēphalios* could there be any hope that others would *return to sobriety*, or "recover themselves (*ananēphō*) out of the snare of the devil" (2:26; page 284). This attitude he must maintain "in all things".

"Endure afflictions, do the work of an evangelist": No difficulty, no hardship, no opposition or unpopularity must stand in the way of the work. So Paul had exhorted in 1:8 and 2:3 (pages 239, 261). Timothy must give himself whole-heartedly to the work of an evangelist. The title of "evangelist" is applied twice more in the New Testament. Philip, one of the seven chosen to "serve tables", was so called, no doubt after his preaching mission to Samaria and the baptism of the Ethiopian eunuch (Acts 6, 8 and 21:8). From Ephesians 4 we would gain the impression that evangelists had a specialised function like that of pastors or teachers. We note in passing that in that reference Paul is emphasising not a difference in function of ecclesial servants, but the *unifying purpose* of God working through them.

Most probably we are not to seek for a specialised interpretation of Timothy's function as "evangelist" in the Ephesus of some years later. The point at issue was defence of the true Gospel in opposition to "another gospel", which was not the Gospel at all. Timothy had to exemplify that Gospel in his life and conduct as well as preach it in all its aspects: it was a "good deposit" and he must preserve it (pages 200-202, 221); he must understand it and "rightly divide" it, giving due emphasis to its doctrinal content and practical implications. He must live it as "an example of the believers", so that—and this is a vital point for our consideration in these days when we witness in some other communities a zeal and devotion to their particular cause which may not appear so evident at all times in us—"he that is of the contrary part" may be ashamed, having no evil thing to say against him: and he must be "apt to teach" it, with the patience and longsuffering of the Teacher himself.

The accumulated imperatives of the preceding verses have the force of military commands, to be obeyed implicitly by the servant of the Lord: Timothy was to "make full proof of thy ministry". These words are, in effect, the end of the Letter, so

clear and emphatic is "the charge" they convey. The full responsibility for the guidance and pastoral care of the ecclesia at
Ephesus now rested upon Timothy, being vested in him by the
authority of an apostle of the Lord Jesus Christ. In fact, the
following verses, linked to the foregoing as they are by a powerful
"For", must have left the young man in no doubt of what, before
God and with His help, he must now bear alone.

4:6-8—The End of the Race

Verse 6: *"For I am now ready to be offered"*: A language like ours
normally uses personal pronouns with verbs and so the force of
their special use in languages such as Latin and Greek where they
are normally omitted can often be missed. We must not miss the
emphasis here. *Su de*, "But thou" (verse 5), is parallelled with *Ego
gar*, "For I"—introducing no egotistical boasting, but a simple
statement of the facts. Timothy had to "take up the burden and
the lesson": Paul's course was run.

The Apostle knows that death is near. For him, however, it is
not an end but a consummation: his sacrifice is complete. The
offering to which he refers is in fact a drink offering, as the verb
spendomai indicates—he was "already being poured out", as the
Revised Version margin has it. In a sense his whole life had been
a sacrifice, a partaking of the sufferings of Christ, and the libation
of wine was now being poured upon it, as upon "the continual
burnt offering, which was ordained in Sinai", the offering which
represented the total dedication of the offerer and what he offered
(Numbers 28:3-8).

"The time of my departure is at hand": In the whole of the Greek
Bible this is the only occurrence of the noun *analusis*. The idea is
that of the breaking up of a feast with the departure of the guests,
the striking of a camp, or the loosing of a vessel from its moorings.
Perhaps here what Paul has in mind is his being set free from a
bondage. During his earlier imprisonment he had written to the
Philippians of having "a desire to depart (*analusai*), and to be with
Christ" (1:23). He had been released from that prison, as he had
himself expected (see the discussion on this point on pages 1, 2),
but for a variety of reasons already suggested (see also on verse
18 below) he knew that the only release from the cell he then
occupied would be in death.

Verse 7: *"I have fought a good fight"*: The metaphor is from the athlete and not the soldier. The Revised Version translates correctly as *"the* good fight", or *"contest"*, which refers not to the Apostle's personal life, but to his apostolic ministry and discipleship—"the race set before us" (see page 188 and Essay 21, page 210; also page 127). There is a closer connection between the symbolism of the offering and the contest than at first appears, since from the earliest times the Greek games were held in honour of some god. The "good contest", therefore, had a special sacrificial quality: it was in the service of the living and true God.

A Race well Run

"I have finished my course": The type of contest is now particularised: it was the foot race. It was required above all of Christ's athletes that they finish their race. For there was no question of being "first past the post", as in the Classical games, where "they which run in a race run all, but *one* receiveth the prize" (1 Corinthians 9:24). It is a matter of running with patience, of enduring unto the end, of overcoming and especially of "striving lawfully" (2:5), which is implied in Paul's *"I have kept the faith"* in this same verse.

As we have seen above, such a declaration on oath was required of the Olympic athlete at the end of his twelve months preparation for the searing few minutes of the actual race. The Apostle could make it at the end of his long feat of endurance, with all the rich meaning both of "the terms of discipleship" and "the faith committed to my trust". The tense of the Greek verb implies that all was now complete. There was nothing more he could do but endure the brief painful interlude of his execution. His faith would stand firm and he would not be found wanting. He had triumphed even over himself, as he had declared to the Corinthians:

> "I therefore so run, not as uncertainly; so fight I, not as one that beateth the air: but I keep under my body, and bring it into subjection: lest that by any means, when I have preached to others, I myself should be a castaway (that is, found unable to stand the test)." (1 Corinthians 9:26-27)

Verse 8: *"Henceforth there is laid up for me a crown of righteousness"*: The "henceforth" represents a favourite word of the Apostle's, who uses it on ten of the fourteen occasions when it appears in the New Testament. *Loipon*, often translated "finally" (2 Corinthians 13:11; Ephesians 6:10; Philippians 3:1; 2 Thessalonians 3:1), here means in effect, "Now nothing remains but for me to receive the crown". This confidence would enable him to endure the approaching execution with courage and sustain him over the period of waiting in the prison cell. The crown was "laid up", as being already his. It was not the kingly diadem but the *stephanos* or victor's crown, the reward of faithful striving, which would be for Paul the true consummation of his labour in the Lord. The athlete strove for "a corruptible crown" of leaves varied according to the location of the games; "but we", said Paul, "an incorruptible", even eternal life itself (1 Corinthians 9:25).

Four Crowns

Four crowns are mentioned in the New Testament: there was "the crown of rejoicing", to be shared by the Apostle with all those among whom he had laboured in the Gospel and in whose salvation he would rejoice when they all stood together in the presence of the Lord at his coming (1 Thessalonians 2:19); there was "the crown of life", to be bestowed upon the man who endured the testing of his character (James 1:12); there was "the crown of glory, that fadeth not away", which the Lord will bestow "when the chief Shepherd shall appear" (1 Peter 5:4); and this crown of righteousness. It is evident that in effect all the crowns are the same since they are to be bestowed "at his coming", and all represent the reward of faithful continuance in well-doing, or righteousness. The varying descriptions amount to differences of emphasis which suit the context of the writer's usage. See the exhortation entitled "That no man take thy crown" (*The Christadelphian*, 1969, page 49) which offers a fuller consideration of these crowns, together with a fifth—the crown of thorns.

There is, however, another shade of meaning to be applied to "the crown of righteousness", especially when it is to be received at the hands of *"the Lord, the righteous judge"*. The "judge" is the umpire or referee at the games, who decides whether a man has "striven lawfully", according to the rules. His verdict finally decided who was the victor and with his own hands he then crowned him. Paul had not always been understood nor did his motives go unquestioned, even by those for whom he had toiled and suffered anxiety. There had been plenty to challenge his authority and seek to undermine his work. The Letter to the Galatians and the Second Letter to the Corinthians offer abundant proof of this. To come to his final imprisonment with the defections listed later in this chapter and with no man willing to stand with him at his trial, might well have depressed the spirit of a lesser man.

Moreover, had he been his own judge he would still have been "the chief of sinners", in captivity to the law which made the hated evil frustrate the longed-for good. But the final judgement lay with the Lord, the righteous judge, who will make no mistakes and who has power to "present us faultless before the presence of his glory with exceeding joy". Perhaps the Apostle also had in mind the contrast between the Lord, in whose hands his case really rested, and the judge before whom he had already appeared once and who would condemn him to death.

The Crown of Rejoicing

"And not to me only": The crown Paul would receive was in every respect different from the corruptible crown for which the athlete disciplined himself and "kept under his body". Not only would this crown be incorruptible, but it was reserved for *"all them also that love his appearing"*. All knew that "they which run in a race run all, but *one* receiveth the prize" (1 Corinthians 9:24). It was not so with the race for life. All who were willing could "so run" that they might "receive the prize".

There is surely in this final clause of Paul's expression of confidence in his last epistle an echo of 1 Thessalonians, in all probability his very first. There the Lord's appearing (Essay 22, page 213) is the climax of every chapter. The believers in Thessalonica had "turned to God from idols, to serve the living and true God; and to wait for his Son from heaven" (1:9,10); the Apostle would share the rejoicing of his redeemed fellow-disciples "in the presence of our Lord Jesus Christ at his coming" (2:19); the disciples' sanctification would be complete "at the coming of our Lord Jesus Christ with all his saints" (3:13); their true comfort in sorrow lay in the promise of the resurrection of the dead when "the Lord himself shall descend from heaven with a shout" (4:15-18); and God would preserve them blameless and entire "unto the coming of our Lord Jesus Christ" (5:23).

337

With this expression of faith and hope the "charge" to Timothy comes to an end. The torch is handed on and the younger man is invested with all the responsibility and the burden laid down by "Paul the aged" (Philemon 9). The remainder of the Epistle is occupied by necessary instructions which of themselves reveal much of the breadth of the Apostle's interest in the work of the first century ecclesia and the extent of the work itself. In this connection the words of Spicq (*Les Epîtres Pastorales*) provide a convenient summary:

"The letter is finished, but cannot be concluded without some instructions of a practical nature, which are singularly revealing of the number and extent of the journeys undertaken by the early Christians as well as the apostolic dimension, if we may so say, of Paul's own soul as he bore the burden of all the churches. In a few verses his thought ranges over Thessalonica, Gaul, Dalmatia, Ephesus, Troas, Corinth, Miletus. He calls one disciple and sends another on his way. These last words of his last epistle are almost a complete résumé of his life."

4:9-22—Final Instructions and Farewell

Verse 9: *"Do thy diligence to come shortly unto me"*: Perhaps the journey had already been agreed upon in principle (1:4), but now the Apostle's circumstances had made the matter urgent. The appeal is repeated with greater earnestness in verse 21, with the addition of the words "before winter". Once the travelling season was past, several months would elapse before the longed-for meeting could take place. As it was we have no idea whether Paul ever saw Timothy again.

Verse 10: *"For Demas hath forsaken me"*: The coming of Timothy was all the more desired because Paul was feeling his increasing isolation from his friends, who were absent either on necessary duties among the ecclesias or, like Demas, had left him on personal grounds. Demas, together with Mark and Luke, is mentioned as a fellow-worker in Philemon 24, and in conjunction with Luke in Colossians 4:14, although some commentators contrast the bare reference to his name in the second passage (both Colossians and Philemon were written during the *first* Roman imprisonment) with the warm commendation of Luke.

Be that as it may, Demas had deserted Paul in his hour of need, since his departure was evidently not of Paul's design. There is

no suggestion of apostasy as such, but simply of a preference for
ease or comfort instead of the dangers and privations of association with Paul the prisoner. Contrast *"having loved this present
world"* with "who have loved his appearing" above.

"And is departed unto Thessalonica": It is possible that Thessalonica was home to Demas, or that he rationalised his conduct by
professing to be going to support the ecclesia there.

"Crescens to Galatia": It is not known who Crescens was, or
whether Galatia here is Gaul or the Asiatic province. Crescens
by tradition was counted as the founder of churches in Southern
France.

"Titus unto Dalmatia": Had Titus been with Paul in Rome?
From Titus 3:12 (see page 417) we learn that he had been sent for
to meet Paul in Nicopolis, on the Greek mainland south of
Dalmatia. The same urgent appeal had been sent ("Be diligent
... for I have determined there to winter") when the earlier letter
had been written to him, and it is possible that Paul had been
arrested in Nicopolis (see page 225).

Verse 11: *"Only Luke is with me":* The faithfulness of Luke,
travel-companion, fellow-worker, spiritual biographer, and
"beloved physician", is here re-emphasised. He had been with
the Apostle during his first imprisonment (Colossians 4:14) and
remained with him till the last. Of his background we know next
to nothing, although it was almost certainly Gentile; his name was
a diminutive of the Roman Lucius. It has been argued that he was
the brother of Titus, on which see Essay 42 (page 373) and the
articles in *The Christadelphian* referred to there. It is clear,
however, that Luke joined the Apostle's party at Troas, where the
"we" passages begin in the record (Acts 16:10), perhaps in the
first instance to render professional services to Paul. At any rate,
we have seen that in the course of their long and fruitful conversa-
tions on the things of the spirit, Paul acquired from Luke a whole
vocabulary of medical terms, which applied to the health of the
Body of Christ (Essay 4, page 46).

The Healing of a Rift

"Take Mark, and bring him with thee": Much has been written on
the subject of the dissension between Paul and Barnabas over
Mark, "who departed from them from Pamphylia, and went not

with them to the work " (Acts 15:37-40). Here we are reassured by the knowledge that Mark, who by the time of the first imprisonment had qualified for the title of "fellow-worker", was so highly regarded by Paul, that he could take comfort in his coming to him. For not only do we see the breadth of Paul's own spirit in his willingness to alter his opinion in the light of circumstances, but we can ourselves take comfort from the knowledge that Mark rehabilitated himself in the Lord's service—there is hope for all disciples who are rightly disciplined by the realisation of their own weaknesses. Whether the word *diakonia* means 'personal service' which the Apostle would be glad to receive at Mark's hands, or "the ministry" in the more technical sense of service to the Gospel, who would not be glad to hear such a man as Paul declare us to be *"profitable to me for the ministry"*?

"And Tychicus have I sent to Ephesus": Was Tychicus the bearer of the Second Epistle itself? Such would be consistent with the kind of service he had frequently rendered as the trusted messenger of the Apostle. He joined the party which preceded Paul to Troas (Acts 20:4), carried the Letters to Colossae and the Ephesians, as "beloved brother, and a faithful minister and fellowservant in the Lord", who would declare unto them "all my state" (Ephesians 6:21; Colossians 4:7). There had been the possibility that he would be sent to join Titus in Crete (Titus 3:12), and there was now the probability that he would remain at Ephesus while Timothy responded to the urgent request in this letter to come to Rome before it was too late.

Verse 13: *"The cloke that I left at Troas with Carpus, when thou comest, bring with thee"*: The visit to Troas must have taken place between the two imprisonments, since that mentioned in Acts 16 was at least six years earlier; of Carpus we know nothing further. The cloak in question was probably a *paenula* or travelling cloak, of which the military counterpart was also used as a blanket for sleeping in. Anyone who has descended into the Mamertine Prison by the Roman Forum, the traditional site of Paul's imprisonment, will have felt the damp cold strike through him, even though the hot Italian sun blazes outside. If that were not the actual cell Paul occupied his must have been similar, and the cloak would have been necessary to make the winter even barely tolerable.

"The books, but especially the parchments": There have been many speculations concerning the nature of these documents, and the reader must ultimately decide for himself on the basis of probabilities and spiritual issues. The "books" would in fact have been written on papyrus, which though less durable than parchment was still very expensive—a *drachma* a sheet in Paul's day, equivalent to the Roman *denarius* or a day's wages! The New Testament letters would almost certainly have originally been written on this kind of "paper". The parchments (*membrana*, the sole occurrence of the word in the Bible) were of vellum and very much more expensive; these *especially* were to be brought.

A Well Stocked Mind

The "books" could have been documents of some importance, the Apostle's certificate of Roman citizenship, for example; and the "parchments", scrolls of the Old Testament, which the Apostle would try to read by the dim light of an oil lamp guttering in the dark cell. If Paul had no copies of these with him, then it is plain from the rich allusions of his writings from prison that his mind was well stocked with the Scriptures.

But there is another possibility: he had obviously been allowed access to writing material in order to write the letter to Timothy, and he could have been contemplating yet more work; perhaps the parchments were not Scriptures, which he would hardly have referred to simply as *ta membrana*, but skins prepared on which he would continue his writing to the very end. In any event, the intrinsic value of the materials themselves, without the richer content of the writing upon them, has surely a lesson for a generation which squanders reams of paper every minute in the publication of God-dishonouring rubbish, and has no regard for the sacred heritage of the God-breathed Word.

Verse 14: *"Alexander the coppersmith did me much evil"*: The identity of this Alexander cannot be established for certain. It was a common enough name and there was at least one member of the ecclesia at Ephesus who bore it. It seems unlikely that the one in this verse is to be identified with the Alexander of Acts 19:33, in view of the passage of time since the events described there, but the brother "delivered unto Satan" of 1 Timothy 1:20 is a distinct possibility. He was either known to Timothy or one with whom he was likely to come into contact. The nature of the "much evil" is equally uncertain: perhaps Alexander had been instrumental in bringing about Paul's arrest, or had been one of those who had testified against him at his trial. He evidently had it in his power to harm Timothy as well.

"The Lord reward him according to his works": Most texts except that of the Authorised Version make the verb a future tense, in which case the Apostle's words are a statement and not an imprecation. *Apodōsei* matches the verb in verse 8: the Lord *"will render"* (RV) the crown to those to whom it is due and evil to those who have merited it. The allusion to Psalm 62:12 should not be overlooked: "Also unto thee, O Lord, belongeth mercy: for thou renderest to every man according to his work."

Verse 15: *"Of whom be thou ware also"*: This verse confirms the impression that Alexander could prove a threat to Timothy and that he had opposed Paul personally—*"for he hath greatly withstood our words"*.

4:16-18—The Final Deliverance

Verse 16: *"At my first answer no man stood with me"*: We do not follow the view that "first answer" here refers to Paul's first imprisonment from which he had apparently been set free. What is known of the ordinary procedure of a Roman trial coincides perfectly with the impression that Paul is referring exclusively to his immediate circumstances. If the presiding judge, after hearing the charge against the prisoner and calling witnesses to testify, needed to make further enquiries, he closed the session with the pronouncement *Non liquet*, 'It is not clear', or *Amplius*, 'More'— that is, 'More evidence needed'. This verdict ended the *prima actio*, or first hearing, and a *secunda actio* was then called for. The case stood adjourned, often for some considerable period, and Paul could well have considered that Timothy would have had the time to come to Rome in the meantime.

"To stand with someone" was a technical term for the services of an advocate or witness in favour of the accused. "Advocate" means literally 'one called to one's side'. There was no-one, however, not even amongst those of his friends actually present, to perform this service for Paul. Possibly their courage failed them as they stood in the awesome *Basilica Julia* where important cases were heard, often by the Emperor in person. If the Emperor Nero were in fact presiding, then the trial often proceeded more on the basis of the expedient and the politic than on the principles of the law. This may explain why Paul, who had been released five years earlier through lack of evidence against him was now condemned. For the climate of opinion against the Christians had altered considerably since the Great Fire of Rome in AD 64. The lack of witnesses for the defence would have weighed heavily against Paul as he made his *apologia* or speech in reply to the charge.

"But all men forsook me": There is a close similarity between the Apostle's case and that of the Master, of whom it is written: "And they all forsook him and fled." And like his Master, Paul showed his capacity for forgiveness when he said, *"I pray God, that it may not be laid to their charge"*.

Verse 17: *"Notwithstanding the Lord stood with me, and strengthened me"*: Yet there had been one silent and unseen Advocate, he who had promised his disciples that in the hour of crisis they would be given words to speak (Matthew 10:19,20). It was he who had spoken to Paul in a vision in Corinth, saying, "I am with thee" (Acts 18:9,10), and had called for the angel of God to stand by him on the heaving deck of a ship in peril on the sea (Acts 27:23). The promise of Matthew 10:24-33 was completely fulfilled, for with courage rising the Apostle looked around at the crowd thronging the Basilica, drawn from every nation under heaven, and turned his *apologia* into a spirited preaching of the Gospel: *"that by me the preaching might be fully known, and that all the Gentiles might hear"*.

The words that had "gone before" on Paul in Acts 9:15,16 were now both literally and symbolically fulfilled: the Lord had shown him how great things he had had to suffer for his name's sake and his mission to the Gentiles was now fully accomplished. The word for "fully known" is rare outside Biblical usage— in verse 5 it is translated "make full proof (of thy ministry)" —and here suggests that Paul had done the same by rounding off his life of service and devotion in this last dramatic proclamation of the Gospel.

"And I was delivered out of the mouth of the lion": Various possibilities have been suggested to explain this sentence. For example, Paul could have established his Roman citizenship at his "first answer", and so would have been granted the privilege of

dying by the sword instead of in the amphitheatre; or, "the lion" was the Emperor from whose adverse judgement the Apostle was temporarily delivered. It is better, however, to recognise in the saying the Biblical expression for deliverance from extreme peril, as in Psalm 22:21—"Save me from the lion's mouth."

2 Timothy 4 and Psalm 22

It has been pointed out that in these closing verses Paul has had the sufferings of the Lord as expressed in Psalm 22 very much in mind, and has drawn comfort from them. The parallels are indeed close, as the following table shows.

Psalm 22		2 Timothy 4
Verse 1	forsaken	Verse 10, 16
5	delivered	17, 18
9, 21	delivered	17, 18
11	forsaken	16
13, 21	lion's mouth	17
21	preserved	18
23	glorify	18
27	Gentiles hear	17
28	kingdom	18

Verse 18: "*And the Lord shall deliver me from every evil work*": If it be argued that Paul was not in fact delivered since he went forth to his death, then this verse should put all in true perspective. The Lord will indeed deliver him as he had done in the past, not simply from danger and distress but from death itself, when he giveth him the victory in the day of resurrection. He had learned that the Lord's strength was made perfect in weakness, and that he who had spread the tabernacle of his power over his apostle (2 Corinthians 12:9, RV margin) would lead him safely through the valley of the shadow.

"*And will preserve me unto his heavenly kingdom: to whom be glory for ever and ever. Amen*": This word for "heavenly" is used almost exclusively by Paul in the New Testament, and is the opposite of that which is "of the earth, *earthy*". No doubt his thoughts run here on the hope of the resurrection, on which he had dwelt at some length in 1 Corinthians 15. He who had borne the image of the earthy now waited for his liberation from his earthly tabernacle in the kingdom of his heavenly Father. The Apostle was given to outbursts of praise and thanksgiving (see Romans 11:33-36; 1 Timothy 1:17; 6:16, with notes on pages 35, 196, 215-219). What more appropriate than that here the phrases which spring so spontaneously to his mind are taken from the prayer which the Lord taught his disciples to pray, and in which every duty, every proper request and every ascription of praise is summed up: "Deliver us from evil. For thine is the kingdom, the power, and the glory, for ever and ever. Amen."

4:19-22—Final Salutations and Farewells

Verse 19: "*Salute Prisca and Aquila, and the household of Onesiphorus*": The Epistle comes finally to a conclusion with a characteristic list of greetings, to Prisca and Aquila and to the household of Onesiphorus. For the note on the latter see 1:16-18 and pages 247-249. Prisca, or to give her more usual diminutive name, Priscilla, and Aquila were old friends and fellow servants of the Apostle, with whom he had once lodged and who had evidently breathed the very spirit of the Truth wherever they set up their abode, offering hospitality and instruction; and evidently in Rome there had been an ecclesia in their house (Acts 18:2,18,26; Romans 16:3; 1 Corinthians 16:19). Why Paul should use the more formal name of *Prisca* here we cannot tell, but it is fitting that she and her husband should be in his last thoughts.

Verse 20: "*Erastus abode at Corinth*": There was an Erastus who was city treasurer of Corinth (Romans 16:23). The one referred to here was more likely the travel companion of Timothy on the way to Macedonia (Acts 19:22). On the other hand the "*Trophimus*" whom Paul had "*left at Miletum sick*" had companied with Tychicus (Acts 20) and with Paul in Jerusalem (Acts 21:29), where the sight of the two men together led to Paul's arrest. Paul in effect resumes from verse 12 his explanation of the absence from Rome of some of the former members of his company whom we should have expected to be with him in his last crisis.

Verse 21: "*Do thy diligence to come before winter*": The urgent request is repeated and with it he joins the greetings from brethren and sisters, perhaps members of the community at Rome. It would appear from Romans 16 that there was more than one ecclesia there, since besides that in the house of Aquila and Priscilla there seem to have been at least two other groups (verses 5,14,15; possibly also 10).

"Eubulus saluteth thee, and Pudens, and Linus, and Claudia, and all the brethren" (RV): There is little to identify those named beyond what tradition has to offer. Linus was said to have been "the first bishop of Rome" for twelve years after Paul's death, and is usually listed after Peter amongst the heads of the Roman Catholic Church. We are more concerned with the real if unknown figures who were our brethren in the first century and who drew their spiritual learning from the beloved Apostle. It is fitting that "Amen" ("The Lord say so too"—see 1 Kings 1:36 and Jeremiah 28:6) should figure twice in this short chapter, which probably contains the last words Paul ever wrote. It seems as though the Apostle is thinking of him in whom "all the promises of God are Yea, and in him Amen" (2 Corinthians 1:20). And through the medium of the Scripture he sends to us, as he did to Timothy, his final greeting:

Verse 22: *"The Lord Jesus Christ be with thy spirit. Grace be with you. Amen."*

ESSAY 38

The "Word of God" in the New Testament

IT IS important that we should briefly survey the usage in the New Testament of the phrase "the word of God", or sometimes as here (2 Timothy 4:2), simply "the word". We do not here distinguish the subjective sense—*the word which came from God*—and the objective—*the word which tells us about God*—since for reasons we have discussed before these two meanings can ultimately only amount to the same thing. There is nothing that can be known of God which God Himself has not revealed. "Canst thou by searching find out God?" (Job 11:7). "Even so the things of God knoweth no man, but the Spirit of God . . . For who hath known the mind of the Lord, that he may instruct him?" (1 Corinthians 2:11-16).

It will be convenient for this brief study to follow the classification given by J. H. Bernard in his notes on 1 Timothy 4:5 in the small volume on "The Pastoral Epistles" in the series on *The Cambridge Greek Testament for Schools and Colleges*. This book, now long out of print, is itself a testimony to the change in attitude towards the Scriptures since the close of the nineteenth century, since no school text-book of today approaches the study of them with such detail, insight and reverence for their Divine origin, even where all the author's conclusions are not equally acceptable.

In the Old Testament "the word of the LORD" refers almost invariably to the word which God had actually spoken or caused to be spoken through Moses or the prophets.

In the New Testament this is still the primary sense, but it is possible to distinguish between *ho logos tou theou* and *to rhēma tou theou*, both translated as "the word of God". *Rhēma* is more strictly a special utterance for a special purpose, as in Luke 3:2:

"The word of God came unto John the son of Zacharias in the wilderness"; in Matthew 4:4—"Every *word* that proceedeth out of the mouth of God"; and notably in Acts 11:16—"Then remembered I the word of the Lord (Jesus), how that he said, John indeed baptized with water; but ye shall be baptized with the Holy Spirit". A concordance will reveal many similar passages, and it is interesting to note in passing that what the angel in fact said to Zacharias in Luke 1:37 was not that no *thing* shall be impossible, but "With God no *word* (RV) shall be impossible"!

The Whole Revelation of God

The more familiar New Testament phrase is *ho logos tou theou*, "the word of God", which also has as its primary idea 'the word which came from God'. But its meaning developed into 'the whole revealed message of God to the world'. In this sense it is a synonym for the Gospel as preached by Christ and the apostles. Luke, for example, uses it four times in his Gospel record and 12 times in the Acts. So the seed in the parable is the word of God, and there is a blessing pronounced upon those who both hear and do it. The word is preached, proclaimed, taught and spread abroad, to be received with open heart and obeyed. Paul often uses the phrase in the same sense, as in the Letters to Corinth (1 Corinthians 14:36; 2 Corinthians 2:17; 4:2), and in 1 Thessalonians 2:13 it is contrasted with the word of men.

In the Apocalypse the same idea is contained in such verses as "(John) bare record of the word of God, and of the testimony of Jesus Christ, and of the things that he saw" (1:2; also 1:9; 6:9; 20:4). In the same book (19:13) and also in John's Gospel (1:1-3), the word is the Word that is "made flesh", the manifestation in life among men of all the fulness of God's purpose and glory, which through the written and spoken word has been conveyed to men.

It is noteworthy, however, that throughout all these shades of meaning, the foundation lies in the word spoken in the past and brought to a fulfilment in the message preached: the apostles spoke "none other things than those which the prophets and Moses did say should come" (Acts 26:22). Paul had a "dispensation of God ... *to fulfil the word of God*" (Colossians 1:25).

348

The Scriptures and the Word

What is important for us all is the undoubted fact that the term "Word of God" is correctly applied to the Scriptures, which are the written record of what God has revealed, whether originally by the living voice from heaven, in the words spoken through the prophets and apostles, or in the life of the Word made flesh. Statements like "the Bible is not the word of God, although it contains it" are neither helpful nor accurate, and in view of the Apostle's emphasis on *the inspiration of the Scripture* (Essay 27) are downright misleading. We can add the testimony of the Lord Jesus when he contrasts the writings of men with those of God: "Thus have ye made the commandment of God of none effect by your tradition" (Matthew 15:6), he says on more than one occasion, often clinching an argument with "Have ye never read ...?" or repelling the tempter with "It is written", and confirming his words with "And the scripture cannot be broken".

The vital importance of "the word", then, in the form in which it has come down to us, cannot be exaggerated. For the problems and pressures of the last days there can still be no better, more solemn command, than "Herald forth the word", with all the zeal, effort and constancy we can command. There is no more effective advice that can be offered us.

The Letter to Titus

INTRODUCTION

THE Letter to Titus belongs to the same period as those written to Paul's other staunch travel companion and supporter, Timothy. The charge given to Timothy concerned the ecclesia in Ephesus; Titus, however, had the task of ordaining elders "in every city" in Crete (1:5). There is no certain record of any apostolic mission to Crete such as is suggested in this epistle (see page 1). Probably the early preaching in the island had been undertaken by those Cretan Jews of the Dispersion who had been present in Jerusalem on the Day of Pentecost (Acts 2:11). If this be so, then the ecclesias which had sprung up may well have been organised—insofar as there was any organisation at all— after the pattern of the synagogue, or even of the Jerusalem Ecclesia. Such organisation, however, would have been without the authoritative guidance of the apostles and have known nothing of the developments described in Acts 6:1-4. Nor would they have had the benefit of such care as Paul and Barnabas exercised on the First Missionary Journey, when they "returned again to Lystra, and to Iconium, and Antioch . . . And when they had *ordained them elders* in every church, and had prayed with fasting, they commended them to the Lord" (Acts 14:21-23).

It is possible that Paul's brief sojourn at Fair Havens, near the city of Lasea in Crete, on his journey to Rome (Acts 27:8), had been sufficient for him to gather some news of the brethren there and kindle the desire to return should opportunity permit. At any rate, we must assume a later visit, together with Titus, in the period between his first acquittal and his final imprisonment. Further evidence for this assumption we shall glean from a consideration of the text itself. In our "Suggested Table of the Last Years of Paul's Life" (page 13) we have set the date of the Letter to Titus somewhere between that of the First and Second Letters to Timothy, probably in AD 67.

The Letter to Titus

CHAPTER 1

Organising and Edifying the Ecclesias in Crete

1:1-4—Superscription, Address and Salutation

Verse 1: *"Paul, a servant of God":* This is the only occasion when the Apostle describes himself as a servant of *God.* In Romans 1:1 he uses the title of "servant of Jesus Christ" and in Philippians 1:1 he and Timothy, like Jude (Jude 1) are both "servants of Jesus Christ". See also Galatians 1:10. James was "a servant of God and of the Lord Jesus Christ" (1:1). Why this term is preferred uniquely in the superscription to Titus may become plain by a brief consideration of its Old Testament usage: see Essay 39, page 367.

"An apostle of Jesus Christ": For a more detailed discussion of this title and the reasons for its use in such personal letters, see the commentary on the opening verses of the two Letters to Timothy (pages 14 and 227). It was an important addition to the title described above, since it was the Lord Jesus who had commissioned him for the work of preaching. It was in this capacity that Paul wrote to Titus, who was to carry out the ministry in his absence, and the sphere of the servant of God's authority is specifically defined by his apostleship: it lay in the work of building up and consolidating the ecclesias in Crete, whether they were Jew or Gentile.

"According to the faith of God's elect": We have seen this use of the word *kata*, 'according to', before in the Second Letter to Timothy. This phrase means much more than "in accordance with the faith". It is true that Paul's apostleship was entirely consistent with the faith embraced by those whom God had chosen and,

indeed, throughout his ministry the apostle's emphasis was always upon the importance of preserving that faith intact. "Faith unfeigned" (1 Timothy 1:5) was an essential part of the love which Timothy was to help develop in Ephesus. In the superscription in 2 Timothy 1:1, Paul describes himself as "An apostle of Jesus Christ ... according to *(kata)* the promise of life", which means virtually "for the furtherance of the hope". The same idea lies behind the phrase "according to the faith". It was to the preaching of that faith and the promotion of it that Paul's service was dedicated. The significance of that concept as the superscription to this Letter will become plain as we proceed.

"Elect" in Isaiah is a term used both of God's servant (42:1) "in whom my soul delighteth" and of Israel (45:4; 65:9,22). In the New Testament, *eklektos* is applied to the saints by the Lord Jesus in the Olivet prophecy, where almost by definition they are the only ones who are not beguiled by the false teachers (Matthew 24:24). It is therefore an appropriate term to use in the Letter to Titus. No-one can "lay anything to the charge of God's elect" (Romans 8:33), who must "put on therefore, as the elect of God, holy and beloved", all the qualities described in Colossians 3:12-13. They are those whom "he hath chosen ... in him before the foundation of the world, that we should be holy and without blame before him in love" (Ephesians 1:4). "Elect according to the foreknowledge of God" the saints may be (1 Peter 1:2), but they may still fail of the grace of God if, being "called, and chosen *(eklektos)*", they are not "faithful" (Revelation 17:14). Hence the urgency of the Apostle's exhortations in these Letters.

"The acknowledging of the truth which is after godliness": Knowledge of the truth becomes saving knowledge when men *acknowledge* it in humble submission to God's will. This is true "godliness", in the apostolic sense of the word—"to do justly, and to love mercy, and to walk humbly with thy God" (Micah 6:8). For a fuller treatment of this phrase, see Essay 34 on "The Acknowledging of the Truth" (page 296) and also the note on 1 Timothy 2:2 (page 58) for a discussion of the word "godliness".

Verse 2: *"In hope of eternal life"*: Godliness has "promise of the life that now is, and of that which is to come" (1 Timothy 4:8). The promise and the hope figure prominently in the Pastorals. See note on 2 Timothy 1:1 (page 227), where Paul, in prison under sentence of death, dwells upon this promise of eternal life. It is the very will of God from the beginning— *"promised before the world began"*—that life should be given to men through Christ Jesus. It is interesting to note that God created man capable of living for ever upon earth, as is evident from the fact that He took active steps to prevent him from doing so in his sinful state (Genesis 3:22-24), yet ensured that "the way of the tree of life" was kept for those (the elect) who would eventually be granted the right "to eat of the tree of life, which is in the midst of the paradise of God" (Revelation 2:7).

The apostolic preaching revealed a whole way of life in Christ, "who hath abolished death, and brought life and immortality to light through the gospel". Paul himself was "a pattern to them which should hereafter believe on him to life everlasting" (1 Timothy 1:16; see also 6:12, with note on page 188).

"God, that cannot lie": This emphasis upon the faithfulness of God is appropriate in all these Letters, dealing as they do with the unfaithfulness of men. For their warning is not directed against the world's unbelief but against those—"of your own selves"— who by their teaching were in effect "denying the Lord that bought them" (2 Peter 2:1). The "Fourth Faithful Saying" of 2 Timothy 2:11-13, discussed in Essay 32 (page 289), declares that "God cannot deny himself". Moreover, "the foundation of God standeth sure, having this seal, The Lord knoweth them that are his" (2:19, with note, page 275).

It is significant, therefore, that the superscription to Titus proclaims the same truth, in view of the fact that it concerns "Cretans (who) are alway liars" (verse 12). Eternal life has been promised by "God, that cannot lie". The word *apseudēs* is an adjective, literally 'not-lying', and makes a play upon words with *pseustai* ('lying') applied to the Cretans. It is a Pauline "oncer", used here only in the Greek New Testament and borrowed from Classical literature, where it refers to the reliability of an oracle.

Verse 3: *"But hath in due times manifested his word":* The faithfulness of God had already been seen in the fulfilment of His promise to send forth His Son into the world "when the fulness of the time was come" (Galatians 4:4). Of the appointed day yet to come, He has also "given assurance unto all men, in that he hath raised him from the dead" (Acts 17:31). The firstfruits of them that sleep is the guarantee of all "the golden harvest ... ripened by his glorious sunshine, from the furrows of the grave".

So Paul emphasises "the due times" to illustrate that God cannot lie and to exhort those to whom the grace of God has appeared to learn of its significance for their behaviour (Titus 2:11-15); see fuller note in Essay 40, page 369.

"Through preaching which is committed unto me": The importance of the apostolic ministry is underlined by these words. For the eternal life that was in God's Son was manifested to some directly: it was "that which was from the beginning, which we have heard, which we have seen with our eyes, which we have looked upon, and our hands have handled, of the Word of life" (1 John 1:1). It needed to be declared, however, to those who were afar off, in distance or time, or as strangers from the covenants of promise. This was the word—or the Word—which was manifested through preaching. "Preaching" is *kērugma*, literally 'heralding', and relates to the more formal proclamation of an apostle, rather than "the work of an evangelist", or preacher who carried on the witness once it had been formally proclaimed.

Such emphasis is laid upon his apostleship by Paul in these Letters that it will be useful to consider the view he took of his calling: see Essay 41, "Paul, the Apostle of Jesus Christ", page 371.

Verse 4: *"To Titus, mine own son after the common faith"*: For this form of address see 1 Timothy 1:2, with note on page 16. The same term, *gnēsios*, is used in both passages, and is a term peculiar to the writings of Paul, and here has the sense of 'true-born', 'legitimate'. We can deduce that Titus was written before 2 Timothy from the fact that, although according to 1 Timothy the two brethren are addressed in the same terms, later when in prison and "greatly desiring to see thee (Timothy), being mindful of thy tears", the Apostle calls the younger man "my dearly beloved son" (2 Timothy 1:2,4; see commentary on page 228). From the Titus passage alone do we discover that Paul converted Titus, the Gentile believer who was to become one of his able lieutenants.

Their mutual faith is described as *koinos*, 'common'; this implies more than "the faith preached everywhere", or even "the same things we both believe". It is rather "the faith we share", "the faith which binds us in fellowship (*koinonia*) with the Lord and with one another".

"Grace, mercy, and peace, from God the Father and the Lord Jesus Christ our Saviour": This salutation, with "mercy" in addition to the usual "grace and peace", appears in all three Letters (though some texts omit it in Titus, for no good reason). It was a natural development in the thought of the Apostle, as he grew ever more mature in the faith, as explained in the commentary on 1 Timothy 1:2 (page 16).

Strengthening the Things which Remain

Verse 5: *"For this cause left I thee in Crete"*: The word for "left" means "left *behind*", that is, after the two men had visited the island together. The most probable time for such a visit would appear to have been towards the end of the five-year period between Paul's release from prison in Rome and his subsequent recapture, possibly while he was awaiting Titus at Nicopolis (Titus 3:12). See Chapter 1 on the Background of the Letters and the chronological Table on page 13; see also Essay 42, page 373.

It seems unlikely that Paul himself had tarried long in Crete, at least if he had had any intention of trying to complete his programme of revisiting the ecclesias he had founded and eventually going on to Spain (Romans 15:24,28; tradition says he did make this visit). The "For this cause" is most emphatic in its position in the Greek sentence and Titus could have been left in no possible doubt as to what his responsibilities were, since the sense of the opening is, "If I have left thee behind, it is for this very purpose . . ." Some have regarded the Letter as a reply to one sent by Titus, but its general form and tone make it plain that, while addressed to him and containing some personal allusions, it constituted an authoritative document for his use amongst the ecclesias in carrying out what Paul had already begun, or at least discussed with him (compare 1 Timothy 1:1-2 and note, page 14).

"That thou shouldest set in order the things that are wanting": It seems that the word for "set in order" is one of those medical terms which Paul learned from his faithful companion Luke, "the beloved physician" (page 7). *Epidiorthoō* appears here only in all the Greek Bible and the root word, as used by the author of a famous treatise on medicine in the Ancient World, Hippocrates, refers to the setting of a broken limb. The prefix *epi-* indicates that Titus is to *continue* the process of correction. The basic idea here

is of reformation, which is how *diorthōsis*, another "oncer" (compare "orthopaedics"), is used in Hebrews 9:10. Paul has left Titus to bring to completion the process of organising the ecclesias which had been already begun.

"And ordain elders in every city, as I had appointed thee": It comes as something of a surprise to realise that Paul never uses the word "elders" in any of his epistles except the Pastorals. For that matter it is only there and in Philippians 1:1 that he uses the term "bishops". He was, of course, familiar with the concept of eldership and oversight, as a rôle distinct from that of apostle, for he introduced that system into the ecclesias he himself founded (Acts 14:23; 20:17; cf. Acts 15:2,4,6,22,23; 16:4, where the two offices are mentioned together). So his special emphasis on the term in these Letters is a measure of the importance he attached to the function of elders in maintaining the spiritual health and growth of the ecclesias in Ephesus and Crete.

Until the appointment of responsible elders was completed on the island there would still be "things that are wanting". "As I appointed thee" is an indication that Paul had discussed these matters with Titus before he left, and was now committing his verbal instructions to a document which gave Titus his authority to carry them into effect.

One Hundred Cities

According to Homer, Crete, where the civilisation was even more ancient than that of mainland Greece, as twentieth century excavations have disclosed, had "one hundred cities". Even allowing for poetic exaggeration and the fact that there were not necessarily ecclesias to be found in all the centres of population, it is still evident that there was much to be done, and no doubt Titus, like Timothy, would understand that "the things that thou hast heard of me (Paul) among many witnesses", he would need to commit "to faithful men, who shall be able to teach others also" (2 Timothy 2:2). "In every city" is better rendered "city by city", a reasonable systematic breakdown of a process which would take some time. The fact that Paul said *"and* appoint elders" suggests that there were other aspects of reform which would also need Titus's personal attention.

In 1 Timothy 3 the office of the deacon and the necessary qualifications for it were discussed at equal length with those of the bishop, or overseer, whereas deacons are not mentioned at all in Titus. This supports the view advanced above, that the ecclesias in Crete were founded by some who had been present in Jerusalem on the Day of Pentecost, who knew nothing of the later introduction of deacons into the organisation of the ecclesia there, as described in Acts 6. Paul, the apostle to the Gentiles, was careful in his arrangements to avoid "building upon another man's foundation" in the predominantly Jewish ecclesias of Crete (Galatians 2:7-9; Romans 15:20; 2 Corinthians 10:14-16), but introduced necessary reforms into an existing organisation which had suffered some neglect.

1:6-9—The Qualifications for Ecclesial Eldership

Five vices to be avoided and seven positive qualities to be displayed are set out in these verses, which should be carefully compared with the seven positive qualities and corresponding negatives in 1 Timothy 1. The reader is invited to re-read the notes on that chapter as well as Essays 10 and 35 on "The List of Qualifications for Ecclesial Office" (page 107) and "Catalogues of Vices" (page 313), for a detailed study of the earlier references. We shall note here mainly the points in which the list in Titus differs and offer some explanation for the variations. For convenience we give in Essay 43 (page 375) a comparative reference list.

The Authorship of the Pastoral Epistles

The higher critics who deny that Paul was the writer of the Pastoral Epistles (see "The Vocabulary of the Letters", page 5) point to the differences in the lists of qualifications in 1 Timothy 3 and Titus 1 as further evidence of their thesis. The evidence is in fact entirely the other way, since a forger would be careful to avoid variations and slavishly imitate the style of his author. The purpose of both lists is manifestly the same, but Paul is writing a semi-personal letter, not copying from a previously composed document, and so introduces words and shades of meaning and emphasis appropriate to the Cretan situation rather than to that in Ephesus.

Verse 6: "If any be blameless, the husband of one wife, having faithful children ...": The structure of this sentence appears to be awkward, until we realise that the whole of this verse is a quotation or a reference back to the verbal instructions he had already given Titus: "Any that are blameless . . . they are the ones to be appointed." Thus the word *anengklētos*, 'irreproachable', is first used as a general term of which two examples are given, and then repeated in verse 7 as the summary definition of the complete list of vices to be avoided and positive qualities to be displayed. In the Cretan situation, the elder must be more than blameless in his own character: nor must there be anything in his family life either which enabled reproaches to be levelled at him. Thus he was to be the husband of one wife, in the sense discussed on page 110, and it was equally essential that he should have his household in subjection (page 93), if he was to be "of good report of them which are without" (1 Timothy 3:7), as well as taking care of the house of God.

"Children that are faithful" could mean "children who are believers" (as the Revised Version suggests) and against the background of verse 9, which implies that an aptitude for teaching was necessary, which surely should have been exercised at home also, that seems the likely interpretation. At any rate, the behaviour of the children was to display nothing which would bring the family or the ecclesia into private or public disrepute. Unruliness, or insubordination (from *anupotaktos*), is mentioned in 1 Timothy 1:9 (page 23) and the word is peculiar to these Letters and to Hebrews 2:8, where it simply means "not under subjection".

Verse 7: *"A bishop . . . the steward of God"*: A bishop is, of course, the same as an elder, charged with the oversight of an ecclesia. There is no authority whatever for seeing in the introduction of the title here a reference to some member chosen from amongst the elders to take overall charge of the "diocese of Crete" as their superior, after the manner of the orthodox churches today. In Philippi there were "bishops and deacons", in the plural, all on a level with "all the saints" (Philippians 1:1). For there were to be no "lords over God's heritage" (1 Peter 5:3), only "good stewards of the manifold grace of God" (4:10), and "stewards of the mysteries of God. Moreover, it is required in stewards, that a man be found faithful" (1 Corinthians 4:1-2).

The *oikonomos*, therefore, while he indeed serves the ecclesia, does so in discharge of a duty to God, whose house (*oikos*) the ecclesia is (see on 1 Timothy 3:4,15, pages 93, 101; also Essay 25, "The Good Deposit", page 221).

"Not soon angry": Violent or hasty temper, like a readiness to resort to blows *(striker)*, is often a characteristic of those who are *"given to filthy lucre"* and *"given to wine"*, and can be no part of the character of elders, who have to exhort and convince with all meekness and longsuffering (verse 9; 2 Timothy 2:25; Essay 33, "The Meekness of the True Disciple", page 293).

Verse 8: *"A lover of hospitality . . . sober, just, holy, temperate"*: Evidently the need to display hospitality was as great in Crete as it was elsewhere in the Ancient World (1 Timothy 3:2, pages 88, 89; Hebrews 13:2); moreover, the elder, as a *philagathos*, 'lover of good men', would seek only the company of those whose standards were his own, the holy, the just and the responsible. We have written in some detail on the word for 'sober', *sōphrōn*, which is found only in the Pastorals, and the reader is referred to pages 71, 88 and 89. We shall consider how the word is again used to great effect when we come to Titus 2:1-6. The Greek philosophers made a distinction between the words *engkratē*, 'temperate', 'master of oneself', and *sōphrōn*. The first they classified as describing one who *endures* either physical or mental suffering and the second, one who *overcomes*, resisting evil thoughts and temptations, which they considered a much harder task.

Verse 9: *"Holding fast the faithful word"*: The Cretan ecclesias, like the one in Ephesus, were troubled by problems of conduct arising from false or inadequate beliefs. The "gainsayers" were like the "other-teachers"; their doctrine was not so much an outright denial of the Gospel truth, but an adulteration of it with other elements which, in effect, made it into no Gospel at all. Great importance was to be attached, therefore, to the faithfulness of the elders.

"Able by sound doctrine both to exhort and to convince the gainsayers": Titus himself was to set an example and speak "the things which become sound doctrine" (2:1,7). For a detailed comment on this characteristic expression in these Letters see Essay 4 (page 46). The elders were to hold fast to the words of the faith *"according to the teaching"* (RV), which, in view of the emphatic nature of the Greek word used, *didachē*, must here mean the apostolic teaching. They were to respond, as those converted by Peter's words on the Day of Pentecost had done, by "continuing stedfastly in the apostles' doctrine *(didachē)* and fellowship" (Acts 2:42). Any of

the Cretans present on that day who had later brought the Gospel back from Jerusalem, should have been fully aware that that was what it was essential for them to do. The fact that Paul assumes there will be some who would respond is an indication that, in spite of his assessment of the Cretan character in general, as it appears from verses 11-12, there could still be found some men of the right calibre in the ecclesias. Compare also 2 Timothy 3:14, and note (page 310):

> "But continue thou in the things which thou hast learned and hast been assured of, knowing of whom thou hast learned them."

Statements of the Faith

Two other points are worthy of notice here. First the expression, "the faithful word" reminds us of those five distinctive "faithful words", or "statements of the faith", which appear in these Letters (the fifth in Titus 3), which point to the existence of a recognised collection of fundamental truths to be believed and obeyed, as discussed in Essay 5, page 49. Second, the word for "hold fast" is a powerful exhortation in itself, as may be seen from its other uses in the Greek Bible: as in "*holding to* one (master), and despising the other" (Matthew 6:24; Luke 16:13), "*laying hold* upon wisdom" as a tree of life (Proverbs 3:18, Septuagint) and, appropriately for elders exercising pastoral care, making sure they "support the weak" (1 Thessalonians 5:14).

"Both to exhort and convince the gainsayers": This is in effect the same command as that given to Timothy:

> "The servant of the Lord must not strive; but be gentle unto all men, apt to teach, patient, in meekness instructing those that oppose themselves."

(2 Timothy 2:24-25, pages 280-282)

For Titus and the true elders in Crete also there would need to be a constant struggle against the heretical teachers and since the aim was to win men over, it would not be by "fighting fire with fire", or to use the Scriptural metaphor from these epistles, by engaging in *logomachiai*, or 'word-battles' (1 Timothy 6:4; 2 Timothy 2:14; see pages 180, 268). The Jews had always shown a tendency to be "a disobedient and gainsaying people" (Romans 10:21), as Paul knew from personal experience, even as there had been many of their ancestors in the wilderness who had "perished in the gainsaying of Core" (Jude 11). For all his forbearance and meekness, however, the man of God has to set a limit to the process of exhorting and instructing; it is a limit in fact set by the gainsayer himself, who, like Korah, is usually a heretic, or leader of a faction within the ecclesia:

> "A man that is *hairetikos* (a Biblical "oncer") after the first and second admonition reject; knowing that he that is such is subverted, and sinneth, *being condemned of himself.*"
>
> (Titus 3:10,11; see also Essay 52, page 426)

Now as then, responsible elders, or by whatever title we choose to call those we nominate to manage ecclesial affairs, ought to be able to exercise the same triple function prescribed by the Apostle: to *teach* sound doctrine, to *exhort* the faithful and to *refute* error.

1:10-16—The Other-Teachers of Crete

Verse 10: *"For there are many unruly and vain talkers":* It will be seen at once that this second major section of the chapter is closely linked to the first; the introductory "For" gives the reason why Titus must exercise such great care in his ordaining of elders and why the qualifications they must possess are so stringently laid down. At every point they must be able to counter the opposition of the gainsayers, the 'speakers against' all that is good and right, who were without self-restraint in any respect. As the Lord had warned in his Olivet Prophecy (Matthew 24) and the Apostle himself had told the elders of Ephesus (Acts 20), such people would become *"deceivers"* of the elect and do untold damage to the flock (see Essay 1 on "The Other-Teachers", page 41).

One word in this verse in particular sums up the whole content—or lack of content!—of such teaching: its proponents were *mataiologoi*, "vain talkers". Like its corresponding verb, *mataiologein* (1 Timothy 1:6, "vain jangling"), this is a Biblical "oncer", and found only infrequently in ordinary Greek. It serves Paul well here as a description of those who, in spite of their impressive oratory and apparent learning, as far as the Gospel is concerned have nothing to say.

The current theme is consistent with that to be found throughout these Epistles, written as they were specifically for ecclesias under pressure in the second half of the first century and so relevant for those in the second half of the twentieth.

The Letters emphasise the close connection between truth and righteousness, between error and unrighteousness. Those who spurn the authority of the Word of God in favour of their subjective "experience" drift further away from the truth and eventually abandon it completely. There have been several modern examples of those who, having made "joy" (that is, "exuberance") their basis of faith and the "motions of the Spirit" their guide in matters of conduct, have sadly had nothing to support them in days of adversity and have eventually cast off religion completely. Sadly too, they have sometimes succeeded in "subverting whole houses" in the process (verse 11).

"Specially they of the circumcision": In the early years the principal opposition to the Gospel preaching from without was led by the Jews, as the record in Acts reveals. This tendency on their part also manifested itself within the ecclesias in the activity of the Judaisers. In Galatia, which like Crete was not a single ecclesia but a region in which there were several communities, it was they who made the Gospel "other" than what it truly was, to the point of preaching what was a "no-gospel". From the beginning Paul lost no time in condemning this movement in the strongest possible terms:

"I marvel that ye are so soon removed ... unto another gospel: which is not another; but there be some that trouble you, and would *pervert the gospel of Christ.* But though we, or an angel from heaven, preach any other gospel unto you than that which we have preached unto you, *let him be accursed.* As we said before, so say I now again ... *let him be accursed."*

(Galatians 1:6-9; cf. 2 Corinthians 11:3-4,13-14)

The Jews in Crete

From the point of view of statistics alone it would be probable that the gainsayers in Crete would be mainly "they of the circumcision". The ecclesial membership, like the island population, contained a significantly high percentage of Jews (Josephus, *Antiquities,* xvii). The Roman historian, Tacitus, went so far as to assert that the people derived their Latin name of *Iudaei,* or *Judaei,* from *Idaei,* dwellers on Mount Ida, the island's famous mountain! We shall consider the Jewish element in the "other-teaching" under verse 14 below.

Verse 11: "Whose mouths must be stopped": the use of this most emphatic of "oncers", *epistomizein*, is consistent with Paul's warning to the Galatians above: the factionists must be muzzled, since the tongue is a source of great evil and, unlike the horse, the gainsayers could not be turned about with a bit in the mouth (James 3:3). Although the word is entirely different, the idea is the same in Matthew 22:34, where by his use of the Scriptures which his critics could quote but did not "know", and therefore "erred", the Lord "put the Sadducees to silence". Compare also, in the same context of the factionists, Jude 10-11:

> "But these speak evil of those things which they know not: but what they know naturally, as brute beasts (the Cretans were "evil beasts"), in those things they corrupt themselves."

Also 2 Timothy 3:7-9 (pages 305-307):

> "Ever learning, and never able to come to the knowledge of the truth ... so do these also resist the truth, men of corrupt minds, reprobate concerning the faith. But they shall proceed no further: for their folly shall be manifest unto all men."

"Teaching things which they ought not, for filthy lucre's sake": Greed for wages is the mark of the hireling shepherd, according to the Lord in his simile of the Good Shepherd (John 10:12), and the overseers, or the elders, had to be seen to be free from the vice of covetousness (1 Timothy 3:8). The heretical teachers supposed "that godliness is a way of gain" (1 Timothy 6:5). Please refer to the notes on these two passages on pages 92, 97, 182; also 162, 163). No doubt covetousness was also a trait of the Cretan character in general; hence this double reference to "filthy lucre" (verses 7,11).

Verse 12: *"Cretans are always liars ... "*: A consideration of the unfavourable reputation of the "Cretians" (RV, Cretans) is taken up in Essay 44, page 377. For Paul's quotations from contemporary poets, see Essay 45, page 380.

Verse 13: *"This witness is true. Wherefore rebuke them sharply"*: The Cretan ecclesias had evidently been influenced to a considerable extent by their environment, and Titus, like Timothy in Ephesus (2 Timothy 4:2), was called upon to "reprove, rebuke, exhort with all longsuffering and doctrine". The spirit in which this was done was to be the same as that of the Lord himself—"As many as I *love*, I rebuke and chasten" (Revelation 3:19)—since the object of the rebuking was to bring about repentance, *"that they may be sound in the faith"*.

Verse 14: *"Not giving heed to Jewish fables"*: Although the reference to *"commandments of men"* might suggest that the controversy was still with the Judaisers it is more likely that it was the followers of those influenced by the Jewish syncretist, Philo, who are in view here. Philo flourished about AD 40, so it could well be that his theories had been gaining ground in the ecclesias for ten or fifteen years.

The word "circumcision" is used only once in the Pastoral Epistles, here in Titus 1, and is more of a generalised epithet for Jews than for a "circumcision party" who were insisting upon the observance of the Mosaic ritual by Gentiles as a condition of their salvation. The question of myths, genealogies and Jewish fables is discussed in Essay 2, page 42; the men who followed them caused people to *"turn from the truth"*, for which expression see notes on 1 Timothy 1:6 (page 21).

Verse 15: *"Unto the pure all things are pure"*: Even though the controversy might not be about a rigid adherence to the Mosaic ritual, there was still an element of false asceticism in the heretical teaching. This was apparent in Ephesus also, and was discussed under 1 Timothy 4:2-5 (pages 123-125). In Scripture all "commandments of men" are regarded as making the Word of God of none effect (Isaiah 29:13; Matthew 15:6 etc.).

The principle behind this verse 15 is the one which Paul maintains in all his discussions of matters of conscience: it is "not that all things are pure *in the judgment* of the pure, but that all things are pure *for their use*" (Bernard). The whole of Romans 14 is a commentary on this principle, which is summed up in verses 20-23:

"All things indeed are pure; but it is evil for that man who eateth with offence ... Happy is he who condemneth not himself in that thing which he alloweth. And he that doubteth is damned if he eat, because he eateth not of faith: for whatsoever is not of faith is sin."

And in 1 Corinthians 8:6-7:

"But to us there is but one God, the Father, of whom are all things, and we in him ... Howbeit there is not in every man that knowledge."

365

"But unto them that are defiled and unbelieving is nothing pure": The converse must of necessity be true, as Paul expresses it forcefully here. It is important to realise the stress that he is laying upon the connection between faith and behaviour, a teaching he proclaims especially in letters such as these which deal specifically with the other-teaching. Paul invariably links faith with a good conscience (1 Timothy 1:5; 6:5; pages 44 and 181); and Peter, standing before the council of the elders in Jerusalem who were discussing the conversion of the Gentiles, said:

"God, which knoweth the hearts, bare them (that is, the Gentiles) witness, giving them the Holy Spirit, even as he did unto us; and put no difference between us and them, *purifying their hearts by faith."* (Acts 15:8-9)

Verse 16: Thus it was useless for the unruly Cretans to *"profess that they know God; but in works they deny him".* That merely showed that they were *"unto every good work reprobate"*, or entirely void of judgement. "Good work", or "good works", has a particular connotation in the context of the Pastoral Epistles, which has already been discussed in some detail. See the parallel expression "throughly furnished unto every good work" in 2 Timothy 3:17 (RV); also 1 Timothy 2:10 (pages 71, 72 and page 7 for the meaning of *kalos* in this connection. The word *adokimos*, 'reprobate', is a common word in Paul's writings; it means an inability to distinguish between good and evil. It is like having one's conscience "seared with a hot iron", as discussed in the note on 1 Timothy 4:2 (page 123). On the other hand, those who are mature in the faith "by reason of use have their senses exercised to discern both good and evil" (Hebrews 5:14). See also Paul's uses of the word *adokimos* in Romans 1:28; 1 Corinthians 9:27 and 2 Corinthians 13:5.

ESSAY 39

The Servant of God

THE use of the term *doulos*, 'slave' or 'bondservant', as it appears in Titus 1:1, is to be understood in the Old Testament sense rather than in that of the Greek world, where it described a social status. It was never used in pagan circles in connection with divine service or worship but in Israel its equivalent, *ebed*, often designated a position of privilege as well as of service. The high-ranking servant represented his master and promoted his honour in fulfilling his commission (cf. Abraham's steward, Eliezer of Damascus, Genesis 24).

The patriarchs were all the LORD's servants, as were the prophets (Genesis 26:24; Deuteronomy 9:27; Psalm 105 throughout; Amos 3:7), and Israel himself (Isaiah 49:3). But even amongst all those who were bound to the LORD by His covenant with them, there were some outstanding figures who occupied a key rôle in the Divine purpose. David, for example, has the title applied to him more times than any, especially in the Psalms, and it was God Himself who set "my servant Moses" apart even from His other servants, the prophets (Numbers 12:6-8). Note also Nehemiah's use of the word to describe both his own status and that of Moses (Nehemiah 1:6,8,11).

"Faithful in all his house"

Moses, who was "faithful in all his house" (Hebrews 3:2), occupied a position of supreme authority in Israel. He became the representative and the special mouthpiece of God after the elders of Israel, on behalf of all the people at Sinai, had pleaded that they should no more hear the voice of the living God Himself (Exodus 20:18-19; Deuteronomy 5:23-28). The LORD invested him with

His own authority and, on occasions, with His own power, so that he could speak to them in "the word of the LORD".

The highest amongst the servants of God, however, was the Lord Jesus Christ himself, as he is presented to us in the prophecy of Isaiah. "Though he were a son", he took upon himself "the form of a servant", and became obedient even unto the death of the cross. Of him the Father said, "Behold *my servant*, whom I uphold; mine elect, in whom my soul delighteth; *I have put my spirit upon him*: he shall bring forth judgment to the Gentiles" (Isaiah 42:1). So being the firstborn of the LORD, as well as perfect in his obedience, the Lord Jesus was highly exalted, to become supreme in all things—"that in all things he might have the pre-eminence" (Colossians 1:18).

In becoming "an apostle of Jesus Christ to the Gentiles", Paul exercised the privilege and function of "a servant of God", in this Old Testament sense, and so was "not a whit behind the very chiefest apostles", that is, 'those who were commissioned to go' (2 Corinthians 11:5; 12:11). He was expressly commanded by the Christ to whom "all power in heaven and in earth had been given", to carry out the commission which the Lord himself had been charged with as the servant of God. The commandment echoed some of the very words used in the prophecy concerning the Lord Jesus, thus proclaiming Paul also to be "a servant of God":

"But rise, and stand upon thy feet: for I have appeared unto thee for this purpose, to make thee *a minister* and a witness both of these things which thou hast seen, and of those things in the which I will appear unto thee; delivering thee from the people, and from the Gentiles, unto whom now I send thee, to open their eyes, and to turn them from darkness to light, and from the power of Satan unto God, that they may receive forgiveness of sins, and inheritance among them which are sanctified by faith that is in me."

(Acts 26:16-18, with Isaiah 42:7; Acts 9:15; 22:21)

Thus, in using his significant title of "servant of God" in the superscription to this Letter to Titus, with all its overtones of Mosaic status in the execution of a Divine commission, Paul proclaims his authority in terms readily acceptable to the predominantly Jewish membership of the ecclesias in which the problems were to be regulated (see 1:10,14).

ESSAY 40

"In due times"

THE Lord told his disciples that the Father had put "the times" and "the seasons" in His own power (Acts 1:7). The immediate reference was to a time still future, that of the restoration of the kingdom to Israel, but Scripture is full of the evidence that the Creator has a plan of the ages, of which certain events have been both a stage in the fulfilment and a guarantee of all that was yet to come.

Whatever other purpose, as yet hidden from our eyes, there may be in the planets, with all the stars in the vastness of outer space, from the foundation of the world they were given for the regulation of the life of man and for his guidance on land and sea (Genesis 1:14-18). There was a Divine covenant linked with the recurring seasons in the time of Noah (Genesis 8:22). The promise to Abraham and his seed was confirmed under the stars of heaven, and linked to the covenant of day and night was the promise of the restoration of Israel (Genesis 15:5; Jeremiah 31:35-37).

As with day and night, so with the passing years:

"I will certainly return unto thee *according to the time of life*; and, lo, Sarah thy wife shall have a son ..." (Genesis 18:10)

"Thy seed shall be a stranger in a land that is not theirs ... but *in the fourth generation* they shall come hither again." (Genesis 15:13-16)

"I Daniel understood by books *the number of the years*, whereof the word of the LORD came to Jeremiah the prophet, that *he would accomplish seventy years* in the desolations of Jerusalem." (Daniel 9:2)

369

"Know therefore and understand, that from the going forth of the commandment to restore and to build Jerusalem unto the Messiah the Prince shall be *seven weeks, and threescore and two weeks.*"

(Daniel 9:25)

"Blessed is he that waiteth, and cometh to *the thousand three hundred and five and thirty days.* But go thou thy way till the end be: for thou shalt rest, and stand in thy lot at *the end of the days.*"

(Daniel 12:12-13)

Those who understood "the due time" were "waiting for the consolation of Israel", because her "warfare was accomplished". They "looked for redemption in Jerusalem" and were not disappointed, for the child was born, heralded by a star in the east, and he "gave himself a ransom for all, a testimony *in due time*" (Luke 2:25, with Isaiah 40:1-2; Luke 2:38; 1 Timothy 2:6, with margin). This inaugurated "the last time", or the period of opportunity for "all men everywhere to repent: because he hath *appointed a day,* in the which he will judge the world in righteousness" (Acts 17:30,31). John speaks of "the last time" in connection with the antichrists and the deceivers who had gone forth into the world, which links up with the background to Paul's Letter to Titus. Like Daniel, the apostles and all the saints who came after them have known that it is the last time, even where they needed to be gently taught that though the vision is true, the time appointed may be long (Daniel 10:1).

The Coming Day

As mentioned in connection with Titus 1:3 (pages 354, 355), Paul emphasises "the due times" to illustrate the certainty of God's purposes and to draw out appropriate exhortations for his readers. For the promise will be consummated in the day that is to come, the day of—

"the appearing of our Lord Jesus Christ: which *in his times* he shall shew, who is the blessed and only Potentate, the King of kings, and Lord of lords; who only hath immortality, dwelling in the light which no man can approach unto; whom no man hath seen, nor can see: to whom be honour and power everlasting. Amen."

(1 Timothy 6:14-16; notes on pages 64, 195, 196)

ESSAY 41

Paul, the Apostle of Jesus Christ

"THE first three verses of the Epistle to Titus are, from the point of view of doctrine, to be reckoned amongst the most concise in all Scripture: they treat of the principal truths of Christianity, and above all contain the fullest definition of apostleship given anywhere by Paul" (Spicq, *Les Epîtres Pastorales*).

From these three verses we are taught that apostleship had its origin in God Himself, and had as its purpose the bringing of men to that eternal life promised from the beginning. Paul received his own commission *"according to the commandment of God our Saviour"* (Titus 1:3). It was, therefore, an extension of the work of the prophets, in whom the Spirit of Christ had spoken beforehand, for the apostles could "preach the gospel . . . with the Holy Spirit sent down from heaven" and report the things that were signified by that Spirit in "the sufferings of Christ, and the glory that should follow" (1 Peter 1:10-12). "God our Saviour" is a characteristic expression in the Pastoral Letters and we have commented upon it more fully in the notes on 1 Timothy 1:1 and 2 Timothy 1:9 (pages 15 and 255). From 1 Timothy 2:3,7 we see how the title "God our Saviour" is closely linked with Paul's ordaining as "a preacher (*kērux*, 'herald'), and an apostle . . . a teacher of the Gentiles in faith and verity". The ecclesia was thus "built upon the foundation of the apostles and prophets, Jesus Christ himself being the chief corner stone" (Ephesians 2:20). Indeed, Christ is "the Apostle and High Priest of our profession" (Hebrews 3:1).

The salvation was *promised* from the beginning. The verb *epaggellesthai* and its related noun *epaggellia*, 'a promise', are from the same root as *aggelos*, 'a messenger', and linked with the

Gospel, or the glad tidings (*euaggelion*).* In Titus 1:1-3, therefore, the promises to the fathers and all the Messianic prophecies—the whole revelation of Christ in the Old Testament—are summarised as the "hope of eternal life". The chosen apostles themselves speak with all the authority of "the Holy Spirit sent down from heaven". The word for "commandment" here (*epitagē*) is one of Paul's characteristic words, used by no other New Testament writer, and carries the overtones of apostolic authority, such as he and Barnabas received when the Holy Spirit said: "Separate me Barnabas and Saul for the work whereunto I have called them" (Acts 13:2). The situation in view in Ephesus and Crete called for an exercise, through his deputies armed with these authoritative documents (pastoral though they are in intent), of the authority granted him. See 1 Timothy 1:1 and note (page 15). So Titus will be able to "exhort, and rebuke with all *epitagē*" (2:15).

With so great a privilege and responsibility, and with so great an end in view—the salvation of mankind, the heralding of the life to come and the promotion of the glory of God—no wonder that the Apostle regards his commission as a sacred trust: "Woe is unto me, if I preach not the gospel!" (1 Corinthians 9:16-17). "Committed" or "entrusted" in verse 3, comes from the same root as "faith" and "belief"—*pistis*. So the proclamation of *the faith* which leads men *to believe* unto salvation must be carried out by those who are "allowed of God to be *put in trust* with the gospel" (1 Thessalonians 2:4). This sense of responsibility Paul conveys to Timothy and Titus, since they too must handle, with all meekness yet with all authority, "the ecclesia of God, which he hath purchased with his own blood" in giving His only begotten Son (Acts 20:28).

For further comments on the apostolic trust see Essay 25, "The Good Deposit" (page 221).

---

* In Greek -gg- is pronounced as -ng-. Thus *aggelos* is the word for 'angel'.

ESSAY 42

Why is Titus not Mentioned in the Acts?

WE have plenty of information about Paul's affection for Titus and his confidence in his ability to carry out the difficult tasks assigned to him, but little that enables us precisely to identify the man himself. He is mentioned nine times in 2 Corinthians (2:13; 7:6,13,14; 8:6,16,23; 12:18), twice in Galatians (2:1,3) and once in 2 Timothy (4:10, page 339).

From these passages we learn that Paul sent Titus on a mission to Corinth, bearing a letter to the Corinthians, and that he had no rest in his spirit until "Titus my brother" returned to refresh him with good news from the ecclesia: "God, that comforteth those that are cast down, comforted us by the coming of Titus." Titus himself had "the same earnest care" for that ecclesia as the Apostle himself had. He was probably the bearer of the Second Letter, if not also Paul's amanuensis in the writing of it. With another brother, not identified by name, Titus had charge of the organising of the "great collection" taken up in Corinth for the poor saints. He evidently combined certain administrative skills with a wealth of sympathy and understanding and Paul had no hesitation in describing him as "my partner and fellowhelper concerning you".

Titus, with Barnabas, accompanied Paul to Jerusalem for the important meeting with James, Cephas and John, when they gave Paul "the right hands of fellowship" (Galatians 2:9), in support of his mission to the Gentiles, of whom Titus himself was one. Unlike Timothy, who was half-Jewish, Titus was not circumcised by Paul, who indeed resisted the suggestion (which seems to have come from the Judaisers) that this should be done.

In spite of the importance of Titus in the work of the Gospel and his evident qualifications for the difficult assignment in Crete, he is never mentioned by name in the Acts of the Apostles (except possibly in 18:7, where, on the strength of some ancient authorities, the Revised Version refers to *Titus* Justus). One theory advanced to account for the omission is that Titus was Luke's brother, and that therefore the "beloved physician" suppressed Titus' name together with his own. The evidence for this theory is discussed, and apparently approved of, by John Carter in an article entitled "Luke and Titus—Were they Brothers?" (*The Christadelphian*, 1960, page 296).

Readers are referred to that article for a full discussion of the topic, which includes evidence brought by conservative Biblical scholars as well as from early tradition. The points in general are that the reference in Galatians, one of the earliest epistles, points to the possibility that Titus was baptized early on in the mission at Syrian Antioch. He is named several times as being in co-operation with an un-named but well-known brother, "whose praise is in all the churches", and the pair journeyed together to Corinth. The phrase in 2 Corinthians 12:18, "with Titus I sent a brother", is literally "the brother", which Greek idiom would allow us to translate as "his brother" in this case.

Moreover, according to 2 Corinthians 8:22 the delegates who went on ahead of the Apostle on his return to Syria with the proceeds of the collection included the two brethren from Corinth, Titus and "our brother (Luke?), whom we have often-times proved diligent in many things, but now much more diligent, upon the great confidence which I have in you". In the list which Luke gives in Acts 20:4, however, there appear the names of Sopater of Berea, Aristarchus and Secundus of Thessalonica, Gaius and Timothy of Derbe and Tychicus and Trophimus of Asia—everybody, apparently except the delegation from Corinth. Was Luke modestly omitting his own name and that of his brother?

There is as yet no more positive proof of any relationship between Luke and Titus than this deductive evidence provides, but we may rest assured that enough information has been given for us to assess the quality of all those men of God, through whose work the ecclesias were shepherded and strengthened. Named or anonymous, they offer us examples to follow in our day.

ESSAY 43

Comparative List of Qualities required for Eldership

IN connection with 1 Timothy 3, and in Essay 10, "The Lists of Qualifications for Ecclesial Office" (page 107), we have already considered this vital topic; "Eldership and Rule in the First Century Ecclesia" was, moreover, the subject of Essay 17, page 170. We shall now compare the similar list of virtues in Titus 1 with those in 1 Timothy 3; and, by way of contrast, the corresponding negative vices (2 Timothy 3), which are to be characteristic of the "last days". Page numbers are given for reference:

TITUS 1	1 TIMOTHY 3	2 TIMOTHY 3	PAGE
Blameless *anengklētos*	Blameless *anepilempton* (v. 2) *anengkletoi* (v. 10) Having a good report from without (v. 7)		87, 110
Husband of one wife	Husband of one wife (v. 2; v. 12)		110
Having faithful (believing) children, etc.	Managing well his own house, and children, etc. (v. 4; v. 12)		
The steward of God *oikonomos*	Take care of the church of God (v. 5)		94
Not self-willed (self-pleasing)		Lovers of their own selves (v. 2)	299
		Lovers of pleasures (v. 4)	302

375

TITUS 1	1 TIMOTHY 3	2 TIMOTHY 3	PAGE
Not soon angry			
Not given to wine	Not given to wine (v. 3; v. 8)		91, 97
No striker	No striker (v. 3)		92
Not given to filthy lucre *mē aischrokerdē*	Not greedy of filthy lucre *aphilarguron* (v. 3) *mē aischrokerdē* (v. 8)	Covetous (v. 2) *philarguroi*	92
A lover of hospitality	Given to hospitality (v. 2)		89
A lover of good men *philagathos*		Despisers of those that are good *aphilagathoi* (v. 3)	301
Sober, or self-controlled	Sober, or self-controlled (v. 2)		71, 88
Just, holy		Unholy, blasphemers, traitors (v. 3; v. 4)	300
Temperate *engkratē*		Incontinent *akratēs* (v. 3)	301
Holding fast the faithful word	Holding the mystery of the faith (v. 9)		98
Able to exhort and convince gainsayers	Apt to teach (v. 2)		90

ESSAY 44

The Reputation of the Cretans

EVEN *"one of themselves, a prophet of their own"* (Titus 1:12, RV), presented the character of the Cretans in a most unfavourable light. The "prophet" was the philosopher Epimenides of Knossos, a Cretan who flourished about 600 BC: the reputation was evidently one of long standing! He was regarded with great veneration and one ancient author states that the Cretans even offered sacrifice to him "as to a god". The actual reference in Titus, *"The Cretans are always liars, evil beasts, slow bellies"*, was written in hexameter verse in the no longer extant *Oracles of Epimenides*, and partly imitated by the poet Callimachus in his *Hymn to Zeus*, which some think was the source of Paul's quotation in Acts 17:28 (but see Essay 45, page 380).

The Three Worst Ks

The Cretans were reckoned amongst the *tria kappa kakista*, the three worst Ks (in English spelling, Cs) of the Greek world —Crete, Cappadocia and Cilicia. They had a reputation for gluttony, corpulence and a sullen disposition, and their renown as liars was satirised in the famous quip that they claimed to have the tomb of Zeus on the island, whereas everyone knew that Zeus was immortal!

Such judgements on presumed national characteristics were common enough in the Ancient World, and words were coined like "to Cretise", to behave like a Cretan, which was parallelled by "to Corinthise", or to indulge in the factious, profligate and immoral behaviour notorious in Corinth which forms part of the background to the First Letter to that ecclesia.

Thus, while the epithets were not necessarily to be applied to all who lived in Crete, either Jew or Gentile, the members of the ecclesias there were as much exposed to the distinctive pressures of their contemporary society as were the brethren and sisters in Corinth, or for that matter in the world of the twentieth century. The background of the society in which the first century ecclesias grew up is reflected with extraordinary accuracy in the apostolic letters, which is what makes them so valuable as sources of exhortation, warning and advice for those who live in the pagan society of today.

Syncretism

There was another word which Crete gave to the Greek language which may be of even greater importance for our present study: it is represented in English by the word *syncretism*. The original verb, *syncretise*, referred to the process of federation of Cretan communities, but by extension of meaning *syncretism* came to mean a combining together of different ideas into a unified system of thought.

In Crete, as in Ephesus, all the currents of religion, philosophy and pagan culture, Greek, Asiatic and Roman, flowed together and syncretist philosophers sought to fuse these ideas into a comprehensive system, a philosophy of life which embraced all the diverse elements. In the tolerant society of the first century there were many superficial converts to Christianity, such as Simon Magus (Acts 8:9), who were never completely delivered from their old allegiances (Essay 36, "Magic, Miracles and Mighty Works", page 317), and in one sense the Roman Church's attempts to fuse Christianity and pagan worship is another example of the syncretist process.

Also Philo, known as "the Jewish Plato", was a Jewish philosopher of Alexandria, who no doubt had access to its famous library of ancient learning. He too sought to assimilate into one comprehensive system both pagan philosophy and the teachings of the Mosaic law, or rather of the Rabbinical tales and traditions which obscured the true teaching of the law.

Syncretism, therefore, presented as serious a threat to the true Gospel message and its way of life then as the ecumenical philosophies of today. The importance of the name of Christ as "the only name given under heaven among men, whereby we must be saved" is being submerged under the assumption that all religions are equally valid and that morality based upon the faith in Christ has no place in modern society. And even amongst those who profess adherence to Christianity the ecumenical movement only prospers where there is agreement to compromise on vital issues.

ESSAY 45

Paul's Quotations from Secular Authors

BY his own account Paul quotes twice directly from secular authors, though without naming them, and there is at least one other possible reference to the work of a Greek poet. This raises certain important questions. To what extent was Paul familiar with the literature of the Ancient World? What authority did he attach to it, when, for example, he quotes the *Hymn to Zeus* in a discourse about the true God? Why does he use these quotations at all? We shall best be able to answer these questions after looking briefly at those we can identify.

Poets and Prophets

In connection with Titus 1:12, we have looked (page 377) at the reference to Eumenides, a philospher-poet of the sixth century BC. Paul calls him a Cretan *prophet*, not because he himself so regarded him but because according to ancient theory poets were inspired with a spirit of the gods, and the writings of the more celebrated, especially Homer, were put into the category of "scripture", sacred and authoritative. Indeed, that was all the "scripture" the Greeks possessed, since the ambiguous oracles of Delphi were not written down. For the important distinction to be drawn between the writings of the Classical poet into whom a god was assumed to have breathed, and the Hebrew Scriptures in which it was the writing itself which was "given by inspiration of God", or God-breathed, see Essay 37 (page 322).

Plato, Aristotle and the Roman orator, Cicero, all esteemed Eumenides as an inspired, prophetic man. The translation of his poem as given in F. F. Bruce's *The Book of the Acts*, page 359 in the New London Commentaries series, is as follows:

"They fashioned a tomb for thee, O holy and high one—
The Cretans, always liars, evil beasts, idle bellies!
But thou art not dead; thou livest and abidest for ever;
For in thee we live and move and have our being."

The last line can be recognised as appearing in Acts 17:28. It has been attributed to another poet, Callimachus, but is almost certainly quoted by him direct from the Cretan "prophet". In the speech on the Areopagus the line is followed by a quotation from the *Phainomena*, written by Paul's fellow-Cilician, Aratus (277 BC):

"For we are also his offspring."

There is some confusion even about this attribution, however, since the line may have been borrowed from a contemporary of Aratus, one Cleanthes, who also wrote a *Hymn to Zeus*. Since Cleanthes was a disciple of Zeno, the founder of the Stoic philosophy, the theory has some probability in the context of Paul's speech before this particular assembly.

The other identifiable quotation is to be found in 1 Corinthians 15:33. It has been attributed to Menander, an Athenian comic poet, who possibly in his turn borrowed it from the Athenian tragic playwright, Euripides. At any rate, Menander was renowned in his day for the fact that "he did not disgrace his compositions, like Aristophanes, by mean and indecent reflections and illiberal satire, but his writings were replete with elegance, refined wit, and judicious observations" (Lemprière, *A Classical Dictionary*). His writings could scarcely be otherwise if he was true to his own counsel:

"Evil communications corrupt good manners."

While looking at 1 Corinthians 15 it is interesting to note that when Paul refers to "fighting with beasts at Ephesus" (verse 32) as "after the manner of men", he means, "to quote the proverbial saying", much as we might use the expression, "bearding the lion in his den". There may even be another such allusion in the same verse. During the *commissatio*, the drinking session with which every pagan dinner party concluded, a small skull and crossbones in marble or plaster, called a *memento mori* ("Remember you are mortal!"), was passed among the guests as a reminder that life was short and so they should make the most of the occasion and "live it up". Sometimes the same figure formed part of the mosaic floor decoration on the dining-room floor, as a permanent reminder that life was for living and there was neither eating nor drinking in the tomb. Is Paul then emphasising the supreme importance of the resurrection of the dead by saying, in effect: "If the dead rise not, then we too might just as well 'eat and drink; for tomorrow we die', as the saying goes!"? It is true that the saying has its roots in Isaiah 22:13, but both Jew and Gentile would see the force of his argument.

With how much Greek literature was Paul in fact familiar? Tarsus, his birthplace, was one of the "university towns" of the Ancient World (the others were Athens and Rhodes). Thus he would have been brought up in an intellectual background. His "higher education", however, would not have been received at the university of Tarsus, but in Jerusalem, where he sat "at the feet of Gamaliel", to be educated in the Divine law, in the widest sense of that term. It was the best education, in human terms, that a Jewish boy could have been given at that time. Paul was indeed a man of culture, fluent in both Hebrew and Greek (and possibly Latin) as most educated Jews of the Dispersion would have been. He certainly had the ability to read the Greek authors if he ever set eyes on them, but with one possible exception there is in fact no evidence that he was widely read in any of the literature of the pagan world. The probability is all the other way, for the serious Jew had neither the time nor the inclination to read such works, for books were expensive and library facilities restricted to the rich or the influential.

How then did he know what certain of their own poets had said? It would have been impossible to avoid becoming familiar with those very many expressions, taken from the poets or philosophers, which had become the common coinage of everyday speech—the proverbial saying, the trite aphorism or the cliché on the lips of a populace for whom it was still part of a religious festival to throng the theatres and hear the works of the great dramatists. The old lady in the story, who saw Shakespeare's *Hamlet* for the first time, but was not impressed "because it was all made up of quotations" is representative of many today whose vocabulary is more widely based upon standard authors than they ever suspect!

To come closer to home, to make their point many Christadelphian lecturers have quoted "the well-known statement by Bertrand Russell about the Christadelphians", or "the Archbishop of Canterbury's attack on the doctrine of the immortality of the soul", without ever having read Russell's book on *Power*, or the treatise on *Towards the Conversion of England*, or even knowing the actual source of their quotations! So we need not assume that in an age when the man in the street knew more about his authors, when borrowings were freer and acknowledgements of sources much scarcer than today, every use of a quotation presupposed a detailed acquaintance with the original.

"Authoritative" Quotations?

The question of "authority" attached to such quotations rests upon the interpretation of that word. For Paul there was only one source of authoritative information and guidance in all matters of faith and conduct—the God-breathed Scriptures which are able to make a man wise unto salvation and throughly furnish him unto every good work. On none of these matters had either Homer or Epimenides anything at all to say. A statement can be true, however, even though it lacks that authority, as Paul says of the quotation about the Cretans: *"This witness is true."*

A moment's reflection will enable us to see how effective the use of such a quotation would be. We often find that a present-day reference to a newspaper paragraph, or a Parliamentary speech, in which someone recognised by others as an authority and in touch with the subject under discussion is supporting the point to be made, is an effective way of introducing what the Bible has to say about current affairs. How much more difficult for the Cretans to quarrel with Paul's assessment of their situation when "a prophet of their own selves" had said the same thing about them long before!

In Athens Paul showed himself to be sufficiently familiar with the arguments and outlook of those who had done him the courtesy of inviting him to address them, to be able to take them on their own ground. It is possible that he had indeed "read up" the Stoics and the Epicureans, since the thought of the Ancient World leaned mainly in the direction of one or the other of the two schools, certainly in Athens. The "masters of those who knew" were in any event carrying out the lawful function of the Court of the Areopagus, in examining his preaching. And as a good steward of the grace of God he must present his case as effectively as possible and speak to the occasion. So although he makes no concessions to their learning and builds his argument entirely upon allusion to the Old Testament, albeit with no direct quotation from it, since it would have been lost upon that audience, he does in fact show them that what they had all the time been grasping after had eluded them; the secret of the Universe lay in the Gospel message, if only they would look there for it. Their materialist philosophers, concerned only with the intellect, had not come so close to the truth as their poets, who dealt in the things of the human spirit; for "the world by wisdom knew not God". Yet He, the Lord of heaven and earth, and not Zeus, was "not far from every one", "if haply they might feel after him, and find him".

It was all of a piece with what he wrote to the Romans:

"That which may be known of God is manifest in them; for God hath shewed it unto them. For the invisible things of him from the creation of the world are clearly seen, being understood by the things that are made, even his eternal power and Godhead; so that they are without excuse ..."

(Romans 1:19-20)

So the Apostle knew how to present the truth in Jesus to the Jews in the synagogue, to the Gentile God-fearers, to the folk who spoke only the dialect of Lycaonia, and to the philosophers of Mars Hill. The Lord had chosen his man, who could travel the Ancient World and stand before kings as well as humble folk. And when all was said and done, it was not the wisdom of this world which turned men's hearts, though wise men could respect Paul's understanding: it was the foolishness of preaching.

384

The Letter to Titus

CHAPTER 2

Positive Exhortations and their Doctrinal Basis

2:1-10—Mutual Relationships in the Ecclesias

Verse 1: *"But speak thou the things which become sound doctrine":*
It is a great mistake to think that organisation of itself produces a spiritually sound ecclesia. It is true for the ecclesia as for us individually that we should:

"Let our ordered lives confess
    The beauty of Thy peace."

Order, however, is not a question of rules and regulations, though no human society can do without them. But as the Apostle says in effect in 1 Timothy 1:7-10 (pages 22-25), law is good if it is recognised for what it is, a means of regulating things when they go wrong: "The law is not made for a righteous man, but for the lawless and disobedient." The disciplined man or woman cultivates a respect for the right and the good as part of a whole way of life. Titus was to set the example himself—this is enlarged upon in verse 7—and, in sharp contrast to the unruly and vain talkers ("But *thou* . . . ") was to proclaim only that which would be for the spiritual health of the ecclesias. Like Timothy, by taking heed unto himself as well as to his teaching, he would both save himself and them that heard him (1 Timothy 4:16).

In the earlier days the Apostle had, as a "wise masterbuilder", been concerned with the building up, or edifying, of the body of Christ as the house of God (1 Corinthians 3:11; Ephesians 4:12-16). Now his great emphasis is upon keeping the ecclesia healthy as a spiritual body, and he uses the verb *hugiainein* (compare "hygiene"), 'to be sound or healthy', and the adjective *hugiēs* frequently in these Pastoral Epistles, always in the context of doctrine or faith. It is used nowhere else in the Bible with this connotation. The complete list of references is as follows: 1 Timothy 1:10; 6:3; 2 Timothy 1:13; 4:3; Titus 1:9,13; 2:1,2,8. In view of the frequent reference to be made in the following verses to "sound doctrine", and to the words *sōphrōn* and *sōphrō nizein*, 'to be temperate', please see the commentary on the earlier passages and especially pages 7, 46, 71 and 78. For a discussion of the word *prepein*, 'to become', see Essay 46, page 397.

Verse 2: *"That the aged men be sober, grave, temperate ... "*: The very words used, *presbutas*, and its feminine counterpart *presbutidas* in verse 3, show us clearly that Paul is not speaking here about ecclesial elders but about the older members of the ecclesia. There is, of course, a connection between the two since the elders would normally have been recruited from amongst the older, though not necessarily the aged, men. Certainly in Israel there was a respect due to people of advancing years as well as that which it was proper to pay to anyone in a position of authority. There were sound spiritual reasons for this, to which we have already alluded (pages 143-147). In this passage, however, the Apostle is commanding Titus to see that by their influence and example the older members of the ecclesia set the very highest standards.

We shall gain a clearer concept of the force of the Apostle's exhortation here if we follow the play upon the word *sōphrōn* in verses 2-6 (see page 71). With the primary meaning in Classical Greek of "a command over bodily passions, a state of perfect self-mastery in respect of appetite", *sōphrōn* is usually translated as "sober". In Titus 2:2 it is "grave"; in a verb-form in verse 4 it is "teach to be sober", followed by the ordinary adjective ("discreet") in verse 5. Finally in this sequence, another verb-form is "to be sober-minded" in verse 6. Paul uses it to indicate a true sense of responsibility in the disciple in both his personal and ecclesial life. So then we may paraphrase the main thrust of the command to Titus as follows:

> "Teach the older men to behave responsibly, the aged women likewise, so that they may inculcate a sense of responsibility in the younger women, who will then also be responsible in their behaviour, and the young men must have the same responsible attitude."

The Practical Effects on Behaviour

We may now consider the practical effects on personal behaviour which such a sense of responsibility in the disciple's calling should produce.

"The aged men" were to be "sober" or "temperate" (*nephalios*). The adjective was briefly discussed in connection with the list of qualifications for eldership (1 Timothy 3:2,11, the only other known uses of the word; page 88). Primarily the word refers to temperance with respect to wine, but here and in 1 Timothy it is extended to every aspect of self-control, both for a "bishop" and for a deacon's wife. It is especially appropriate in Titus, for it contrasts the saint's behaviour with the celebrated gluttony of the Cretan (1:12) and with general Greek moral standards. *Semnos*, 'grave' or 'honest', has also been discussed in connection with its noun, *semnotēs*, in 1 Timothy 2:2; 3:4,8,11 (pages 59, 94).

"Sound in faith, in charity, in patience": The above qualities were to be enriched by a healthy commitment to the faith (see above on *hugiēs* etc.), a stability not easily shaken by the sensations of novelty such as troubled the ecclesias, notably in Crete and in Ephesus, in the second half of the century. The helpful note on the word *hugiainontas* in this verse, which Spicq offers in *Les Epîtres Pastorales,* is worth reproducing here: "(The older men) were in short to display a healthy morality befitting men who have reached maturity (*hugiainontas,* cf. 1:13; contrast with *noson* ('sick'), 1 Timothy 6,4; and *asthenounta* ('weak in the faith'), Romans 14:1). The nuance of the word is that of vigour and strength—appropriate for men whose physical strength is declining."

Verse 3: *"The aged women likewise ... "*: This verse contains several "oncers"—the words for "aged women", "behaviour" and the single word (*hieroprepeis*) for *"as becometh holiness"*. The Apostle's emphatic use of "likewise" here, as in 1 Timothy 2:9; 3:8,11, indicates that the older women were to practise the same virtues as the men, but adapted more specifically to their nature and calling.

We have already dealt at some length with the complementary rôles of brethren and sisters in the ecclesia, when discussing 1 Timothy chapters 2, 3 and 5 on pages 76-80, 85, 99, 143-161. All of this material throws valuable light upon the current passage. The word *hieroprepeis* is worth special mention, however,

387

since it is plainly related to the verb *prepein*, 'to become', discussed in Essay 46, page 397. In a sense it sums up all the demeanour and spiritual deportment of the saints, whether men or women: they behave as people manifesting that "holiness, without which no man shall see the Lord" (Hebrews 12:14). It is perhaps appropriate that the single use in Scripture of the word should be applied to aged women in particular, since Paul manifests a great respect for them as well as showing a deep sensitivity towards the emotional side of the feminine nature. He, like Peter (1 Peter 3:1-7; the whole passage together with Ephesians 5 forms a useful commentary on these verses in Titus), understands the woman's natural preoccupation with the question of adornment, a concern which "The Virtuous Woman" of Proverbs 31 extended to all her family. Both apostles exhorted sisters to concentrate upon that adornment which would have permanent results, so that even though time might take its toll of physical appearance the older folk could, in their work and worship, manifest "the beauty of holiness" (Psalm 29:2; 96:9).

They were also to be *"teachers of good things"*. The word *kalodidaskalos* (another "oncer") is, like *heterodidaskalein* ("otherteach" in 1 Timothy 1:3; 6:3), apparently unique in all Greek literature to the Apostle Paul. The coining of both words especially for these Letters shows the great importance laid upon sound teaching in both the moral and the doctrinal spheres if the health of the ecclesia is to be maintained. "Other-teaching" and the significance of the word "good" (*kalos*), "the quality of beauty and nobility that springs from excellence", is discussed at some length on pages 41, 22, 72, 177 and 178.

Verse 4: "That they may teach the young women ... ": The wisdom and propriety of this command to Titus are as apparent as in the similar instruction to Timothy (page 147), especially against the background of social conditions in Crete. The purpose of this spiritual education was to guide the younger women in their true rôle in a community in which there were no distinctions in status but only of function:

> "There is neither Jew nor Greek, there is neither bond nor free, there is neither male nor female: for ye are all one in Christ Jesus." (Galatians 3:28)

The above passage has its counterpart in Colossians 3:11, where it is immediately followed by those injunctions for husbands and wives, parents and children, masters and servants, which declare that the spiritual life is to be expressed in all the varied circumstances of daily living. That this is so becomes evident in what follows in our Titus passage.

Preserving the Honour of Their Calling

"That the word of God be not blasphemed": Once more this important principle is set before the members of the ecclesias, this time for the benefit of the younger sisters. A similar caution with respect to "the name of God and his doctrine" was given to servants in their behaviour towards their masters (1 Timothy 6:1; page 176). Throughout these Letters great emphasis is laid upon the disciple's reputation amongst those outside the ecclesia, for the sake of the honour and glory of the Lord God Himself. Isaiah had said of Israel's behaviour in the sight of the surrounding nations:

> "For thus saith the LORD, Ye have sold yourselves for nought . . . Now therefore, what have I here, saith the LORD, that my people is taken away for nought? they that rule over them make them to howl, saith the LORD; and *my name continually every day is blasphemed.*" (Isaiah 52:3-5)

In Ezekiel the message is equally clear:

> "And when they entered unto the heathen, whither they went, *they profaned my holy name,* when they said to them, These are the people of *the LORD*, and are gone forth out of *his land* . . ." (Ezekiel 36:20,23)

Such passages were no doubt in the mind of the Apostle Paul when, apparently in an ecclesial context of tension between Jew and Gentile disciples, he pointed out the terrible consequences of making a profession of righteousness which was not matched by appropriate conduct:

> "For the name of God is blasphemed among the Gentiles through you, as it is written." (Romans 2:24)

We may well ask, therefore, Why in the immediate context should this principle be emphasised for the young women? Essay 47, page 399, will offer an answer to this and some related questions.

Verse 6: "Young men likewise exhort to be sober minded": As in verse 3 the "likewise" is emphatic, showing that the exhortation to one section of the ecclesia was in effect an exhortation to all: their "sense of responsibility" would ensure that the high standard set by the Head unto which they were all to grow up would be exemplified in conduct appropriate to the age and condition of each individual member.

At a time when the debate rages in the outside world as to the extent to which "the church" should pronounce upon, or involve itself in, political or social affairs, and all kinds of ecclesiastical decisions are being made in the name of "equality" and "human rights", it is refreshing to be reminded so forcefully that for the first century disciple Christianity was to be a spiritual force rather than a social or political one, concerned with eternal and not temporal affairs.

2:7-8—A Personal Charge to Titus

Verse 7: *"In all things shewing thyself a pattern of good works":* The sound judgement shown by the Apostle in selecting his men is frequently underlined in these Letters. The choice was critical, for both Timothy and Titus would have to display in themselves all the qualities which they would exhort others to cultivate (pages 128-132). The "pattern" (*tupos*, 'type') is almost equivalent to what we would call a template, an exact outline from which identical shapes can be fashioned. The "good works" are not simply acts of charity in the modern sense, although these may well be included, as has already been amply discussed (1:16, page 366). That there was a doctrinal basis for them is evident from what follows.

"In doctrine shewing uncorruptness, gravity, sincerity": The Revised Version has "in thy doctrine", showing that Titus's *didaskalia*, or *manner* of teaching, was to reinforce its content, the "sound speech" or *logos hugiēs* of the next verse. By taking heed to himself in this way he would, like Timothy, both save himself and them that heard him (1 Timothy 4:16). In all true teaching, especially that of the Gospel, the enthusiasm, straightforward demeanour and integrity of the teacher should shine through.

Verse 8: *"Sound speech, that cannot be condemned":* There could be only one foundation upon which Titus was to build his teaching: the apostolic deposit of the faith which, in controversy, would not represent his own opinion but the authoritative message of the Gospel as a basis for belief and conduct. Such a teacher, like his

390

very words, must then be *akatagnōstos*, 'not open to just rebuke' (a New Testament "oncer", found elsewhere only once in the apocryphal Old Testament).

"That he that is of the contrary part may be ashamed": There were many "of the contrary part" in both Ephesus and Crete. Amongst them were "the vain talkers", "the other-teachers", the preachers of "the cankerous word" and those who delighted in "word battles". In reply to the healthful teaching and irreproachable conduct which Paul enjoined upon Titus and all who heard him, such adversaries could find *"no evil thing to say of you"*. If we follow the Revised Version here ("no evil thing to say of *us*") we see that Paul is in effect commending a course which he had proved for himself by experience. The word for "evil", *phaulos*, always implies evil deeds rather than words, so Titus's good works (*kala erga*) were to be truly "the beauty of holiness", the right conduct which was the index of true belief.

2:9-10—A Special Exhortation to Slaves

Verse 9: *"Exhort servants to be obedient unto their own masters":* The foregoing exhortations affected primarily relationships within the ecclesia, although those for married women were to be followed even when they had an unbelieving partner, in the spirit of what Paul had written to the ecclesia at Corinth (1 Corinthians 7:13-16). The lowest and most despised class in society, however, had to live out their lives as the property of someone else. The reader is referred to Essay 18, page 204, for a brief discussion of the responsibilities of Christian slaves who had believing masters. The addition of the word "own" in this passage seems to suggest that here we have more specific instructions for those with unbelieving masters.

"To please them well in all things: not answering again": Arduous though his lot might be, the Christian slave was not to vent his feelings by grudging service or truculence, as was only too common amongst slaves with easy-going masters or even those with harsh lords if driven to desperation. The disciple's attitude to those in any kind of authority—whether parents, magistrates, lords or kings—was not dependent upon the worthiness of the superior but upon the principle that honour and respect to them rested upon a divine obligation. The simple sanction for most of the precepts regulating such things in Israel—obedience to

parents, rising up before "the hoary head", purity and chastity in all forms—was "I am the LORD". The slaves' service to difficult masters went beyond the merely satisfactory: they were to *"please them well"*.

The Temptation to Steal

Verse 10: *"Not purloining, but shewing all good fidelity"*: There was good reason why purloining should be singled out for special mention: it was almost the hallmark of the average slave! In Latin the word FUR, or 'thief', was often used as a synonym for slave, and one caught in the act might well be branded with the word, thus becoming known as "a three-letter man" (see also on 1 Timothy 4:2, page 123). Not all slaves were of low intelligence and many were given responsibility in various household departments, or as teachers of children at a preparatory level (the *paidagōgos*, or "schoolmaster" of Galatians 3:24) and even as managers of their master's business. The opportunities for purloining were therefore many, and hard masters were considered fair game. There was, however, another cogent reason why a slave should seek to line his pockets. He was permitted to amass a certain amount of personal wealth, known as *peculium* (cf. God's *peculiar* people, the nation which He bought for His very own), which he could use to buy his freedom under certain conditions. Thus theft could prove a short cut to freedom—unless he was detected first!

No such short cut, however, was permitted to the slave who had been "bought with (another) price". He was already the Lord's freeman, and although if he could legitimately be free from slavery he should "use it rather", where that was not possible he should abide in his original calling "with God" (1 Corinthians 7:20-24).

From such conduct a wonderful and wholly unexpected result would follow, in sharp contrast to that which caused the Word of God to be blasphemed. Accustomed to regard himself as base in the sight of men, not even master of himself but entirely at the disposition of a sometimes unpredictable owner, the slave too could contemplate the beauty of holiness: he could be an ornament to a spiritual society, and actually *"adorn the doctrine of God our Saviour in all things"*. There were not infrequent cases where a bond of affection grew up between master and slave, or a slave might even become an adopted son; it is to be hoped that in a believing master's household that was not uncommon. But to adorn the doctrine of God! To be amongst that number to whom God had respect, saying, "To this man will I look, even to him that is poor and of a contrite spirit, and trembleth at my word" (Isaiah 66:2)! For such men and women God Himself "was not ashamed to be called their God"; and the Lord Jesus, who had "made himself of no reputation, and took upon him the form of a bondservant", was "not ashamed to call them brethren" (Philippians 2:7, margin; Hebrews 2:11; 11:16). Such grace was granted to all those who were numbered amongst the faithful followers of the exhortations in this chapter, as the introductory "For" of verse 11 clearly indicates. Moreover, it was the *"grace of God that bringeth salvation"*. This theme is expanded in Essay 48, page 401.

2:11-14—The Doctrinal Pivot of the Epistle

These verses may be compared with those in 1 Timothy 3:14-16 which, in Essay 12 (page 113), we described as the *caesura* of the Letter; that is, the dividing point which gives it significance. The Titus passage likewise forms the bridge between (a) the practical exhortations and instructions of the first part, which deal with the function and life of the ecclesia, and (b) the second part, which is concerned more with the disciple in society, furnishing us also with the doctrinal basis upon which both parts are founded. It is therefore the key passage to the whole of the epistle, and the fifth "faithful saying" of 3:4-7 takes up the same thought to emphasise it once more. Indeed, that saying could almost be described as a "Statement of Faith" version of the present passage.

Verse 11: "Hath appeared unto all men": Whether one follows the Authorised Version in attaching "unto all men" to "appeared", or the Revised which attaches it to "salvation" (*anthrōpos* in effect means 'mankind'), is a matter for grammatical discussion. We would say that the weight of probability favours the Revised Version but either rendering is justifiable from a Scriptural point of view. Certainly in view of what has gone before, it is clear that all men without distinction of rank, or nation, social status or sex come within the scope of God's purpose. Any distinction is based upon the *response* of the individual concerned, as the following verse shows. The point is dealt with at greater length when discussing Paul's reference to "God our Saviour, who will have all men to be saved" (1 Timothy 2:4; pages 60-61).

Verse 12: *"Teaching us that, denying ungodliness and worldly lusts, we should live soberly":* Nothing could be plainer. The responsible behaviour (*sōphrōnōs*) enjoined upon the ecclesia, although supported by Paul's full apostolic authority, is not a code of conduct devised by any rule of man, such as might be appropriate to a guild or a club. It was the proper response to the grace of salvation which the dayspring from on high had revealed. The better rendering of this verse is, "Instructing us to the intent that, having once and for all put away ungodliness and worldly lusts, we should live . . ."

Israel were taught by the redemption from Egypt that they should be like the God who had made a covenant with them. As we have already seen, "I am the LORD" was a sufficient reason for all the commandments governing their worship and their social behaviour. It is possible to see in *"soberly, righteously (justly) and godly"* the respective social and spiritual aspects of one's own behaviour—that towards neighbours and that towards God, although this point cannot be pressed. The contrast between "ungodliness", which we have put away, and the "godly" life cannot be more marked, especially since "the mystery of godliness" was "manifest in the flesh", the very nature from which we too must banish "worldly lusts". The word for"deny", or "put away" means 'renounced', 'categorically refused', and is found nowhere else in Paul's Letters. It is used to great effect, however, here, and in 1 Timothy 5:8; 2 Timothy 2:12,13; Titus 1:16, and especially in 2 Timothy 3:5, where the man of God is to "turn away" from those professing a form of godliness. It is fitting that the doctrinal pivot of this Letter is the same as that of 1 Timothy. See further the note on "Godliness" (page 58) and Essay 13, "Great is the Mystery of Godliness" (page 116). "Grace is the very foundation of education in the house of the living God" (Spicq).

Verse 13: *"Looking for that blessed hope, and the glorious appearing of the great God and our Saviour Jesus Christ":* Many of the terms employed in the Pastoral Epistles have a contemporary background, and were therefore comprehensible to any speaker of the Greek *koinē*. The Apostle, however, gives them a fulness of spiritual meaning which makes them distinctive of the early ecclesias' faith and hope. We have already seen, for example, how the qualifications for elders (page 107) and the catalogues of vices (page 313), the "good deposit" (page 221) and even words like *eusebia* for 'worship', or 'godliness', had their counterparts in the Hellenistic World. So likewise the word which we considered above, *epiphania*, was a technical term in Greek culture (see page 196 and Essay 22, page 213). It referred to the 'manifestation', or 'acclamation' of the ruler, and was therefore most appropriate to the historical event when the voice from heaven said, "This is my beloved Son, in whom I am well pleased", adding later, "Hear ye him". But the *epiphania* was also the accession to power of the Emperor, and therefore was vividly expressive when Paul used it to describe the Lord's second appearing, "the brightness of his *coming*" (2 Thessalonians 2:8).

This is "the glorious appearing", or more accurately, "the appearing of the glory", which has been "the blessed hope" of the saints from the beginning. "We are saved by hope", said the Apostle (Romans 8:24) and it is a hope which is produced by "the patience and comfort of the Scriptures". The downtrodden and the oppressed, such as the poor and the slave, and indeed all who vex themselves with the wickedness of the times, which is thrown into relief by what "the grace of salvation" teaches, all who long to see the glory of the Risen Lord "face to face", echo the age-old cry, "How long, O Lord?" For the "blessed hope" is in fact "the hope of blessedness", first for those who are Christ's at his coming and ultimately for all nations.

We consider the concluding phrase of this verse in Essay 49, "The great God and Saviour Jesus Christ" (page 405).

Verse 14: "Who gave himself for us, that he might redeem us from all iniquity": These words take us to the heart of the whole matter of our redemption and, taught by Paul in Philippians 2, we can catch even more of the spirit of the exhortations of this chapter. For it was indeed "with the precious blood of Christ, as of a lamb without blemish and without spot" (1 Peter 1:18-19) that we were redeemed. It must not be forgotten, however, that "Christ . . . through the eternal Spirit *offered himself* without spot to God" (Hebrews 9:14). We are redeemed from "all lawlessness", for as John reminds us: "Every one that doeth sin doeth also lawlessness: for sin is lawlessness" (1 John 3:4, RV).

The Lord's Own People

Paul and Peter agree that the effect of redemption was to deliver us from "vain conversation (way of life)", to "purge our conscience from dead works", or to *"purify unto himself a peculiar people"*. The words of the LORD to Israel and later applied to the saints in 1 Peter 2:9 (note the "marvellous light") are echoed here in Titus. The purpose of redemption was to make men and women the Saviour's *private possession*. So in one of his last letters Paul continues the clear line of his teaching about the people of God—another proof, incidentally, of the authenticity of these Letters. All Christians, of whatever race they sprang, were all sons of God and all one in Christ Jesus, in whom they constitute one holy nation (Galatians 3:26; 1 Corinthians 12:13; Colossians 3:11).

For this purpose Christ's people had to be *purified unto himself*; or, as it is written in Hebrews 2:11, "Both he that sanctifieth and they who are sanctified are all of one: for which cause he is not ashamed to call them brethren."

It is not sufficient, however, to be purified from sin. He purges our conscience *from* dead works *to serve* the living and true God. Thenceforth one must therefore be *"zealous of good works"*. The word *zēlōtēs* (cf. "zealot") implies both a zeal and a desire towards something, as when it was said of the Lord Jesus, "The zeal of thine house hath eaten me up" (Psalm 69:9; John 2:17). And so:

"The love of Christ constraineth us; because we thus judge, that if one died for all, then were all dead: and that he died for all, that they which live should not henceforth live unto themselves, but unto him which died for them, and rose again."   (2 Corinthians 5:14-15)

Verse 15: *"These things"* Titus was to *"speak, and exhort, and rebuke with all authority"*, no doubt suiting the form of his exhortation to the needs of the flock at the time. There seems little doubt that Titus was an older man than Timothy; nevertheless the addition of *"Let no man despise thee"* (cf. 1 Timothy 4:12) suggests that he was still relatively young for a task which involved the responsible leadership of older people. In any case, like Timothy, he was given an apostolic commendation for a difficult and arduous work.

ESSAY 46

"Thus it becometh us . . ."

THE use of the word *prepein*, 'to become' (Titus 2:1), is almost an exhortation in itself. It is not to be confused with the other English word 'become', in the sense of 'to come into being', 'to be made into', which is represented by an entirely different Greek word. Our word here means 'befitting', 'seemly', 'the only proper thing to do'. The Lord Jesus used it when John demurred at his request for baptism: "Suffer it to be so now: for thus it *becometh us* to fulfil all righteousness" (Matthew 3:15). There was a Divine standard to be met by the only begotten Son of God, in the honouring of which he set the example for all who would be his disciples and "follow his steps". For his baptism was a commitment to the path of obedience unto death, according to his Father's purpose. This the Father acknowledged when, for the first time since Sinai, the voice of the living God was heard from heaven. It said:

"This is my beloved Son, in whom I am well pleased."

The Psalmist and the prophet had both looked forward to this when they wrote:

"Thou art my Son; this day have I begotten thee."
(Psalm 2:7)

"Behold my servant . . . in whom my soul delighteth."
(Isaiah 42:1)

The action befitting the revealed purpose—to try to keep the sense of beauty and holiness which lies behind the thought, we could almost say the *comely action*—is referred to in a similar context in Hebrews, this time applied to the Father Himself. How was it possible to bring men and women compassed about with

397

the infirmities of the flesh into fellowship with Him who is holy? There was only one fitting way:

"For it became him, for whom are all things, and by whom are all things, in bringing many sons unto glory, to make the captain of their salvation perfect through sufferings."

(Hebrews 2:10)

There was yet more. For, having given His only begotten Son for the redemption of the world, God established him as a great High Priest, who ever liveth to make intercession for those whom he is not ashamed to call brethren, weak and liable to err though they be. So it was made possible for those who are sanctified— who *need* sanctification—and him who sanctifies, being himself "the holy one of God", to be made one with the Father:

"Wherefore he is able also to save them to the uttermost that come unto God by him, seeing he ever liveth to make intercession for them. For such an high priest became us, who is holy, harmless, undefiled, separate from sinners, and made higher than the heavens ... the Son, who is consecrated for evermore."

(Hebrews 7:25-28)

What force, then, lies behind the words with which Paul exhorted Titus to speak, "alway with grace, seasoned with salt" (Colossians 4:6), those *"things which become sound doctrine"*!

ESSAY 47

Relationships between Men and Women in the Ancient World

RELATIONSHIPS between old and young, between husbands and wives, and between brethren and sisters—topics introduced again in Titus 2:1-5—have been considered before (pages 147-148). It was precisely in the matter of the relationship between the sexes and the conduct of both in their respective spheres that disciples could lay themselves open to the greatest criticism. This is true even today, where there is less general respect paid to questions of morality and conduct than perhaps at any time since the first century (cf. Romans 1). For the *public figure*, the *religious leader* and *those who profess high standards* come under severer censorship and always to the detriment of their political party, their church or their particular cause. The members of the ecclesia of the first century, surrounded as it was by detractors both pagan and Jewish, were exposed to an even harsher light.

Christian women, therefore, like Christian men had to strike the right spiritual balance between their liberty in Christ and their proper social obligations. They were "all one in Christ Jesus", and women achieved a status in the ecclesia and from the point of view of salvation which transcended anything to be found in the social strata of the Ancient World, certainly in Greece.

Even although Roman society offered women a greater freedom of assembly together with men, there was still a certain austerity and reserve about it and especially in the drinking of wine. In practice even married women did not join in the *commissatio*, or wine-drinking which followed the dessert at a formal meal. Moreover, they did not drink the same kind of wine as the men, but rather the *mulsum*, a mixture of wine and honey more suited to their taste and far less potent in its effects.

In dealing with 1 Timothy 2 (pages 69-80, 83) we have endeavoured to show at some length that the mutual responsibilities of men and women in the ecclesia were firmly based upon spiritual and emotional concerns and not on questions of superiority or inferiority. It was sufficiently necessary, however, for all to guard against the danger of using their liberty "for a cloke of wickedness" for Peter to refer specifically to it (1 Peter 2:16, RV).

So in a world where the Greek woman was in effect imprisoned at home, more of a servant than a partner to her husband, and the Roman matron gained her greater liberty after marriage only within the context of her family life, for the young sisters not to be "keepers at home" outraged both sections of "them that are without" and what were perceived as decadent standards would be attributed to the influence of their religion. The greatest circumspection had to be exercised, therefore, within the context of their liberty in Christ, especially when they sat to partake of bread and wine together in "the communion of the body and blood of Christ". They had to display a higher standard in their communal worship and give evidence of a deeper, more spiritual quality of family life so that, like the slaves mentioned below, they would "adorn the doctrine of God".

The reference to younger women has particular relevance in this passage in Titus, but it should not be forgotten that the same *sobriety*, or sense of responsibility, is called for throughout these Letters on the part of all, men and women, young and old alike. To be "given to wine" was a disqualification for eldership, as was improper behaviour on the part of their wives; if widows exercised their freedom from marital responsibility by "wandering about from house to house", as "tattlers and busybodies" it disqualified them from enrolment in the list of the ecclesial benevolent fund; while "with all purity" was to be the watchword of a Timothy or a Titus in all his dealings with older and younger women alike. Only thus could they all "give none occasion to the adversary to speak reproachfully" (see 1 Timothy 2:8-15; 3:3-12; 5:6,11-14, together with the relevant notes).

ESSAY 48

"The grace of God that bringeth salvation"

THE expression *"The grace of God that bringeth salvation"* (Titus 2:11) is in effect an exposition of the Name of the "God that cannot lie" who promised eternal life "before the world began" (Titus 1:2). In the Old Testament the word *chen* (with its related adjectival and adverbial forms) is usually, though not invariably, translated as "grace" when used in connection with God, and "favour" at other times. The basic meaning is the same although, as we shall see, the *quality* of the attribute, if we may so speak, is different. The adjective "gracious" and the adverb "graciously" are also almost always used of God; indeed, there are only about three exceptions to this principle out of more than 30 occurrences of the words in all Scripture, and one of them refers to the gracious words spoken by the Lord Jesus.

It is a remarkable fact that the word "gracious" is almost always coupled with the attributes of mercy, compassion or long-suffering when used of God's relationship with men. How can sinful man find favour with the Holy One unless He looks upon him with mercy and compassion? As has been demonstrated elsewhere*, the Name of the LORD, being the covenant-name of God, is always used in connection with the relationship between God and men and this can only be on the basis of God's provision for the forgiveness of man's sins. The wonder of God's grace is that He reveals it in the context of judgement upon sin and mercy for the sinner who repents.

From the time when the Spirit of God "hovered (*rachaph*) upon the face of the waters" in Creation, as it was later in the desert

---

*See Chapter 7 of *The Name that is Above Every Name*, published by The Christadelphian Office, 1983.

401

to "flutter *(rachaph)*" over the people to whom He declared, "I bare you on eagles' wings, and brought you unto myself", the LORD clearly loved what He had made, whether it was the world with man upon it or the nation which was His "peculiar treasure" (Genesis 1:2; Deuteronomy 32:11; Exodus 19:4-6). God yearns deeply over man in whom He put His spirit, or breath of life, especially when He sees him become a friend of the world, and therefore an enemy of God (James 4:4-5; see also Genesis 6:3 with RV marginal notes).

All the fulness and majesty of the Divine attributes and purpose—"the glory of the LORD"—were revealed to Moses when the LORD proclaimed His Name, declaring what their God was and would be for His people:

> "The LORD, the LORD God, merciful and gracious, long-suffering, and abundant in goodness and truth, keeping mercy for thousands, forgiving iniquity and transgression and sin, and that will by no means clear the guilty; visiting the iniquity of the fathers upon the children, and upon the children's children, unto the third and to the fourth generation."
>
> (Exodus 34:6-7)

There is a comparable passage in Numbers, where after the hardened rebellion of Korah and company and the leader's intercession for the people caught up in their transgression, Moses describes the power of the Lord *(Adonai,* Creator and Possessor of heaven and earth), who will fill the earth with His glory as the waters cover the sea:

> "And now, I beseech thee, let the power of my Lord *(Adonai)* be great, according as thou hast spoken, saying, The LORD is longsuffering, and of great mercy, forgiving iniquity and transgression, and by no means clearing the guilty, visiting the iniquity of the fathers upon the children unto the third and fourth generation. Pardon, I beseech thee, the iniquity of this people according unto the greatness of thy mercy . . . And the LORD said, I have pardoned according to thy word."
>
> (Numbers 14:17-20)

So the glory of the LORD was revealed in His power, His grace, His mercy and His compassion, which implied far more than the forgiveness of individual acts of sin and transgression. The LORD who had revealed Himself to be Israel's strength and song was actually to become their salvation, as the exodus from Egypt had foreshadowed (Exodus 15:2) and as had been confirmed in the Psalms and prophets:

"The LORD is my strength and song, and is become my salvation ... I shall not die, but live, and declare the works of the LORD ... I will praise thee: for thou hast heard me, and art become my salvation." (Psalm 118:14,17,21)

"Behold, God is my salvation; I will trust, and not be afraid: for the LORD JEHOVAH is my strength and my song; he also is become my salvation ... for great is the Holy One of Israel in the midst of thee." (Isaiah 12:2-6)

God our Saviour

It is noteworthy that the title "God our Saviour" is characteristic of the Pastoral Epistles and of no other letters of Paul (see on 1 Timothy 1:1, page 15; also Essay 29, page 255), and where it is coupled with the name of Christ it signifies that the LORD would become our salvation in him: "For God so loved the world that He gave His only begotten Son, that whosoever believeth in him should not perish, but have everlasting life." So in the fulness of time Jesus—"The LORD is Salvation"—was born and:

"The Word was made flesh, and dwelt among us (and we beheld his glory, the glory as of the only begotten of the Father), full of grace and truth ... And of his fulness have all we received, and grace for grace. For the law was given by Moses, but grace and truth came by Jesus Christ." (John 1:14-17)

The Brightness of His Coming

The passage we are considering in Titus yields even more beauty in its meaning. *"That bringeth salvation"* is a single word in the Greek. The phrase is therefore literally "saving grace", linking "grace" and "salvation" together even more closely—which is indeed what we should expect from what has been said above. But this grace did not simply appear: *it shone forth. Epiphanē* is the word used for the appearance of the sun and the stars (see the negative of this in Acts 27:20, where neither appeared for many days of the storm) and it is Paul's favourite word in these Letters for the manifestation or coming of Christ (Essay 22, page 213). Immediately all the Scriptures concerning the light that shineth in the darkness, the light which the darkness was unable to put out, the daystar that arises in our hearts as well as over all the land, that lightens all the Gentiles, the Sun of righteousness with healing in his beams—all are focused on this verse in Titus in which the light of life and hope shines into the life of ordinary people who believe, whether Jew or Gentile, old or young, male or female, bond or free. And the message of the Gospel was like that of the great forerunner of the Lord:

"To give knowledge of salvation unto his people by the remission of their sins, through the tender mercy of our God; whereby the dayspring from on high hath visited us, to give light to them that sit in darkness and in the shadow of death, to guide our feet into the way of peace." (Luke 1:77-79)

There is one more point to consider: the English translation, "the grace of God that *bringeth* (not *sendeth*) salvation" emphasises an important aspect of our theme. In our quotation from Psalm 118 above—"The LORD ... is become my salvation"—the words are those of the Lord Jesus himself. He cried unto Him that was able to save him from death, and was heard in that he feared. So, as the title of "God our Saviour" in the Pastoral Letters indicates, "God was in Christ, reconciling the world unto himself". So the LORD became his salvation but also "bringeth in the firstbegotten into the world" to be the Saviour of all them that believe. Truly, "God is the LORD, which hath shewed us light" (2 Corinthians 5:19; Hebrews 1:6; Psalm 118:27).

ESSAY 49

"The great God and our Saviour Jesus Christ"

THE expression in Titus 2:13 which forms the subject of this essay has given rise to much discussion. The title of "the great God" here is unique in the New Testament, although it is found in the Old, especially Isaiah and the Psalms (cf. Exodus 18:11; Deuteronomy 10:17; Nehemiah 1:5; Daniel 9:4 and the frequent expression "Great is the LORD"). In many of these passages the true greatness of Israel's God is being contrasted with the weakness of the gods of other nations for whom the title was claimed, as it was for Diana of the Ephesians (Acts 19).

Faced with the apparent attribution to Christ of the title of "the great God" we tend to side with those textual expositors who separate the two titles, applying "great God" to the Father and "our Saviour" to the Son. Whether this is the correct interpretation of the text as it stands turns upon fine points of Greek grammar and the use of the definite article. Expositors usually follow the one which suits what they have already decided on other grounds is the meaning. When it is pointed out that further explanation is required if it is the appearing of two persons at the Second Coming that is intended, we usually reply that it is the *glory* of both God and the Lord Jesus which appears.

It will be of great value for us to pursue this matter briefly, not solely for the purpose of deciding a matter of translation but of considering the wonders of the theme of "God was in Christ" which runs through these Letters in the frequent ascription to God of the title "Our Saviour". Possessed as we are of an almost unique understanding of the Scripture teaching of God's manifestation of Himself in Christ and fortified by our study of the way in which throughout these Letters the title of Saviour truly belongs to the Father but is the very name of the Son, Christadelphians have no need to be embarrassed by any questions of grammatical difficulty. In our proper emphasis upon the unity of the Godhead and the human nature of the Lord Jesus it is important that we do not fail to recognise the exalted status of the Son of God, or forget that "he that honoureth not the Son, honoureth not the Father which hath sent him".

The Name above every Name

The truth is that the Father has not only given His Name— "the name that is above every name"—unto His Son but some of the titles which go with it. "King" is a good straightforward illustration: "The LORD is King" throughout the Psalms, yet we find no difficulty at all with the Scriptural ascription of that rank to the Lord Jesus. "Lord" is another example, and here we do not mean as a translation of "the LORD" (Yahweh) but as a title of supremacy. It was the Father Himself who made "that same Jesus ... both Lord and Christ" (Acts 2:36). In stating these facts we do not diminish the glory of the Father: we recognise it as even greater, as Paul plainly emphasises in Philippians 2. There he applies to the name of Jesus what God had declared of His own name in Isaiah 45:23:

> "Wherefore God also hath highly exalted him, and given him a name which is above every name, that at the name of Jesus *every knee should bow ... and every tongue confess* that Jesus Christ is Lord, (adding significantly) to the glory of God the Father."
>
> (Philippians 2:9-11)

The glory of Him who is always "My Father" and "My God" to the one to whom He has given great glory must always be the greater. The important thing to realise is that for Christ such a name and titles were not underived as they were for his Father: he received them by *inheritance*. Is it right then that he should be ever be referred to as "God" as well as "King" and "Lord"? The question has been answered many times in the Truth's literature, from the days when Robert Roberts actually had to defend Dr. Thomas in *The Christadelphian* from the charge laid by certain brethren that he was a Trinitarian(!) up to our own times. We shall content ourselves here with an extended quotation from

The Letter to the Hebrews by John Carter, page 20, which is both informative about the subject in hand and helpful in its approach to similar topics. The actual passage under review is the quotation of Psalm 45:6-7 in Hebrews 1:8-9—"Thy throne, O God, is for ever and ever . . ."

"The Psalm speaks of the king as enthroned for ever. He is a ruler who exercises authority in righteousness, having in a time of probation loved righteousness and hated iniquity. Because of this God has exalted him to the position wherein he is worshipped, and his name remembered in all generations (verses 11,17).

"Various expedients have been resorted to to explain away the use of 'God' as applied to Christ. Needlessly so. It is better to ascertain the Biblical meaning and usage of its own terms. The judges of Israel were called 'gods' (Exodus 21:6; 22:8,28—see RV). The judges are referred to in Psalm 82: 'God standeth in the congregation of the mighty; he judgeth among the gods.' And in judging them he rebuked them in the words: 'I have said, Ye are gods; and all of you are children of the most High. But ye shall die like men, and fall like one of the princes.' The 'God' who judges is the chief ruler. Christ was such when he stood in the midst of Israel's leaders, and quoted this very Psalm in defending his claim that he was Son of God. Isaiah speaks of a 'God' who discerned Jehovah's purpose amidst prevailing failure to do so. 'From of old', he says, 'men have not heard, nor perceived by the ear, neither hath the eye seen, O God, beside thee, what he (Jehovah) hath prepared for him that waiteth for him' (64:4). Paul comments upon this lack of understanding on the part of the rulers of his day in crucifying the Lord of Glory, and quotes this passage in support. He then adds, 'But God hath revealed them unto us by his Spirit . . . that we might know the things that are freely given to us of God' (1 Corinthians 2:10,12). The 'O God' of Isaiah is Christ who saw clearly what God's arrangements were. Paul omits 'O God, beside thee' in his quotation, but immediately adds that there were some who saw and heard by means of the Spirit's revelation. The 'us' of Paul is the Christ-body, which shares to some extent the discernment of the Head.

"What is wanted then, is not to alter the translation (as the RV suggests in the margin of Psalm 45), but an understanding of the scriptural usage of the terms."

Unlike the doctrine of the Trinity, which confuses persons with their titles and diminishes the glory of both Father and Son, the above enhances the glory of the Father in its exalted view of the Son (John 5:23; 13:31-32). If we follow the excellent reasoning and exegesis here it is consistent with the doctrinal thrust of these three Epistles and also with the background of imperial times. The Emperor and some contemporary lesser monarchs (Ptolemy of Egypt, for example) gave themselves various titles such as *Euergetēs* (Benefactor; see Luke 22:25), *Sotēr* (Saviour) and *Divus* (The Divine, or God). Their *epiphany* was simply worldly pomp for none of them could bring salvation, their benefits accrued largely unto themselves and they "all died like men". What blessings had already been bestowed by "the grace of God that bringeth salvation"! What great hopes were centred on the "appearing of the glory" of the Lord Jesus—*to the glory of God the Father*!

The Letter to Titus

CHAPTER 3

Life in the World
for the Sanctified Believer

THE preceding chapter was mainly concerned with the personal conduct of brethren and sisters and their ecclesial relationships, although they were to realise that even in that they would come under public scrutiny. Paul now turns to their behaviour in society and their attitude to the ruling authorities. Their subjection was not to be out of mere necessity—because rulers are "sent . . . for the punishment of evil-doers, and for the praise of them that do well" (1 Peter 2:14)—but because of an attitude of mind which governed behaviour towards all men, whatever their status or condition.

3:1-2—Attitude towards Rulers and All Men

Verse 1: "Put them in mind to be subject . . . to obey . . . ": The injunction to remind the Cretan brethren especially of the duty of obedience is entirely consistent with what we have already learned of their background from chapter 1. They had no doubt been made aware of it when the Gospel had first been preached, since it was a fundamental duty of the believer to "render unto Caesar the things that are Caesar's", which included obedience as well as the payment of taxes and tribute. This is made abundantly clear in such extended passages as Romans 13 and 1 Peter 3 and 4:15-19. We have already commented fully on 1 Timothy 2:1-2 (pages 54-59, 81), but there is an important additional point to be made here.

Well aware though the Cretan ecclesias might have been of their duties, the social climate rendered such powerful reminders as Titus was to give both necessary and timely. Both Jews and

Greeks felt there was good cause to resist the authorities, the Jews for the same reason that made them seditious particularly in Judaea itself, the Greeks for a similar historical reason. A proud and independent people looking for a Messiah to deliver them, hated the Roman yoke. A people with a long democratic tradition found subservience to the emperor equally distasteful, for the Romans, like all non-Greeks who could not speak Greek without "barbaring" or mispronouncing it, were regarded simply as *barbarians*, for all their military prowess. Add to this the fact that, according to the Greek historian Polybius (vi. 46,9), the Cretans were outstanding for their character and revolutionary spirit and the Apostle's concern for the brethren and sisters living in such a society is readily understood. Thus while in 1 Timothy the reasons why we should pray for rulers are given, in Titus the elementary duty of obedience is stressed. Since "rulers are not a terror to good works, but to evil" (Romans 13:3), disciples are *"to be ready to every good work" (agatha)*. The "good works" of verse 8 are *kala*, on which see 1:16 and notes.

Verse 2: *"To speak evil of no man . . . shewing all meekness unto all men":* Here the scope of self-disciplined behaviour is extended. It imposes the highest possible standards upon ecclesial members which are not always readily perceived by us even today. So often "zeal for the truth" or the need to dissociate oneself from certain beliefs and practices, within or without the Brotherhood, is taken to be a licence for downright rudeness. A moment's reflection upon this verse should disabuse us of any such idea and a consideration of the doctrinal foundation for the opposite kind of behaviour set out in the following verse should banish it for ever.

We may readily concede that we should be *"no brawlers"*, and that not even for the sake of the Truth can the protest march, the "demo" or any political strife form part of the disciple's life. But to "speak evil of no man" is "not an easy precept to observe, if we are surrounded by persons whose principles of faith and conduct we believe to be quite unsound and mistaken" (J. H. Bernard, *The Cambridge Greek Testament for Schools and Colleges*). *Blasphēmein* and its cognate words carry this sense of evil speaking against men as well as God in the Pastoral Epistles and characterises the "perilous times" of 2 Timothy 3 (verse 2)— significantly, likely to be manifest in the ecclesia itself!

Instead, the attitude was to be one of meekness and forbearance. Moreover, the attribute was to be *a recognised characteristic* of the Christian, to be displayed beyond the limits of the household of faith: "Let your *forbearance* be known unto *all men*. The Lord is at hand" (Philippians 4:5, RV). Verse 3 introduces us to the reasons why.

Verse 3: *"For we ourselves also were sometimes foolish, disobedient, deceived"*: "Sometimes" should read "sometime" or "afore-time", for the verse refers to behaviour which should by now have been put far behind us, though we should still remember what it had been like to be so in bondage to the flesh—slaves to *"divers lusts and pleasures"*. The fearful list of effects of that past conduct are spelled out as *"living in malice and envy, hateful, and hating one another"*.

The truth of this assessment of human nature is seen in every aspect of private and public life, in domestic tragedy, social disorder and political strife. "And such were some of you" the Apostle had said of some of the grosser forms of misconduct (1 Corinthians 6:9-11), but he could never forget that even he himself, though as touching the law, a Pharisee, "was before a blasphemer, and a persecutor, and injurious", "breathing out threatenings and slaughter" and showing himself to be "exceedingly mad" against the disciples. Indeed, the "for *we ourselves*" makes it clear that he is associating himself with this description of the Cretan brethren's former state.

That Paul was no longer in such condition was because "the grace of our Lord was exceeding abundant with faith and love which is in Christ Jesus", a grace which had made him what he was, transformed from being "the chief of sinners" into a great apostle. In this context, as in Titus 3, Paul gives us, in the first of the "faithful sayings", the doctrinal basis for such a trans-formation in conduct and status:

"This is a faithful saying, and worthy of all acceptation, that Christ Jesus came into the world to save sinners; of whom I am chief. Howbeit for this cause I obtained mercy, that in me first (i.e. as chief) Jesus Christ might shew forth all longsuffering, for *a pattern* to them which should hereafter believe on him to life everlasting."

(1 Timothy 1:15-16; pages 27-35, 49)

411

3:4-7—The Doctrinal Basis of the Foregoing Commandments

In Titus 3:4-7, the fifth "faithful saying" (see Essay 50, page 420), the Apostle emphasises the same point: we were all "concluded under sin" until *"the kindness and love of God toward man appeared"*. This *philanthrōpia* of God should have found a response in the behaviour of those renewed by it with their own philanthropy towards all men. As we have said (page 393), this is in effect a "Statement of Faith" version of the doctrinal statement of 2:11-14. The "Faithful Sayings" in general form the subject of Essay 5 and the first four are discussed in the notes on the relevant verses.

The use which the Apostle has made of this statement of faith is masterly in its context. Throughout the Letter to Titus the "God that cannot lie" is contrasted with "the Cretans always liars" (1:2,12). The failure of men in general to respond to the offer of salvation by the God whose very nature it is to save men through His kindness and love-toward-man (*philanthrōpia*), does not alter the purpose of God, but only limits its application to those who believe. This was beautifully expressed in the metrical Greek of 2 Timothy 2:12,13 (Essay 32):

"If we deny him, he also will deny us.
 If we believe not, yet he abideth faithful:
 He cannot deny himself."

Hence the urgent exhortations in Titus 2 to continue in the hope of the everlasting life promised before the world began, and to adorn the doctrine of God our Saviour in all things. This passage in chapter 2 is therefore the pivot of the whole epistle, and it is reinforced by these words of the "faithful saying".

When we look now at the content of the saying in closer detail we see the great depth and beauty of the teaching it enshrines.

Verse 4: "But after that the kindness and love of God our Saviour toward man appeared": The words for "kindness" and "love-toward-man" in combination were familiar enough in the philosophical writings of the Hellenistic world. But as we have seen before in these Letters, the Apostle Paul, while often using the vocabulary of the educated speaker or writer of the period, invariably imparts to the words a profound spiritual meaning which has its roots in the Old Testament rather than in contemporary thought. Sadly a later generation has tended to work in the opposite way by weakening the force of Scriptural words in an effort to make them "relevant".

The root meaning of the Greek words *chrēstos*, 'kind', and *chrēstotēs*, 'kindness', is "useful" or "profitable", and is also translated by all the words italicised below in this paragraph. It is a quality, therefore, which goes far beyond a simple generous impulse towards others, for it is a fruit of the Spirit (*gentleness*, Galatians 5:22), it is a distinctive quality of that deep love or charity of 1 Corinthians 13—"love is *kind*"—and is above all an attribute of God Himself: "If so be ye have tasted that the Lord is *gracious*" (1 Peter 2:3). We are immediately back in Psalm 34, invited to "taste and see that the LORD is good: blessed is the man that trusteth in him", and many other Old Testament Scriptures proclaiming the goodness of God come into mind. It is from this goodness, kindness, and gentleness that the saving work of God in Christ takes its origin; for it is out of "the riches of his *goodness* and forbearance and longsuffering" that "the *goodness* of God leadeth thee to repentance" (Romans 2:4). The frequent exhortations to Christ's followers to manifest the same spirit to one another, and indeed to all men, form the background to our verse in Titus 3.

> "And be ye *kind* one to another, tenderhearted, forgiving one another, even as God for Christ's sake hath forgiven you. Be ye therefore followers of God, as dear children, and walk in love, as Christ also hath loved us, and hath given himself for us."   (Ephesians 4:32—5:2)

> "Put on therefore, as the elect of God, holy and beloved, bowels of mercies, *kindness* ..."   (Colossians 3:12)

This kindness and love of God, like the grace of God of which it is the expression, "shone forth" (*epiphanē*).

Verses 5, 6: "*Not by works of righteousness which we have done*": Israel were frequently reminded that it was "not for thy righteousness, or for the uprightness of thine heart, (but) ... that he may perform the word which the LORD sware unto thy fathers" (Deuteronomy 9:5) that God had become their salvation. Paul makes the same point here as he had done to the ecclesia at Ephesus:

413

"... that in the ages to come he might shew the exceeding riches of his grace in his kindness (*chrēstotēs*) toward us through Christ Jesus. For by grace are ye saved, through faith; and that not of yourselves: it is the gift of God: *not of works*, lest any man should boast. For we are his workmanship, created in Christ Jesus unto *good works*, which God hath before ordained that we should walk in them. Wherefore remember, that ye being in time past Gentiles in the flesh ..." (Ephesians 2:7-11)

No doubt Paul had in mind that the root meaning of the Old Testament word for "mercy" (*chesed*) is "covenant love", for the sake of which the LORD was prepared to "perform the truth to Jacob and the mercy to Abraham" which He had sworn unto the fathers from the days of old. So he adds, *"but according to his mercy he saved us"*.

"By the washing of regeneration, and renewing of the Holy Spirit": It does not affect the meaning if, with the Revised Version margin, we speak of the "laver" instead of the "washing" (cf. also Ephesians 5:26). Either meaning is supported by the text, but "laver" seems to point more clearly to a bath for immersion and has overtones of the priestly laver through which all who would minister in the tabernacle had to pass.

That the two elements, water and Spirit, are essential to the baptism which is true regeneration, or rebirth, is abundantly clear from the Lord's own words to Nicodemus: "Except a man be born of water and of the Spirit, he cannot enter the kingdom of God" (John 3:5). This is borne out by the Apostle Peter when he writes of being "saved by water, the like figure whereunto even baptism doth also now save us (not the putting away of the filth of the flesh, but the answer of a good conscience toward God) by the resurrection of Jesus Christ" (1 Peter 3:20-21).

That this does not involve any concept of receiving the Spirit in the Trinitarian, or even evangelical, sense has been amply demonstrated above. Nevertheless, baptism is more than a dipping of oneself into water. Accompanied by faith in, and therefore a participation in, the promises of God, the once-for-all act is a genuine death unto sin and a rising to newness of life. The best explanation of the Titus passage is provided by the words of Scripture itself:

"Seeing ye have purified your souls in *obeying the truth through the Spirit* unto unfeigned love of the brethren, see that ye love one another with a pure heart fervently: *being born again,* not of corruptible seed, but of incorruptible, *by the word of God,* which liveth and abideth for ever ... And this is the word which by the gospel is preached unto you."

(1 Peter 1:22-25)

Or, as Paul expresses it in Ephesians 5:25-26, in words which virtually offer a parallel definition to those from Titus:

"Christ also loved the church, and gave himself for it; that he might sanctify and cleanse it with *the washing of water by the word.*"

Verse 7: *"That being justified by his grace, we should be made heirs ... ":* Only through this grace could "he that sanctifieth and they who are sanctified be all of one" (Hebrews 2:11), heirs of God, and joint-heirs with Christ and thus, though by nature sinners, made partakers of a righteousness which is not their own. The inheritance is none other than that "eternal life, which God, that cannot lie, promised before the world began" (1:2).

What God can *do* for us, what He can *make* of us, prompts the exploration of a rewarding Scriptural theme. By divine workmanship the sinful can become sanctified; this "vile body" can become "fashioned like unto his glorious body". We follow through this train of thought in Essay 51, page 423.

"Washing of regeneration"

To conclude the comments on this section of Titus the two passages, from Ephesians 5 and Titus 3, are set out below in a way which demonstrates that "by the word" and "renewing of the Holy Spirit" are parallel expressions. This brings out the meaning of the second passage and shows how clearly linked it is with the birth of water and of spirit of John 3:5. Grammatically, the expression "the washing" or "the laver" can cover both "regeneration" and "renewing", so that the sense is, "the laver of being born again and of renewing of, or by, the Holy Spirit". Thus a man or woman is renewed by the power of God through Christ at the time of baptism. It is not a bestowal of the Holy Spirit but essentially a renewal of the mind, as in Colossians 3:10, Romans 12:2 and Ephesians 4:22-24.

415

EPHESIANS 5:25-27	TITUS 3:4-7
"Christ also loved the church, and gave himself for it, that he might sanctify and cleanse it with the washing of water by the word, that he might present it to himself a glorious church, not having spot, or wrinkle, or any such thing; but that it should be holy and without blemish."	"But after that the kindness and love of God our Saviour toward man appeared ... according to his mercy he saved us, by the washing of regeneration, and renewing of the Holy Spirit; which he shed on us abundantly through Jesus Christ our Saviour; that being justified by his grace, we should be made heirs according to the hope of eternal life."

3:8-11—Final Commands for the Ecclesias

Verse 8: "These things I will that thou affirm constantly": The reason for this constant affirmation becomes clearer the more we contemplate what has gone before. The Revised Version says "confidently unto the end" for "constantly", which adds to the idea of persistence, in the certain knowledge that the hope will be realised by those who endure. In the discharge of his own responsibility to the brethren and sisters in Crete Titus must be unwearying. For God cannot lie and Titus could be "confident of this very thing, that he which hath begun a good work in you will perform it until the day of Jesus Christ" (Philippians 1:6). The essential thing was that *"they which have believed in God might be careful to maintain good works"*. Appropriately, as we have observed before, the word for "good" here is *kala*, carrying the sense of beauty and grace in action. It is used 24 times in the Pastoral Epistles, usually in connection with work or works.

"These things are good and profitable unto men": The word for "profitable" is not found anywhere in Scripture outside the Pastoral Epistles. It occurs in 1 Timothy 4:8 and 2 Timothy 3:16, in both cases applied to the Scripture which is profitable to the man of God. The full force of the expression is discussed in the respective notes, especially on page 312.

Verse 9: "But avoid foolish questions ... for they are unprofitable and vain": The things to be avoided are parallel with those already spelt out in 1 Timothy 1:4, with the additional qualification that these things are folly. The separate elements of these aspects of unhealthy teaching— *"genealogies, and contentions, and strivings about the law"*—

416

are dealt with in the notes on 1 Timothy 1, and their unprofitable nature is discussed under 1 Timothy 6:3-5 (pages 41, 42, 180-182; also 2 Timothy 2:23). All such questions and disputings are *"vain"* because they never lead to any settled conviction.

Verses 10-11: *"A man that is an heretick . . . reject":* Paul now passes from the "other-teaching" to the man who propagates it. The reader is referred to the notes on "From such withdraw thyself" (page 182) and "Flee these things" (page 186). At a time when questions of "heresy" are being widely discussed in the Brotherhood it will be profitable to look closely at this apostolic injunction: this we do in Essay 52, page 426.

3:12-15—Fraternal Communications and Farewell

Verse 12: *"Be diligent to come unto me to Nicopolis":* Of the Artemas named in this verse nothing outside tradition is known. Tychicus, on the other hand, is mentioned several times as a companion or messenger of Paul. With Trophimus he came with Paul from Greece to Jerusalem (Acts 20:4) and as "a brother and faithful minister of the Lord" he was sent to Ephesus to bring tidings of Paul and comfort to the ecclesia there. He performed a similar mission to Colossae (4:7) and was later sent back to Ephesus (2 Timothy 4:12). From the fact that this was after Paul had been imprisoned once more we may surmise that it was in fact Artemas who was sent to relieve Titus in Crete. The form of the expression *"When I shall send Artemas"* refers to some time, certain but up to that point still undefined, for which Titus was to be prepared. Similar instructions were given Timothy (see the end of the Second Letter) which make it plain that the respective commissions of both these men were to set things in order in Ephesus or Crete and then commit the ecclesias "to faithful men able to teach others also", while they executed other commissions.

Of the three cities called Nicopolis the one mentioned here is most probably in Epirus; it derived its name of "City of Victory" from the decisive battle of Actium which confirmed Augustus as Emperor. Did Paul actually go there *"to winter"*, to be joined by Titus? And was it at Nicopolis that he was arrested and taken back to Rome in company with Titus who later went on to Dalmatia (2 Timothy 4:10)? Or was that winter in fact the one he would be spending in the chill Mamertine prison at Rome, comforted by the prospect of the coming of Timothy with the warm cloak he was asked to bring with him (2 Timothy 4:13,21)?

Verse 13: *"Bring Zenas the lawyer and Apollos on their journey diligently":* We do not know whether Zenas was skilled in Greek or Hebrew law; of Apollos, however, there is much recorded. He is the same "eloquent and learned Alexandrian" who learned the truth from Priscilla and Aquila and played a leading rôle in the ecclesia at Corinth (Acts 18:24; 19:1). Tradition has it that he retired to Crete to escape the controversies at Corinth, but it seems most improbable that any of the Apostle's men should adopt that method of avoiding personal unpleasantness. All we know is that Paul was unable to persuade him to return to Corinth at the time of the writing of the First Letter, although there was a promise that he would visit there "when he shall have convenient time" (16:12). We do not know what was the journey envisaged in this verse in Titus.

The New Testament Letters are full of the commendations of brethren and sisters to and from various ecclesias, together with requests that they be given all necessary assistance for their journey, *"that nothing be wanting unto them"*. The unsavoury atmosphere in the inns and taverns and the possibility of being robbed or molested on the way made the offering of hospitality a prudent act as well as a gesture of fellowship. Even in our safer times the generous welcome is still offered throughout the worldwide fellowship.

Verse 14: *"And let ours also learn to maintain good works":* The Apostle here is not simply repeating the exhortations of the preceding chapters, although they are implied as well. Rather is it a reminder that all of "our people", and not just Titus alone, should cooperate in the work of hospitality and welfare. The Revised Version suggests that they were to "profess honest occupations" in the spirit of 2 Thessalonians 3:7-13. It seems more probable that the *"necessary uses* (RV, wants)" were the acts of hospitality and response to similar needs which would become apparent from time to time and in which they should be prepared to offer assistance. In this way their fellowship would be a genuine sharing together and *"not unfruitful"*.

Verse 15: *"All that are with me salute thee. Greet them that love us in the faith":* The "thee" tells us that this was a personal message to

Titus from all who were personally acquainted with him or knew him by repute. It breathes out the very spirit of worldwide fellowship which transcends both space and time. In those days there were closer links than we perhaps realise between "all that in every place call upon the name of Jesus Christ our Lord, both theirs and ours" (1 Corinthians 1:2); and with very many of those called to be saints in the "churches in God the Father and in the Lord Jesus Christ" we have a sense of closer affinity than with any in the outside world of our twentieth century.

"Grace be with you all. Amen": For the general pattern of first century correspondence and the apostolic use of it, see the Introduction, page 8. After the emphasis upon the grace of God throughout this epistle what more appropriate farewell and benediction could there be?

ESSAY 50

The Fifth Faithful Saying

THE last of the faithful sayings is perhaps the most difficult of them all to define, since the statement which precedes the characteristic formula "This is a faithful saying" (Titus 3:8) is much longer than any we have considered and does not have the same quality of terseness. For this reason some commentators take the actual words of the saying to be verse 8:

"That they which have believed in God might be careful to maintain good works."

The verbal construction used in this verse is plainly a purpose clause, however, and it seems obvious that it expresses what is to be Titus's aim in constantly affirming that actual "word of the faith" which has gone before in verses 4-7 and urging those who have believed in what God has done in the work of salvation to express their faith in works consistent with it.

The saying itself is noteworthy because it emphasises the part played by baptism in the salvation wrought by God in Christ, and is one of the few passages in the Pastoral Epistles where the title of Saviour is applied to Christ as well as to God (see page 255). In fact, this "word of the faith", with its reference to the renewing of the Holy Spirit, is a confirmation of the fact that the Lord's command to baptize "in the name of the Father, and of the Son, and of the Holy Spirit" (Matthew 28:19) was well understood in the early ecclesias, not necessarily as a set formula to be used at every baptism but as a description of the end and aim which would be secured in and through baptism.

This whole point has received extended treatment in two articles on "The Lord's Command to Baptize" by L. G. Sargent in *The Christadelphian*, 1963, pages 152 and 202, where the authenticity of the Matthew passage and the importance of the linking together of Father, Son and Holy Spirit are ably discussed. In view of its relevance to our own comments on the Titus passage, we reproduce the following extracts:

"The difficulty, of course, comes in the words 'in the name of the Father, and of the Son, and of the Holy Spirit', commonly referred to as the 'Trinitarian formula'. Yet this is not unique: the three are named together several times in the New Testament, and (as will be shown later) at least twice in direct connexion with baptism. The existence of Father, Son and Holy Spirit is inwrought into the New Testament. We cannot deny that there are three, or that they are intimately related. We need not turn to paganism to find a 'threeness'. What we can and must deny on scriptural ground is that they are three co-equal and co-eternal persons. It is this belief which constitutes the Doctrine of the Trinity, and has corrupted and distorted the theology of the Church. This we must repudiate decisively. Our concern is not whether there are three, but what is their nature and what is the relationship between them. Here we must affirm with Paul that there is 'one God, the Father, of whom are all things, and we in him; and one Lord Jesus Christ, through whom are all things, and we through him'; and 'one Spirit, even as also ye were called in one hope of your calling' (1 Corinthians 8:6; Ephesians 4:4, RV). Yet the Son is born at a point in history, and the Spirit is defined as 'the power of the Highest' (Luke 1:35) rather than a distinct Person. The Spirit, as the words used for it indicate, is indeed the 'outbreathing' of God. This character it retains, even though (like 'the Word') it can sometimes be spoken of as though it were in some way independent and acting on its own . . .

"(The passage in Titus) names (1) 'God our Saviour', (2) the Holy Spirit, and (3) 'Jesus Christ our Saviour'. Of God it is said, 'According to his mercy he saved us'—a past act; His salvation is on His part an accomplished fact, whatever men do with it. His kindness and love to man have been made manifest. The saving is 'through the washing of regeneration and renewal of the Holy Spirit'. It is a washing of rebirth and renewal through or by means of the Holy Spirit. If verse 6 ('which he poured out upon us richly'—RV) seems to be an allusion to Pentecost, it cannot mean that all are recipients of a Pentecostal outpouring at baptism, for that would be accompanied by visible signs. Nor did the Holy Spirit come on that day upon those who were baptized as it had come upon the apostles. It was truly said to them, 'Ye shall receive the gift of the Holy Spirit', but the 'gift' was that of the Holy Spirit's redeeming action. No mention is made of those three thousand converts receiving 'spirit gifts' or such visible outpouring as had endowed the apostles with their powers, or indeed in any obvious sense 'receiving the spirit' at all.

"In what way can it be said, then, that there is an 'outpouring' for us now? First it is to be noted that the outpouring is for us 'through Jesus Christ'. Whether or not he bestows Spirit gifts, he is the channel through whom the Spirit is active. Receiving the Spirit without measure and accomplishing the work of the Spirit in his death and resurrection, and being presented to us as the object of our faith, he is the Spirit to us. In him the Spirit works for our salvation; and through the grace that is in him we are justified and made heirs in the hope of eternal life. Thus Father, Son and Holy Spirit are all actively involved in our salvation, which has its beginning in our new birth through baptism.

"So far, then, from Matthew 28 being unique in the New Testament in its mention of the threefold Name, the redemptive activity of God through the Holy Spirit in His Son is essential to Paul's doctrine of baptism. Whether or not he has the threefold Name in Matthew directly in mind—as indeed he may—Paul's teaching on baptism forms an exposition of the words spoken by the Lord. That teaching, so far as it concerns the threefold Name, can hardly be better expressed than in the ascription of glory which concludes one of our hymns—a hymn which surely could only have been written by a Christadelphian steeped in Scripture and in the writings of Dr. Thomas:

> Glory to the Father be
> By the Son's supremacy
> In the Spirit's mystery:
> Hallelujah! Yea, Amen."

ESSAY 51

"For we are his workmanship"

AS we noted when cosidering Titus 3:3 onwards, the Apostle associates himself and Titus with the Cretans when describing the transformation in status and behaviour which the grace of God that bringeth salvation could bring about. It is as though he is encouraging us with the greatest examples of the workings of this grace. Even the Cretans, with their national reputation and natural disposition, even an apostle who was a persecutor and injurious (the latter word in 1 Timothy 1:13 is almost equivalent to being a "bully"!), were not beyond the scope of God's mercy and indeed were the living proofs of its efficacy. He cannot restrain the expression of his praise for the grace he had received: "Now unto the King eternal, immortal, invisible, the only wise God ('our Saviour', Jude 25), be honour and glory for ever and ever. Amen" (1 Timothy 1:17).

God, therefore, was able to "make something of them"; or as it is expressed in Ephesians 2:10, "We are his workmanship". The word for "workmanship" appears twice only in the New Testament, here and in the plural in Romans 1:20, translated there as "the things that are made". When we learn that the word is *poïēma*, the usual word for "poem", we become aware that it means more than a mere work of construction. In Greek the word "poet" means a "maker", and in its artistic sense refers to someone who takes the basic material of words and language and, by means of rhythm, metaphor and symmetry, fashions a thing of beauty which expresses his own feelings and personality.

This is exactly what God our Maker has done. The Scriptural meaning of glory, indeed the very Hebrew word, implies all that God is—His substance, weight, honour and majesty. So Paul contrasts "light affliction" with the "far more exceeding and eternal weight of glory" which God will reveal in His sons (2 Corinthians 4:17). So "the heavens declare the glory of God; and the firmament sheweth his *handywork*" (Psalm 19:1), and "the invisible things of him from the creation of the world are clearly seen, being understood by *the things that are made*, even his eternal power and Godhead" (Romans 1:20).

So out of the material things of the universe God set in order something of beauty, described by the greatest of earthly poets as covering himself "with light as with a garment", "stretching out the heavens like a curtain", "laying the beams of his chambers in the waters", "making the clouds his chariots" and "walking upon the wings of the wind" (Psalm 104).

In God's Image

"God hath made every thing beautiful in his time" (Ecclesiastes 3:11) and the crown of His work was man. Out of the dust of the ground man was fashioned "in his image, and after his likeness", an image soon to become sadly disfigured and a likeness overlaid with something which became fashioned according to man's own lusts (cf. 1 Peter 1:14).

Then, like the poet, who out of the letters which make words fashions something beautiful, so God sent forth a man "born of a woman", yet in very truth His only begotten Son, "the brightness of his glory, and the express image of his person". He was the Alpha and Omega, the A to Z of God's purpose, the very Word expressed in human form; "and we beheld his glory, the glory as of the only begotten of the Father, full of grace and truth". God's purpose was to bring "many sons unto glory", men and women of flesh and blood who, "having escaped the corruption that is in the world through lust" could "become partakers of the divine nature".

Thus the people redeemed by God's grace in Christ Jesus to become His very own, a "peculiar treasure", should be truly beautiful in their holiness and gracious in their speech and actions, in hope of eventually having their vile body changed, to become "fashioned like unto his glorious body", the perfect expression of God in them as He was in Christ. For they are "God's *poem*, created in Christ Jesus unto good works, which God hath before ordained that we should walk in them".

"We shall be like him"—pure in heart, and sinless;
But his redeeming mercy ends not there;
These bodies like to his shall then be fashioned,
And we his resurrection glory share.

A final thought in this connection: "rejoicing in his present gift of grace", we are even now able to appreciate something of the beauty of music and poetry, particularly that of the "psalms and hymns and spiritual songs" of our worship. How much will that appreciation be enhanced, how much deeper will be our enjoyment when, in God's mercy, we ourselves become the instruments sounding forth the pure tones, the rich harmonies and the gracious words of the new song unto the Lord!

ESSAY 52

"A man that is an heretick"

HAIRETIKOS ('heretic') is a "oncer", used here (Titus 3:10) only in all Scripture, while *hairesis* ('heresy') is a term in the New Testament frequently translated as "sect". From its basic meaning of 'choice' or 'selection' it also carries the meaning of 'faction' or 'preferred opinion'. Christianity was regarded by its detractors as a sect of Judaism (Acts 24:14; 28:22) when in reality its adherents were the true "seed of Abraham". Judaism itself had the sects of the Pharisees—"the most straitest sect of our religion"—and the Sadducees, between whom there were deep cleavages in practice and fundamental belief. The Scriptural evidence is that the existence of these factions brought nothing but disunity, as witness the uproar in the council that sat in judgement on Paul (Acts 23:6-10). It is ironic that the few records in the New Testament of their consenting together—even joining with the Herodian faction—was in condemnation of the Lord Jesus!

Faction in the early ecclesias was equally debilitating and came under the strongest apostolic censure. The opening of the First Letter to Corinth, for example, gives us an insight into the nature of such divisive tendencies, which were not founded on points of doctrine but of personal preference. The Corinthians needed to be exhorted to be "perfectly joined together *in the same mind and in the same judgement*" (1:10). There was nothing "theological", so to speak, in a partiality for Apollos or Paul (or whoever the actual ecclesial members in question were, whom Paul delicately declines to name, using the names of Apollos and himself "in a figure"). Yet the result of such division of opinion was contrary to that doctrine not specifically included in formal "statements of the faith"—the fundamental doctrine of unity.

426

1 Corinthians 11:3-17 is equally instructive in this matter and, set as it is in the same chapter which deals with thoughtless behaviour at the breaking of bread, which obscured the true meaning of their coming together for those involved, offers a classic example of both the nature and effects of "heresy". The first part of the chapter deals with the question of sisters' head coverings, the real point of which seems in modern times to have been lost in the discussion of what constitutes a "covering" and precisely what is an assembly of the ecclesia.

"No such custom"

The resolution of these questions is not the subject of our present comment. We point out simply that there was an attempt being made to discount the principle altogether and, after setting it out once more Paul appeals to the widespread tradition and practice of the ecclesias to clinch the matter—we offer F. F. Bruce's *Expanded Paraphrase* of 1 Corinthians 11:16:

> "However, if anyone is minded to argue the point further, this is all we have to say: we have no such custom as you are trying to introduce, and neither have the churches of God elsewhere."

Later, in dealing with the "cliques" at the Lord's table, he makes the surprising point that the rise of faction in human society is inevitable, but has at least the beneficial result of showing who are the truly spiritually minded ones: they are those who refuse to be party to it (verse 19):

> "For there must be also heresies among you, that they which are approved may be made manifest among you."

Throughout these Epistles Paul has been dealing with the question of "other-teaching", especially of the kind which seeks support for a variant opinion in a misuse of Scripture, such as the "cankerous word" of Hymenaeus and Philetus (2 Timothy 2:17). Whatever their specious reasoning on the basis of wrested texts, their conclusions were contrary to the received body of doctrine passed on by apostolic ministry. Their teaching was therefore mere *dogma*, or opinion, and the attempt to draw away disciples after them was *heresy* in the Scripture meaning of the word. See also the notes on the subject of heresy elsewhere (pages 304, 362 and 417).

We can deduce from the foregoing that either teaching or conduct on the part of one who seeks to form a "party", or lead a dissident group, often in the name of "enlightenment", which runs contrary to the Brotherhood's code of faith and practice or even the arrangements of an ecclesia for its smooth running and discipline, would come under the apostolic censure. There was an apostolic procedure for dealing with it also: *"After the first and second admonition reject"* (Titus 3:10). For only a wilful determination to go against the agreed wishes of the ecclesia, or the hope that by persistence sufficient support would be found for the opinion to triumph, could lead one to refuse such admonition. It was the mark, says Paul, of one with a perverted mind—and he knew it (verse 11): *"Knowing that he that is such is subverted, and sinneth, being condemned of himself."*

EPILOGUE

THE subtitle to our book on the *Letters to Timothy and Titus* is "Sound Words for Ecclesias under Pressure". While it was being written the needs of the twentieth century ecclesias were kept very much in mind, in the belief that the timeless nature of Divine principles makes these Letters for first century ecclesias a valuable document for our own times. A great deal of the background to life in the first century has been presented in order to show the value of the Pastoral Epistles as contemporary writings and to help us to relate them to the problems and needs of the present-day ecclesia. Much of that material is contained in the Essays, which have also provided the opportunity to expound at greater length the Scriptural basis of many a passage in the Letters and to reveal a depth and richness in many a phrase, unsuspected beforehand by this author at least.

The Subject and Scripture Indexes at the end of this book give some idea of the range of spiritual topics covered and the extent of the Biblical quotations. But that of course would be entirely expected by those who believe that—

"All Scripture is given by inspiration of God, and is profitable for doctrine, for reproof, for correction, for instruction in righteousness: that the man of God may be perfect, throughly furnished unto all good works."

May we all continue in the things which we have learned and have been assured of.

SCRIPTURE INDEX

SUBJECT INDEX

435